WORLD ENGLISHES
IN ASIAN CONTEXTS

Asian Englishes Today

Series Editor: Kingsley Bolton
Professor of English Linguistics, Stockholm University
Honorary Professor, The University of Hong Kong

The volumes in this series set out to provide a contemporary record of the spread and development of the English language in South, Southeast, and East Asia from both linguistic and literary perspectives. Volumes in this series reflect themes that cut across national boundaries, including the study of language policies; globalization and linguistic imperialism; English in the media; English in law, government and education; 'hybrid' Englishes; and the bilingual creativity manifested by the vibrant creative writing found in a swathe of Asian societies.

The editorial advisory board comprises a number of leading scholars in the field of World Englishes, including Maria Lourdes S. Bautista (De La Salle, Philippines), Susan Butler (Macquarie Dictionary), Braj Kachru (University of Illinois, Urbana-Champaign), Yamuna Kachru (University of Illinois, Urbana-Champaign), Shirley Geok-lin Lim (University of California, Santa Barbara), Tom McArthur (editor of *English Today*), Larry Smith (co-editor of *World Englishes*), Anne Pakir (National University of Singapore), and Yasukata Yano (Waseda University, Japan).

WORLD ENGLISHES IN ASIAN CONTEXTS

Yamuna Kachru and **Cecil L. Nelson**

香港大學出版社
HONG KONG UNIVERSITY PRESS

Hong Kong University Press
14/F Hing Wai Centre
7 Tin Wan Praya Road
Aberdeen
Hong Kong

Hardback   ISBN-13: 978-962-209-755-1
                ISBN-10: 962-209-755-3
Paperback   ISBN-13: 978-962-209-756-8
                ISBN-10: 962-209-756-1

Secure On-line Ordering
http:// www.hkupress.org

British Library Cataloguing-in-Publication Data
A catalogue record for this book is available from the British Library.

Cover design by Prashast Gautam Kachru of New Delhi, India. The artwork represents a sculpted image of the phenomenal diffusion of world Englishes.

Printed and bound by United League Graphic & Printing Co. Ltd., in Hong Kong, China

To

Amita, Shamit and Sasha K. Kachru

and

JoAnn, Jessica and Joshua Nelson

with love and affection

for making up

our enchanting Inner Circle of world Englishes

Children who are born into homes of privilege, in the way of wealth, tradition, or education, become native speakers of what is popularly known as "good" English; the linguist prefers to give it the non-committal name of *standard* English. Less fortunate children become native speakers of "bad" or "vulgar" or, as the linguist prefers to call it, non-standard English.

Leonard Bloomfield (1933: 48)

For last year's words belong to last year's language
And next year's words await another voice.

T. S. Eliot (1943: quartet No. IV)

The reason I'm so fascinated by the English language is that ... it is so flexible, it is so elastic. It does stretch. It does adapt, and does take on all those Indian concepts and traditions and ways.

Anita Desai (1992: 171)

Wordsworth in the tropics: daffodils mutate.
Out of the parley in the tents, a fresh
Vocabulary, equal, reconciling Englishes
Dismantle white umbras through synonyms
Translating psyches, achieving metaphors,
Defining room for mutual, fresh realities,
A calculus for fellowship of language
As power, as making, as release.

Edwin Thumboo (1993: 109)

... if I'm asked, "Do you write correct English?" I would say, "Of course, it's correct. I'm the one writing it. You're not the one writing it. It is correct." In other words, we have our own — I sense this all the time — we have our own way of thinking. We have our own way of feeling, by which we then use this language called English. So that English is ours. We have colonized it too.

Gemino Abad (1997: 17)

Contents

List of illustrations

Maps

Photographs

Figures

Series editor's preface

This new volume from Professors Yamuna Kachru and Cecil L. Nelson is an important and innovative addition to the *Asian Englishes Today* series. It is an important addition in the sense that it is the first volume in the series that is explicitly designed for use as a higher-level undergraduate or postgraduate advanced resource book. In addition, *World Englishes in Asian Contexts* not only has the potential to serve as a textbook for courses in world Englishes, but also as a companion volume for courses in English language teaching, second language acquisition, and sociolinguistics, or as a stand-alone guide for self-study in the field of world Englishes.

A major area of innovation is the approach adopted throughout this volume. Many earlier textbooks on world Englishes and varieties of English have tended towards a Eurocentric or 'Americentric' perspective in the selection of material and the scope of topics presented. The present book is arguably the first of its kind, as it endeavours to introduce and explore major aspects of world Englishes through perspectives particularly sensitive to the Asian region.

The volume is organized into four parts: Part I, 'Theory, Method and Contexts'; Part II, 'Acquisition, Creativity, Standards and Testing'; Part III, 'Profiles across Cultures'; and Part IV, 'Applied Theory and World Englishes'. In broad terms, Part I introduces key concepts in the theorization and description of world Englishes, and Part II considers the links between Second Language Acquisition research, standards of English, creativity and the teaching and testing of English worldwide. Part III focuses on regional and national varieties with coverage of South Asian, East Asian, Southeast Asian, African, and Afro-American varieties, while Part IV comprises a number of applied studies relating to grammar, lexicography, code alternation, critical linguistics, and speaking, writing, and genre across cultures. The twenty-two core chapters are supplemented by questions and activities designed to exemplify and probe the issues set out in each chapter.

Professors Kachru and Nelson are two acknowledged experts in the field of world Englishes, and this volume has been authored with a combination of thoughtfulness and flair that has characterized the work of these two linguists throughout their careers. For almost four decades, Yamuna Kachru has taught courses at the University of Illinois at Urbana-Champaign on several areas of linguistics, including applied linguistics and discourse analysis, English grammar, the languages of South Asia and much else. Cecil Nelson has taught linguistics, applied linguistics, sociolinguistics and ESL at Indiana State University for more than twenty years. Both are outstanding educators, and the quality of their work and combined talents shines through this volume, which will be of interest, I anticipate, not only to teachers and students of English across Asia, but also to a very wide international audience throughout the world.

Kingsley Bolton
December 2005

Preface

This volume presents a comprehensive picture of the spread, functions and dynamic status of English in the changing Asian contexts. As discussed in the Introduction, *World Englishes in Asian Contexts* comprises in its four parts theoretical conceptualizations and methodological processes utilized in the study of the field, followed by issues in language acquisition, standardization and testing in view of the innovations and creative potential exhibited in the varieties. The regional profiles provide the essential basis for conceptual and applied generalizations regarding the major theoretical, methodological, educational and pragmatic questions related to world Englishes. Finally, the volume presents applications of theories and methodologies to research on grammar, vocabulary and literary style in a number of Englishes. The twenty-two chapters in the volume address the major 'socially realistic' concerns of Englishes in the Asian region.

There are, of course, heated arguments about the present and ever-increasing ascendancy of the medium of English across cultures and languages. Attitudes about the presence of English in Africa, Asia, and Europe are articulated in two major ways. Some celebrate it with slogans of 'triumphalism': English is viewed both as a global medium and a unifying linguistic channel. On the other hand, there is no dearth of people who consider English an initiator of 'language death' and decay, of 'mongrelization' and 'McDonaldization' of the world's languages. Whatever the attitudes and linguistic conflicts, there is no disagreement that the English language has crossed the proverbial seven seas and practically all cultural and linguistic boundaries. It has Englishized almost all the world's languages in contact with it, and as time passes, more and more 'new' varieties of English are being recognized, taught in classrooms, and studied with close attention and excitement.

We also see the world's leading language scholars recognizing the dynamic structural and functional changes in a language that spread from Britain, a location that Thomas Didbin (1717–1841) called 'a right little, tight little island' (cited in Algeo 2004). The dynamics of Englishes — particularly in Asia and Africa — are changing so fast that they are affecting the profile of world Englishes. It was in 1997 that a keen observer of world Englishes, David Crystal, speculated that a 'World Standard Spoken English (WSSE)' might emerge as a model of English (Crystal 1997: 136–7). However, in 2004, in a seminar organized by the British Council in New Delhi, Crystal expressed a reconsidered awareness of the functional realities of world Englishes when he predicted: ' "Hinglish" will soon become the most commonly spoken form of the language globally ...' (*The Times of India*, 11 October 2004).

Whether Crystal's prediction is realized or not, what is true is that '[English] is the leading language of science, medicine, technology and academic publication' almost everywhere and that '[most] of what takes place around the world is unregulated and haphazard, part of people's day-to-day actions and needs and of the social forces that operate on them' (McArthur 1998: 38). There is greater multiplicity than ever before in the forms and uses of English in the twenty-first century.

The spread and functions of English among its 1,500 million speakers has resulted in unparalleled research activity in the scholarly fields concerned with acquisition and uses of English across the world. This volume brings together the strands of research on world Englishes, especially in the linguistically and culturally pluralistic Asian context — an area of the globe that comprises almost a quarter of the world's population. One of our main aims has been to represent the voices of major Asian linguistic and literary scholars, and those of creative writers and educators. We have attempted to make the Asian contexts meaningful and relevant for our own and our readers' better understanding of theoretical and applied sociolinguistic generalizations based on world Englishes. It is our hope that this work will encourage other such studies for other parts of the English-using world.

World Englishes in Asian Contexts is primarily designed for advanced undergraduate and beginning graduate courses. Its organization and content, we believe, make it an appropriate resource for courses in, for example, world Englishes, sociolinguistics, language in society, language convergence and change, literary creativity, and 'additional' language education. In a broad sense, *World Englishes in Asian Contexts* is a major resource for anyone interested in cross-cultural diffusion of languages and the implications of such diffusion. We hope it will stimulate a thoughtful consideration of the concerns of the world Englishes community among a wide variety of professionals and readers.

Yamuna Kachru and Cecil L. Nelson
Vasant Panchami, 2006

Acknowledgements

The genesis, completion, and production of *World Englishes in Asian Contexts* owes gratitude to several individuals and institutions: To Kingsley Bolton, the initiator of the series, *Asian Englishes Today*, for his enthusiastic endorsement for the idea of this volume, and his continued invaluable advice and suggestions; to Clara Ho of Hong Kong University Press for her understanding and patience, for obtaining the permission of the Hong Kong writer Agnes Lam to reproduce her picture, and for her help with the entire process of production of the book; to Prashast Gautam Kachru for the cover design, which he did with his usual elegance, love and vision, and for the seven sketches of Asian and African creative writers which he completed with his friend, Karim; to the cartographer of Hong Kong University Press for producing the maps of the regions represented in the volume; Maria L. S. Bautista, Braj Kachru, Bapsi Sidhwa, and Edwin Thumboo for their permission to reproduce their pictures; to Margaret Courtright for her permission to use selected parts of her unpublished PhD dissertation in Chapter 10; to our research assistants, Heeyoun Cho, Jamie S. Lee, Wooseung Lee, Theeraporn Ratitamkul, and Seok-Youn Yoon, for their invaluable help at various stages of completion of this volume; to the Research Board of the Graduate College, University of Illinois at Urbana-Champaign, which has provided research support to Yamuna Kachru over the years; to the anonymous reviewers of the book proposal whose constructive suggestions were of immense value; and last, but not least, to our "inner circle" to whom we owe an enormous debt of gratitude, Larry Smith, Braj, Amita and Shamit Kachru, and JoAnn, Jessica and Joshua Nelson, whose constant encouragement, generous support, and bright humor contributed to the completion of *World Englishes in Asian Contexts*.

List of abbreviations and symbols

Abbreviations

AfrE	African English
AmE	American English
AusE	Australian English
BrE	British English
CE	Chinese English
CbE	Caribbean English
CM	Code-mixing
CS	Code-switching
ESL	English as a Second Language
EFL	English as a Foreign Language
ELT	English Language Teaching
IE	Indian English
IVE	Indigenized Variety of English
MexE	Mexican English
NE	Nepali English
NgE	Nigerian English
NS	Native Speaker
NNS	Non-Native Speaker
PE	Pakistani English
SAE	South Asian English
PhE	Philippine English
SgE	Singaporean English
SLA	Second Language Acquisition
SME	Singaporean-Malaysian English
TESOL	Teaching English to Speakers of Other Languages
TOEFL	Test of English as a Foreign Language
TOEIC	Test of English for International Communication

Symbols

'	signals that the syllable following it is stressed.
CAP lc words in sequence	The word in capital letters bears emphatic stress
Bold face word(s)	the focused element in the sentence
[ ]	phonetic representation
/ /	phonemic representation
θ	Voiceless inter-dental fricative as the *th* in *thin*
đ	Voiced inter-dental fricative as the *th* in *this*
š	Voiceless palatal fricative as the *sh* in *shade*
ž	Voiced palatal fricative as the s in *measure*
ʃ	Voiceless labio-dental fricative as the *f* in *fare*
υ	Voiced labio-dental fricative as the *v* in *very*
w	Voiced bilabial continuant as the *w* in *wet*
ə	unrounded low-mid vowel as the *a* in *above*
ø	zero; absence of any sound
:	lengthens the segment preceding it
ā, ī, etc.	long vowels
ṭ, ḍ, etc.	Retroflex plosives
ṛ	Retroflex flap
~	signals nasalization

Map of Greater Asia

Introduction

The notion 'world Englishes' provides the major conceptual framework for a useful and reasoned understanding of the spread and functions of the English language in global contexts. This concept also forms the theoretical and methodological basis for the twenty-two chapters of this volume. Earlier proposals for such a conceptualization — not necessarily using the term 'world Englishes' — were presented in studies that include B. Kachru (1982b [1992d], 1986a), Smith (1981, 1983, 1987), and Strevens (1980). Since then, the area of research labelled world Englishes (WEs) has grown rapidly and has produced a great number of publications on many aspects of WEs, e.g. Görlach (1991–2002 [4 vols.]), Jenkins (2003), Melcher and Shaw (2003), Schneider (1997 [2 vols.]), Smith and Forman (1997), and Thumboo (2001b).

The diffusion of English has resulted in the emergence of three broad categories of regional varieties of English. The first set includes the varieties in the countries where the English language has its origins and those where it is the dominant language as a result primarily of population migration, e.g. Australia, Canada, New Zealand, the UK and the USA, which were inhabited by migrations of English-speaking people in large numbers from the British Isles. The second set comprises the varieties that have developed in countries where English has a long history, essentially due to colonization, in which the language has undergone acculturation and nativization, has a body of creative writing, and has an official status, e.g. India, Nigeria, Singapore, the Philippines, and others (B. Kachru, 1985; Crystal, 1987: 357). The third set consists of the varieties that are developing in countries where English is used primarily for international purposes, but is fast becoming an instrument of identity construction and artistic innovation (e.g., in the People's Republic of China, Japan and Korea). These three sets have been termed the Inner-Circle, the Outer-Circle and the Expanding-Circle varieties in the Concentric Circles model (B. Kachru, 1985; see Chapters 1 and 2 for more on the circles). The conception of the circles is that they are dynamic; historically, each circle has demonstrated its changing character (see Chapter 2).

World Englishes

The term 'world Englishes' is inclusive and does not associate any privilege with English in any one circle or in any one of its specific varieties. It simply denotes the historical facts of origin and diffusion of English around the world. It has correctly been pointed out that this term emphasizes the equality of all the varieties used in the Inner, Outer and Expanding Circles (McArthur, 1998) and focuses on inclusivity and pluricentricity in approaches to the study of English in its global contexts (Bolton, 2004). In this respect it is decidedly unlike the terms 'World English' (Brutt-Griffler, 2002), 'English as an International Language' (Jenkins, 2000) and 'English as a Lingua Franca' (Seidlhoffer, 2001), all of which idealize a monolithic entity called 'English' and neglect the inclusive and plural character of the world-wide phenomenon.

The topic of 'World Englishes in Asian Contexts' is of great interest for several reasons. As Dissanayake (1997: 136) asserts, 'World Englishes ... presents us with a vibrant site where cultural articulations of the mutual embeddedness of the local and the global are given comprehensible shape'. Furthermore, the Asian region encompasses all three circles. Australian and New Zealand Englishes, part of Greater Asian Englishes, are Inner-Circle varieties; Philippine, South Asian, and Singaporean Englishes exemplify Outer-Circle developments; and varieties such as Chinese, Indonesian, Japanese, Korean, Malaysian, and Thai Englishes are parts of the Expanding Circle. By now, Asian English users represent the largest number of English users in the world (see Chapter 1). The fast-developing functions of and innovations in English in this region are of great interest to linguists, literary scholars, educators, educational administrators, and those fields and professions that are involved in international or global enterprises.

Asian Englishes

Our treatment of Asian Englishes in this volume needs some explanation. We have included discussions of the spread and functions of English in Australia and New Zealand, East Asia (China, Japan, Korea), South Asia (Bangladesh, India, Nepal, Pakistan, Sri Lanka) and Southeast Asia (Indonesia, Malaysia, the Philippines, Singapore, Thailand), but have not said much about some parts of Southeast Asia, e.g., Vietnam, still less about West Asia (or the Middle East), or the states in Asia that were formerly parts of the USSR. It has not been easy to find systematic treatments of English language-related topics for many of these countries, and it is difficult to be comprehensive and encompass the vast region of Asia in one volume of this size in any case.

The justification for including Australia and New Zealand is that they share the southern hemisphere with Asia and are intimately connected with Asia in population migration patterns and in economic ties. To give just one example of Australia's increasing economic ties with Asia, according to an official white paper, Asia took 56 percent of Australian merchandise exports in 2002, seven out of ten top Australian export markets are in Asia, and increasing importance is being attached to economic relations with Japan, China, the Korean Peninsula, Indonesia and India. As regards the recent population profile of Australia, there is an ever-increasing immigration from the People's Republic of China, Hong Kong, Indonesia, Malaysia and the Philippines. Australia is seeking close cooperation with organizations such as the Association of South East Asian Nations (ASEAN) and Asia-Pacific Economic Cooperation (APEC). Additionally, it is increasingly becoming a major force in the field of English language education in the region, and is attracting a large number of college and university students in other fields from East, South and Southeast Asia.

We are quite aware of the fact that when we talk of South Asian or East Asian or Southeast Asian English it does not mean that 'South Asia', or 'East Asia' or 'Southeast Asia' is a monolithic entity. These labels do not represent unitary categories any more than 'the West' or 'Europe' or 'America' do. Nevertheless, it is true that in spite of the differences across the larger region, there are shared spaces and cultures that have to be acknowledged and have been recognized in a variety of scholarly studies (e.g. B. Kachru 2005).

Resources on world Englishes

The publications in the area of WEs are of several types. Some are broad generalizations about WEs (e.g., B. Kachru, 1982b [1992d], 1986a; Kachru and Nelson, 1996; Platt, Weber and Ho, 1984; Schneider, 1997; among others), whereas others deal with issues raised in relation to specific regional or national varieties (e.g., Bell and Kuiper, 1999; Baumgardner, 1993, 1996b; de Klerk, 1996; Collins and Blair, 1989; B. Kachru, 1983; 1994a; Mesthrie, 1992; Rahman, 1990; Tay 1993b), or with detailed grammatical descriptions of national varieties (e.g., Bautista [1997b, 2000] on Philippine English; Bolton [2003] on Chinese Englishes; Stanlaw [2004] on Japanese English; B. Kachru [1983] on Indian English; and Rahman [1990] on Pakistani English). Some scholarly journals publish a great deal on variation in English within the Inner Circle (e.g., *English World-Wide* [John Benjamins, Amsterdam], *English Today* [Cambridge University Press, Cambridge]), while others devote a larger share to the Outer and Expanding Circles (*World Englishes* [Blackwell Publishing, Oxford], *Asian Englishes* [ALC Press, Tokyo]).

A major topic that has been treated in the available literature is the indigenization of English in descriptions of a particular regional variety's or sub-variety's phonology, lexicon, syntax, or use (see the References). Some topics within grammar have been compared across Inner-Circle varieties as well (e.g., Australian vs. American and Australian vs. British, as in Collins [1991]). Other studies have explored lexical and semantic differences between Inner-Circle Englishes and Englishes across the circles (e.g., Grote, 1992; Ho, 1992).

In studies on discourse, there have been discussions of communicative styles (Y. Kachru, 2001a), speech acts (e.g., Y. Kachru, 1998; K. Sridhar, 1991) and writing conventions, ranging from expository prose (e.g., Y. Kachru, 1987 *ff.*) to literary works (e.g., Dissanayake, 1985; B. Kachru, 1986b, 1987, 1994, 1997, 2002; Tawake, 1990, 1993, 1995a; Thumboo, 1992; Valentine, 1991, 1995). Research in genres across varieties is also making a beginning (Bhatia, 1997), and another interesting sub-area of research has been intelligibility among different varieties (e.g., Smith and Rafiqzad, 1979; Smith and Bisazza, 1982; Smith and Nelson, 1985; Matsuura, Chiba and Fujieda, 1999).

Ideological issues that have been raised include the following: (a) attitudes towards and controversies surrounding norms, standardization and codification of Outer-Circle varieties (e.g., Bamgboṣe, 1982, 1992; B. Kachru, 1985, 1988; Pakir, 1997; Quirk, 1985, 1988, 1989); (b) teaching English in non-Western contexts (Strevens, 1980; B. Kachru, 1986a, 1995b) and in Western contexts (Seidlhofer, 1999); (c) English textbooks currently in use in the world (Baik, 1994; Tickoo, 1995a); and (d) the power and politics of English, especially in relation to the propagation of English through official and non-official agencies (e.g., Berns et al., 1998; Canagarajah, 1999; Dissanayake, 1997; B. Kachru, 1976, 1987, 2005, *inter alia*; Pennycook, 1994, Phillipson, 1992).

Each of the several strands that make up the total picture of research on Englishes makes a significant contribution to the understanding of the phenomenon of Englishes around the globe. The selections of topics and sources in this volume, taken as a whole, represent the entire area of research. The guiding principle of *World Englishes in Asian Contexts* has been a representation of varied viewpoints in addition to a presentation of the distinct sub-areas of research on WEs in the Asian contexts.

Structure of this book

This volume does not present Asian Englishes in isolation. The geographical area in focus is Asia, but we have included one chapter on African Englishes to show the shared characteristics of Englishes in the Outer and Expanding Circles. African Englishes exhibit the same processes of indigenization in linguistic structures, language use, and literary creativity as do Asian Englishes. Africa and Asia raise similar issues in codification, standardization, and ideological concerns with regard to the use of English in education and other domains of life.

We have also included one chapter on a sub-variety — African American Vernacular English (AAVE) — to help drive home an awareness of the fact that no national variety is unitary; there is significant variation within varieties in all English-using countries, certainly including 'American' or 'British' English. The choice of AAVE was motivated by several factors: (a) there is a long tradition of research in this variety, (b) AAVE raises interesting issues in the historical, descriptive, ideological and pedagogical fields, and (c) more than any other comparable variety, AAVE has stimulated discussions of ethnic identity expressed through language. These are important considerations for all WEs.

While we have included references to so-called 'non-standard varieties' wherever possible, there are no chapters on English-based pidgins and creoles in this book, not because we did not think they were important, but because of limitations in terms of the size of the work. These varieties are as much a part of world Englishes or Asian Englishes as are other regional, social or ethnic varieties. Much has been published in recent years on the importance of creoles and minority dialects in education in the contexts of Australia, the UK and the USA which is also relevant for the Asian contexts (e.g., Nero, 2001; Siegel, 1999).

This book is divided into four parts on the basis of our conceptualization of the best way to unfold the research areas of WEs. The first part contains chapters on theoretical formulations of and methodological approaches to the field in response to issues that have arisen due to the diffusion of English and the emergence of varieties in various cultural contexts. The second part discusses concerns in the areas of language acquisition, standards and testing and draws attention to the creative and innovative aspects of varieties of Englishes. The third part presents profiles of regional varieties, including their distinct historical backgrounds, societal statuses, and formal and functional characteristics. The fourth part includes chapters on the applications of theory and methodology to researching various aspects of WEs. Each chapter is followed by suggested activities to stimulate discussion, consideration of alternative viewpoints, and investigations of various sorts.

The annotated bibliography lists resource materials that are helpful in exploring facets of WEs, and the list of Web sites facilitates an examination of further material. The lists of select literary works in various Englishes identify additional resources for building an awareness of the creative potential of regional varieties.

This book is designed to be useful to anyone interested in English studies. It is perhaps of most relevance to advanced undergraduate and beginning graduate students of English and English-language education, including those who are undergoing preparation for teaching English as an additional language. It is also suitable for use in courses on sociolinguistics, multilingualism, and language contact and convergence. Professionals other than teachers and students of English who are training for international activities in Asia (e.g., in business, journalism and tourism) may find this volume helpful in developing sensitivity to language use and cultural conventions of interaction in Asian Englishes. The suggested activities are designed to promote active participation, contemplation and critical thinking on issues related to language use in general and, more specifically, in pluralistic contexts.

Although the chapters are structured in a way that allows selection for use in a specific context of teaching and study, we feel that the first part of the book, Chapters 1–5, are essential for conceptualizing forms and functions of Englishes in the world. Chapters 6–10 in Part II are of special interest to those who are English language teaching professionals or are preparing to enter the profession. The sketches of various regional varieties in Part III, Chapters 11–15, are sources of examples and analyses for those engaged in English studies. Chapters 16–18 in Part IV emphasize research areas and provide information about the formal study of Englishes which can be broadly applied. Chapters 18–21 are crucial for an appreciation of cultural differences in interaction through the modes of speaking and writing. And Chapter 22 invites closely considered attention from a wide variety of practising professionals and readers, including students, teachers and scholars of Englishes, and sociolinguists, sociologists and political scientists interested in language-related issues. The conclusion points out the current trends and poses questions that suggest future directions of research.

It should be kept in mind that the approach taken in this book derives primarily from the theoretical foundations and methodologies of sociolinguistics (see Halliday 1973, 1978; Halliday and Matthiesson 1999; B. Kachru 1986) rather than from those of sociology of language or language policy and planning. Although no prior knowledge of formal linguistics is assumed for the users of the book, it is expected that readers will have an interest in language-related issues and will give serious consideration to questions of language ownership and languages as vital instruments of achieving pragmatic and imaginative social goals.

Part I
Theory, Method and Contexts

1
World Englishes today

World is crazier and more of it than we think
Incorrigibly plural. I peel and portion
A tangerine and spit the pips and feel
The drunkenness of things being various.

Louis MacNiece, 'Snow', from *Selected Poems* (1990: 23)

Introduction

The latter half of the twentieth century saw an amazing phenomenon — the emergence and acceptance of a single language as an effective means of communication across the globe. English by now is the most widely taught, learnt and spoken language in the world. It is used by over 300 million people as a first language in Australia, Canada, New Zealand, the UK and the USA, and by over 700 million people as a second or additional language in the countries of Africa, Asia, Europe, and Latin America, and of the island nations of the world (Crystal, 1985a; B. Kachru, 1999).

The world-wide diffusion of English

The spread of English has been viewed in terms of two diasporas (see B. Kachru, 1992d; also see Chapter 2). The first arose as a consequence of the migration of English-speaking people from Great Britain to Australia, North America, and New Zealand. The second resulted primarily from the diffusion of English among speakers of diverse groups of peoples and languages across the world as a result of colonialism and other political and economic factors; only a small number of English speakers carried their language, as colonial officials, missionaries and businessmen. The two diasporas have distinct historical, sociocultural, ideological, linguistic, and pedagogical contexts. These different contexts of diffusion have given rise to various phenomena that need careful study.

The field of English studies, whether in the first or the second diaspora, is fraught with debates and controversies. Questions ranging from 'What is English?' and 'Whose language is it?' to 'Which English should we learn and teach?' rage, and not only specialists but everyone active in areas such as politics, academia and media, has an opinion. Although most discussions tend to present issues in terms of binary categories such as *standard* vs. *non-standard*, *native* vs. *non-native*, British vs. American, and so on, the patterns that the global spread of English presents are much more complex than such an either-or view can realistically or usefully handle.

English has more centres than just America and Britain by now, and as linguists and language learners and teachers, it is important that we study the nature of this 'various' language. One useful way of conceptualizing this pluricentricity is to look at the English-using world in terms of three concentric circles, as B. Kachru (1985: 12–3) suggests. The Inner Circle comprises the 'mother country' — England and the British Isles — and the areas where the speakers from Britain took the language with them as they migrated — Australia, New Zealand and North America. The Outer Circle comprises the countries where the language was transplanted by a few colonial administrators, businessmen, educators, and missionaries, and is now nurtured by the vast majority of indigenous multilingual users. They use English as an additional language for their own purposes, which include many national and international domains. The Expanding Circle represents the countries (e.g., People's Republic of China, Japan, Korea, Thailand, countries of Europe, the Middle East, and Latin America) where the language is still spreading, mainly for serving the need for an international medium in business and commerce, diplomacy, finance, and other such spheres (see Chapter 2). English in this circle, however, is also finding increased use in internal domains of academia, media and professions such as medicine, engineering, etc. (see Chapters 4 and 12).

Language, dialect and variety

When we say English has become a global language, we are using the word 'language' to cover a great deal of territory. The term 'language' represents an idealization. Individuals do not speak a 'language', they speak a 'variety' of a language, or a 'dialect'. We identify the national varieties by terms such as American English, Australian English and British English. Within each nation, we identify varieties by regions. In the UK, we speak of Scots, Northern, Central and Southern dialects. In the US, Wolfram describes eighteen dialect areas of the Atlantic seaboard, including a distinct dialect spoken in New York City (1981: 44 *ff.*).

Dialect variation is generally understood to be based on geography. However, there are other factors that lead to variation, too. For example, there are differences in the speech of different classes, ethnic groups, age groups, and genders, and there are differences between educated and uneducated speech. In the US, there are dialects such as African-American Vernacular English (Labov, 1998; see Chapter 15). In the UK, the dialect known as Cockney has a class basis: Trudgill (1990: 46) calls it 'the Traditional Dialect of working class London'. In South Asia, there are dialect differences based on castes and religions, so that one speaks of a Brahmin dialect and a non-Brahmin dialect of, say, Tamil, and of Hindu versus Muslim Bengali or Kashmiri (B. Kachru, 1969; Shapiro and Schiffman, 1983: 150–76; Ferguson and Dil, 1994). There are dialects that are identified with both religion and caste; for instance, within Hindu and Christian Konkani there are Brahmin Hindu vs. non-Brahmin Hindu Konkani, and Brahmin Christian vs. non-Brahmin Christian Konkani (Miranda, 1978).

For attitudinal reasons, the term 'dialect' is not the preferred way of referring to national Englishes, such as American English and British English. Instead, linguists and lay people alike use the term 'variety'. No matter which term we use, some people may still contest the superiority or inferiority of one variety or another. For instance, as recently as 1995, Britain's Prince Charles observed that the American version of the language was 'very corrupting', and that the English version was the 'proper' one. He told the British Council that 'we must act now to ensure that English and that, to my way of thinking, means English English, maintains its position as the world language well into the next century' (*Chicago Tribune*, 24 March 1995, Section 1, p. 4).

Accent

The feature commonly used as a criterion in talking about variation is 'accent'. Accent refers, in addition to the pronunciation of sounds, to stress and intonation, or to the rhythm of speech. Just like variety, accent also leads to controversies about which one is superior, desirable, and so on. As the British phonetician David Abercrombie observes (1951: 15): 'The accent bar is a little like a colour-bar — to many people, on the right side of the bar, it appears eminently reasonable. It is very difficult to believe, if you talk RP yourself, that it is not intrinsically superior to other accents.' Actually, the RP accent, though intimately associated with standard British English, has always been a minority accent. According to McArthur (1992: 851), it is 'unlikely ever to have been spoken by more than 3–4% of the British population'. This is true of other standard or 'upper-class' accents, too.

When people talk about variation in language, they do not really make a distinction between 'dialect' and 'accent'; there is a consistent pairing of dialect and accent in people's minds. As Strevens (1983: 89) observes, '[s]ince dialect + accent pairs co-exist in this way, it is not surprising that most non-specialists, and even many teachers of English, habitually confuse the terms *dialect* and *accent*, and observe no distinction between them.' The confusion, to some extent, is understandable: the pairing of dialect and accent, however, breaks down in the case of standard languages; e.g., the presidents of the United States in the last two decades have all had different accents, but they may all rightly be considered speakers of Standard American English. The same is true of the BBC news anchors and reporters who have regional accents, often identifiable as Irish or Scottish, but they are all considered speakers of standard or educated British English as opposed to, say, American English.

Varieties of world Englishes

The varieties of English that are commonly accepted and are considered 'legitimate' for educational purposes all over the world are American and British English. The other varieties, Australian, Canadian and New Zealand English, are still trying to achieve legitimacy (Bell and Kuiper, 1999; Collins and Blair, 1989; Turner, 1997; Hundt, 1998). The national varieties used in countries of Asia and Africa where English has official and societal status raise even more debate and disagreement. Table 1.1 gives some idea of the range of countries across the world where English has official status and is used for intra-national purposes (B. Kachru and Nelson, 1996: 75).

Diffusion and variation

The global spread of English and its unprecedented success as a language used in many domains all over the world have created both elation and consternation among language experts. For some there is a great deal of satisfaction that people, at last, have a viable medium for international communication in place of the tower of Babel. There is, however, an equal measure of concern at the perceived variation among Englishes and the apprehension that ultimately this will lead to the decay and disintegration of the English language. Of course, what is at stake here is not *English* per se, but *Standard English,* however we may choose to define it. The last statement is valid in view of the fact that there already is a great deal of variation in what is known as English, as has already been pointed out; there are regional variations in, e.g., American and British Englishes, and there are variations related to age, gender, etc.

Table 1.1 Functional domains of English across the Three Circles

Functions	Inner Circle	Outer Circle	Expanding Circle
Access code	+	+	+
Advertising	+	+/-	+/-
Corporate trade	+	+	+
Development	+	+/-	+/-
Government	+	+/-	-
Linguistic impact	+	+/-	+
Literary creativity	+	+/-	+/-
Literary renaissance	+	+	+
News broadcasting	+	+/-	+/-
Newspapers	+	+/-	+/-
Scientific higher education	+	+	+/-
Scientific research	+	+	+/-
Social interaction	+	+/-	+/-

[NB: The above table shows the presence and co-existence of World Englishes with other languages in various functions in bilingual or multilingual contexts. The depth of presence in each function varies from region to region and country to country. The '+' indicates an exclusive use of English in the domain, the '+/-' indicates co-existence of other local languages along with English, and the '–' signals the absence of English in the domain.]

Standards

Overarching all the discussion of variation within, say, the UK and US are the concepts of Standard British English and General American English, which are codified in grammatical descriptions, dictionaries, and manuals of usage. According to those who voice concern with respect to the developments of Outer- and Expanding-Circle Englishes, it is the 'standard' language which is in danger of being diluted by these new varieties.

The concerns of standards and codification become clearer and more fruitfully discussed in the context of emergence of indigenized Englishes outside the Inner Circle. The debate between those who see a deterioration in standards and therefore reject notions of indigenized Englishes, and those who argue that indigenized Englishes demonstrate the acculturation of English to varied contexts and celebrate the creative potential of its users, has been going on for over two decades now. The questions raised are not only relevant to world Englishes but also to sociolinguistics in general as well as to the more immediate concerns of learners, parents and teachers — those of educational policy and planning.

The history of how the notion of 'standard' language arose and became established is both interesting and instructive, and is discussed elsewhere (see

Chapter 7). The issues of standards and the codification of indigenized varieties in the Outer and Expanding Circles are of more immediate relevance here.

External models in the Outer and Expanding Circles

A number of scholars have been aware of the fact that the notion of standard in language has more to do with ideological than with linguistic factors. For example, Marckwardt (1942: 309) wrote that 'the acceptance as a standard of one type of speech over another is based not upon linguistic considerations but rather upon political, cultural, and economic factors'. He went on to suggest that London English may be a satisfactory standard for most Southern English speakers, but 'there is no excuse for its adoption in New York, Chicago, Atlanta, or San Francisco, when these cities in themselves constitute powerful centers which affect in many ways the behavior of culture of the inhabitants within their sphere of influence'.

Similar arguments are applicable to justify an Indian, a Nigerian, or a Singaporean model for the respective countries. However, there are well-known scholars who are in favour of maintaining an external norm — American or British — for the Outer and Expanding Circles on the basis of arguments such as the following.

First, a uniform standard world-wide is essential for maintaining 'world English' or 'international English' or 'global English' as a viable means of communication (a *lingua franca*). Acceptance of multiple norms would lead to fragmentation of the language and leave us again without a common language for interaction across cultures. The leadership of Outer- and Expanding-Circle countries (e.g., presidents and prime ministers) is not in favour of internal norms, anyway, which they view as non-standard.

Second, there are already varieties that have been codified after extensive and intensive research. There is an abundance of instructional and reference materials in American and British English. Other Englishes, such as Indian or Singaporean, have yet to be codified. In any case, educated spoken varieties across these regions are not so different from American or British varieties, or from one another, and even less differentiated are the written varieties. People in the Outer and Expanding Circles use English for restricted purposes, for which the models of English currently available are quite adequate. Therefore, there is no need to look for new, internal norms in India, the Philippines, or Singapore.

Third, the relationship between language and culture is organic, and all this talk of nativization and acculturation does not change the fact that English necessarily reflects British and/or American culture. The creativity of the Inner-Circle user or native speaker remains unmatched in the Outer- and

Expanding-Circle varieties, as they are not used in all the domains of human activity. Literary creativity in the Outer and Expanding Circles has value in sociological and anthropological terms (the works represent the exotica), but African, Indian, Philippine, Singaporean and other literatures are on the periphery of American and British English literatures, which define the literary canon.

Fourth, the case in favour of regional norms, such as South Asian, African, South-East Asian, etc., reflects 'liberation linguistics' ideologies and is motivated by considerations of power.

Internal models in the Outer and Expanding Circles

Contrary to these views in favour of external models, the supporters of internal models in the Outer Circle present the following arguments.

First, the development of American English and now the progressive movement towards claims of independent status for Australian, Canadian and New Zealand Englishes demonstrate that acculturation of language to new contexts is unavoidable. To quote Mencken (1936: 3), '[t]he first American colonists had perforce to invent Americanisms, if only to describe the unfamiliar landscape and weather, flora and fauna confronting them.' Given this intuitively reasonable view, it is easy to see that there is even stronger justification for 'inventing' Indianisms, Nigerianisms, Philippinisms, Singaporeanisms, etc., considering how socioculturally different India, Nigeria, The Philippines and Singapore are from North America and Britain. The claim that English is used for a narrow range of purposes in the ESL contexts has also directly been questioned, for example, by Kennedy in his comments (Quirk and Widdowson, 1985: 7): 'whenever there has been careful research on the use of English in an ESL context, an organic complexity has been revealed in the functional range, use and purpose ... . Surely it is what the users of the language do, not what a small elite would like them to do which counts in the end.'

Second, languages do not owe their existence to codification, they exist because they are used by people. Just as Americanisms were noted and commented upon long before grammars and dictionaries of the American language were compiled, features of African, South Asian, Southeast Asian and other Englishes have increasingly been catalogued by careful researchers. Dictionaries of many of the varieties are already available or are being compiled (see Chapter 17) and partial grammatical descriptions are also accessible in existing reference resources (see Chapters 3 and 16). The International Corpus of English or ICE (Nelson, 2004), comprising data from varieties of English from fifteen countries (Australia, Canada, East Africa, Great Britain, Hong Kong, India, Ireland, Jamaica, Malaysia, New Zealand, Philippines, Singapore,

South Africa, Sri Lanka, USA), will lead to research on these varieties. Meanwhile, the users of these varieties are making use of the resource in ways they find serve their purposes best. At the time Nelson (2004) went to press, the following corpora were available for academic research: Great Britain, East Africa (Kenya and Tanzania), India, New Zealand, Philippines, and Singapore, and rapid progress was being made by the compilers of corpora from Hong Kong, Ireland, Jamaica, Malaysia, and South Africa. (The following Web site contains detailed information about the availability of these corpora: http://www.ucl.ac.uk/english-usage/ice/index.htm.)

Third, as users of English keep enlarging its range and depth in the Outer and Expanding Circles and the language becomes acculturated and transforms itself into localized varieties (see Chapter 2), the question of the organic relationship between *American* or *British* culture and English becomes moot. Both linguists researching the varieties and authors writing in African, Indian, Philippine and Singaporean Englishes have pointed to the need for moulding the language to their respective experiences (see Chapter 10; Dhillon 1994; B. Kachru, 2002). The strength of the English language has been its ability to represent effectively the contextual experiences of those who use it (see Chapter 8). This is true of all languages of wider communication, but even more so in the case of English.

Fourth, it is worth repeating the point that, ultimately, the issue of standard has more to do with power and ideology than with language; as Crystal observes (in Quirk and Widdowson, 1985: 9), '... all discussion of standards ceases very quickly to be a linguistic discussion, and becomes instead an issue of social identity'. The assertion of status of Indian, the Philippine or Nigerian English is an assertion of sociolinguistic reality and a claim of identity. The evidence for the reality and the justification for the claim of identity are in the unique characteristics that English has acquired and the uses that it is being put to around the world.

Fifth, as for the increasing differentiation among varieties and issues of intelligibility, as Crystal puts it (1997: 136–7), 'A likely scenario is that our current ability to use more than one dialect would simply extend to meet the fresh demands of the international scene ... Most people are already "multidialectal" to a greater or lesser extent.'

Teaching methods and materials, selection of teachers, including the desirability of importing 'native speakers' as instructors or assistants, and types of tests are all intimately dependent upon the resolution of the controversies discussed above. If an education ministry, school committee, or school administration believes in the primacy of an Inner-Circle English, the decisions that those bodies make will be quite different from those in a system that is oriented towards regional or local norms (see Chapter 9 for discussion of these issues). While debates rage and policies are formulated or changed, the use of English in different contexts is transforming the English language in various ways.

Ideological perspectives

There is another side to the spread of English, which is not purely linguistic or sociolinguistic, and which brings in troubling questions of power and ideology. Both Inner- and other-Circle scholars and researchers have been grappling with the impact of English on other languages and cultures.

As a language with transnational presences in various configurations of institutionalization, ranges of functions, and depths of penetration in societies, English lends obvious advantages to its users. On the other hand, it is not surprising that such access to a global language comes with costs of various sorts. English is the paradigm modern language of political and economic power. As such, some observers assert that the power of English is the factor responsible for disenfranchisement of a vast majority of populations in the third world, and a major cause of the 'deaths' of hundreds of minority languages.

Phillipson (1992: 17 *ff.*) asserts that '[t]he advance of English, whether in Britain, North America, South Africa, Australia or New Zealand has invariably been at the expense of other languages', and claims that 'the monolingualism of the Anglo-American establishment blinds its representatives to the realities of multilingualism in the contemporary world and gives them a ... false perspective'.

He divides the communities of the English-using world into two collectives: the *core* and *periphery*. The core, according to his characterization and listing of countries, matches the Inner Circle of B. Kachru (1985). The periphery is subdivided into two categories: those countries that 'require English as an international link language', such as Japan and Korea, and those that use English for 'a range of intranational purposes', such as India and Singapore. The latter sub-category comprises former colonial countries where English is a desirable medium, and access to it is actively sought by many people. Citing B. Kachru (1986a), Phillipson observes: 'those in possession of English benefit from an alchemy which transmutes [language] into material and social ... advantage. Not surprisingly, attitudes to the language tend to be very favourable.'

However, English replaces and 'displaces' other languages in both core and periphery countries. Displacement occurs when 'English takes over in specific domains', such as education or government (Phillipson, 1992: 27). This evaluative view of the nature of the spread of English is further examined in Chapter 22.

Pennycook (1994: 73) explores the sources of what he refers to as 'discourse of English as an International Language (EIL)', and also the nature of Linguistics and Applied Linguistics as disciplines. 'Discourse' in his use (see his f.n. 1 on p. 104) seems to be about knowledge as power, and about who controls any body of knowledge, thus not only accruing power to themselves, but also controlling who will be admitted to the club or acknowledged as having a share in power.

Pennycook's thesis is that the power and prestige of EIL came about largely because of what he terms 'a will to description' (1994: 73). That is, the English-speaking colonizers were also in part linguistic codifiers, and gatekeepers with respect to people who wished to share in the economic and other benefits of becoming English users. With reference to how English was regulated by its colonial 'owners', Pennycook makes the following observations about 'the extent to which linguistics is a very particular European cultural form':

> From the cultural politics of linguistics has emerged a view of language as a homogeneous unity, as objectively describable, as an isolated structural entity; meaning is taken either to reside in a world/word correspondence that is best articulated in English or within the system itself (and typically in the brain of the native speaker); monolingualism is taken to be the norm; and speech is always given priority over writing. (Pennycook, 1994: 109)

The second arm of regulating language was the importance attached to language standardization, because of 'the belief that language reveals the mind and that to speak the common or "vulgar" language demonstrated that one belonged to the vulgar classes and thus that one was morally and intellectually inferior' (p. 112). Standardization in the colonial period thus served to make it easy to tell who was who in social hierarchies. Pennycook further comments that:

> [t]he view of the spread of English as natural, neutral and beneficial is made possible by the dominance of positivism and structuralism in linguistics and applied linguistics, since these paradigms have allowed for the concentration only on a notion of abstract system at the expense of social, cultural or political understandings of language. (Pennycook, 1994: 141)

Phillipson and Pennycook represent views of English and of English teaching and learning which have raised important questions that contribute to the entire debate on the benefits and drawbacks of the spread of English.

Literatures in world Englishes

The ideological stance on a 'legitimate standard' extends from forms of language to canonicity of literatures. Approaches to literatures in English have for a long time recognized at least American and British streams of productivity. This, of course, was not always the case, but it is certainly true today. In the same way, English literatures produced in Africa and Asia 'have both a national identity and a linguistic distinctiveness' (B. Kachru, 1986b:

161). Just as American writers diverged from previous literary styles and genres to express new settings and relationships, Outer-Circle authors such as Rao and Achebe exploit linguistic, social and cultural features which allow them to express realities, themes and settings 'to delineate contexts which generally do not form part of what may be labeled the traditions of English literature'. Deviations from familiar genres and norms of the Inner Circle have been disturbing to some observers; but for others, it seems reasonable that English take on new forms and functions as it is transplanted into multilingual settings (Ashcroft et al., 1989; Talib, 2002).

Having made the choice to write in English to start with, multilingual authors have to pay attention to the forms and functions they assign to their English usage. As Thumboo observes:

> But language must serve, not overwhelm, if the Commonwealth writer is to succeed. Mastering it involves holding down and breaching a body of habitual English associations to secure that condition of verbal freedom cardinal to energetic, resourceful writing. In a sense the language is remade, where necessary, by adjusting the interior landscape of words in order to explore and meditate (*sic*) the permutations of another culture and environment. (Thumboo, 1976: ix)

Monolingual authors make the same sorts of choices, of course, e.g., in considering the usage of characters' dialogue on the basis of geography or education; but the decisions of the multilingual author are more complex, as they involve more potential variables, including those of multiple literary traditions. For example, Southeast Asia has cultural and literary traditions inherited from Sanskrit, Malay, Chinese, Javanese, Portuguese, Dutch, Spanish, to name just a few, which manifest themselves in English literary creations of the region. As Thumboo points out (1976: xvi), it is not possible to erase the traces of these traditions: 'cultures, especially those with a long history, have a hard core, conservative and self-protecting and not likely to yield'. This is especially true of the local languages, Chinese and Sanskrit in the context of, say, Indonesia, Malaysia and Singapore.

Multilingual English users

All language use is at its heart 'creative'; this insight, now a commonplace observation, was a part of the paradigm shift in formal linguistics in the 1960s: most utterances are novel utterances, and hearers are able to decipher such novel messages at a first hearing most of the time. Multilingual language users have more options of codes, strategies, and nuances since they control more than one linguistic system.

To take an example from literature, the following passage from Raja Rao's novel *Kanthapura* (1963: 10; cited in B. Kachru, 1986b: 165) depicts the character Jayaramachar telling *Harikatha*, traditional religious stories, in which a connection is made between ancient Indian legends and contemporary events leading towards independence:

> "Today," he says, "it will be the story of Siva and Parvati." And Parvati in penance becomes the country and Siva becomes heaven knows what! "Siva is the three-eyed," he says, "and Swaraj too is three-eyed: Self-purification, Hindu-Moslem unity, Khaddar." And then he talks of Damayanthi and Sakunthala and Yasodha and everywhere there is something about our country and something about Swaraj ...

In this passage, names such as *Siva* and *Parvati* contain 'reference to the multitude of the pantheon of Hindu gods', while the word *Khaddar*, 'handspun cloth', is a contextually meaningful reference to an element of anti-Raj protests — making cloth for clothing by hand in India, rather than buying it from British purveyors. Such texts raise '*interpretive* difficulties' (B. Kachru, 1986b: 165–6) because readers from outside the context do not have straightforward access to the assumptions that make the allusions work effectively as parts of the overall text. Such use of the language extends the cultural load of English words to Asian and African myths, folklore, and traditions. It universalizes English, and to that extent 'de-Englishizes' it.

Multilingual people's grammars are best thought of in terms of 'verbal repertoires'; they use 'a formally and functionally determined range of languages ... as part of their competence for linguistic interaction'. One of the salient devices available to such users is 'the faculty and ease of mixing and switching [of codes], and the adoption of stylistic and discoursal strategies from the total [available] repertoire' (B. Kachru, 1986b: 164). The passage cited above from Raja Rao's *Kanthapura* illustrates this (for code-mixing and switching, see Chapter 18).

Issues in English language education

Challenges to English language teaching (ELT) from a world Englishes perspective are many. As soon as one recognizes the pluralistic nature of English across the world today, the possibilities become numerous. The concerns turn on nativization and standardization, concepts explored in this chapter and throughout this work from various perspectives.

Tawake's Symposium on World Englishes in the Classroom (1995) reveals some of the more specific terms in which these concerns about teaching of world Englishes have been addressed. Brown's paper in the symposium explores the basic questions of whether 'to teach or not to teach' world

Englishes. Bhatt investigates how prescriptivism and creativity interact and conflict in approaching the teaching of world Englishes. Baumgardner uses Pakistani English to present an investigation of 'acceptability and the norm' in a non-Inner-Circle English. Nelson addresses concerns raised with regard to intelligibility in teaching English composition to mixed-background students. Tawake brings out the importance of 'cross-cultural reader response' in assigning comprehensibility and interpretability to texts. She concludes, 'If readers from different cultures create vivid, dynamic, but different, imaginative experiences from the same text and reach very different interpretations of the meaning of that text, our approach to teacher training in literature should be guided by that reality' (1995a: 296).

A study by Smith (1992: 86) provides evidence that 'many native and nonnative speakers of English would label most educated speakers of nonnative English as users of Standard English'. For those who share this view, the definition of 'Standard' is one that conforms to the reality of world Englishes; those who do not share this view face the difficult task of trying to *rationally* explain away what Strevens (1983: 88) referred to as the 'evolution', as opposed to conscious fashioning, of standard English (see Chapter 7).

However, many 'fallacies' in facing the realties of ELT in the post-Inner-Circle English-using world still remain (B. Kachru, 1992b: 357). Among these are the mistaken belief that English is a means to interacting with and becoming involved in the cultures of Inner-Circle users, or that Inner-Circle users have any large degree of input in ELT in the Outer and Expanding Circles (1992b: 358). It is not in fact obvious that most global users of English have any desire to speak or write like Americans, Canadians, British or Australians. The challenges to ELT in the future perhaps begin with settling codified models and norms for 'local' Englishes.

It is not necessary for everyone in every part of the world to be able to communicate as readily with an American or an Australian as they do with fellow countrymen. But users familiar with several varieties of English can make accommodations with other users they come in contact with, to the greater satisfaction of all participants. This means that ELT professionals have a responsibility not to limit their students' creativity, but to help to shape it, through increased awareness of others and ever less complacency about 'my English'.

Conclusion

As this brief survey shows, the areas of study of world Englishes and the approaches to those areas are many and complex. From description of the language to evaluation of its impact, formal and functional categories of knowledge are available for analysis or waiting to be brought to light. The concepts and information outlined here will be treated in detail in the following chapters.

Familiarity with variation creates awareness among users of all varieties of English to the extraordinary ranges of possibilities for expression by those who can draw on multicultural and multilingual experience. Such awareness makes demands on monolinguals, as well as on anyone unfamiliar with the variety of English employed by a speaker/writer from an unfamiliar part of the English-using world. Variations in genres, styles, and devices have their effects on English as a whole. It is in this sense that English is becoming an ever more 'universal' language, not in the sense that it is one code which can be acquired in one place and then transferred to another as a whole, unadapted structure (B. Kachru, 1986b: 170).

Suggested activities

Read the following paragraph and discuss the questions that follow (Bolton, Kingsley, 2000, The sociolinguistics of Hong Kong and the space for Hong Kong English. *World Englishes* 19(3), 265–85):

In this article, Bolton applies the defining characteristics suggested in Butler (1997) to define a variety of English to determine if Hong Kong English, one of the world Englishes, is a variety, and goes on to say that the discussion of whether the 'criteria' are sufficiently persuasive or powerful to make a distinct 'variety' evident is less important than 'the desire to create a new space for discussion and discourse on Hong Kong English. Such a space would encompass not only the global and cosmopolitan, but also the local and ludic [playful], not just one variety of localised English, but a number of different voices' (p. 281).

a.   How important is it for users and teachers of English and researchers in the field to become aware of *all* variation in their region and across the regions?

b.   A great deal of importance is attached to standard language, and dialects — whether geographical, or based on factors such as ethnicity, gender, age, etc. — are either totally neglected or less valued in 'high culture' contexts of academia, government, legal system, etc. What are the consequences of this sociolinguistic practice? What is your reaction to Bolton's plea for creating 'space' for not only the more standard-like variety but also the 'playful' varieties in your own region?

c.   Unlike the 'high culture' contexts mentioned above, literature and media (popular or the 'high' variety) exploit all variation for creative purposes. Discuss the reasons for such use of variation and its significance for the societal view of 'standard' language.

2
Conceptual framework

English is the lingua franca that Asians now share with one another and with the rest of the world. One should add however that this English is now also manifestly an Asian language in its own right. It has been thoroughly indigenised. One might consequently say that whereas the centre of gravity of English as a native language continues to be the North Atlantic (in insular Europe and continental North America), the centre of gravity of English as a second language or lingua franca is manifestly Asian (especially in the South and East).

McArthur (2003: 22)

Introduction

Concepts of varieties and variation must be examined from a number of points of view in order to give anything like a complete picture of contemporary world Englishes. Chapter 1 presented a brief overview of the development of varieties of English across the world diasporas, and Chapter 3 explicates the characteristics of varieties, e.g., phonological and grammatical features. This chapter presents the basic theoretical concepts that must be understood in order to hold a clear view of the status of English as an inclusive entity, and of the relationships of the many various Englishes extant in the world today. The focus here is on re-examining the concepts that have been the mainstay of the ELT profession regardless of the context of teaching, learning and using the language, and the status of those concepts in the new context of growing research on world Englishes.

The reality of native vs. non-native

For a long time, the designations that served the ELT profession were 'native' vs. 'non-native' speaker(s). This distinction is not unreasonable on its face. In the US, for example, university departments of 'English' have always been quite different from departments of 'Foreign Languages', which are sometimes specifically named, as, the Department of Romance Languages, or of French, German, etc., and they are virtually always administratively separate from one another. The same is true of China or Japan, where Departments of English, French, German, etc., are within the realm of 'foreign' languages.

The worth and advisability of teaching students another language as opposed to 'refining' their own has often been intuitively regarded as an acceptable matter of argument. Therefore, if American students studied French as a foreign language — the modifier has always been left unspoken, at least in the US — it stood to reason that students learning English where it was historically not an indigenous language were learning it as a foreign language. And, since their accents, most immediately, and also their lexicons, etc., were different from 'ours', whether 'our US' or 'our British', they were automatically 'non-native speakers'. These polar designations persist in widespread professional and casual use today, in spite of a great deal of discussion about doing away with them (see, e.g., Paikeday, 1985). The relevance of this distinction to linguistics and language teaching still evokes a great deal of discussion and debate.

In a recent monograph, Davies (2003) takes up the whole question of the reality of the native speaker as a construct and examines it from various perspectives, including its psycholinguistic, linguistic and sociolinguistic conceptualization. After examining the 'common-sense' and empirical criteria, he concludes that 'the fundamental opposition [between native speaker and non-native speaker] is one of power and that in the event membership is determined by the non-native speaker's assumption of confidence and of identity' (p. 216). That is, the basic criterion remains the long-asserted requirement of exposure in early childhood, variously referred to as 'mother tongue', 'first language' and 'home language' (pp. 16–8). All other criteria are what Davies terms 'contingent issues' (p. 212); that is, for example, it is possible, though perhaps difficult, for someone for whom English was not the *mother*, *home* or *first* language to acquire access to intuitions about his/her own grammar, facility in creative performance, and so on. The 'contingencies' reside in parameters such as contact with other speakers of the language, opportunities for active use of the language, and attitudinal evaluations of the user's language by others (p. 211).

As for non-native speakers, it is legitimate to ask if the construct represents a monolithic reality, as does the 'native speaker'. The answers have varied, as the following discussion shows.

EFL vs. ESL: The prevailing view

In the middle-to-later years of the twentieth century, it became apparent to the ELT profession that the situations of 'non-native' users of English around the world were not all the same. A clear distinction was to be made, for example, between students of English in Africa or Asia, who already had other languages at their disposal, and were learning English for limited purposes, and immigrants into the US, Canada, etc., who were taking up English as their language for all necessary business and most if not all social interaction, to the point that the language of 'the old country' was set aside, with children not being encouraged to learn it, or even being forbidden to do so. Thus, the distinction between English as a Second Language (ESL) for immigrants to the Inner Circle and as a Foreign Language (EFL) for learners world-wide in their own contexts arose to account in some broad ways for differences between situations of acquisition (learning) and use of English in various contexts (see, e.g., the discussion of this topic in Strevens, 1992).

EFL users were those who learned English at a distance from any 'native' speakers and for limited utility, e.g., for reading knowledge to keep up with Western science and technology. ESL users studied the language more intensely and intimately, and they could speak it, which the EFL person was not necessarily expected to be able to do. There was an implicit association of proficiency-level and comparison, which made EFL something less than ESL. Most departments, programmes, and textbooks use 'ESL' as a generic inclusive label for teaching English to those who already speak other languages, though sometimes the EFL/ESL distinction is made explicit, as in the title of Celce-Murcia's *Teaching English as a Second or Foreign Language* (1991).

This is one view of the EFL/ESL dichotomy among non-native speakers. Strevens (1992: 35–7) expressed a more sophisticated view in which he distinguished between *primary* and *secondary* languages. For someone who grew up in an English-speaking household, neighbourhood, or larger community, English was the 'primary' language. Wherever a language was acquired or learned for purposes of business, diplomacy, education, etc., it was 'secondary'. Then, among users for whom English was a secondary language, those in communities, countries or regions in which English was not a medium of formal public instruction, not an accepted code for administration, medium of education, legal affairs, broadcasting, print media, public and private discourse, and so forth, it was a foreign language.

In ESL countries such as those of South Asia, Southeast Asia and Anglophone Africa the secondary language is not 'just another language'; it has special standing as a language of education and of other officially designated functions (see the discussion of *institutionalization* below). In this case, the usage of the community necessarily comes into the picture, since by definition the individual users are strongly influenced by the language as they hear and read it in their sociolinguistic environment. The increased use of the language in education eventually leads to its use in the private domains and in creative literature. A great deal of the divided thinking in the ELT profession may have been caused by this failure to accept the fact that the models and norms for learners' English were quite different in EFL and ESL situations, with a consequent insistence on 'native' English norms in both types of situation. The FL/SL designation makes, or should indicate, a significant difference in the status and nature of English in a given context. Strevens sums it up:

> [The EFL/ESL distinction] affects the extent of the learner's prior familiarity with English, ... the learner's expectations of success, and ... both the average level of attainment ... (higher overall in ESL than in EFL countries) and the ultimate norms or goals for success which learners and teachers set themselves (aspiring to L1-like in EFL countries, aspiring rather to an NNS target in ESL countries). (Strevens, 1992: 36–7)

Speech community and speech fellowship

Both EFL and ESL countries, together with the countries where English is the primary language, belong to the same speech community. Within the wider speech community, there are speech fellowships that are marked by local contextual features (B. Kachru, 1995b). The idea of a *speech community* refers to a wide-ranging 'association' of varieties which would be conceded to be different from one another in particulars, but which are subsumable as 'sub-varieties' under a broad label. For example, American, British, Australian and New Zealand English are different from each other and are being codified as distinct varieties, but all these speech fellowships are members of the same English-speaking speech community. At a slightly more restricted level, there is an American English speech community, with speech fellowships representing regional speakers from the Northeast (Maine), the Southwest (New Mexico), the Northwest (Oregon), or Southeast (South Carolina). The speakers from these regions exhibit noticeably distinct dialectal features of pronunciation, lexicon, and so on. Despite their empirically measurable differences, all of them would be labelled members of 'the US speech community'. Obviously, this concept is very abstract (see B. Kachru, 1985: 23); however, imprecise as the definition may be, it accords well with the attitudinal basis of people's judgements of acceptability/non-acceptability of non-standard regional or social varieties recognized to be exponents of the community and of ESL and EFL varieties. The NS/NNS and ESL/EFL designations, by definition, play an exclusion game by not allowing speakers from certain regions into the 'club' of the speech community. Looking at varieties of English in terms of speech communities and fellowships, B. Kachru says, 'brings us closer to the real world of English users, their underlying distinct differences, and also their shared characteristics' (1995b: 16).

Looking at language forms or functions in terms of dichotomies is rarely useful or capable of withstanding long-term and in-depth scrutiny, and this has been true of the distinctions between NS/NNS or ESL/EFL outlined above. A more rational way of categorizing and discussing the many varieties of English across the world is provided by the concept of Englishes in terms of their developmental and functional characteristics.

The Three Circles

B. Kachru (1985: 12–3) introduced the three circles concept of world Englishes. It is an interpretation that rests not only on a valid historical view of the spread of English (see Chapter 1), but also on sociolinguistically viable interpretations of the status and functions of English in its many contexts. In some ways, the circles overlap former notions of NS/NNS and EFL/ESL, but they serve explanatory needs better in research and in pedagogy. The three circles are a conception of the status and functions of Englishes, including their identity-conferring capacities, that is dynamic and not presumed to be controllable by any agency or group, 'native' or otherwise.

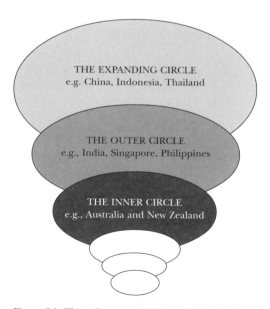

Figure 2.1 Three Concentric Circles of Asian Englishes

The Inner Circle refers to English as it originally took shape and later was spread across the world in its first diaspora. In this transplantation of English, speakers from England carried the language to Australia, New Zealand, and North America, as well as to the extended British Isles or UK. In the countries of this mnemonically apt Inner Circle, English was the primary, indeed, with the exception of Canada, the sole language of education, of officialdom, and of society at large. Its stability in this position is a matter of fact, to the point that, for example, the US Constitution made no mention of it as an 'official language' to the exclusion of any other: the status of English simply did not have to be mentioned.

The Outer Circle of Englishes was produced by the second diaspora of English, which spread the language through colonization in Asia and Africa. This was accomplished via a relatively small number of users sent to parts of the world far removed from the societies where English was the medium of daily use. Yet, because of the imposed economic, political and military realities, English became *the* additional language for many indigenous residents of countries such as India and Nigeria. The British Empire later crumbled away, but English did not: it had made itself indispensable. In the multilingual and multicultural nations and regions which were its newer homes, English took on functions which other languages had not performed. For example, in some places English became a medium of higher education which was available to young people from all sub-regions, no matter what their first, or home, languages were. English became for many people the primary language, in Strevens' term, in certain domains. Outer-Circle countries and regions such as the Caribbean, India, Nigeria, Pakistan, the Philippines, and Singapore are now routinely characterized as 'English-using', and it is a surprise to a visitor when a resident cannot speak at least some English, rather than the reverse. It is in these countries and regions that a vibrant tradition of literary creativity flourishes and many writers have been awarded prestigious literary prizes, including the Nobel Prize, for their creative works in English.

The Expanding Circle represents the further diffusion of English propelled by the political and economic influence of Britain and the USA in East Asia, Middle East and Latin America, in addition to Europe and the island nations of the world. In the nations of the Expanding Circle, English has limited roles in the public life, basically in higher education in science and technology, and very restricted functions in the personal domain. This, however, may be changing as more and more nations in Europe and Asia are adopting the policy of introducing English at early stages of schooling to compete in the global technology and service-oriented market (for details of the European situation, see the following section; for developments in East and Southeast Asia, see Chapters 12 and 13).

The concept of circles, as B. Kachru (1985) makes it clear, does not grant any central status to the Inner Circle and does not put the Outer and

Expanding Circles in the periphery, in spite of the criticism of the notion levelled by scholars such as Mufwene (2001b: 139). The labels merely indicate the historical contexts of the varieties — their original habitat and later spread, and the population movement vs. other factors that were responsible for their further development.

Range and depth

Within the contexts of the Outer and Expanding Circles, two dimensions need to be considered in order to substantively characterize the status and functions of English in communities: *range* and *depth* of the spread of English. These considerations make available another, pragmatically more informative and usable, face of the 'nativeness' dichotomy: According to B. Kachru:

> In defining the nativeness of Englishes, yet another distinction is useful: between genetic nativeness as opposed to functional nativeness … One refers to the historical relationship and the other to the nativeness of a language in terms of its functional domains and range and its depth in social penetration and resultant acculturation. (B. Kachru, 1997: 217)

Range in this context of analysis and discussion refers to all the functions which English has in a given community context, e.g., in education at all levels, business, legal system, administration, etc., as well as in more intimate domains of family and other social networks whose members may or may not share another language. Range also comprises the shifting of varieties across or within a speech event, such that appropriate lectal and other choices are made by participants, in terms of establishing and maintaining identity, group cohesiveness, and so forth.

Depth of societal penetration refers to the uses of English that are available to people with varying degrees of education who are at different socio-economic levels, with different jobs and professions. English may be expected to be used by well-educated (perhaps Western-educated) academics. Is it also used by top-level business people, management, employees, and professionals such as doctors, nurses, engineers? Do shopkeepers, taxi-drivers, and blue-collar workers use it? A cline of proficiency may be associated with societal penetration, so that people with less contact with users of 'fuller' varieties of English may speak a *basilectal* form, with gradations up the economic and social scales to an *acrolect*.

Institutionalization

In societies of the Outer Circle, English is said to be *institutionalized*. This term refers to the official recognition and acceptance of English. Its status is explicitly recognized and, while its use may be denigrated by some observers (who may very likely be users themselves), it is in fact encouraged by legislation and in use. In the Anglophone Caribbean, English is the *de jure* official language and is used in addition to the English-based creole and immigrant languages. In Kenya, English is the second national language with a status lower than that of Swahili, which is the official language. In Nigeria and Zambia English is one of the state languages. In India, English is an associate official language with Hindi, which is the official language. English in India co-exists with national languages (e.g., Hindi, Marathi, Tamil) of the vast territory; it also has the status of a national language for the purposes of, say, the national academy of letters, and it is the official language of eight Union Territories, directly controlled from New Delhi.

The position of Europe is interesting in that claims are being made about the emergence of a distinct Euro-English variety (Cenoz and Jessner, 2000; Modiano, 1996). This is understandable in view of the fact that English and French are the two working languages of the European Union; fluency in English is a prerequisite for EU employees, and French is employed by the permanent staff. Delegates from member countries use English for communication, including in EU meetings (Hoffman, 2000: 11). English has a very high profile in Belgium, Germany, the Netherlands and the Scandinavian countries, and 90 percent of all EU pupils learn English as their first 'foreign' language.

In countries of the Expanding Circle, English exists in *performance varieties*, that is, it is not institutionalized as in the Outer Circle. This situation obtains in, for example, Korea, Japan, mainland China, and Indonesia. In contrast to the institutionalized status of English in Outer-Circle countries, the language has no official sanction (except as a required or encouraged school subject), and indeed may be militated against. For example, Stanlaw (1992: 194) reported that the Japanese 'Ministry of Education's Department of National Language, *as a matter of policy* "has never published anything that contains loanwords of Western origin" (Sibata, 1975: 169)' (emphasis added). Yet English in the Expanding Circle is very much a fact of life; it is the most frequently studied foreign language in China, Korea and Japan (see Cheng, 1992; Baik and Shim, 1995; Stanlaw 1992). Even in Japan the official policy has given an extended role to English in the educational system of the country in recent years (see Chapter 12).

Norm-providing and norm-accepting

A way of seeing the categorization of the circles is in terms of where the norms for the communities come from. In Expanding-Circle countries, as has been mentioned, the norms still come from outside, from the Inner Circle. This is basically true of China, Japan, Thailand and Korea in Asia and in most of the countries in the Middle East, a large part of Europe and Latin America. Thus, the Inner-Circle Englishes may be spoken of as 'norm-providing' — they provide norms and, less abstractly, teaching models and physical materials such as textbooks — to the Expanding Circle, which may then be termed 'norm-accepting'. This is the situation in Korea, for example, where US English is considered the prestige model (see Baik and Shim, 1995); cf. Cheng's (1992) remarks on the Chinese switch from British to American English as the target of teaching and learning. Historically, British and American English have been the two prestige models, but the situation is 'dynamic', as B. Kachru (1997: 220) terms it: exposure to various Englishes is becoming technologically easier, and 'variational pluralism' is taking hold in some contexts (e.g., the codification of Australian English, as discussed by Butler, 1997).

In the Outer Circle, the situation regarding norms is more complicated; attitudes having to do with cultural and political identities make themselves felt, with some spokespersons advocating outright banishment of English, others, adoption of one or another Inner-Circle model, and still others, adoption of a regional or local model. This is the ambivalent situation that B. Kachru terms 'norm-developing' and applies to many countries in South Asia and Southeast Asia.

Although attitudes vary and debates continue, the English language is going through the natural processes of nativization of sounds, vocabulary, grammar and conventions of using language to perform various acts. The nativized variety is what is being used in everyday life, in media, and in other domains of national life. Along with the process of nativization of English, the process of English influencing the local languages continues, which has been termed 'Englishization' (B. Kachru, 1979).

Nativization and acculturation

As Alatis and Lowenberg concisely put it in their afterword to Thumboo (2001b), 'Nativization brings forth a new variety of English, and Englishization causes changes in the native language' (p. 428). Both processes are triggered by language contact and the natural inclination in users to mould the medium to express relevant contextual realities. Nativization affects the structure of language (e.g., sound system and rhythmic patterns, vocabulary and sentence structure) and use of language (e.g., conventions of speaking and writing). It is the process of nativization that is responsible for the differences manifest in pronunciation, lexico-grammar and literary creativity among various Englishes. Numerous examples of the phenomenon are discussed in Chapters 3, 4, 8, 17, and 21, in addition to the description of regional varieties in Part II.

Bilinguals' creativity

In the countries of the Outer Circle, taking English to themselves without limitations on its possible functions has quite naturally included using it, along with other languages of the available repertoire, in creative ways. 'Bilinguals' creativity' is perhaps most readily thought of as 'creative writing', whether of prose in stories or novels, poetry, or plays for the theatre. It is certainly the case that, following the first public attempt at such creativity in the early nineteenth century, Outer-Circle writers have made names for themselves across the English-using world. B. Kachru (1997: 222–3) gives this representative list of world-class literary prize winners: Nobel Prize in Literature — Wole Soyinka (Nigeria), 1986; Derek Alton Walcott (Trinidad), 1992; V. S. Naipaul (Trinidad), 2001; Neustadt Award — Raja Rao (India), 1988; Booker Prize — Salman Rushdie (India), 1995; Chinua Achebe (Nigeria), 1987; Michael Ondaatje (Sri Lanka), 1992; Ben Okri (Nigeria), 1991; Arundhati Roy (India), 1997.

Creative use of language is certainly not limited to fiction, though. Journalists in many countries ply their trade in English (see Chapter 12); there are over 3,600 English-medium newspapers in India (B. Kachru in McArthur, 1992: 510), and 21 in Pakistan (Baumgardner, 1993: 255). In these contexts, English sometimes takes on new functions (as, the often-cited matrimonial advertisements in South Asian periodicals), and in every case exhibits the characteristics that define a particular regional or national variety. Consider, for example, this excerpt from *The Nation* (1989), a Pakistan daily published from Lahore:

> ... the Soviet Deputy Foreign minister, currently shuttling in the region to find a solution to the Afghan problem, met Sahabzada Yaqub Khan this morning for about 45 minutes ... [S]ources at Pakistan's Foreign Office are adamantly evasive to comment on the progress made ... (cited in Kachru and Nelson, 1996: 75–6)

English also plays a significant role in broadcast media in many contexts. As K. Sridhar (1989: 7) observes, although radio news bulletins and special-topic programming in India are offered in many minority languages, the major emphasis is on English and Hindi for pan-Indian programmes.

The examples above are from India and Pakistan; the same situation exists in most of the countries in South and Southeast Asia, as is made clear in subsequent chapters (see, e.g., Chapters 11 and 12). The aspect of creativity in world Englishes is discussed in greater detail in Chapter 8. In view of the functions of English in the national life and the transformations that the language has undergone in various regions, the issue of models achieves greater relevance in these contexts. The advocates of maintaining the integrity of British or American English have yet to appreciate the implications of these factors.

Multilingualism and models

A key realization for ELT professionals in the Inner Circle is that there are very important differences between being a monolingual and a multilingual person: the multilinguals, who have English as only one member of their linguistic repertoires, have much greater funds of resources for developing and augmenting their Englishes. One aspect of this is that the language changes and undergoes adaptations in the Outer Circle that naturally make it sound and look and even work differently from the way it does in the Inner Circle. Attitudinally, when it comes to what one regards as one's *own* language, 'difference' is often automatically regarded as 'deficiency' when it manifests in the language variety used by someone else. Monolingual speakers may be baffled by the observation that multilinguals do not use the same language in all domains; this variability is taken as a sign of lack of proficiency in the total range by speakers of any single language of the multilingual repertoire.

The other aspect of multilingual language use that is mystifying to monolingual speakers is the facility with which multilinguals mix and switch between languages in their repertoires. This has already been briefly mentioned in Chapter 1, and is discussed in some detail in Chapter 18. Such mixed language is often viewed as 'impure' by many observers. The same sort of attitude about language purity may be observed in examinations of diachronic stages of language, in that really old versions of the language may be regarded with respect, while contemporary, on-going changes in a community or fellowship are likely to be seen as 'decay' and 'crumbling standards'. This attitude may be exacerbated in observations about English in contexts that are considered outside the commentator's own preferred speech community.

Conclusion

While it may be said that there are as many 'types' of English as there are users of it, it is possible and useful in various ways to sort out classifications in terms, first, of historical criteria, and then with regard to functional parameters that have to do with the users of English and how they employ the language. English falls into legitimate paradigms of use, and it is doubtful whether any purpose is served by regarding the language as the exclusive property of the old Inner-Circle users — who, historically, have been unable to fully accept one another's Englishes themselves. The statuses of English in the Outer and

Expanding Circles must be viewed from a 'sociolinguistically realistic' point of view, rather than one that is predetermined by self-serving senses of 'ownership' or considerations of economic advantage and power. B. Kachru (1997: 215) clarifies the concept in this way: 'The term "world Englishes" is not intended to indicate any divisiveness in the English-using communities but to recognize the functions of the language in diverse pluralistic contexts.' Such a point of view removes the stigma of lack of proficiency and performance from varieties of English, and respects the fact that people take English as they find it and use it as they will.

Suggested activities

1. There are two views about the goal of acquiring English as an additional language in the Expanding Circle. Andreasson (1994: 402) claims: 'Speaking English is simply not related to cultural identity. It is rather an exponent of one's academic and language-learning abilities. It would, therefore, be far from a compliment to tell a Spanish person that his or her variety is Spanish English.'

    Contrary to this view is the following from Baxter (1980: 42):

    > A Japanese colleague, a university professor of English language and literature, went on a three-month trip to America and Britain. Upon his return, he recounted how he had been told in America that he spoke like an Englishman. In Britain, he was likened to an American English speaker. My colleague grasped the significance of this: the external reference groups were exercising their "right" to evaluate his manner of speaking English. His reaction? "I'm not an American, nor British. I'm Japanese and Japanese English is perfectly good as an international language."

    Discuss the following points with your colleagues/teachers:
    a. Is it true that using a second or additional language in the Expanding Circle is not related to one's cultural identity?
    b. Is it true that an American should feel proud if identified as a speaker from New York or Boston or Chicago, but a Spanish or Chinese speaker if identified as such should feel his/her speech is 'non-standard' and reflects poorly on his/her language learning ability?
    c. If you agree with Andreasson, how would you identify 'native speakers' whose English will serve as *the* model for the Expanding Circle? Consider 'native speakers' from Australia, Canada, New Zealand, English-speaking South Africa, the UK and the USA.

3
Structural variation

The lecture is very important, whatever your predicament, if you must be safe from end of semester *banging* from *hackeous* lecturers. If you ever *bang* for more than is safe, the school is ready to *fashee* you. To avoid this, you must go beyond attending lectures; you must be a *mad jacker* if you do it too much, you will end up as an *aro* in *B1* some do *burst* lectures *shao!* Those are the *Nfites*. Certainly, as a *jambite*, don't try it.

Longe (1999: 239)[1]

Introduction

For the users of the English in the Outer and Expanding Circles, English is either a second language, or, if they are multilingual, it is one of the languages in their linguistic repertoire. As such, their English is in constant contact with the languages of the regions which they inhabit. Consequently, these varieties of English are influenced by the local language(s) in various areas of their grammars and exhibit specific phonological, lexical, syntactic and discoursal characteristics. The excerpt above from a text in Nigerian English exemplifies features that are not familiar to users of other varieties of English. The text is, of course, coded in the student slang of a particular campus. As such, it illustrates the uses of the language localized to suit the purposes of a specific site in Nigeria. The features of Outer- and Expanding-Circle Englishes may extend or restrict the rules of the Inner-Circle varieties of English. Findings of research in identifying and describing these characteristics are summarized briefly here.

Phonology

There are phonological differences across all varieties of English. When we speak of someone having an 'accent', what we mean is that the person exhibits a characteristic pronunciation that we do not share. The differences are in stress and rhythm as well as in segmental features.

Stress and rhythm

Stress assignment in words in the Outer and Expanding Circles does not follow the rules that operate in the Inner-Circle varieties. Word stress in the Outer- and Expanding-Circle varieties may seem idiosyncratic from the perspective of a speaker from the Inner Circle, e.g., *'success* for *suc'cess* (Nigeria), *recog'nize* for *'recognize* (India, Nigeria), etc. Actually, as most such varieties have a syllable-timed rather than a stress-timed rhythm (Bamgboṣe, 1992; B. Kachru, 1983), it is probably the case that the stress assignment follows the values attached to the *morae* (weight of syllables in terms of duration) in these varieties. This seems to be the case in South Asian English (SAE). Since the vowels in *re-* and *-cog-* are short and not as 'weighty' as the diphthong in *-nize*, the primary stress goes with the heavier syllable (e.g., for Philippine English [PhE] see Bautista, 2000; Tayao, 2004).[2]

Rhythm in varieties of SAE is based on the morae of the syllables; long syllables are twice as long as short ones, but the quality of the vowels in long as well as short syllables remains the same. In the case of a word with several long syllables, all the syllables are pronounced long, irrespective of their stressed or unstressed character. This is in contrast to the Inner-Circle varieties, where the stressed syllable in a word has a longer duration as compared to the unstressed syllable; in fact, the characteristic rhythmic pattern of British English is such that in a multi-syllabic word, the duration of the several unstressed syllables is roughly equivalent to that of the one stressed syllable.

Speakers of Outer- and Expanding-Circle varieties arrive at values for syllables following the conventions of their first languages and assign stress accordingly. For instance, in words such as *biology*, speakers assign the value to syllables as follows: *ba-yo-lo-ji* and both *'bi-o-lo-gy* and *bi-o-'lo-gy* are possible. Such stress placement is attested in SAE, PhE and Singapore-Malaysian English (SME); see B. Kachru (1983), Llamzon (1969, 1997), Platt and Weber (1980), and Zuraidah Mohd Don (2000) for further discussion of these phenomena.

In addition, speakers of these varieties do not utilize stress to make a distinction between nouns and verbs in pairs such as Inner-Circle *'import* and *im'port*. They do not utilize contrastive stress for focussing, either (Bamgboṣe, 1992; Gumperz, 1982a, 1982b). Instead of *JOHN did it*, Nigerians say *It was John who did it* (Bamgboṣe, 1992) and Indians say *John only did it* (Gumperz, 1982b). Both sets of speakers are utilizing a familiar device for emphasis. Nigerians use the cleft-sentence pattern 'It was X ...' and Indians use an emphatic particle 'only' as in their native languages. Emphasis and focus, as well as the distinction between *given* and *new* information, are signalled by utilizing pitch and intonation in ways which are very different from those utilized by the Inner-Circle varieties (Gumperz, 1982a; 1982b).

In most Outer- and Expanding-Circle varieties, there exists the phenomenon of 'spelling pronunciation'. For instance, a word such as *plumber* is pronounced with a medial *-mb-* cluster since the word is spelled as it is. As English is learned in schools from local teachers, the tradition of local pronunciation continues. Although the pronunciation of segmental sounds in the Outer- and Expanding-Circle varieties hardly ever leads to communication breakdown or even serious misunderstanding, the following information about the characteristics of sounds in these varieties may be useful.

Sounds

In pronunciation, most Outer- and Expanding-Circle varieties display differences from the Inner-Circle varieties, similar to those found between regional dialects within the Inner-Circle varieties. Some of these differences lead to grammatical consequences which may affect comprehension. One such feature is the simplification of final consonant clusters in Singapore-Malaysian English, e.g., [*lef*] for *left*. By itself, in most contexts, there will probably be no serious difficulty. It is noteworthy, however, that this feature leads to the loss of past tense endings on verbs, e.g., *pick* for *picked*, and to the loss of plural markers on nouns, *bed* for *beds*. There is potential for misunderstanding in such cases. These features occur not only in the Outer- and Expanding-Circle varieties, but also in certain varieties of American English (e.g., African-American Vernacular English [AAVE], see Chapter 15).

Some English sounds that are pronounced differently in the Outer- and Expanding-Circle varieties are as follows. Only widely shared features are listed; this is not an exhaustive description of any particular regional variety.

Consonants and vowels are different as compared to the Inner-Circle varieties in the following ways:[3]

1. Voiceless plosives, *p t k*, lose their initial aspiration so that the speakers of Inner-Circle varieties often perceive them as *b d g*.
2. Fricatives *f v θ ð š ž s z* are often replaced by other sounds: *f* by *ph* (Indian English [IE]), *v* by *bh* or *w* (IE), θ by *t* (Chinese English [CE], SME, PhE) or *th* (IE), *ð* by *d* or *z* (CE, SME, PhE), or *d* or *dh* (IE), *z* and *ž* by *j* in most varieties; *s* and *š* are not kept distinct in many subvarieties, and *s, z, š* and *ž* may all be pronounced as *s* in PhE.
3. The clear and dark *l* (as in *like* and *dull*) are not distinguished in most varieties.
4. Some speakers of Expanding-Circle varieties do not distinguish between *r* and *l*.
5. Final consonant clusters are simplified in most East and Southeast Asian

varieties. In some varieties, initial consonant clusters with initial *s* are either simplified by inserting a neutral vowel between the two consonants or pronounced with an initial vowel so that the cluster is no longer initial, e.g., [səporṭ] for *sport*, [islo] for *slow* (IE).

6. Almost all Outer- and Expanding-Circle varieties simplify the diphthongs and triphthongs of the British variety, e.g., *ei>e* as in *paid, ou>o* as in *bowl, au>aw* as in *our*, pronounced [awər].

7. Stressed and unstressed vowels are not distinguished.

8. In several varieties, *ī* and *i,* and *ū* and *u* are not distinguished, therefore, *sleep* and *slip* have identical pronunciations, and so have *pool* and *pull.*

Occasionally the grammatical differences in the new varieties combine with the differences in rhythmic patterns to cause serious problems in communication between speakers of Inner- and other-Circle varieties. However, all users of English arrive at some accommodation as they become more familiar with the variety in use among the interlocutors (Smith, 1992). Awareness of variety differences thus promotes successful communication across varieties. The media have unintentionally started playing a role in creating such awareness, as multinational channels such as the British Broadcasting Corporation, Public Radio International and Cable News Network employ more and more local reporters with a variety of accents to report on local and regional events.

Grammar

The grammatical features that are common to a large number of varieties are described below in comparison with the grammars of the American/British varieties, not because they are being treated as 'the norm', but because they are extensively codified in grammars (e.g., Quirk et al., 1985) and dictionaries (e.g., Webster, Random House, Longman), and most students of English are familiar with them. What follows is a brief discussion of features that are widely but not uniformly shared.

Nouns

The grammar of nouns deals with the dependency between articles and singular count nouns and the distinction between count/mass and singular/ plural.

◆ Articles and determiners

English articles belong to a category that is defined in relation to nouns. For example, the articles *a(n)* and *the*, though written as independent words, do not really have the privilege of occurring as independent words. Similarly, singular count nouns such as *boy, book, chair*, etc., cannot occur in a sentence without an article or some other determiner such as *this, that, any, each*, etc.

There is nothing comparable to the articles of English in many of the languages of the world, though most languages have demonstratives such as *this, that*, etc. Furthermore, it is not quite clear to most teachers and learners of English in these regions what the semantic bases for the use of articles in English are.

The article in Inner-Circle English has three sets of functions: a set of purely grammatical functions, a set of semantic functions, including reference, and a set of pragmatic functions. The grammatical functions in themselves are quite complex; when the interlocking semantic and pragmatic functions are added, the description of the article system becomes even more formidable. The basic grammatical functions are listed below:

1.   a count noun in the singular must be preceded by an article if not preceded by some other determiner (e.g., *A dog makes a good pet*);
2.   a predicate nominal in the singular must be preceded by the article *a* or *an* (e.g., *My friend is a graduate student*);
3.   certain proper nouns must be preceded by the article *the* (e.g., *The Hague, The Rhine*).

The semantic functions are basically related to reference, signalling the meanings of definite/indefinite and specific/non-specific as well as generic/ non-generic reference.

The conventions of use of articles with nouns can be stated as follows:

*   *a(n):* indefinite non-specific, or indefinite specific, or generic (with count nouns in the singular)
*   *the:* definite specific (with count and mass nouns), or non-specific generic (with count nouns only)
*   *some:* indefinite non-specific, or indefinite specific (with count nouns in the plural, with mass nouns)
*   *ø:* generic (with count nouns in the plural, with mass nouns)

It is clear that there is considerable overlap among the forms of articles and the meanings they signal, as well as interaction across articles themselves and other aspects of grammar. For example, generic reference is not signalled by the articles exclusively: the tense-aspect of the utterance is relevant, too (cf. *A tiger roars* vs. *A tiger is roaring*, or *A tiger roared;* only the first sentence has a generic meaning).

There are two factors that complicate the acquisition of this system of articles for learners of English. First, in the Inner-Circle varieties of English, either the indefinite or the definite article can be used to signal generic reference, since the generic is a function of the non-specific and all the articles can signal this meaning. Second, in many languages of the world, the definite specific noun is not marked; it is usually the *indefinite* noun that is marked, and the generic is a function of the definite specific. Additionally, there is no one-to-one correlation between the forms (i.e., *a*, *the*, *some*) and the meanings they signal. It is, therefore, difficult for learners of English to arrive at the principles underlying the use of articles.

The picture is further complicated by the fact that, depending upon speaker intentions, the choice of articles may vary in what appears to the learners as the same context. For instance, both the following sentences are grammatical and appropriate, depending upon the context in which each one is used: *He has written a grammar of English*, or *He has written the grammar of English*. The first one is a simple description of the grammar of a language someone has written, the second one signals a particular speaker intention. The speaker is either saying that the author has produced a *definitive* grammar of English (signalling high praise for the author), or is using *the* contrastively, i.e., in clarifying that the author has written a grammar *of English* and not of any other language(s) or that the author has written the grammar and not the thesaurus that is also being talked about.

◆ Count/mass

The above discussion may suggest that nouns are inherently either count or mass and that the use of articles is determined by these properties of the nouns. That is not true, of course. As has been said earlier, there is a relation of mutual dependency between articles and nouns; as Huddleston (1984: 246) observes, there are general usage rules that can be applied to all determiners and '[c]ountability has to do with a noun's potential for combining with various types of determiner ...'

According to Allan (1980), there are eight different classes of nouns in English in view of: (a) their potential for combining with the following types of determiners: the zero determiner; unit determiners such as *a(n)*, *one;* fuzzy quantifiers such as *several, about fifty;* the determiner *all* in the sense of 'completely'; and (b) their potentiality for being marked as plural, either inflectionally or in terms of agreement features. According to Huddleston (1984: 245), there are six classes of nouns exemplified by *equipment* (fully mass), *knowledge* (almost mass, but occurs with *a*, e.g., *a good knowledge of Latin*), *clothes* (occurs with fuzzy quantifiers such as *many, few*, hence is more count-like), *cattle* (occurs with fuzzy quantifiers and large round numbers, e.g. *a thousand [head of] cattle*), *people* (collective nouns which have plural forms, e.g., *peoples*, but are not fully countable, as they do not occur in a singular form), and *dog* (fully count).

Thus, the English system of countability is complex. Further, the conventions of marking countability differ across languages. In English, mass nouns (*equipment, sugar*) are inherently singular, in Sinhalese and Swahili, they are treated as plural. In African, Caribbean, East, South, and Southeast Asian varieties of English, the complex system of marking count/mass distinction in English is simplified. Perceptually countable items such as *furniture, equipment, luggage* are regularly used with a plural marker to denote more than one piece (see examples and discussion in B. Kachru, 1982b; 1992d). Also, since neither the determiner nor the countability system is clearly described in teaching texts, there is a great deal of variation across varieties in the usage of determiners and the categorization of nouns. For variation in Inner Circle, see Ilson (1995); Rastall (1995).

Verbs

The grammar of verbs deals with not only the tense-aspect distinctions, but also with semantic categorization of verbs in terms of stative:dynamic, factive:non-factive, volitional:non-volitional, etc. These categorizations do not coincide in all the varieties of world Englishes.

◆ Stative vs. dynamic

According to Quirk et al. (1985), the distinction in terms of stativity is central to the grammar of verbs in English. Stativity of the verb interacts with the aspectual and mood systems of the English verbal construction, e.g., stative verbs do not occur in the progressive aspectual form, so sentences such as the following are ungrammatical: **You are resembling your brother, *They were knowing all the answers.* Also, the following imperative sentences are strange: *?Know Russian! ?Resemble your mother!*

Many languages of the world, however, do not express stative vs. dynamic meanings through verbs, and the Outer- and Expanding-Circle varieties of English most often do not make such a distinction, either. Sentences such as the following are perfectly grammatical in these varieties: *He is having two cars, I was not knowing him then, She is not recognizing you.* Characterizing such uses of the progressive as 'non-standard' ignores a vital semantic motivation at work in many Englishes.

◆ Factivity and volitionality

In addition to the stative/dynamic distinction discussed above, there are other distinctions, partly semantic and partly grammatical, that are made in the verb systems of human languages. For instance, English makes a distinction between *factive* and *non-factive* verbs as in *Peter regrets that he was rude to Bill* vs. *Peter believes that he was rude to Bill.* Negating the main-clause factive verb *regret* does not affect the interpretation that it was a fact that *he was rude to Bill,* but negating the non-factive *believe* negates the whole sentence, cf. *Peter did not regret that he was rude to Bill* (from the perspective of the person who utters this, Peter was, in fact, rude to Bill); *Peter did not believe that he was rude to bill* (the speaker is not asserting that Peter was, in fact, rude to Bill). Other languages may make a distinction between *volitional* and *non-volitional* verbs, i.e., verbs that assert that the subject was responsible for the action expressed by the main verb of the sentence and those that do not imply such responsibility. Declarative sentences such as 'Bill is sick' may have grammatical markers that indicate whether the speaker is asserting it as a fact or merely reporting it as something she heard. Such distinctions may be reflected in the English sentences produced by speakers of such languages as well.

◆ Tense and aspect

In East Asian as well as Southeast Asian languages, verbs are not inflected for tense. The distinction between present and past time reference, for example, is expressed by adverbs. In several South Asian languages, tense, aspect and mood have complex interactions which are not exhibited in the Inner-Circle English tense/aspect systems. Matters are further complicated by the fact that most English language teaching texts do not explain the semantic and pragmatic factors involved in the choice of a tense form. The multilingual users of English base their systems on the system they know best, that of one or more of the other languages in their repertoires. As a result, there is a great deal of variation in the use of the tense-aspect markers of English across its varieties. For instance, it is common to come across definite past-time adverbs with the present perfect tense (e.g., *I have written to him yesterday*) in many of the African and Asian varieties; East and Southeast Asian varieties leave out the tense-markers and signal the time reference with time adverbs (e.g., *I talk to her yesterday*); the aspectual meaning is signalled with adverbs such as *already* ('completive') and *last time* ('formerly') in the Southeast Asian varieties (e.g., *Last time working in Golden Mile* 'I used to work in Golden Mile'; SME).

Differences across varieties sometimes may cause serious problems in a different variety context. Gumperz (1982b) discusses two court cases in the USA involving a Filipino doctor and two Filipino nurses, respectively, in which the Filipino subjects were perceived as being untruthful. The doctor, in fact, was sued for perjury. A linguist was called in to point out that in PhE, tense distinctions are not as important as aspectual distinctions. P. B. Naylor's work (1980: 'Legal testimony and the non-native speaker of English' [Typescript]) is cited in Gumperz (1982b: 173) to explain that the use of present and past tenses in PhE, different from AmE, is due to substratum influences from local languages.

In addition to the use of tenses, the sequence-of-tenses phenomenon is almost always absent in the Outer- and Expanding-Circle varieties. In a narrative, tense forms seem to vary from present to past to future to present or past with dizzying frequency from the point of view of a speaker of an Inner-Circle variety. Nelson (1985) documents such usage in creative writing in IE and Y. Kachru (1983) relates this feature to the fact that in Indian languages the tense forms in successive clauses are determined by the natural sequence of events in time. In a long narrative or conversation with a speaker of an Inner-Circle variety, this creates problems, especially when combined with prosodic clues that differ significantly from those of the Inner-Circle variety (see Mishra, 1982).

Selected syntactic patterns

In the case of the Filipino doctor's problem in the US courts mentioned above, the difficulties with tense forms were further compounded by the use of a question-answering system that does not operate in American English.

◆ Question-answering systems

According to Pope (1976), there are two types of question-answering systems in human languages. In one, the answer follows the polarity of the question, i.e., if the question is in the positive, the answer confirming the assumption of the questioner is in the positive, the answer disconfirming the assumption is in the negative. If, however, the question is in the negative, the answer confirming the assumption of the questioner is in the negative as well, while the answer disconfirming the assumption of the questioner is in the positive. This is called the *positive-negative system*. There is another system, which many languages in various parts of the world follow, in which an answer confirming the assumption of the questioner is always in the positive to signal agreement, while a negative answer expresses disagreement with that assumption. This is called the *agreement-disagreement system*. The difficulty that speakers who follow the positive-negative system face in interacting with those who use the agreement-disagreement system is that they are never sure how to interpret the *yes* or *no* of the response unless the *yes* or it is followed by a full clause to clarify what the person answering the question intends to say (e.g., *Yes, I think you're right, No, that's not so*).

Filipino English follows the agreement-disagreement system, which led to the difficulties in the court case discussed in Gumperz (1982b). This system is shared by many other Outer- and Expanding-Circle varieties, e.g., African English (AfrE, Bokamba, 1992: 132–3), SAE (e.g., B. Kachru, 1983), SME

(Lowenberg, 1984; Platt and Weber, 1980: 80), PhE, and CE (Li, 1995: 55) and is often mentioned in Inner-Circle anecdotes as causing problems in interaction with Asian and African users of English.

Tags

In addition to direct questions, the other device that the Inner-Circle varieties of English use to request confirmation of assumptions is tags. Tags are used with question intonation following statements, e.g., *You are coming to the party, aren't you?* The tags are formed in AmE or BrE following very general principles, e.g., the subject of the sentence is copied as an appropriate pronoun form, the tense and aspect are copied in an auxiliary, and the polarity is reversed; e.g., *John hasn't arrived yet, has he?* There is agreement between *John* and *he*, the present perfect auxiliary *has* is repeated in the positive form, instead of the negative of the statement.

In the Outer- and Expanding-Circle varieties, a general tag, *is it, isn't it* or *no*, is often used universally: the following are grammatical in SAE, SME, and many other varieties:

i.   A: I want it at six o'clock.
      B: At six, is it? (Tongue, 1974:42)

ii.   You are not going home, is it? (Platt and Weber, 1980: 76)

iii. You didn't want to come, isn't it?

In SME, the tag *is it* signals a request for confirmation or agreement, whereas the tag *isn't it* seems to signal a straightforward question that requires a yes-no answer.

Complementation

The Outer- and Expanding-Circle varieties of English use adjective, noun and verb complements differently from the Inner-Circle varieties. The differences are attributable to two major grammatical factors. In the Inner-Circle Englishes, complements are either full clauses, or, if reduced, either gerunds or infinitives. Specific verbs, prepositions and adjectives are associated with specific forms of complements: the verb *say* takes a full clausal complement, *enjoy* takes a gerund as a complement, and *want* takes an infinitive as a complement: e.g., *Peter said that Bill would be late, Martha enjoys playing tennis, Dorit wants to mail the packet herself.*

In many languages, complements have only two forms: full clause and infinitive. In South Asian English, for example, infinitives and gerunds are used differently from the way they are used in the Inner-Circle Englishes. The examples cited below illustrate this phenomenon; Pakistani English (PE) examples are from Baumgardner (1987) and Indian English (IE) are from Nihalani et al. (1979):

i.   IE, PE   They were not at all interested in democracy ... and were only *interested to grab* power at any cost.

ii.   IE, PE   She said that her party *wanted that* we should not intervene in internal affairs of Afghanistan:

Complements of nouns exhibit different usage patterns, too, as in the following:

iii. PE   Pakistan has no *control to influence* affairs inside Afghanistan.

Purpose adverbials use the preposition *for* followed by a gerund instead of the infinitive:

iv.   IE, PE   He *went* to China *for learning* Chinese.

Since the complement types do not seem to be clearly linked to any semantic differences, and some verbs such as *like* govern both gerunds and infinitives (*I like to swim* and *I like swimming*), variation in this area of English grammar is only to be expected.

Linkers

In the Outer- and Expanding-Circle varieties, various types of linkers are used in ways that are unfamiliar to the speakers of the Inner-Circle varieties. This feature is illustrated with prepositions as they are used to link nouns with each other, or predicates with adjuncts in a sentence.

◆ Prepositions

According to Quirk et al. (1985), the meaning of place prepositions in English can be described in terms of location at a point, along a line on a surface, or in three-dimensional space. Also, prepositions signal location as well as motion. Whereas signalling location vs. motion is important in all languages, signalling the difference between dimensions — location at a point or on a surface — may not be as important since that distinction is contextually obvious. The orientation for location, etc., may be with reference to the person of the speaker rather than to the reference point established in the utterance by the speaker. The semantic extensions of the place prepositions to time and other dimensions may not follow the same principles either. All these divergences lead to difficulties in the use of prepositions across varieties, especially because the use of prepositions is determined partly by their meaning and partly by formal grammatical requirements with no reference to meaning. And grammars of English have very little to say about their use in general. The following exemplify the use of prepositions in Outer- and Expanding-Circle varieties:

SME (Tongue, 1974: 53)

> We can give some thought on the matter.
> The matter has been studied with a view of further reducing the risk of fire.

PhE (Peña, 1997: 92–3)

> Call some students to answer ...
> Review on pronouns by playing ...
> What could have happened with him?

PE (Rahman, 1990: 51)

> to combat against/with poverty

According to Rahman, 100 percent of PE-using subjects judged the use of *against* grammatical, and 70 percent judged the use of *with* grammatical in the phrase above. They also judged the following sentence perfectly grammatical:

> What is the time in your watch?

Nepali English (NE, Verma, 1996: 82–7)

> Rasthriya Panchayat Members Discuss on Food Problem
> N. Korea, Sri Lanka to Discuss about Reopening the Mission

S. Sridhar (1996: 58–9) quotes the following from educated IE speech:

> She [a woman] was not allowed to appear in front of other men.
> Now look the difference between ...

V. Bhatia (1996: 170) has following examples from SAE:

> The students ... are trying to escape out from this monster of severe disorder.

For the differences between AmE and BrE use of prepositions, see Quirk et al. (1985): notes on pp. 667, 673, 678, 702, 707 *ff.*

Discourse

Varieties differ across several aspects of discourse, both in terms of micro- and macro-structures, i.e., in terms of overall structure and that of sub-parts such as paragraphs of the text. Textual organization is especially crucial for structuring information, which in turn has consequences for grammatical structure.

Thematic information

The organization of information that the sentence conveys is different in the Outer- and Expanding-Circle Englishes. This is obvious if we look at the devices utilized for expressing *focus* and *theme.*

Focus and theme

In the Inner-Circle Englishes, the initial element in the sentence in the unmarked case usually signals the *theme,* and the element that follows the main verb is in *focus;* e.g., in the following exchange, the element in italics is the theme, and the element in boldface is the focus, in the context of the question:

7.   Q: Where did Sue go yesterday?
     A: *She* went to **the beach**.

The Outer- and Expanding-Circle varieties utilize different devices to signal focus and theme. Consider, for example, the following sentences from different varieties:

i.   *Certain medicine* we don'(t) stock in our dispensary
ii.   *One subject* they pay for seven dollars
iii. And *weekend* you can spend with your brother.
iv.   *My daughter* she is attending the University of Nairobi.

Examples (i-ii) are from SME (Platt and Weber, 1980: 73); (iii) is from IE (Gumperz, 1982b: 34); and (iv) is from AfrE (Bokamba, 1992: 131). The front-shifting of the direct object (in i) and the prepositional object (in ii) is for focus. In (iii), the front-shifting seems to be for the purpose of definitization

(Gumperz, 1982b: 34), which is consistent with thematization. The front-shifting in (iv) is for thematic purposes as well. In these varieties, the device of front-shifting is utilized both for thematization and focus or emphasis.

Conclusion

Many more areas of English grammar can be explored in greater detail, and many more examples can be extracted from available literature, but these few are sufficient to establish the fact the speakers of different varieties use English differently. This fact has to be appreciated before any progress can be made in successful cross-cultural communication through English and in our understanding of the differences in their own terms, not as 'deficiency'.

Suggested activities

1. Look at the following excerpts from English newspapers and determine how they differ in grammatical terms from the variety you and your community use:

    A.   From *The Guardian*, Lagos, 6 April 2000: Letter to the Editor

    > Let me declare that I never in my worst thoughts ever imagined that the leadership of this country would be so unkind as to simply watch as we slide inexorably into the dark ages of no electricity. There were power outages during the Nigerian civil war period but by no means were they any where near what we are experiencing now.
    >
    > Factories are idle, thus leading to mass retrenchments. Resourceful graduates who for lack of jobs, branched into barbing, pure water manufacturer, or fashion designing, are forced to close shops as they cannot even earn enough to pay the rents, let alone the operations. Those of us who have computers in our offices now find ourselves paralised. Thank God, I didn't dump my old manual typewriter and it comes in handy.

    B.   From 'English Plain and Simple', by Jose A. Carillo, 'The Assaults on Our good Sense', *The Manila Times*, 7 July 2003:

    > ... Because we allow pseudoscience to rule our political life, we have become a nation of petty deceivers. We allow pollsters-for-hire to play around with the nation's destiny by directly equating popularity with fitness for high public office. We allow them to validate the illogical, absurd thinking of the misguided many and make it look like it's preordained, inevitable. Their modus operandi, as always, is anchored on this classic non-sequitor question: 'Here's a list of 20 mentioned as presidentiables. If elections were held today,

who among them will you vote for?' Do they ever indicate if those listed are fit, competent, or morally qualified for the presidency? Never! That's why the cult of popularity rules this country.

2. Read the following and comment on the differences, if any, from your variety:

> She regarded her two sons beside her, Bit-tik — fresh like a newly baked jar but browned like his father with the taint of soil and the sun's rugged scheme. At her right sat Istak, hunched before the low eating table, no higher than a stool but if he stood his full height, he was as tall as the rod by which one may measure the sky. His brow was high and implied a keenness of mind which he had. Hadn't he stayed in the convent for ten years teaching catechism to Captain Berong's children and helping in the mass? Couldn't he read Latin now and dispense with wisdom which the priest brought from beyond the seas? His hair, though cropped short, did not stand bristly like a pig's, but was soft and pressed flat and shiny by coconut oil which made not only his hair but also his skin shine in the sallow light. Ay — he was the marked one, and on his face which was pale once like the banana's inner trunk, Mayang's eyes lingered. (Jose, 1968: 18)

4

Contexts and identities

Susan: So, I'll come round at eleven o'clock, OK?
Takeshi: OK, I'll be waiting at the corner.
Susan: Why? I can come to your place. It's no problem.
Takeshi: Oh, then I'll be standing at the gate.
Susan: Look, it's cold out. Why don't you wait inside? It's really no problem
          ... unless you don't want me to come to your flat ...

Koyama (1992: 96)[1]

Introduction

It is clear from the exchanges between Susan and Takeshi cited above that the negotiation of meaning between the two participants is not going well. Both, of course, are equally proficient in English; however, it is doubtful that they share the same *competence* in using their linguistic *proficiency* for communicating across cultures.

Unlike proficiency, which generally refers to a control of linguistic structure, competence in language has several components, at least three of which can be discussed in broad terms under the labels of *linguistic competence, pragmatic competence,* and *sociocultural competence.* Linguistic competence refers to the knowledge of language that speakers have, i.e., the grammar and vocabulary of the language. Pragmatic competence encompasses knowledge of how to use the language to express one's intents and purposes and to recognize others' intents and purposes in any interaction using language. It involves knowing how to get others to do things, offer to do things for others, express gratitude, appreciation or regret, compliment someone or complain about things, and achieve many other such objectives through the use of language. Sociocultural competence comprises the knowledge of who to interact with, what to say why, when and how, how to negotiate, and also when to be a non-participant. Although it is convenient to divide up what we mean by our overall competence as users of language in this way, all the components of each of these competences are interlinked. This will become clear as the discussion in this chapter progresses. It will also become clear why, as any one factor changes, whether it is the language, the ways of using language for expressing one's intents and purposes, or the sociocultural context in which one uses language, the change affects the entire nature of interaction and creates a potential for negotiation of meaning to minimize misunderstandings. The characteristics of the linguistic knowledge that is relevant to world Englishes has already been discussed in Chapter 2. In this chapter, the focus is on pragmatic and sociocultural competence. These aspects of language use are discussed with reference to two major components, the conventions of speaking and of writing.

Conventions of speaking

Conventions of speaking in a society from a sociolinguistic point of view have to be discussed with reference to several areas of research: the *cooperative principle* (Grice, 1975); *speech acts* (Austin, 1962; Searle, 1969), *politeness* (Brown and Levinson, 1987); and *conversation analysis* (Sacks, Schegloff and Jefferson, 1974).

The Gricean cooperative principle presents a general, socioculturally neutral framework for structuring what people do when they interact using language. The cooperative principle comprises four *maxims* with several sub-axioms:

Gricean Maxims

Quantity: Make contributions to communication as informative as required; do not give more information than required.

Quality: Do not say what you believe to be false: do not say that for which you lack adequate evidence.

Relevance: Be relevant.

Manner: Be perspicuous, i.e., avoid obscurity of expression; avoid unnecessary ambiguity; be brief, be orderly.

The cooperative principle is not to be construed as prescribing how interactions should be conducted or asserting that all interactions conform to these maxims. They simply point out that if any of the maxims is violated, the violation leads the participants to infer something about the intent behind the violation. An example may make this clear:

1. Professor A: What do you think of X's research paper?

    Professor B: It has a lot of artwork, beautiful graphs and charts, and it is bound elegantly.

It is clear that Professor B's response has violated both the maxims of quantity (it gives more information than is required) and relevance (the observations about the paper are not exactly relevant to a reply to the question posed) by not giving a straightforward reply to Professor A's question. It is, however, unlikely that any proficient speaker of English would think of characterizing Professor B's response as a frivolous remark. It is highly likely that Professor A and others who may happen to overhear the exchange would draw the conclusion that Professor B does not think much of the intellectual content of the research paper, but did not wish to make a bald statement as to how unsatisfactory she found the paper to be. Perhaps the reason for avoiding the bald statement is politeness: Professor B may be treading cautiously so as not to offend Professor A, in case A's opinion is more favourable to X's research paper, for example.

Politeness

Politeness involves considerations of maintaining *face*, one's own as well as the addressee's. *Face* is defined as the 'public self-image that every member wants to claim for himself' (Goffman, 1967: 5). Brown and Levinson (1987), working with the notion of face, identify two aspects of politeness in verbal interaction, *positive face* (presentational) and *negative face* (avoidance). Positive face indicates a want or need to be desirable to others; therefore, it functions as a strategy of friendliness or camaraderie. Negative face indicates a want or need not to be impeded by others; therefore, it functions as a distancing strategy of formality. All members of a speech community use positive and negative *politeness strategies* to save, maintain, and enhance face. Brown and Levinson (1987) describe a number of strategies and their linguistic realizations that maintain and enhance positive and negative face of interlocutors in conversation.

In order to soften a *face-threatening act* (FTA), i.e., to diminish the effects of imposition on the addressee, positive politeness strategies claim common ground for both speaker and addressee and emphasize that they belong to the same set of individuals with similar wants. Negative politeness, on the other hand, addresses the hearer's 'want to have his freedom of action unhindered and his attention unimpeded. It is the heart of respect behavior, just as positive politeness is the kernel of "familiar" and "joking" behavior' (Brown and Levinson, 1987: 129).

Leech (1983: 15–6) discusses the use of language under *rhetoric* as a count noun and defines it as the study of 'effective use of language in its most general sense' and proposes two rhetorics, *interpersonal* and *textual*. The proposal subsumes the Gricean cooperative principle, politeness, and a third parameter, the *irony principle*, under interpersonal rhetoric, and introduces many more maxims, such as the maxims of *tact, generosity, approbation* and *modesty*. The framework proposed in Leech (1983) leaves the possibility open for more principles and has not been applied as widely in cross-cultural studies as the others cited here, though the notions of *tact* and *modesty* seem quite useful in describing some of the observed cross-cultural differences in language use.

Coming back to exchanges like that in (1) above between the two professors, we may assume that the Gricean cooperative principle was violated due to politeness considerations. Such violations, however, may not lead to the same kind of inferences across the three circles. For example, Rose (1999: 72) narrates an incident involving himself and a Korean couple who lived next door to him. As the author returned from the hospital after a night of very little sleep following his daughter's birth, he met the couple in the parking lot. When they heard the good news, the woman said, solemnly, that the author 'looked much older'. The author was taken aback at first, but then realized this was her way of paying a compliment: he was a father now, with greater responsibility, and therefore entitled to the dignity of being older. Had the author had no prior contact with Korean culture, he would have been perplexed, perhaps even offended by such a personal remark. 'Looking older' does not have the same connotation in American English as it does in Korean English.

In the excerpt from a conversation between Susan and Takeshi cited at the beginning of this chapter, there is no apparent violation of Gricean maxims. However, it is clear that the two participants have two different notions of politeness. For Takeshi, it is important to show consideration for Susan's gender; he does not want her to come to his place as that may compromise her reputation. In Asian cultures, generally, single young women do not visit single young men in their places of residence, and vice versa. For Susan, Takeshi's reluctance to allow her to pick him up at his place suggests that she is unwelcome there for some reason mysterious to her; this threatens her face and she naturally feels offended. The misunderstanding is due to the difference in Australian and Japanese cultural conventions of polite behaviour rather than to proficiency in English.

Speech acts

The notion of speech acts comes from the observation that a linguistic utterance, i.e., saying something like *Open the door!* does not merely signal the production of the sounds, words and sentence pattern that the utterance is composed of, but also the act of commanding the addressee to open the door.[2] And it is uttered only when one is reasonably sure the addressee will in fact carry out the action. Thus, the utterance signals a series of three acts: a *locutionary* act of uttering the linguistic expression, an *illocutionary* act of commanding, and a *perlocutionary* act of influencing the addressee's behaviour. One can also rephrase the above by saying the locutionary act of uttering a linguistic expression of appropriate form (i.e., imperative) has an illocutionary force associated with it (i.e., of command) and has a perlocutionary effect resulting from the illocutionary force (i.e., obeying the command). Similarly, an interrogative utterance has the illocutionary force of seeking a response and a perlocutionary effect of obtaining the response.

Conventions regarding which linguistic expressions are appropriate for which speech acts differ across cultures, as is shown by the following example and also later in the chapter. For instance, in the context of a Chinese offer of a gift and final acceptance (Zhu, Li and Qian, 2000), the sequence of offering and acceptance is as follows: offer-decline-reoffer-redecline-reoffer-redecline-reoffer-final acceptance. The declining or reluctance to accept gifts is to show modesty and lack of greed on part of the recipient. Final acceptance is accompanied by expressions such as:

2. a. Don't do that again in the future. Otherwise don't come anymore.
    b. You make me really uncomfortable.
    c. Our boss brought me quite a few (computer disks). You take them back with you.

The directives (i.e., imperatives) while accepting a gift in (2a) and (2c) and the complaint in (2b) may not be appropriate in many cultures when accepting a gift; rather, a speech act of thanking (i.e., expression of gratitude) may be considered more appropriate. However, they seem to go along with offer of gift and acceptance in the Chinese cultural context. Gift offers in the Chinese context are always verbal so as to give the recipients an opportunity to decline a gift, if they so wish.

Conversation analysis

In addition to the research areas of the cooperative principle and speech acts, studies in conversation analysis are relevant to this discussion of conventions of speaking. The methodology of conversation analysis, based on ethnomethodology, is concerned with uncovering what people know of their own societies and practices as they structure their interactions. Instead of generalizations, as in linguistic pragmatics, conversation analysis aims at the dynamics of co-construction of sociocultural meaning as participants interact.

All participants evaluate what others say and modulate their own responses accordingly, which in turn are evaluated by the others, and so on. There are conventions for creating in-group solidarity as there are conventions for promoting camaraderie across diverse groups. This becomes clear when we look at interactions across ethnic and gender groups.

The interactional sociolinguistic approach to analysing verbal exchanges reveals many differences across cultures. For example, Japanese participants use *backchannel* cues (expressions such as *yeah, mhmm, really?*, etc. that indicate that the addressee is paying attention to the speaker) much more frequently than do American English speakers in a conversation, and they use such cues in different topical contexts (Yamada, 1992), leading to American English speakers feeling they are being interrupted. On the other hand, the Japanese speakers interpret the lack of backchannel cues as lack of interest on part of the American English speaking hearer. Inner-Circle speakers of English observe the rule of not interrupting another speaker's turn in conversation; the speaker's right to have the *floor* is respected (except in heated exchanges, for example, on political topics on TV talk shows in the USA). Japanese, Indians and many others overlap a great deal, but these overlaps in turns are not viewed as interruptions (Hayashi, 1996).

Such differences, however, are not only between, say, the Americans and the Japanese, or the British and the French. Differences show up between different groups within cultures, e.g., teenagers versus adults, men versus women, or New York Jewish versus non-Jewish participants in conversations (Tannen, 1984). Studies in speech acts and conversation analysis using data from world Englishes illustrate this point clearly.

Speech acts in world Englishes

English is used in the three circles for various purposes — as a home language, a medium of education, in professions, media, diplomacy, trade and commerce, and for literary creativity. For achieving success in all these areas of activity, users of English have to do various things with language. They have to use it for performing various acts, such as imparting information, negotiating, persuading, agreeing, disagreeing, demanding, apologizing, etc., in different contexts. The question naturally arises as to whether speakers of all varieties of English perform the same speech acts in the same contexts using the same linguistic tools.

Although there is a large body of research available in speech acts across languages, not much has been published as yet comparing speech acts across varieties. A study that looks at speech acts across varieties is Y. Kachru (1998); another study (K. Sridhar, 1991) investigates the speech act of request in Indian English. A large-scale study that compares a specific speech act in English by speakers of Brazilian Portuguese in Brazil and the USA, and American English speakers in English and Brazilian Portuguese is Silva (1998). The study by K. Sridhar (1991) is summarized below to illustrate the methodology of such studies.

Request in Indian English

K. Sridhar (1991) describes a study that investigated the speech act of request in Indian English in a limited setting in India and reports on the reaction of two judges, both American English speaking teachers of ESL, to the linguistic devices used by Indian English speakers.

The setting of the study was Bangalore, the so-called Silicon Valley of India, a cosmopolitan city in the state of Karnataka in south India. The subjects were 164 undergraduate students enrolled in three different colleges: Mount Carmel College (MCC), a Christian missionary institution with students primarily from Westernized families with English-medium education in 'convent' schools; Vijaya College (VC), with students from more traditional families and regional language background; and NMKRV College (NMKRV), with students from mixed backgrounds, with many from English-medium school education. They were administered a set of questionnaires which elicited approximately 1,100 examples of 'request' strategies in Indian English. The seven situations were as follows (pp. 311–6):

Situation 1:   Asking a friend's mother for a glass of water while visiting her home

Situation 2:   Asking for a menu from the waiter in a local fashionable restaurant for ordering snacks

Situation 3:   Asking for movie tickets from the person in the ticket office

Situation 4:   Asking a shopkeeper to show merchandise when buying clothes (sarees, shirts, etc.) from a fashionable shop

Situation 5:   Asking for a particular book from the person at the desk in the British Council Library

Situation 6:   Asking what time it was from a schoolboy with a watch

Situation 7:   Asking for a transcript (*mark sheet* in IE) from the person at the desk in a college office

The responses were analysed 'with reference to (1) the variables incorporated in the stimulus situations; (2) the sociocultural background of the students themselves; and (3) the conventions governing the performance of equivalent speech acts in their own languages' (p. 309).

In order to obtain all the information needed for the analysis, the questionnaire was divided into three parts (p. 309): the first part elicited background information (students' native languages; area of study; earlier training in English; use of English, mother tongues or regional languages in the various domains; how comfortable they felt in using English). The second part consisted of the seven situations, which involved a number of sociocultural variables, such as deference, Westernized versus traditional setting, differences in the social status of the person who the request was addressed to, etc. The third part asked respondents to indicate whether they would use their mother tongue, English, or both languages in each of the seven situations.

The students represented various language groups that included major Indo-Aryan and Dravidian Languages. A majority of students (73 percent) spoke Kannada or another Dravidian Language as their first language. For almost 97 percent of the students, English was the medium of instruction at high school and college, i.e., they had studied English for at least six years. A majority of them (90 percent) claimed they used English most often with their friends; an even higher number (98 percent) claimed they felt comfortable using English (p. 310).

Strategies of request in Indian English

For situation 1 (requesting a glass of water from a friend's mother), the term of address *Aunty* was used by 92 percent of the respondents. Use of a kinship term is a marker of politeness in Indian languages, and is extended to English in India. The American ESL teachers found it strange, but for educated, upwardly mobile, middle-class people in urban India, use of *uncle* and *aunty* for friends' parents functions as a mark of Westernized sophistication. This seems to be true of other Asian and Southeast Asian Englishes also.

The linguistic strategies used show the following pattern: indirect requests in interrogative forms (e.g., *Can I have a glass of water?*, *Could you please give me a glass of water?*) were the most common (86 percent), followed by direct imperatives (e.g., *Give me a glass of water, Get me some water*) with or without the word *please* (10.4 percent); expression of one's want or need (e.g., *I want/need …*) was the least common (2 percent).

In situation 2 (requesting a menu at a fashionable Westernized restaurant), the preference was, again, for indirect request forms (*May I have … ?*, *Can/could you?*) though direct imperatives (*give us …*) and 'want' statements (*I want …*) also occurred. Several instances of direct orders of snacks and other invalid responses showed up as well, since in traditional restaurants, the menu is recited orally and the orders are placed following the recitation. Direct orders are also motivated by the fact that the status of waiters is low on the social hierarchy, and in traditional contexts it is not felt necessary to use softeners such as *please* with indirect requests or direct commands addressed to such interactants. In situation 3 (request for movie tickets), since the addressee is a low-status individual, a majority of responses were just a noun phrase, *5 tickets (please),* followed by indirect requests (*Could you give me ... ?, Can/may I have ... ?,* 36 percent).

Situation 4 involved shopping for clothes in a fashionable, Westernized shop. The pattern of responses here was revealing in that the number of indirect requests was high (87.5 percent for MCC respondents, 95.3 percent for NMKRV, and 54 percent for VC). Within the category, the number of conventional indirect requests (*Can/could/would you ...*) was much higher (77.5 percent, 81.5 percent and 46 percent for the three groups) than the less preferred *Will you show me ...* (10.2 percent, 13.8 percent and 8 percent, respectively, for the three groups). Secondly, the VC group used direct imperatives also (Table 21.8, p. 314). There are two possible explanations for this behaviour on part of the VC group: a direct imperative is not an impolite form in Indian languages, as the ending on the verb indicates politeness levels. Alternatively, the subjects may have been thinking of a sales clerk of the store as the addressee, in which case, the status difference would justify the use of the less polite form. Although small in number, instances of the strategy of using *Will you ... ?* as an indirect request are noteworthy. While the use of modal *will* in this context is considered 'petulant or rude' (p. 314) in the Inner Circle, it does not necessarily carry that meaning in the Indian social context. In Indian languages the use of the future inflection on the imperative verb is considered polite. Since *will* has the function of marking future tense, it is equated with the future inflection by subjects. It is worth remembering that there are no textbooks that describe the pragmatic uses of modals in English.

Situation 5, requesting a book from the clerk at the British Council library, was a rather unusual situation for this group of subjects. The library charges a membership fee and stocks only English books; it is used mainly 'by ambitious, upper middle class students' (p. 315). Indirect requests with *can/ could/would you* were the most frequent in this context. Situation 6 involved a neutral setting with a child as the addressee and the content of the request fairly routine, about the time. The responses from subjects were as follows: indirect requests (*Can/could/would you* and *may I*) were the most frequent, followed by direct questions, *What's the time,* and a few instances of just the noun phrase (*Time [please]*). Two features of this group of responses are noteworthy: the *May I know the time* by more than a third of the MCC subjects is unexpected in that 'the structure would be regarded as overtly polite when addressed to someone younger in the Indian context'.

The last, situation 7, was more formal. The pattern of responses was as follows: indirect requests with *can/could/may I have* is the most frequent followed by *would/ could/ can you, I want to have,* and *I need/want a copy.* Close to a third of MCC and 44 percent of the VC students felt the need to offer some kind of explanation before requesting the transcripts.

The major characteristics of requests in IE are the following: First, the requesting strategy in IE is different from that in Inner-Circle varieties of

English. This is seen most clearly in the less frequent use of indirect requests and more frequent use of straightforward questions, direct commands and desiderative statements in IE. Second, many of the differences between Inner-Circle and IE patterns of requesting have their sources in the conventions of requesting in Indian languages. Thus, if variation theory is to include varieties of a language, the speaker's mother tongue has to be recognized as a major variable, analogous to factors such as class, region, and age, which are conventionally recognized in the paradigm. Third, even when an Outer-Circle variety uses a structure that is apparently identical to one that may be employed in a native variety, the 'social meaning' of that structure may be different in the two contexts. This is illustrated by the use of the *Will you ...* question in Indian English.

Fourth, variation studies must pay attention not only to the differences between Inner- and Outer-Circle varieties, but also to variation within an Outer-Circle variety. In this connection, sociocultural factors such as *degree of Westernization* and *stratification within the specific Outer-Circle society* function as variables differentiating one variety of Outer- and Expanding-Circle English from another. Fifth, one of the most important differences between the Inner-vs. Outer- and Expanding-Circle varieties is that the latter involve 'partial linguistic/communicative competence'. The Outer- or Expanding-Circle speakers do not need English to perform a great many speech functions — their mother tongue (or other languages in their repertoire) is used for these purposes. Consequently, a number of speech functions are performed at best awkwardly (from the point of view of the Inner-Circle speaker), or, rather, in ways that involve a direct extension of either the speaker's limited second-language competence or the speaker's mother-tongue competence.

This study, like the studies by Y. Kachru and Silva referred to above, validates the claim (Gumperz and Cook-Gumperz, 1982: 6) that bilinguals create new communicative strategies by juxtaposing two sets of forms, one from each of the codes in their repertoire.

Conventions of writing

Just as conventions of speaking differ across groups and cultures, so do conventions of writing. The concepts of the cooperative principle, speech acts and politeness are as applicable to writing as to speaking. This will become clear in the following discussion.

It is worth remembering that not all cultures around the world are literate cultures. A large number of languages have no scripts and no tradition of writing. Even where there is a long tradition of writing, it may not be identical, or even similar from culture to culture. Historically, writing was restricted to specific groups all across the world, whether in Africa, Asia, or Europe. Until very recently, the skill of writing and access to written records were associated with religion and with rulers' or traders' record-keeping. Mass literacy postdates the Industrial Revolution, and universal literacy is a twentieth-century phenomenon.

A close look at different societies shows that *genres*, whether oral or written, differ across cultures. For instance, there is nothing comparable in other varieties of English to the oral genre of 'signifying' in African-American English (Mitchell-Kernan, 1972: 315 *ff.*). Similarly, until very recently, there was no genre of written instructions (e.g., recipes, instructions for operating mechanical devices, assembling furniture or equipment, or sewing, knitting, etc.) in the Indian languages (Y. Kachru, 1997b).

Since academic writing is a major concern of writing research, we will consider this area in some detail. The development of what has been termed *essay-text literacy*, with its emphasis on explicit, decontextualized, impersonal language (Gee, 1986) in academic settings in the Inner Circle is not necessarily the preferred mode in the Outer and Expanding Circles. Research on contrastive rhetoric (e.g., Martin, 1992) and genres (e.g., Bhatia, 1993) reveals that a direct, linear, straightforward exposition is viewed as less imaginative and scholarly in many cultures (see Asante, 1987; Gee, 1986; Y. Kachru, 1997b; Lisle and Mano, 1997). For instance, it has been claimed that Chinese students are taught to devote the opening paragraph of an essay to statements of universal truth following which it is appropriate to broach the topic of the paper (Lisle and Mano, 1997: 16). In the Japanese and Korean traditions, an essay consists of at least one tangentially related sub-topic, 'brought up with few overt transition markers' (Hinds, 1987: 150).

In Arabic rhetoric, verbal artistry and emotional impact are the primary measures of persuasive power: rhythm, sound, repetition, and emphatic assertion carry more weight than factual evidence, and the organization may depend more on metaphor and association than on linear logic (Lisle and Mano, 1997: 17). Sa'adeddin (1989), writing about the Arabic tradition, makes a distinction between two different modes of text development: aural and visual (pp. 38–9). The former has the features of recurrent and plain lexis, exaggeration, repetition of syntactic structures, loose packaging of information, and a lack of apparent coherence, that is, a style that signals informality and solidarity, highly valued in the Arabic tradition. The latter, on the other hand, has the features of linearization, progressive development of a thesis, logical coherence, and syntactic cohesiveness, all of which are highly valued in the Western tradition.

According to Asante (1987), indirection and circumlocutory rhetoric are a part of African discourse strategy. 'By "stalking" the issues, the speaker demonstrates skill and arouses hearers' interest. The person who gets directly to the issues is said to have little imagination and even less flair for rhetorical style' (Asante, 1987: 51).

The Indian tradition is characterized by a spiral development (Y. Kachru, 1997b) of topic instead of a linear presentation. According to Heimann (1964: 170–1), one position is first presented, 'then confronted and denounced by a second, a third and further *pakshas* "wings" or "viewpoints". Finally the highest, or at any rate the at-present no-more-refutable notion is reached.' Quotations from the classics and stylistic flourishes are highly valued as they provide evidence for the writer's being learned, cultured and sophisticated in his/her use of language (Y. Kachru, 1997b). For example, Vyas, Tiwari and Srivastava (1972) in their standard textbook on Hindi grammar and composition explicitly state that the purpose of the deliberative essay, comparable to the argumentative essay in the Anglo-American context, is *not* to *provide solutions* and *convince* the audience of their rightness; rather, it is to *lead* the readers to find the right solutions.

As far as argumentation and persuasion goes, in most Asian cultures, the aim is not to convince the readers of one's own position, but to present all aspects of a problem, and to suggest all possible solutions, pointing out the strengths and drawbacks of each so that readers are able to make up their minds about the best possible solution (Y. Kachru, 1999; 2001b). In the last several decades, genre analysis emerged in a distinct area of research within academic writing and has had more purpose-orientation. The theoretical and methodological characteristics of genre analysis are discussed in detail in Chapter 21.

Conclusion

The question may arise as to how desirable or practical it is for all users of world Englishes to acquire linguistic, pragmatic and sociocultural competence in all varieties of English. The answer must be that it is of course desirable, but whether it is practical may depend on several factors. One important precondition is the acknowledgement and awareness of the variation in conventions of language use that exists. Once this precondition is met, ways can be found to introduce material in teacher training programmes and textbooks to expose students of English language in all the circles to various conventions of speaking and writing.

Suggested activities

1. What kind of response does the news of a birth typically elicit in your sociocultural context? Some possibilities are:
    a. Expressions of congratulations
    b. Demand for sweets or a party

    c.   Expressions of happiness at the news

    d.   Anxious inquiries about the health of mother and infant

    e.   Offer to help with household chores, etc.

    f.   A combination of some of the above

    g.   Any other response

2.   These activities are designed for groups of students rather than an individual.

    a.   Select two groups of subjects from two different linguistic and cultural backgrounds. Design a questionnaire to elicit speech act data (on any speech act, such as an apology, an invitation to dinner, congratulating a colleague on a significant achievement, apologizing for failing to meet a deadline) and interview the two groups of subjects to see if they view the questions in the same way. The focus should be on:

       (i)   the groups' perception of relations between the speaker and the addressee in terms of social status, rank and role, i.e., whether the relation is viewed as intimate, friendly or distant; and

       (ii) the groups' perception of the situation, whether it is in the intimate, social or professional domain.

    b.   (i)   Fine-tune the questionnaire in light of what you find out about the comparability of the instrument across cultures and pilot it to test its usefulness in eliciting data. Pay special attention to the factors that define the context in which the target speech act is to be performed.

       (ii) Following data elicitation, interview a subset of subjects to confirm their intentions and compare these responses to see whether they match what you inferred from the elicited data.

    c.   Write up a report of your findings and present it for class discussion. See Blum-Kulka and Olshtain (1984) for more information on cross-cultural speech act research.

5

Parameters of intelligibility

I stopped in at the local turf accountant — a charming British euphemism for "bookie" — to place a bet on the famous horse race called the Derby (rhymes with "Barbie"). I picked a horse, filled in the tout slip and laid 5 pounds on the counter. To my delight, my horse came romping home at 7-1 odds.

Instead of the 35-pound ($60) windfall I had every right to expect, though, my winnings barely exceeded 8 pounds. When I complained, the clerk explained: "Your chit was an each-way, mate. A four-way punt. Quarters your quid."

"But, but, I don't understand why ..." I sputtered before he cut me off.

"Don't go whingeing about like some yobbish wally," he said. "Don't you ... Yanks know English?"

Reid (1998)[1]

Introduction

A recurrent discussion in world Englishes contexts turns around the likelihood that present or future varieties of English may not be readily intelligible when used outside their home localities, nations, or regions. Much of ESL or EFL teaching is concerned with the development and practice of forms of English such that learners' presentations will be functional across regional and national boundaries. Such concerns perhaps most often have geographical or ethnic bases, though one can readily imagine others — for example, questions about cross-generational intelligibility. We may spend a good deal of classroom time doing 'same or different?' recognition and repetition exercises to help students to distinguish the pronunciations of 'sin' and 'seen', for instance, because such vowel distinctions are commonly regarded and presented as crucial for distinguishing lexical items and, therefore, conveying messages accurately and efficiently.

The word 'intelligibility' has its origin in the Latin verb *intellegere* 'to understand' or 'to perceive'. Discussions of differences across varieties of English lead inevitably to concerns about intelligibility, often broadly taken to mean 'understanding'; if utterances are perceived as 'making sense', they are said to be intelligible. It is commonplace to recognize many different English accents; on the face of it, this implies that there may be intelligibility difficulties across varieties. For example, the accent of Outer Banks North Carolina (US) English is quite different in various details from that of any other area of the country. A social marker of this accent is the vowel in 'high' and 'tide', which is pronounced approximately like that in standard US English 'boy', whence the title of a book by Wolfram and Schilling-Estes (1997) explicating this dialect, *Hoi Toide on the Outer Banks*.

As soon as consideration moves beyond standard national varieties, often involving what may really be professional-academic written varieties, lexis and even grammar may be problematic. Strevens (1983, 1992) motivated and illustrated the analytic and practical efficacy of separating *accent* from the other aspects of language, to which he assigned the label *dialect*. He gave an example from a dialect of northeast England (1992: 40): '*Us had best take us coats: happen it will rain* "We had better take our coats: it might rain".' Not only does this dialect apparently not differentiate first-person-plural subject, object, and possessive forms, but the lexical-grammatical structure *happen X will verb* takes the place of standard *X might verb*. In west-central Indiana (US), a stereotypical phrase that marks a local variety is *My warsher needs fixed*, with an epenthetic *-r-* inserted in *washer*, and the structure *X needs done* as the equivalent of standard *X needs to be done* or … *needs doing*. Such instances are trivial in themselves, but are indicative of the ways in which varieties can differ from one another. Taken in the aggregate and in conversation at ordinary rates of production, they may cause frustration across speakers of different varieties to some degree.

Considerations of intelligibility bring out the social nature and basis of language. That is, the question 'Is this utterance intelligible?' in the abstract has no meaning; one might compare the question 'Is *X* a phoneme?' without reference to any particular language. Degree of intelligibility can only be meaningfully considered in a particular context of participants and situation: who is speaking to whom, when, where, why, and so on. Certainly, intelligibility may be considered in the context of any mode of production or reception; it may perhaps be most conveniently discussed in terms of speakers and hearers.

Intelligibility, comprehensibility and interpretability

Smith (1992: 75) spoke succinctly to the concern about loss of intelligibility across varieties: 'My response … is that for at least the last two hundred years there have been English-speaking people in some parts of the world who have not been intelligible to other English-speaking people in other parts of the world. It is a natural phenomenon when any language becomes so widespread.'

By adopting this commonsense and empirically arguable stance on the issue, Smith does away with recourse to emotional sorts of reactions to the spread of English. The reflexive cry 'something must be done!' is set aside in favour of a reasoned exploration.

Holistic approaches to intelligibility are difficult to carry off: it becomes clear, as illustrated in the examples above, that there are various levels of language and of the perception of language at work in communicating with other speakers of English. Strevens' proposal of separating accent from the other layers of language was a step in the direction of allowing for more specific approaches and an understanding of the parameters of successful verbal interaction. 'I couldn't understand what she was saying to me' could have one or a combination of senses. It might be intended to mean 'couldn't make out the words themselves' because of any number of factors, such as the speaker's pronunciation or volume, or background noise distractions, not to mention the speaker's using another language. It might be intended to convey 'didn't know what some key words meant', as in listening to someone speaking about a technical topic such as setting up a computer. It is important to have clear ways of addressing the specific categories of parameters we wish to investigate.

Smith (1992; see also Smith and Nelson, 1985) analysed the holistic language-in-use notion of understanding, or 'intelligibility' in a broad sense, into three components: *intelligibility, comprehensibility,* and *interpretability.* These components form a continuum of complexity within which *intelligibility* involves the fewest variables and *interpretability,* the most.

Intelligibility in this scheme refers to the level of sound and parsing utterances into recognizable or plausible words, as in the example at the beginning of this chapter. The US writer who places the bet — 'punt' — and the British turf accountant — 'bookie' — each believe the other to be speaking English. That is, an *intelligible* English utterance is one that sounds like English — just that. This categorization allows for the everyday phenomenon of hearing an unfamiliar word or 'not catching' some part of an utterance. In such cases, the entire exchange does not break down; clarification and repair devices come into play, e.g., 'Excuse me?'; 'Would you mind saying that again?'; 'Sorry, I didn't quite catch that'; or the missed element is stored for checking later; or it may simply be passed over, with the hearer relying on the redundancy in the overall message. In a study by Smith and Rafiqzad (1979), for example, subjects heard a tape of a passage and filled in words from it in its printed cloze passage version.[2] Being able to approximate a representation of sounds heard by writing them down was counted as a successful demonstration of intelligibility. It must be said, and kept in mind, that writers very often use the word 'intelligibility' not in this limited, technical sense, but as a holistic cover term for the degree of success in communication.

Comprehensibility, the next level of complexity in Smith's analysis, involves assigning meaning to utterances, approximately the conventional basic sense of 'understanding'. For example, successful comprehensibility involves apprehending an utterance *table* as meaning 'table', the word, and recognizing that it refers to an appropriate category or specific referent in the world so that it fits meaningfully into the current utterance, as in *Please put the package on the table, Invite guests of the committee to the table, Table a motion*, or *Insert data into cells in a table*. It is this level of linguistic interaction that is at risk when, say, unfamiliar technical terms come up in listening to an information technology troubleshooter explain to you why your e-mail is sending all your messages to Nome. In the example above, the American correctly understood that he was risking some money against the chance of a higher pay-off, but did not understand what sort of bet an 'each-way' was. In such cases, the discourse sounds like English, so its *intelligibility* is high; but some of the information is not coming through from speaker to hearer, so *comprehensibility* is lowered.

This is the situation that may arise, for example, in conversations across varieties of world Englishes when speakers introduce a borrowed lexical item, or a short stretch of mixing. For example, B. Kachru cites this example from an Indian newspaper matrimonial advertisement (1992a: 311): 'Correspondence invited, preferably for mutual alliance ... .' Kachru explains: 'The term *mutual alliance* is a culturally significant collocation; it refers to an arrangement by which X's daughter marries Y's son and Y's daughter marries X's son. ... [O]ne obvious advantage is that it restricts the giving or receiving of the dowry.' This 'culturally significant' term is one that would have to be made clear by a knowledgeable informant to someone not familiar with the Indian context, specifically with regard to customs of marriage arrangements. If there is no one to ask, the outsider must rely on further discoursal and contextual clues to infer a meaning for such an element.

The most complex level of communication, and the most important one, according to Smith (1992: 83), is that of *interpretability*. Beyond recognition of the medium and its elements (*intelligibility*) and recognition of meanings which may be reasonably assigned to words and phrases (*comprehensibility*) within a specific context, speakers discern the purpose and intent of an utterance. For example, there is a joke about the writing instructor who tells her class that a double negative such as *don't have no* ... makes a positive, but that a double positive does not make a negative, and a student responds with, *Yeah, right*. A speaker's transforming *yeah* 'yes' plus *right* 'you are correct' into the equivalent of *That's not so* or *I don't believe it* and the hearer's realizing that intent is a demonstration of interpretability at work.

The following passage from the novel *Jasmine* by Bharati Mukherjee (1989: 48) provides some further exemplification of these domains. In this paragraph the protagonist has been made an offer of marriage by the widower referred to in the passage, and her teacher — 'Masterji' is probably transparent to world English readers, if they compare 'schoolmaster' — has come to confer with her father, to insist that she not be married off, but allowed to continue her education:

> Masterji must have heard that he was likely to lose me to the Ludhiana widower. He biked all the way to our adobe compound one Sunday morning, his white beard rolled spiffily tight and his long hair tucked under a crisp chartreuse turban, to confront my father … He was even carrying a kirpan, which meant that for him this was a special occasion. Masterji was a Sikh. All Sikh men in our village … kept their hair and beards, but very few went around with their ceremonial daggers strapped to their chests all day long.

There is no problem of intelligibility here: the few words that may not be familiar to international English readers are plausible English words. Even 'kirpan', not marked as not-English in the text, is readable and pronounceable. The name-ending '-ji' is repeated often enough in the narrative and dialogue of the work at large ('Pitaji' for reference to the father, 'Mataji' for the mother) that the reader may quickly pick it up as a term of respect: that is, it becomes comprehensible with just a little exposure. Similarly, looping back naturally through the passage after encountering the plain assertion '[He] was a Sikh' shows readers some descriptive criteria of such a man, e.g., having a beard long enough to be rolled, having hair long enough to be tucked up, and wearing a turban. And the offered interpretation of those details is made plain by the author's narrative, '… which meant that for him this was a special occasion'. The author employs a similar retrospective device to 'translate' *kirpan*, the one lexical item that might have remained a bit of a mystery, with the reference to 'their ceremonial daggers …'. Multilingual creative authors make decisions about what parts of their texts they will elucidate in such ways, and which to leave more to the reading skills of their audiences. If one imagines transforming this scene into a live play with spoken dialogue, then the features of the text would work in exactly the corresponding ways in the spoken medium.

In the same ways, while the *mutual alliance* phrase in the matrimonial advertisement quoted from just above can probably be dealt with as a matter of lexical meaning (*comprehensibility*), the following one, also from a matrimonial advertisement cited by B. Kachru (1992a: 311) requires an added element of interpretation: 'Matrimonial correspondence invited from respected Punjabi families for my son … clean shaven.' The descriptive phrase, says Kachru, 'has a serious religious connotation: it is indicative of non-conformism with traditional Sikhism in India'. Sikh men, cf. the passage by Mukherjee above, traditionally maintain long hair and beards. Some modern, Westernized Sikhs, however, prefer to be clean shaven. The implications of such a disclaimer can only be sensed by someone with some close degree of familiarity with the relevant cultures.

Researching intelligibility

The findings of intelligibility studies have shown that no 'native' or Inner-Circle English can be considered some sort of primary form among world Englishes, and that the levels of language comprehension and processing interact with one another but are not strictly interdependent. That is, some loss of intelligibility because of background noise, for example, does not necessarily preclude successful comprehensibility or interpretability of an utterance.

The following three paradigm studies of intelligibility conducted by researchers from the Inner, Outer and Expanding Circles will suggest ideas for empirical studies that may be carried out within a mixed classroom where a number of varieties of English are represented. Or, if the class comprises a fairly homogeneous group, data from broadcast media may be recorded and used for testing intelligibility. For comprehensibility and interpretability, written texts may also be used.

Smith and Rafiqzad's study of intelligibility

A study by Smith and Rafiqzad (1979), which employed over 1,300 subjects, showed that the claim 'that a native-speaker variety of English should be the … standard with which to compare all other varieties' could not be supported (p. 371).

The researchers obtained the help of nine collaborators, who each recorded a passage of English speech; the readers were from Hong Kong, India, Japan, Korea, Malaysia, Nepal, the Philippines, Sri Lanka, and the USA. The tapes of the passages were played for groups of listeners in eleven countries in Asia, South Asia and the Pacific, who filled in cloze passages while following along with the readings (pp. 372–3). Thus, this was a test of intelligibility, not comprehensibility.

One important finding emerged immediately. The averages of correct responses from listeners to the reading by the US speaker were so low that the researchers questioned whether the data from that reader were valid. They played that tape for five groups of listeners from various countries as a follow-up check on the results. That test confirmed the US reader as a representative, intelligible English speaker, and the results were used. Smith and Rafiqzad present a striking observation: '[T]he native speaker was always found to be among the least intelligible speakers, scoring [an average of 55%].' The speakers from India and Japan, for example, scored much higher (p. 375). The researchers had confidence in their findings because the intelligibility ratings for readers across groups of listeners remained reasonably consistent. That is, for example, the US speaker was always in the lowest three for all the listener groups, while the Japanese speaker was always among the top five.

One of the study's questionnaire items asked listeners to try to identify the nationality of the speaker they had heard. In the seven cases in which listeners heard someone from their own country speaking, the results were varied. The Korean, Malaysian and Japanese listeners correctly identified their respective countries' speakers 87 percent of the time, while the Hong Kong listeners correctly identified the Hong Kong speaker with only 57 percent accuracy, and the Indian and Philippines listeners scored only in the forties. There may be several explanations of this result; there are more subvarieties within Indian and Philippine English than there are in Korean, Malaysian or Japanese English. Smith and Rafiqzad summarize their study's fundamental importance in this statement:

> Since native speaker [i.e., Inner-Circle] phonology doesn't appear to be more intelligible than non-native [i.e., Outer- or Expanding-Circle phonology], there seems to be no reason to insist that the performance target in the English classroom be a native speaker. (Smith and Rafiqzad, 1979: 380)

This study is rather straightforward in its conception: questions naturally arise about cross-varietal intelligibility in general, and more particularly, whether some accents are 'better' than others in the sense of being more widely acceptable, therefore more 'worth learning'. So the researchers set out to investigate this idea by getting people to listen to varieties of English that were and were not their own. The logistical demands were great, but the basic idea is of the 'why didn't someone think of doing this sooner?' variety. Beyond the results as such, which are in themselves surprising in various ways, the clear indication of Smith and Rafiqzad's research is that there is nothing inherently 'good' or even 'better' about an Inner-Circle or so-called 'native' accent; the definition of 'native' has to be adjusted according to the usage in countries where there are English speakers. The authors' data and interpretations thus suggest a radical revamping of many people's thinking about matters of curriculum and instruction in English as an additional language.

Smith and Bisazza's study of comprehensibility

Smith and Bisazza (1982) examined the comprehensibility of Indian, Japanese and US varieties of English. The study investigated the effects of listening to passages which were 'syntactically identical but phonologically different' because of the variety of English that speakers used (p. 259). The authors hypothesized that a particular speaker might well be more comprehensible to listeners who were accustomed to one English variety rather than another.

Recordings of the Indian, Japanese and US speakers were played for subject listeners in Hong Kong, India, the Philippines, Japan, Taiwan, Thailand and the US (Hawai'i); the readings were three different forms of the Michigan

Test of Aural Comprehension, which asks subjects to select a picture that best matches a passage which they have heard, and to answer questions at the ends of sentence- or paragraph-length passages (p. 260). The authors observe that 'subjects in all seven countries had primarily been trained to interact in English with native (Inner-Circle) speakers and/or with fellow countrymen' (p. 268). The research results indicated that the subjects' variety of English affected their comprehensibility scores. Not too surprisingly, the subjects from ESL countries such as India made higher comprehensibility scores than those from EFL countries such as Thailand (pp. 264–5). Consistent with the authors' hypothesis, there was a speaker effect: 'The American speaker was easiest for the subjects [to understand], and the Indian was most difficult', with the Japanese speaker in the middle (p. 265).

By the nature of this study (i.e., all readers used texts from the Michigan Test), only phonology varied across the reading passages that the subjects listened to. Therefore, intelligibility was shown to have an effect on comprehensibility, since comprehension test scores varied across parameters including which speaker the subjects listened to. This shows that variety exposure is important. For example, as is commonly remarked, Japanese students typically get all their English exposure in the classroom, with little or no interaction with speakers in natural, spontaneous contexts; and, in this test, the Japanese subjects did better when listening to the Japanese speaker than they did when listening to the American or Indian speaker. Smith and Bisazza conclude:

> It seems clear from this study that one's English is more comprehensible to those people who have had active exposure to it. [Nowadays,] with English being used frequently by nonnative speakers to communicate with other nonnative speakers, this study gives evidence of a need for students of English to have greater exposure to nonnative varieties of English. (Smith and Bisazza, 1982: 269)

This study shows that wider exposure to more varieties increases users' ability to comprehend international educated English. These findings are consistent with those from Smith and Rafiqzad (1979): rather than trying to inculcate in students a particular accent which has been selected *a priori* as one that 'should' be the best to use, students should be made aware of and offered practice in as broad a variety of accents and usages as possible if the goal is to equip them to be effective in the international domain of interaction.

Matsuura, Chiba and Fujieda's study of intelligibility and comprehensibility

Matsuura, Chiba and Fujieda (1999) examined the intelligibility and comprehensibility of American and Irish English speakers in Japan. Their findings show that there is a likelihood of mismatch between what speakers think they are understanding, their 'perceived comprehensibility' (p. 58), and their actual measurable intelligibility and comprehensibility.

For this study, three US and three Irish teachers of English recorded 'self-introduction' texts which were played for a total of 106 Japanese students from three universities (p. 50). The US variety was regarded as 'familiar' to most students, and the Irish, 'unfamiliar'. The presentations were tested as dictation exercises, and a follow-up questionnaire was administered to gather the students' subjective impressions of their own performance and comfort-levels (p. 52). The researchers found that clarity and intonation seemed to be factors in achieving successful intelligibility as measured by dictation scores. More important for the students' self-perception of successful communication were 'familiarity and exposure', which 'at minimum, had a positive psychological effect on the listeners'. That is, exposure provided 'less inhibition, less bias and more tolerance toward different varieties of English' (p. 58).

Citing Lippi-Green (1997), who found that the acceptability of accent had an effect on employment opportunities in the US, Matsuura, Chiba and Fujieda wrote that Japanese institutions should make an effort to hire non-Japanese English teachers from places other than North America, in order to expose students to more varieties of accents (p. 58). They recognized that this might not be feasible on any large scale in the public education system, and suggested trying to achieve these ends to some extent with aural media and written teaching materials.

Conclusion

The three components of language introduced here — intelligibility, comprehensibility and interpretability — are intuitively accommodating to various sorts of analytical and pedagogical purposes. Their availability in our technical and conceptual lexicons does away with facile recourse to uninformative ambiguities in such casual observations as 'I couldn't understand a thing they were saying'. How one applies these notions is guided by the purpose at hand, whether, for example, in teaching a range of pronunciation acceptable in the contexts of use of a variety, teaching denotative vocabulary, or practising the use of idioms for desired effects (e.g., how 'let the cat out of the bag' is different from 'disclose secret information').

It is important to keep in mind that there is no implication of an equation of intelligibility and proficiency, for example, or of a defining criterion in terms of comprehensibility in differentiating E-S-L from E-F-L. Smith (1992) has demonstrated that the 'native speaker' may often be the least intelligible to other participants in situations where 'non-natives' are taking part. Success in conversation or writing, i.e., degree of achievement of any one or all of intelligibility, comprehensibility and interpretability, can only be assessed while simultaneously taking the participants into account. Midwestern US and South Asian English speakers, neither having encountered the others' accent and usage before, will be in some degree unintelligible to one another, until some amount of exposure expands their ranges of what is 'acceptable'. But it is important for ELT professionals concerned about world Englishes to keep Smith's closing comment in mind (1992: 8): 'Being a native speaker does not seem to be as important [for Intelligibility, Comprehensibility and Interpretability] as being fluent in English and familiar with several different national varieties.' That is, it is important to expose students to as many varieties of English and to as many contexts of its use as possible, thus broadening their sense of what is acceptable or possible.

The thrust of Smith's work is not a call for 'tolerance', which implies condescension, but for open-minded recognition of diversity and linguistic variation, and of the importance of each English user's attitude towards others' Englishes. The intelligibility-comprehensibility-interpretability framework allows empirical investigation of the world of linguistic *pluricentricity*: there is no one world centre of English correctness or goodness. Each country or region decides, in some terms, where its norms will come from — from within or without. Such a view removes 'native speakers' from their formerly alleged status as owners and directors of English. Looked at in another way, it absolves them of a heavy burden.

The studies reported on here suggest some basic ways of getting at the components of language use. Intelligibility, the level of recognizing the sounds and legitimate sound patterns of language (sounds themselves and syllable shapes, for example), can be checked by asking for written representations of what subjects think they are hearing. Dictation and cloze-passage tests are commonly used devices for these purposes. Comprehensibility is examined by asking for responses to factual questions about the passage that subjects have heard or have read. If subjects read the excerpt from the novel *Jasmine* given in Chapter 4, for example, one could ask 'What do you think a *kirpan* is?' The text provides a clear answer, in this case, though it is not completely straightforward, since it is separated from the lexical item in question by several lines of text; more advanced questions could involve greater degrees of inference. Interpretability, perhaps the most interesting to work with, requires thinking about the implications of what is presented in the text and consideration of the features that provide bases for reasonable inferences. In some cases, these elements may not be at all transparent to someone who is unfamiliar with the cultural context in question and will call for assistance from a 'native speaker' of that variety (see Chapter 10).

Overall, these studies indicate several basic and very important points: the *non*-primacy of Inner-Circle English or its speakers; the importance of lowering one's resistance to receptivity through exposure to as many varieties of English as possible, and the effect of confidence or a positive attitude in believing in one's ability to function in English. They suggest that these are qualities that ELT professionals should make a part of their own view of world Englishes, and seek to inculcate in their students.

Suggested activities

1. Observe or recall and write down an outline of a conversation in which you participated which contained a specific linguistic element or usage that called itself to your attention. Was it a pronunciation that you found unusual, an unfamiliar lexical item, or a question about interpretation? Did the linguistic and/or extra-linguistic context sort out the difficulty for you? Explicate the situation and the working-out of intelligibility, comprehensibility or interpretability, as appropriate; present your observation and analysis to your classmates, and be prepared to contribute your thoughts to a discussion of their presentations.

2. Find a passage of written text from a variety of English not your own which provides features of the same sort as those discussed in the *Jasmine* excerpt in this chapter. You might look, for example, at the editorial pages of major newspapers from various English-using countries, such as India, The Philippines, or Singapore (look up Internet sites, where such publications are readily available).

    Similarly, find a passage of text from your own variety, or one with which you are familiar, and try to predict the sorts of questions that might arise for readers not familiar with it. See how your predictions match the subjective reactions of your classmates when you present the passage and your analysis to them.

3. Following Smith (1992) and Smith and Rafiqzad (1979), discussed above, organize the class into groups according to their respective 'native varieties' of English. Have each group pick a passage to read, and choose a reader to present the passage to the other groups. Prepare copies of cloze-passage text for each selection, and provide it on handouts for all the members of all the groups. Have the cloze passages filled in as the passage is read once at a normal speed. Tabulate the results: do they confirm the sorts of findings discussed in this chapter, or not? If not, what factors may have contributed to the different results?

Part II
Acquisition, Creativity, Standards and Testing

6

World Englishes and language acquisition

SLA — as an apparently hermetically sealed area of study — is in danger of losing contact with research on language and social interaction. This state of affairs is visible in three ways: (a) the narrow spectrum of data types and contexts examined in SLA studies, (b) the methods of analysis and the underlying analytic assumption of 'learner-deficient interactant', and finally (c) the theoretical understanding of what constitutes discourse and communication.

Firth and Wagner (1998)

Introduction

Second Language Acquisition (SLA) emerged as a distinct field of research in the late 1950s to early 1960s (see, e.g., Mitchell and Myles, 1998; Ritchie and Bhatia, 1996) attempting to answer questions such as the following: Is it possible to acquire an additional language in the same sense as one acquires a first language? If yes, are the two processes similar; if not, what is the difference between *acquisition* and *learning?* Are the motivations for people to acquire additional languages primarily *integrative*, or are they *instrumental?* Is there a difference between the end results of the process of language acquisition depending on the nature of motivation? What is the role of instruction (i.e., language teaching) in the acquisition of an additional language? What sociocultural factors, if any, are relevant in studying the learning/acquisition of additional languages?

Theoretical orientation of SLA research

All these issues are directly relevant to investigations in world Englishes, which are by their very nature instances of additional language acquisition (or learning) for the majority of users in the Outer and Expanding Circles as well as significant minorities in the Inner-Circle countries. Treatment of these questions in the SLA literature in general have one thing in common: researchers view the problem of acquiring an additional language from the perspective of an individual. Whether one labels it 'learning' or 'acquiring' an additional language, it is considered an individual accomplishment, and what is under focus is the cognitive, psychological and institutional status of an individual. The spotlight may be on what mental capabilities are involved, what psychological factors play a role in the learning or acquisition, or whether the target language is learned in an instructional setting or acquired through social interaction in a natural sociocultural setting. Even when the study is based on cross-sections of particular populations, generalizations are presented in terms identical to those of individual language acquisition (e.g. Larsen-Freeman, 1976).

The same is true of research that claims to be based on sociolinguistic models of second language acquisition (e.g., Preston, 1989) or is said to take into account notions from pragmatics and communicative competence (see, e.g., discussions of interlanguage pragmatics in Kasper and Blum-Kulka, 1993): the individualistic orientation of learning/acquisition is maintained. Although research in pragmatics is based on speaker intentions, research on second or foreign language pragmatics neglects speaker intentions and analyzes SL speaker utterances solely from the perspective of the hearer, who is presumed to be a *native* speaker of the target language. This leads to notions of 'pragmatic failure' (Thomas 1983), which has doubtful theoretical validity viewed from the perspective of speaker intentions. According to the Gricean cooperative principle (Grice, 1975), speakers and hearers are assumed to be honest in their interaction, and most data discussed in the literature do not provide evidence that second language speakers intend to mislead their interlocutors. Therefore, the focus on 'pragmatic failure' is puzzling.

SLA in multilingual contexts

The world Englishes orientation recognizes that additional languages are learned/acquired in multilingual contexts (here, 'multilingual' is used to include 'bilingual' unless noted otherwise). The uses and functions of the additional language are determined by the needs of the community; i.e., the competence in the target language that a multilingual person acquires is largely a function of the niche the additional language occupies in the linguistic repertoire of the community. Disregard of this fact results in the neglect of a variety of issues related to the learning or acquisition of any language of wider communication, including world Englishes.

World Englishes are entities of functional performance in varied settings across the world; as such, they provide the most extensive 'laboratory to date for applied linguistic and sociolinguistic research' (B. Kachru, 1990a). Observations and analyses in this laboratory bring important SLA concepts and claims into focus and reveal cracks in theory-building.

For example, Mesthrie (1992), on the basis of his study of South African Indian English (SAIE), has shown that the parameter-setting model of second language acquisition (e.g., Flynn, 1987; White, 1989) may not be the most appropriate model for naturalistic second language acquisition.[1] He observes: 'The New English data suggest that we are not dealing with discrete [parameter] settings ('off' and 'on'; 'plus' or 'minus'; etc.), but with a continuum of settings. This makes the acquisition process more fuzzy and susceptible to social conditions than Universal Grammarians would allow' (Mesthrie, 1992: 174).

The world Englishes perspective has shown that concepts such as *interlanguage* (Selinker, 1992), *fossilization* (Selinker, 1992), *input* (Krashen, 1985), and *monitor* (in terms of native speaker competence; Krashen, 1981), as currently formulated are of no relevance to indigenized varieties of English (see below). Indian, Nigerian, or Singaporean English speakers follow the norms of their own varieties rather than the norms of American, Australian, or British English.

While theories of formal linguistics seek the most efficient representations of phrase and sentence structures and theories of bilingualism continue to grapple with basic questions such as how many grammars bilingual people have in their brains, the study of world Englishes reveals the research focus that may be brought about by tying data to theory, rather than the other way around. Consequently, questions of uses and functions of the language, rather than of how it is acquired, come to the fore as the salient face of the inquiry.

SLA and formal instruction

The relevance of world Englishes to issues of language learning/acquisition is clear in the context of the assertion in the introduction to Ritchie and Bhatia (1996: 20) that 'the question of the specific effects of formal instruction can ... be safely ignored in a treatment of theoretical issues'. This ignores S. Sridhar's (1994: 800) observation that '[a] great deal of successful SLA takes place through formal instruction; acquisition through informal exposure is not the only way.' According to Mesthrie (1992: 29), for example, SAIE developed as a distinct variety as a result of several factors, including 'the teaching of English by a French-speaking missionary to Tamil-speaking children via the medium of a Zulu-based pidgin'. This is, and continues to be, true of most former colonial contexts of ELT. Because most acquirers of English as an additional language in the Outer and Expanding Circles learn English in formal settings without exposure to Inner-Circle users or, sometimes, even to materials from the Inner Circle, instruction must be considered an important aspect of SLA with respect to world Englishes.

As instruction is important and there are salient divergences of English in its diasporas across the globe due to the historical — usually colonial — legacy associated with it, the most often addressed questions about English are: Who owns X country's English? Whose English should we teach? How do we define proficiency or success in learning?

Issues of proficiency and communicative competence

While *proficiency* in a hard science may be measured with respect to firmer standards, fluency — ease of performance and interlocutor satisfaction — is often automatically defaulted in SLA to a measurement with respect to *native speakers* or *native English*. This concern is of primary importance in SLA; Gass (1997: 1) argues, '[t]he concept of input is perhaps the single most important concept of [SLA].'

It is understandable how this attitude could come about. Foreign language instruction has always been carried on with respect to 'best' or 'native' models: public school classes in French in the US or UK or anywhere else, for example, do not teach 'Algerian French', or 'Canadian French'. There is not, however, a widespread expectation in the UK and US that one's high school French teacher will be a *native speaker* of French from France.

Regarding world Englishes, however, there has always been a pervasive sense that somehow the language has to be taught by a *native speaker*; it was being tainted by its being taught by *foreigners*. Thus, questions of pedagogical model and what it is that is being learned — UK, US, or *local* English — have been much debated. Although France is not exporting hordes of trained 'French as a Foreign Language Teachers' to America or Britain, *purists* everywhere implicitly seem to hope for that situation for English learners outside the Inner Circle. In reality, however, as S. Sridhar (1994: 801) points out, there are 'millions of L2 users who learn and use second languages in their own countries, from their own (nonnative) teachers, for use primarily with other nonnative speakers, and who may never come across a native speaker face to face'. In short, the *input* for a learner comes from the context in which learning takes place.

The term *native speaker* has an almost inescapable cachet in the parlance of language teachers and researchers. According to McArthur (1992: 682), 'native' has been 'used in this sense since at least the 16c'. In the foreword to B. Kachru (1992d [1982]), Charles Ferguson wrote: 'Linguists, perhaps especially American linguists, have long given a special place to the "native speaker" as the only truly valid and reliable source of language data' (1982/1992: xiii). If a US university department wants to hire an instructor of French or Japanese, the advertisement is likely to read 'native speaker preferred'.

However, the global distribution and functions of English are quite different from those of French or Japanese, or of any other language. The faculties of most academic institutions in the UK, US and other Inner-Circle countries include professionals from an Outer- or Expanding-Circle country whose competence in English is not less than that of *native* users of English. In fact, some of them may even exhibit superior capabilities in their extent of vocabulary, nicety of word choice, colourfulness of expression, clarity of transmission of information, etc., as compared to the *native* speakers. As Mufwene (2001b: 139) observes, 'what linguistics needs as an arbiter of a community's norm is a proficient speaker', which some native speakers may not be.

The accepted standard, seemingly innocuous definitions say that a *native speaker* is someone who acquired a given language as her/his home language, *at mother's knee*, without benefit of formal instruction. She/he has useful *intuitions* about grammatical correctness, and does not have to think about how to say what she/he wants to say, except for occasional searches for the right words, and so on. The notion of an ideal hearer/speaker has been codified as an abstraction for research purposes in formal linguistics; its extension to SLA is another matter.

All of the criteria in SLA rely fundamentally on monolingual notions about language acquisition and secondarily on assumptions about family and other social factors that may not match the ideal at all. Strevens cautions:

> Usually [a] primary language is the language used by the child's mother, which is why the conversational label *mother tongue* is often used — but of course less usually the child may not be brought up by its mother, or the mother may deliberately employ a language different from her own "mother tongue," or ... the child may simultaneously acquire more than one language ... (Strevens, 1992: 35)

These are the sorts of considerations that led Ferguson (1992: xiii) to conclude his remark on the notion with the famous suggestion: 'In fact, the whole mystique of native speaker and mother tongue should probably be quietly dropped from the linguists' set of professional myths about language.' More recently, Davies (2003: 197) observed, 'The native speaker is a fine myth: we need it as a model, a goal, almost an inspiration. But it is useless as a measure; *it will not help us define our goals*' (emphasis added).

If it is too big a leap to drop the notion altogether, we can certainly start by admitting that some better definition needs to be developed, to account for many, many users of English in the Outer and Expanding Circles. If an Anglo-American speaker were addressing a meeting of colleagues at the Central Institute of English and Foreign Languages in Hyderabad, India, she would be identifiable without hesitation as not-Indian. If one can be a *native speaker of American English*, it is only reasonable that one can be, given certain circumstances, a *native speaker of Indian English, Nigerian English*, and so on.

B. Kachru notes the necessity of a distinction between genetic and functional 'nativeness' (1997: 217): if a variety of English has practical sociolinguistic status in its ranges of use in a society, and its users recognize what 'good' English is, and what it is (and is not) good for, then English has become one of the languages functioning in the available repertoire of languages. Genetic (historical, in-line development) considerations are neither here nor there for this situation.

In addition to native speaker, 'communicative competence' of speakers — the ability to use a community's language in appropriate ways to achieve goals and to operate in the society in an intended manner — has been an area of concern since the term was made a 'key word' by Dell Hymes in the 1970s. Notions of communicative competence are analogous to, for example, knowing and acting in accordance with the sociocultural knowledge that if an Indian person hands you something, you should not accept it in your left hand, or that it is unthinkable to go into a Japanese home with your shoes on. Similarly, there are conventions about who speaks when with whom and how; it is not reasonable to assume that what is *polite* or *de rigueur*, etc., in one community will hold for another. A person's being born in a *native-English-speaking* country does not make for a more *competent* communicator in any other context. Instead, wide exposure to varieties of English makes one more amenable to being flexible in one's use of the language and forms the basis for recommendations such as 'a world Englishes perspective should be infused into the TESOL preparatory curriculum' (Brown, 1995: 233; see Chapter 9).[2]

Nativization and Englishization

The concern with effective communication using world Englishes depends on an awareness of *nativization* (B. Kachru, 1983) of English and *Englishization* (B. Kachru, 1979) of the languages in contact with English. Nativization refers to the adaptation of English in particular social-cultural settings, and leads to qualifying descriptors such as 'US English', 'Indian English', 'Singaporean English', and so on. Englishization refers to the manifest influences of English on other languages in a given repertoire; levels of languages from pronunciation through literary genres may be affected in discernable ways. The phenomenon is of concern to some purist observers, a matter of increasing the flexibility of codes of communication to others. Often-quoted statements on this latter attitude include the following one from the Indian philosopher and creative writer Raja Rao:

> We cannot write like the English. We should not. We cannot write only as Indians. We have grown to look at the large world around us as part of us. Our method of expression therefore has to be a dialect which will some day prove to be as distinctive and colorful as the Irish and the American. (Rao, 1938, cited in S. Sridhar, 1982: 294)

Code-mixing and *code-switching* (CM and CS hereafter; changing from one language to another within sentences, and across sentences and larger language domains, respectively) together comprise a major characteristic of the users of world Englishes which is readily observable, but a capacity not easily grasped by monolingual investigators. A monolingual perspective views mixing and switching as unnecessary, even illogical. The reality of the phenomena cannot be discounted, however. Thus, SLA research in the world Englishes framework seeks to answer questions regarding not only how, but when, where, why and with whom CM and CS occur (see Chapters 8 and 18).

Interlanguage and world Englishes

Closely allied to the models, cross-language influence and performance controversies are the hypotheses gathered under the label *interlanguage* (IL). The monolingual stance that is necessary to make the hypotheses internally consistent and universally applicable necessitates regarding all nonnative/ nonstandard forms of language as failed attempts at learning. According to Y. Kachru (1993, 1994a), the basic IL notion may be useful in describing the process of SL learning in instructional settings in which English is not employed for any real instrumental purposes outside the learning situation itself. Interlanguage as a concept, however, has no relevance to 'stable contexts of bi-/multilingualism' across the world (Y. Kachru, 1994a: 796).

In particular, claims that entire varieties of English are not that, but are instead *fossilized* forms of historical precedents, results of *imperfect learning*, fly in the face of assessments of varieties in their own terms, without biases introduced by comparison to chronological antecedents. American English would have to be considered an *imperfectly learned* version of British English under such definitions. Y. Kachru comments on fossilization: 'it is irrelevant to situations in which an additional language has definite societal roles in the linguistic repertoire of its users', in this case, English (1994a: 797; see the ever-growing literature on English in Outer and Expanding Circles, as in Cheshire, 1991; B. Kachru, 1992d; Thumboo, 2001b). Sociolinguistic contexts in which users' multilingual repertoires include English are linguistically as stable as any monolingual societies' contexts: evolving, to be sure, but not subsumed under the learning curves of IL interpretations as fossilized varieties (Y. Kachru, 1994a: 798).

The notion of repertoire has to be seen in ways different from — more complex than — those that give rise to register analyses in monolingual societies or studies limited to monolingual contexts. In the broader language use of a multilingual person, languages complement one another in the same ways that various registers do within their domains of applicability. It is reasonable to assume that one does not discuss knitting, marriage arrangements, and physics in the same languages; in other words, 'no one ... code is appropriate in all domains' (Y. Kachru, 1994a: 798). The models for SLA in the Outer/Expanding Circles are to a great extent the teachers and materials in classrooms. While this modeling situation is the same as for the French classroom in Birmingham or Idaho, the uses to be made of second-language English outside the classroom and the reinforcement/expansion of the classroom learning to be found in the greater society's modeling of English, including the media, make the overall situations entirely different from one another.

Why SLA theories and world Englishes do not connect

Although the vast majority of learners of English learn the language in the Outer and Expanding Circles, their presence and concerns have rarely been acknowledged in building theories of second language acquisition. Most theory-building activities have treated the foreign learners who happen to join an institution of higher learning and the immigrant populations in the Inner Circle (the ESL context) as primary sources of data. That is to say, a vast majority of learners of English in the Outer and Expanding Circles are 'invisible' to the theory construction; worse yet, a large number of factors that are crucial in understanding how languages are learnt and used are being almost totally ignored, as the quote at the beginning of this chapter suggests. Since English is taught in most Outer-Circle countries by indigenous teachers using locally produced materials (e.g., in most of South Asia, East and West Africa), there is little awareness of factors relevant to acquisition of English in these contexts. To the extent that the learners or contexts of learning in the Expanding Circle are mentioned in the so-called English as a Foreign Language (EFL) situation, it is in the context of how to prepare Inner-Circle teachers to deal with them.

Y. Kachru (1994a), S. Sridhar (1994), and Sridhar and Sridhar (1992) question the assumptions of prevailing bases of SLA research and point out the realities that demand attention. Sridhar and Sridhar (1992) observe that the lack of mutual relevance of SLA theories and world Englishes, labelled

Indigenized Varieties of English (IVEs) to each other is based on a number of suppositions (pp. 93–4):

1. The goal of SLA is to acquire native-like competence in the target language, i.e., be as proficient and fluent as a native speaker in pronunciation, grammar, and vocabulary, and also in the sociocultural conventions of language use.
2. The entire range and depth of input is or ought to be available to the learners so that they can achieve the goals of language acquisition defined above.
3. What functions the target language serves in the learners' community is irrelevant to SLA.
4. Learners' previous language(s) are not relevant to SLA except as a source of negative transfer, which is undesirable, or a source of positive transfer, which is acceptable.
5. Success in SLA depends crucially upon integrative motivation, i.e., the desire to become a part of the sociocultural milieu of the native speakers of the target language.

These assumptions, consequently, lead to hypotheses that treat the following as axioms on which all theoretical formulations and empirical research are based:

1. The learners in the ESL settings are expected to acquire the competence to use the language effectively with *native* speakers. The norm is the idealized grammar that underlies the native speaker competence as envisioned in linguistic theory, i.e., the grammars of Standard American or British English; Australian, Canadian and New Zealand Englishes are still rare as norms.
2. The input is or ought to be the entire range of English in the American or British English-speaking situations.
3. Learners are or have to be motivated to acquire the language and the sociocultural norms and values of the models of English they are acquiring.
4. The roles that are or could be assigned to the primary language(s) of the learners are either impediments, or in some cases, facilitators to target language acquisition.
5. Any difference from the American or British models in pronunciation, grammar, vocabulary, or language use is evidence of failure: the grammatical differences are clues to fossilizations and the differences in speech acts, discourse strategies, etc., to pragmatic failure.

Given these assumptions, it is no wonder that only about five percent of learners are expected to achieve native competence in the target language (Selinker, 1992). The others are relegated to the category of users of an interlanguage — a linguistic system that represents neither the previous language(s) nor the target language, but is an intermediary stage on the way towards the target language norms.

The ground realities

From the point of view of a majority of users of Outer- and Expanding-Circle varieties of English, this monolingual approach is not only a depressing but a totally unrealistic and misinformed appraisal of their situation and linguistic competence. The reality of the situation that prevails in the world beyond the Inner Circle has the following characteristics.

The varieties learned in the Outer Circle, and increasingly in the Expanding Circle, are acquired primarily for communicating with other similar users (Smith, 1983a). Inner-Circle speakers of English are not the only, or even primary interlocutors in most situations; Inner-Circle norms are not the most preferred norms as they may be viewed as 'distasteful and pedantic', 'affected or even snobbish' (B. Kachru, 1982b; Bamgboṣe, 1971; Sey, 1973). This is also true of written language, creative literature providing the prime example (B. Kachru, 1986b, 1990b, 1995a).

The input that is available to most learners in the Outer and Expanding Circles is the relevant indigenized variety of English (e.g., Caribbean English, IE, PhE, SME, etc.). The Inner-Circle varieties are available through the audio-visual media to a limited number of learners, but the overwhelming influence is that of the local norm. The teachers, materials and peer group all are indigenous to the learning context. English is just one part of the linguistic repertoire of the learners; they have other languages in their repertoire for many domains, including familial and interpersonal. Therefore, 'the Bloomfieldian ... model of bilingualism, one in which the ideal bilingual has a native-like command of both languages, each complete in itself' is irrelevant in these situations (S. Sridhar, 1994: 801). Typically, in multilingual communities, competence in a second language does not duplicate the primary language competence, it complements it (Grosjean, 1989).

Some of the functions of Englishes in the Outer and Expanding Circle are unique to them. They serve as the High Variety in a diglossic situation, e.g., in formal situations in administration, higher courts of law, tertiary education, etc. In the domains of friendship and social events, they may overlap with other languages in the repertoire of the community; 'code-switching and code-mixing are manifestations of this overlap' (Sridhar and Sridhar, 1992: 96).

Sociolinguistic surveys of attitudes and motivations of learners of English in the Outer Circle have shown that '[t]he reasons for studying English and the skills desired are overwhelmingly the ones normally labeled instrumental' (Shaw, 1981: 121). The effectiveness of instrumental motivation in promoting second-language proficiency has been demonstrated by Lukmani (1972) for a group of non-Westernized women in Bombay, and by Gardner and Lambert (1972) for Filipino learners of English. The generally high level of competence in English attested in the Outer-Circle users of the language seems to render questionable the hypothesis that integrative motivation is vital for achievement in second language acquisition (Sridhar and Sridhar, 1992: 96).

Some of the most creative innovations in the indigenized varieties of English involve differences from the Inner-Circle Englishes in grammar, vocabulary, discourse strategies, and genres and styles. To label them deviations, errors, mistakes, fossilizations, pragmatic failure, etc. is to deny the linguistic and cultural experiences that motivate such innovations.

Acquisition of English in the Outer and Expanding Circles

The gap between the assumptions of classical SLA paradigms of research and the ground realities of acquisition of English in the Outer and Expanding Circles clearly indicates that the concepts and methods of the former are not immediately and totally transferable to the latter situations (Sridhar and Sridhar, 1992: 97). A realistic characterization of acquisition of Englishes outside the Inner Circle and even to some communities within the Inner Circle involves an understanding of the following points.

First, that English is one language among several others in the linguistic repertoires of the multilingual users' Englishes. The domains of use are not the same as among the monolingual speakers of Inner-Circle English, hence the competences the multilingual users of Englishes exhibit are different. They are not *deficient* speakers/writers, they are proficient users of English *plus* other languages in the domains where the specific code or codes are appropriate. English in the rituals of Hindu worship in India is as unexpected as Persian in a Roman Catholic Church service. In the multilingual context of Delhi, a user of Indian English may use, e.g., Punjabi for discussing the dinner menu in the family domain, a regional variety of Hindi with her neighbours, Sanskrit in her daily Hindu worship, Punjabi or Hindi in collective singing of devotional hymns, Standard Hindi and Indian English in her professional environment; she may listen to Urdu *ghazals* (semi-classical vocal music), Hindi popular songs or English pop music for entertainment, read English and Hindi newspapers and magazines, listen to BBC news, and view Hindi TV serials and English movies. There is nothing unusual about such linguistic behaviour; most educated speakers in Delhi in fact code-switch and code-mix Hindi, Punjabi and English with great facility. The same is true in Singapore, where code-switching and mixing among dialects of Chinese, Malay and English are the rule rather than the exception (Tay, 1993a).

A second point is that the input that is available to learners of English in a majority of Outer- and Expanding-Circle contexts is local, as has been said before. Most teachers are proficient in their own varieties of English and teach through the bilingual method, i.e., use the primary language of the students in the classroom to teach English. The resources of the familiar local languages are exploited to teach the unfamiliar language, English, which is an effective strategy. Even the so-called English-medium schools and 'missionary' schools (those run by foreign Christian missions) employ a large number of teachers for whom English is an additional language. Many of the missionary schools in India, Sri Lanka and other parts of the world were and are still run by European missions rather than denominations from Britain or the USA. In fact, one of the early English-medium schools in India was started by a German missionary in Tanjore in 1772 (Sinha, 1978: 13). In contemporary society, print and audio-visual media expose learners to American popular culture, resulting in the development of indigenous versions of local popular cultures, and these have the most impact on young users of English in Delhi, Singapore, or Lagos. The same is true of the internet — the chat rooms that Outer- and Expanding-Circle users set up show local flavour in their creativity in Englishes; there is no evidence for a 'universal' or 'international' or 'lingua franca' (Seidlhofer, 2001) or 'world' English (Brutt-Griffler, 2002).

Another point is that the concepts of 'interlanguage' and 'fossilization' are not the appropriate models for researching world Englishes, as has been pointed out. Interlanguage is an unstable system, whereas Indian, Nigerian, Singaporean and Ghanaian English in many respects are as stable as American or British English. Secondly, users of these varieties are not trying to achieve some other 'target' variety. Thirdly, those characteristics that are labelled 'fossilizations' are stable, normal features of these varieties; unlike the fossilized pronunciation or structures of language learners, they do not appear only when the speakers/writers are careless, or under stress, or anxious. The indigenized varieties do not illustrate a process of creolization, either. Creolization is achieved mainly by children and results in a first or primary language (Bickerton, 1983). The Outer- and Expanding-Circle varieties are not the first or primary languages in their settings; they are essentially second or additional languages.[3]

Fourth, the attitude towards and the appraisal of the role of first or primary languages in SLA need to recognize the fact that in multilingual situations, primary languages have a very positive part to play in the acquisition of the additional target language. All languages in the communities' repertoires have mutually complementary and sustaining roles. The innovations in lexicon, grammar and discourse inspired by the primary languages contribute to building the learners' communicative competence in the target language on the one hand, and acculturation of the target language to the local context on the other. The substrate languages and the target language enhance each other's style potential and release creative energies of a language in a unique way (e.g., Y. Kachru [1989] discusses the stylistic exploitation of mixing with indigenous dialects, Sanskrit, Persian and English in modern Hindi poetry; see also B. Kachru [2005], Thumboo [1985, 1992]).

Finally, integrating world Englishes into the paradigms of SLA demands that attempts at theory building take into account the facts of multilingualism, functions of language or languages in the total repertoire of communities, and the creative potential of human linguistic behaviour.

It is encouraging to note that the situation outlined above with regard to SLA research may be changing. As Sridhar and Sridhar note:

> Andersen ... lists 'indigenized language' as a distinct 'setting or type of acquisition' in his typology of SLA contexts and processes ... Muysken (1984:101) — working independently of IVEs — advocates a perspective on SLA that corresponds to the paradigm argued for in this chapter ... 'to see second language learning as becoming a member of a speech community, governed in the same way as other forms of verbal behavior by norms that obtain in that particular speech community'. (Sridhar and Sridhar, 1992: 103)

More recently, Jenkins (2000) has suggested that '[t]here is really no justification for doggedly persisting in referring to an item as "an error" if the vast majority of the world's L2 English speakers produce and understand it. Instead, it is for L1 speakers to move their own receptive goal posts and adjust their own expectations as far as *international* ... uses of English are concerned.'

Conclusion

Sridhar and Sridhar conclude (1992: 103): '... there is a lack of articulation between theories of SLA and research on the acquisition and use of IVEs. ... SLA theory has been counterintuitive and limited in explanatory power with regard to a very substantial segment of the second language learner population.' The world Englishes perspective has a great deal to contribute to an understanding of language capacity of humans and enrich the SLA theory.

Suggested activities

1. Do you agree with the claim that the bilingual is not two monolinguals in one person? What evidence would you look for in bilingual performance to justify this claim?
2. According to Y. Kachru (1994b: 590):

Interlanguage hypothesis has some value as a psycholinguistic construct for explaining the stages a learner goes through in the process of acquiring a second or nth language. It has no role to play in discussing varieties such as Singapore English or Indian English or SAIE, which are stable varieties. The users of these varieties are not looking toward any other target language norm. It is true that they are different from the older varieties of English, and do not display the same type or range of dialect variation — whether geographical, or social, or registral — as the older varieties. Nevertheless, they are socially and culturally as institutionalized as the older varieties.

a.   Do you agree with these views? If you do, give at least five arguments in favour of the claim that IL hypothesis is not relevant in the context of world Englishes.

b.   If you do not agree with these views, give at least five counter-arguments to the claim that IL hypothesis has a role to play in discussing institutionalized varieties.

7

Standards, codification and world Englishes

First, all languages *change* in the course of time, and all speech communities change through time in respect to the functional allocations of the varieties of language used in them. Second, all users of language in all speech communities — speakers, hearers, readers, writers — *evaluate* the form of the language(s) they use, in that they regard some forms as 'better' or 'more correct' or 'more appropriate' than others either in an absolute sense or for certain purposes or by particular people or in certain settings.

Ferguson (1996: 277)

Introduction

The global spread of English and its unprecedented success as a language used in many domains by almost all sections of human societies have created both elation and consternation among language experts. There is a great deal of satisfaction that people of the world, at last, have a viable medium for international communication. There is, however, an equal measure of concern at the emerging variation among Englishes used around the world and the apprehension that ultimately this will lead to the decay and disintegration of the English language. Of course, what is at stake here is not *English* per se, but *Standard English,* however we may choose to define *standard.*

The last statement is valid in view of the fact that there already is a great deal of variation in the language; there are regional variations and there are variations related to geography, age, gender, education, socioeconomic class, ethnicity, and other factors within regional varieties. For example, on the basis of geographical distribution of sounds, vocabulary and grammar, the dialect areas identified within the British Isles number thirteen (Trudgill, 1999), and just on the Atlantic seaboard in the USA, eighteen (Wolfram, 1981: 44–68). Overarching all the variation, however, is the notion of General American English or Standard British English codified in grammatical descriptions, dictionaries, and manuals of usage. It is the standard language which is in danger of being diluted, according to those who voice concern with respect to the developments of Outer- and Expanding-Circle Englishes.

Issues of standards and codification in the context of the emergence of indigenized Englishes outside the Inner Circle are fundamental to understanding the opposing views concerning world Englishes. The debate between those who see a deterioration of standards and therefore reject the notion of indigenized Englishes and those who argue that indigenized Englishes demonstrate the acculturation of English to varied contexts and celebrate the creative potential of its users has been going on for two decades now. The questions raised are relevant not only to world Englishes but also to sociolinguistics in general and to the more immediate concerns of learners, parents and teachers — questions of educational policy, planning, and practices. The indigenized varieties represent *change*, and the worries about deterioration of standard reflect *evaluation*, as in the quote from Ferguson at the beginning of this chapter, both of which need discussion.

Standard British English

The notion of a 'standard' arose in the twelfth century in the context of 'a cluster of flags on a ship's mast mounted on a carriage' that flew in the battle between the English and the Scots at Cowton. Subsequently, 'the battle flag of England came to be known as the King's standard', which by the fifteenth century was 'extended to weights and measures guaranteed by the monarch'. It was not until the early eighteenth century that the term 'standard' was applied to language and literature (McArthur, 1998: 102 *ff.*).

There were some attempts to establish academies, comparable to the ones in France, Italy and Spain, to set the standards for English. The earliest one in North America was proposed by John Adams, who suggested that Congress institute a body for 'correcting, improving and ascertaining the English language' (quoted in Mencken, 1936: 7). No formal body, however, was ever constituted to regulate the use of the language either in Britain or in the USA. Instead, a number of phonetic and grammatical descriptions and compilations of dictionaries devised the standards over a period of time (McArthur, 1998). The pronunciation of English words as described by Daniel Jones and known as *RP* (*Received Pronunciation*), the model in Britain, was associated with the pronunciation acquired at the British 'public schools' (in fact, private schools) by the privileged classes from the South of England. It was mandatory for many domains of employment in Britain, and was taught overseas by the British agencies engaged in teaching English. This rigid model began to be relaxed in the 1960s and has since made way for a broader range of educated pronunciation in a number of domains in the UK.

That Standard English was more a matter of grammar than of pronunciation, however, was recognized by many authorities. For instance, Henry Wyld (1907; quoted in Crowley, 1989: 178) observed, '[t]he Grammar of Standard English is practically fixed and uniform, so that among educated speakers, no matter how much they may differ in other respects, Pronunciation, Vocabulary and Idiom, they will generally agree in using the same grammatical forms.' More recently, Strevens clarified that the term 'Standard English' is potentially misleading for at least two reasons:

> First, in order to be self-explanatory, it really ought to be called 'the grammar and core vocabulary of educated usage in English'. That would make plain the fact that it is not the whole of English, and above all it is not pronunciation that can be in any way labeled 'Standard', but only ... its grammar and vocabulary. (Strevens, 1985: 5)

That Standard English is associated more closely with *written* language is clear from statements such as the following (cited in McArthur, 1998):

> Abercrombie (1965: 10): Standard English is a language, not an accent and it is as easily recognizable as standard English when it is written down as when it is spoken. It is, in fact, the only form of English to be at all widely written nowadays.

> Quirk (1968: 99–100): [Standard English] is a complex function of vocabulary, grammar, and transmission most clearly established in one of the means of transmission (spelling), and least clearly established in the other means of transmission (pronunciation). ... it is particularly associated with English in written form, ... there are sharper restrictions in every way upon the English that is written (and especially *printed*) than upon English that is spoken. ... the standards of Standard English are determined and preserved, to no small extent, by the great printing houses ... . As an ideal, it cannot be perfectly realized and we must expect that members of different 'wider communities' (Britain, America, Nigeria, for example) may produce different realizations. ... the remarkable thing is the very high degree of unanimity, the small amount of divergence.

It has also been pointed out that the issue of standard has more to do with matters of power and ideology than with language. As Marckwardt (1942: 310) observes, the acceptance of one type of speech over another as standard is not based upon linguistic considerations; it is based upon political, cultural, and economic factors. He cautions that 'it is a mistaken attitude to ascribe to the standard any logical, aesthetic, or functional virtue which it does not possess'.

External vs. internal models in Outer and Expanding Circles

The four categories of arguments summarized in Chapter 1 are those most often applied to the models controversy by those who see non-Inner-Circle Englishes as deficient. Notions of the primacy of native speakers and historical precedence contribute to such positions. For example, the argument that there should be one world-wide standard does not entail choosing, say, UK or US English to be that standard; yet, that is the usual presumption. Similarly, an assertion that learning and using any sort of English in any context inevitably involves users in one or another Inner-Circle culture is a matter of belief, not of empirically verifiable fact.

Choosing internal models in countries such as India and Nigeria makes pragmatic sociolinguistic sense (see Chapter 1). There are not enough 'native-speaker' English teachers in the world to provide significant degrees of influence on the English learning of the many millions of 'non-native' users of English across the world. Just narrowing the focus of the question provides a clear indication of the reality: English users in New England — the American northeastern states, e.g. Connecticut — exhibit what we think of as identifiably New England English pronunciation, grammar, and discourse characteristics (unless they are immigrants or otherwise belong to subcategories of New Englanders); these characteristics are different in their details from those exhibited by speakers from the northwestern states. More broadly considered, people from both regions are all speakers of 'American' English; there is no good reason to view the Indian or Nigerian English case any differently in these respects.

The discussion, debate and disagreements on standard and codification have many manifestations, some of which are discussed below.

Two constructs of standards and codification

When English is considered in a national, Inner-circle context, it is easier to preserve a working notion of 'a standard' language. This has been the case in education and in 'careful and considered' use, as when references are made to 'the Queen's English', 'US English', or a 'non-standard English', since the last must have some standard to be compared to.

The first great diasporic schism was American English's emergence as a variety recognized, not only by its speakers but internationally, as different from BrE. The spread of English as an institutionalized language in the Outer Circle has raised the question of recognition once more. The basic opposing views are represented here by Quirk (1988) and B. Kachru (1988).

Photo 7.1   Randolph Quirk (left) and Braj Kachru

The Quirk position

Quirk begins by categorizing into three groups the mechanisms and resulting situations of language spread (1988: 229–30). The first type, the 'demographic model', refers to spread that is directly attributable to the movement of speakers of a language; examples are North America and Australia.

Spread 'without much population movement' is termed the 'econocultural model'. Classical examples are Latin, 'the language of learning throughout Western and Northern Europe', and 'Arabic as the vehicle of Islam'. English is being spread nowadays as the medium of much of science and technology and of business. The 'imperial model' of language spread is like the econocultural type in that large-scale movement of people is not a factor: imperial spread involves 'political domination with only sufficient population movement to sustain an administrative system and power structure'. This type is exemplified by several European languages: the spread of Persian and English in India, 'the spread of Russian throughout the USSR', French in some African countries, and Spanish and Portuguese in Central and South America. The econocultural sort of spread applies clearly to English today. This is the situation captured by B. Kachru's category of Expanding-Circle countries. Quirk divides the issues having to do with standards in this area into the 'general' and the 'restricted' (1988: 232 *ff.*).

The general issues have to do with educational concerns: who decides what the standards are, and what major models will be adhered to. Quirk identifies two more specific concerns here: one is the 'increasing unwillingness or inability to identify standards in America or Britain', and the second is the 'false extrapolation of English "varieties" by some linguists'. By varieties, Quirk appears to intend labelling the usage of those with an incomplete command of English — speakers of something 'low on the cline of Englishness' — as, for example, so-called 'Japlish'.

The restricted issues of standards have to do with 'such special uses of English as Soviet broadcasts to Third World countries, the English used in transnational corporations, ... and in such systems as the [maritime English] Seaspeak devised by Strevens and his colleagues'. These uses are what Quirk terms the 'genuinely and usefully international' sense of 'standards' for global use of English.

The imperial model of the spread of English refers to situations such as that of India, in which '[l]ocal elites [speak] the imperial language and [become] the more elite in doing so' (p. 233); thus, the desire and perceived need for English are maintained by those in indigenous power structures who have adopted it.

Quirk recommends 'dispassionate needs analysis' to distinguish econocultural, international motivations for adopting English from internal, link-language motives. The latter would need serious consideration of development and support of a national, or 'local', standard (p. 234).

Analogies between 'designators like American English, or Iraqi Arabic' and Nigerian or South Asian Englishes, for example, are 'misleading, if not entirely false', according to Quirk. Labels such as 'African English' (Bokamba, 1982 [1992]) may mean nothing more than English 'written in Africa by black Africans' (p. 234), and although 'Indian English' is one of the most discussed and written-about putative varieties, 'there is still no grammar, dictionary, or phonological description for any of these nonnative norms that is ... recognized as authoritative ... , a description to which teacher and learner (*sic*) in India could turn for normative guidance, and from which pedagogical materials could be derived' (pp. 235–6). Quirk argues that any candidate for local norm is always 'a desirable acrolectal [variety] which bears a striking resemblance to the externally established norm of Standard English, (p. 236). This is the point at which Quirk's often-quoted lines regarding ESL/EFL occur:

> But, it may be objected, this is to ignore the distinction between English as a foreign language and English as a second language. I ignore it partly because I doubt its validity and frequently fail to understand its meaning. There is certainly no clear-cut distinction between ESL and EFL. (Quirk 1998: 236)

B. Kachru's position

B. Kachru (1988) addresses what he terms 'the sociolinguistic reality of English in the global context' that involves multicultural identities of English in its 'penetration at various societal levels', *depth*, and 'its extraordinarily wide functional domains', *range*. The global situation entails that 'any speaker of English, native or nonnative, has access to only a subset within the patterns and conventions of cultures which English now encompasses' (p. 207). This stance in the debate removes the *native speaker* from any special, primary place in a cline of users.

The crucial point about the diasporas and acculturations of English is that it has called up questions about areas that were previously regarded as axiomatic (or were 'sacred cows'). Kachru notes 'a crucial observation about conceptualizing the spread of English' attributed to Cooper (1982): English did not spread itself, like some sort of glacial accumulation and extension; rather, more and more people began to acquire and use it (B. Kachru, 1988: 208). This conceptualization 'emphasizes the focus on the *user*' and reminds us that language is an 'activity', not an object. From this perspective, it is easier to understand and accept the adjustments that people make in their Englishes to reflect the semantic and pragmatic values of their sociolinguistic contexts. Kachru then begins his discussion of acquisitional, sociolinguistic, pedagogical, and theoretical 'sacred cows'.

In the area of acquisition, the traditional, 'common sense' view that the native speakers are the keepers of primary patterns from which other Englishes are cut with more or less ability to follow the lines has resulted in a no-win situation for the Outer-Circle users. The multilingual speakers of a new variety of English will always be influenced by the other codes in their language repertoires. All the hypotheses related to interlanguage — negative transfer, error analysis, fossilization — have affected how researchers, teachers, and users themselves have viewed divergent varieties of English. Kachru suggests that 'we should seriously evaluate the validity of the generalizations made on the basis of these concepts' (p. 210). Criteria that may apply to a US university student learning French in a classroom setting may well not apply to a Malaysian or Singaporean businessperson who wants to be able to communicate profitably in English with clients and associates from around the Pacific Rim.

In sociolinguistic terms, the spread of English, with its various centres of norm-providing and modelling, has had significant effects in the conceptualizing of 'English' as an entity with very important ideological consequences. Rather than spreading English as a unitary artifact which everyone buys 'as is' and then employs in prescribed ways, 'new canons have been established' in 'literary, linguistic, and cultural' terms (p. 210). When people learn English, they themselves do not seem to become English, or

American or whatever *native speaker* one might mythologize as integrally associated with the language.

Acquiring English allows people to interact with Inner-Circle speakers, as with others from the Outer Circle. The other 'face' of English is that it allows expression of 'national and regional identities', to the extent that English has become in many cases 'an effective tool of national uprisings against the colonizers' (p. 211). This adaptability of English gave it both 'inward-' and 'outward-looking faces', something that cannot be accounted for under the strictures of the old 'native speakers own the language' view. The natural adaptation of English to particular contexts resulted in English becoming 'more and more localized as its regional roles expanded' (p. 212).

These developments have serious consequences in the pedagogical arena, where models, materials and methods have to be evaluated, and it has to be determined whether the learners' motivations can be narrowly categorized. Certain basic concepts utilized in discussing sociolinguistic aspects of English, such as 'speech community', 'native speaker' and 'communicative competence', require rethinking as well (see Chapter 2).

The concept 'speech community' requires re-examination because of issues of users' attitudes towards English and its new 'cultural and interactional roles' (p. 213). A fundamental difference between the Inner and Outer Circles is that the majority of users in the former are functionally monolingual, while those in the latter are necessarily multilingual. The multilingual and multicultural nature of the wider English speech community gives Outer-Circle varieties of English a character altogether different from that in its Inner-Circle contexts. Users of English in each region may feel more comfortable within their own speech fellowship of, say, Indian English or Philippine English. The literature is replete with anecdotes indicating that Africans, Indians, etc. have no desire to be linguistically mistaken as English or American.[1]

The 'native speaker' is characterized by Kachru as 'an age-old sacred cow carrying an immense attitudinal and linguistic burden' (p. 214). The term remains in current and prevalent use, in spite of many sociolinguistics writers pointing out its irrelevance and in spite of the complications that arise if one tries to hold to the native speaker idea and ideal (see, e.g., Paikeday, 1985, and Ferguson's foreword in B. Kachru, 1982b: vii).

The reality is that Outer-Circle users select languages from their available code repertoires as they sense the appropriateness of one or another language for given situations and functions. A monolingual 'native speaker' never has to deal with such choices, beyond the occasional selection of a foreign term or phrase in an attempt to capture 'just the right word' or to try to appear more impressive in some way. Multilinguals bring new dimensions to creativity with the language (see Chapter 8). Such multilingual creativity has always been a part of the sociolinguistics of countries and regions in the spheres of languages of wider communication; compare the traditions in using Sanskrit and Persian in South Asia, for example.

Attitudinal factors may affect 'those who consider themselves the "native speakers" of the language, and ... those who use the language as an "additional" code' (p. 215). As Paikeday (1985: 72) has observed, users do not want to stand out as anything but members of a regional or national linguistic community: '[T]hey would rather affect features of Indian English than be looked down on as foreigners' (B. Kachru, 1988: 215). Besides, the identity as 'native speaker' seems to be fluid: Kachru refers to one of the authors of this volume as 'a speaker of Hindi, Bengali, Marathi, and English' who is 'most comfortable with Bengali, Hindi and English'. Interlocutors would consider her to be a 'native speaker' of Bengali or Hindi in given situations, but typically revert to considering her a 'native' Marathi speaker if they learn that Marathi was her 'home' language as a child (B. Kachru, 1988: 215–6). Varying one's designation of another's 'native' language in such terms takes away any validity the term might have been perceived to have.

The adaptations of English to multilingual contexts are not 'acquisitional deficiencies'; various sorts of 'subtle sociolinguistic messages' are conveyed by the 'diversification' of English. Indigenized-variety use carries a 'distance' message, asserting a regional, national or local identity as distinct from any other variety users, including those from the Inner Circle (e.g. Ooi, 2001). 'Creativity potential' reflects the many and diverse cultural circumstances in which English is used. And the 'Caliban syndrome' is revealed in resistance to Englishes, which may be regarded as a hegemonic intruder, in Ngũgĩ's (1981: 3) term (B. Kachru, 1988: 218).[2]

The diversification of English has made it 'a medium of cross-cultural expression' with the potential for its becoming a vehicle of 'intercultural understanding' (p. 219), but it had to pay a price for this expansion of applications. The literary and cultural bases of the language as it was formerly conceived have lost their automatic implicative character. The various varieties are just that: various, 'showing considerable diversification at the base [of a metaphorical conical structure], or colloquial level, and less diversity as one advances to the apex, or educated level'. The same can be readily observed in comparisons across Inner-Circle varieties, too. Questions of communicative competence must now be related to many more sociolinguistic contexts than were previously considered. This world-wide diversity seems to call for some sort of 'management' related to concerns about 'decay', 'intelligibility', and who the 'guardians' of English are (p. 220). It is a fact that the number of speakers of English across the world is increasing exponentially at all levels of society; access to the language is 'no longer restricted to the privileged urban segments'. It is not possible to claim, simply on the basis of 'an idealized past', that standards for teaching and learning English have fallen.

A constant concern, as mentioned in the introduction of this chapter, is that as English diversifies, intelligibility across its varieties will be lost. It is helpful to reconsider this worry in the light of the findings of the study reported in Smith (1992) which concludes that exposure to more varieties results in lowered resistance to allowing intelligibility to happen (see Chapter 5). It is important that preparation of teachers and researchers include exposure to as many varieties as possible, since we cannot have international uses without internationalization, which entails 'nativization and acculturation' (B. Kachru, 1988: 221).

Finally, English users in the Inner Circle can no longer be regarded as 'guardians' of the language. If nothing else, sheer world numbers of speakers make such an ideal impossible to hold on to. Kachru's discussion ends on an optimistic note: '[w]here over 650 artificial languages have failed, English has succeeded. English has been amenable to adapting, or to being adapted, in terms of identity-shifting, "decolonization", and flexibility for expanded creativity in its lexical range and grammaticalizations' (B. Kachru, 1988: 222).

Issues in standards and codification

The study of world Englishes as grounded in contextually determined criteria has raised the topic of where standards come from as never before. In the Inner Circle it was largely possible to accept at least the myth of standard language as a given, since users of English had little awareness of the difference between prescribed and described language. Now the discussions are motivated by a new impetus, i.e. the need for description — and even prescription — of the institutionalized Englishes, at least in the context of language education. These are discussed below by considering *codification* in the context of the Outer Circle and *standard* in language education in the context of Expanding Circle.

Pakir on codification

Pakir's discussion of codification (1997: 171), following Quirk's econocultural model, opens from the premise that English is the source of financial opportunities across the world, in its diasporas 'growing like a thriving money plant'. This leaves 'the now commonplace questions … : which English and whose English?'

In terms of market share, there is no question that British and American English have had no rivals historically, although Australian English is now beginning to take on significance in the nations of Pacific Asia. As the Outer-Circle Englishes gain more general acceptance in global domains of interaction, standards and codification of these varieties become a real concern. While codification implies standardization, Pakir gives most of her attention to the former, because standardization brings with it considerations that lead into other areas such as 'the status of a particular variety', 'intolerance of variability', associations of 'ideology', and the treatment of a standard language as an abstraction 'rather than a reality' (p. 172). Codification involves by and large more concrete or at least relatively limited concerns, including recognition of 'emerging canons of creativity' and the 'myths' having to do with, for example, anticipated goals of use and idealization of the native speaker.

The Englishes of the Outer Circle exist in multilingual, multicultural environments. Hence, the desire to codify any such English must deal with 'competing norms' involving 'competing values in ... language standardization policy' in terms of a resolution of two contending concepts: what the codification is supposed to do and for whom, and the reception among the users of such codification. Codification efforts will be in the interest of two groups, depending on how those efforts are conceived. An 'instrumental' focus will serve to 'strengthen the elite' of society; such a dynamic is beginning to be the case in Singapore. An 'integrative' motivation will strengthen the local varieties of English, which 'would be a step towards legitimization and liberation, since it will restore the easily marginalized' (p. 174).

Concerning the attitudes of users and institutions, especially governments, towards *de facto* functioning varieties, Pakir observes that so far, governments have chosen to call for maintenance of the traditionally accepted standards, that is, from the UK or US. However, this 'business-as-usual' attitude fails to recognize the sorts of existence that English has in the world today, with more Outer- and Expanding-Circle users than Inner-Circle ones, and most English use occurring without a native speaker present in the mix (p. 174). Along with the change in attitudes and the requisite 'political and economic will' that reality demands from the Outer Circle, there needs to be a concomitant change in the Inner Circle, such that the new English varieties are not disparaged as deviant branches from the wholesome trunk of the language tree.

Five challenges of codification

The 'procedural problems' of codification, how such a scheme might be carried out, involve five main sets of challenges. The oppositions that are normally seen between prescription vs. description of the code, and internal vs. external model, etc., may not be as salient in countries of the Outer Circle, though a few challenges still remain (Pakir, 1997: 175). Codification in the Outer Circle involves deciding on models and pedagogical norms on the one hand, and focusing on the cultural context of uses and users on the other hand; thus, the divide between prescription and description is somewhat blurred.

Outer-Circle English users communicate within their region and with speakers from other circles; this pragmatic observation precludes choosing exclusively either an internal or an external model as *the* standard.

Policy-makers and planners must be aware of the functions of English; codification for purposes of 'mutual collaboration' would indicate a *participatory function*, while 'marking boundaries' of distinct identity would constitute a *separatist function*.

With reference to the *content of standards*, a basic decision is to be made between two possibilities. Staying with one of the traditionally valued codifications, 'the classical canon of British literature, or even American literature' would be the most economically feasible, and the easiest. However, if the choice is in favour of an internal model, there will be an immense amount of work to be done; the reward would come in the self-awareness of identify and opportunities for supported creativity. Furthermore, the *acceptance of standards* is not automatic; '[a]ttitudes towards standards which are locally defined need the approval and support of (a) professionals (b) general population and (c) institutions' (p. 176).

With regard to the concerns of codification, i.e. choice, functions, content and acceptance, Pakir presents characteristics of the situation and possible options in Singapore, where English is an official language, 'a local educated variety of English that is internationally intelligible', but which has yet to be codified, though it is widely used (pp. 176–7).

Codification and teacher education

Seidlhofer (1999) brings the focus of codification into the very practical realms of the profession: how non-Inner-Circle English teachers may see themselves in the context of pedagogical theories, methods and institutions which continue to value the *native speaker* as the ultimate teaching resource. She takes the various 'double' aspects of non-native EFL teachers' professional lives as opening the possibility for 'unique contributions that [they] can make'. Terms with negative connotations are re-examined to reveal their positive meanings for ELT professionals: *double agent, double talk, double think,* and *double life* (p. 235).

The 'doubling' arises out of the 'double standards' under which non-native EFL teachers operate:

> [M]onoculturalism seems to have been replaced by multiculturalism, monolingualism with multilingualism, and targets seem to be criterion-referenced rather than (native-speaker)norm-referenced. (Seidlhofer 1999: 234)

Still, virtually everything that has to do with the day-to-day concerns of working teachers, such as textbooks and reference materials, refers almost entirely to 'native speaker culture as the (uncontaminated?) source providing the language to be taught'. The conceptual definitions of the ELT field are positive and 'inclusive' while the day-to-day working definitions are negative and 'exclusive', driven largely by a market dominated by UK and US people and publications (p. 234).

Given these contradictory conditions, non-native EFL teachers should think of themselves as 'double agents', people grounded in a solid course of teacher training and also members of their communities, with a thorough knowledge of English as it is used in various domains in their societies (p. 235). They have to adapt textbook material, generally having little relevance in their contexts of use, to accord with local cultural norms.

Non-native EFL teachers may find themselves required to teach 'authentic' English, and to function as reliable 'informants' according to the method of 'communicative language teaching', widely regarded as the only reasonable paradigm for inculcating a foreign language (pp. 236–7). There is no recognition of the desirability of appropriateness of materials and methods. Fortunately, the non-native EFL teachers have themselves been non-native EFL learners. 'One could say that native speakers know the destination, but not the terrain that has to be crossed to get there', while non-native teachers have available this background knowledge as a positive resource (p. 238).

'Double talk' can be investigated by teachers in 'double think', i.e. considering the two directions in which non-Inner-Circle teachers are pulled by demands about what kind of English to teach. Newer corpus-based research shows that 'at least some of what existing textbooks contain is wrong, or at best, misleading ...' (p. 238). In reality, the most usual use of English in the Expanding Circle is to deal with participants from the Outer or the Expanding Circle, where 'real' English is not the same as in the UK or the US. Resolving the 'incompatibilities from the vantage point of their learners' needs and interests' becomes the EFL teacher's major task (p. 239).

Teachers as professionals are concerned with achieving a proper 'balance' of language and teaching (p. 239), and this is where good training programmes should be preparing them to make decisions and consider 'the choices that *can* be made' (p. 240). For example, contrary to 'modern' language teaching theory and practice, Seidlhofer holds that translating is useful in that it requires learners to relate the known to the one being learned and students have always done it anyway. Other 'outlawed' activities worth considering in are 'copying ... , repetition and learning by heart' (p. 240). Teacher education should encourage the exploration and development of whatever methods might be useful and effective when prospective teachers leave the safety of the practicum classroom.

The notion of foreignness

Seidlhofer asserts that 'the notion of foreignness is absolutely crucial for FL(E) teachers' self-image' (p. 241). She reports on an empirical study the findings of which are revealing. The study asked two questions of teachers, one regarding the main emphasis in a training programme, whether it was on becoming an effective communicator (i.e. as near-native a speaker as possible) or on becoming an effective foreign language teacher, and the other concerning how confident the respondents felt as teachers of English. Seidlhofer observes that there is so much emphasis on language proficiency in pronunciation and grammatical skills that well over half the EFL teacher population report that they are not happy in their profession.

The few confident teachers have a positive self-image as they emphasize sharing their students' first language; one reported response was, 'I can ... understand typical Germanisms!' However, that confidence was often matched by language insecurity — the idea persists that 'a native speaker can do it better' in modelling and interacting.

Seidlhofer concludes that non-native EFL teachers are 'lead[ing] double [lives] in the best sense of the word' with positive connotations 'of value and strength, ... something that is twice the size, quantity, value, or strength of something else' (p. 243). Non-native EFL teachers are well prepared and inherently equipped to put themselves into the place of their students, as contrasted with the pressure to put themselves into the place of native speakers. She believes that the former should be the aim of ELT professionals in the Expanding Circle.

Conclusion

The issues of standards and codification, choice of models for teaching, teacher preparation, and adoption of texts and materials are still being debated vigorously and will remain a matter of contention in the near future. ELT professionals need to be well-informed about the various positions and come to some conclusions about their own practices in their own contexts.

Suggested activities

1. Bamgboṣe (1998: 4) clarifies:

    I use codification in the restricted sense of putting the innovation into a
    written form in a grammar, a lexical or pronouncing dictionary, course books
    or any other type of reference manual. ... The importance of codification is

too obvious to be belaboured ... one of the major factors militating against the emergence of endonormative standards in non-native Englishes is precisely the dearth of codification. Obviously, once a usage or innovation enters the dictionary as correct and acceptable usage, its status as a regular form is assured.

How crucial is codification for changing the status of a 'variety' to that of a 'language'? What criteria would you apply to define a 'language' as opposed to a 'dialect' or 'variety'?

2. If you are an Outer- or Expanding-Circle user of English, try 'putting yourself into the skin' of an untrained Inner-Circle English speaker to teach a grammar point of your choice to students from your country or region. Remember, this means that, for example, you cannot translate lexical items or compare grammatical structures for your learners (at least, not without their help). What else do you find that you have to give up? In a short essay, report on your experience.
3. Locate one or several teachers of languages that are not their first languages (as, in the US, foreign language departments often include non-native graduate teaching assistants in Spanish, French, etc.). Work with these subjects to replicate or expand on Seidlhofer's 'programme emphasis' and 'confidence/insecurity' investigations. What do you learn from your informants to support or shed new light on Seidlhofer's findings?

8

Creativity and innovations

In this book a number of dialects are used, to wit: the Missouri Negro dialect; the extremest form of the backwoods Southwestern dialect; the ordinary 'Pike-County' dialect; and four modified varieties of this last. The shadings have not been done in a haphazard fashion, or by guesswork; but painstakingly, and with the trustworthy guidance and support of personal familiarity with these several forms of speech. ... I make this explanation for the reason that without it many readers would suppose that all these characters were trying to talk alike and not succeeding.

The Author (Mark Twain 1884/1985: xxxii)[1]

Introduction

It is perhaps legitimate to wonder whether, in the intense and now immense discussions of 'world Englishes', there might not exist an underlying continuation of the alleged dichotomy between the 'native and non-native' speakers. That is, it might be easy to foster an implicit, however unintended, view that Englishes across the world are all very well in their respective places and times, but that 'real' English still resides within the social grammars of the older worlds' users of the language. As the quotation above from Mark Twain's powerful *Huckleberry Finn* shows, this author was keenly aware of the differences among his characters in terms of their societal relationships, levels of education, and so on, and he had a sharp sense of how those differences correlated with his speakers' use of English.

Similarly, Lafcadio Hearn (d. 1904) — referred to in biographical citations as an American-Japanese author who was born in Greece — used English to translate contexts and conversational features of the Japan of his day. For example, the following is a bit of a conversation (however fictionalized), between himself and a man conveying him in a rickshaw (Hearn, 1925: 103):

"O Kurumaya! the throat of Selfishness is dry; water desirable is."
He, still running, answered:

"The Village of the Long Beach inside of — not far — a great gush-water is. There pure august water will be given."

I cried again:
"O Kurumaya! — those little birds as-for, why this way always facing?"

He, running still more swiftly, responded:
"All birds wind-to facing sit."

By all accounts, Hearn never became proficient in Japanese (Ritchie, 1997: 15–6), though he lived in Japan from 1890 until his death in 1904 and married a Japanese (pp. 269–70). However that may be, his attempts to represent Japanese conversation and context in English give a decidedly un-British, un-American cast to his Japanese characters' speech, as the example above illustrates.

Such examples show without any room for question that thoughtful observers and users of English have been aware of social-group and other differences in 'native' Englishes before there was ever any widespread discussion about the legitimacy of English as it might exist or someday come to exist in Asia or Africa. The linguistic creativity of bilingual writers, as opposed to a monolingual-centred idea of an 'imperfect' knowledge of English, is manifested in the use of English internationally. While literate, well-educated people may first think of literature when they hear the qualifier 'creative' used with 'language', a moment's reflection will call up instances of day-to-day linguistic creativity on the part of any speaker.

An early exposition of the nature of literatures written in English around the world, as in the genres of novels and poetry, is in B. Kachru (1986b). Such an investigation raises concerns in terms that are found throughout this volume (see Chapters 1 and 2 for basic issues): Who develops the norms for use of English? Who legitimately judges the worth or 'goodness' of attempts to use English for particular purposes?

Background

The discussion of bilinguals' creativity and contact literatures begins in B. Kachru (1986b) with a review and critiques of the notions of language 'centres' which have been the criteria, sometimes explicit and sometimes implicit, for descriptions of language varieties and for literatures written in them. A core idea associated with centres of English is that of 'the ideal speaker-hearer' for any description of the language of a 'speech community'. The 'community' concept takes on a very homogeneous connotation, since the 'ideal' notion is readily interpreted as representing '*a* variety', and allowance for variability is not easily made unless one is used to it. The problem is, as numerous lines of investigation and interpretation have shown, that monolingualism and monocultural social contexts are not the usual situation globally — or are only applicable to very limited contexts. As, when a US politician speaks of 'the American people', it is all too easy, perhaps even 'natural', for those who hear that phrase to interpret it as 'people who are like me and my family', and not as applying to the myriad of ethnic and other possible classifications of the millions of people in the whole country.

Kachru notes that any variety we can recognize and label has its set of implicit norms and standards. The Inner-Circle English-using world has long recognized two major 'centres' that provide norms to their own and to other regions: the US and England. The spread and the institutionalization of English, says Kachru, have 'naturally resulted in the *pluricentricity* of English' (B. Kachru, 1986b: 159, emphasis added): that is, there are various 'centres' that users implicitly look to for their models, as for example South Asian English, and within that broad array varieties, Pakistani or Indian or Sri Lankan, and even smaller refinements, such as 'South Indian' and 'Kannada'.

The discussion of monolingual and monomodel vs. multilingual and pluricentric interpretations and values is a matter of on-going debate (see Chapters 2, 7 and 22). The users of English more or less consciously choose which model of English to follow and develop; obviously, many writers have decided not to follow Western, Inner-Circle models and have been acclaimed as 'successful' in their work. Not only have identifiable formal characteristics of English been observed to deviate from variety to variety, but also 'thought patterns' or criteria for textual cohesion are different, depending on the cultural traditions of the writers' social circumstances.

In reality, even though English had been influenced by 'foreign' sources long before the diaspora into Asia and Africa, those were all 'essentially European and more or less consistent with the Hellenistic and Roman traditions'. However, in South Asia, for example, Raja Rao's writing may exhibit features of 'Sanskritization'; Tutuola's and Achebe's 'Yorubaization' and 'Igboization' (B. Kachru, 1986b: 160). The speech communities that the writers of such literatures come from are essentially different from those of the Inner Circle: monolingualism provides quite a different world of possibilities than does multilingualism.

Contact literatures

The 'national identity and a linguistic distinctiveness' of a 'contact literature' are exhibited in various ways (p. 162). The 'contact' is between English as matrix medium and the new cultural features, types of discourse, and so on, that it is called upon to represent. As B. Kachru puts it:

> Thus contact literatures have several linguistic and cultural faces: they reveal a blend of two or more linguistic textures and literary traditions, and they provide the English language with extended contexts of situation within which such literatures may be interpreted and understood. (B. Kachru, 1986b: 161)

Examples of such 'extensions' in an African context are offered by Gyasi (1991) for Ghanaian English. For instance, at the lexical and morphological levels, functions and forms of elements may change (see examples also in Chapter 14):

> Your behavior *tantamounts* to insubordination.
> It *doesn't worth* the price.

In these instances, the lexical categories of *tantamount* and *worth* have been extended to include their functions as verbs. Governed complement forms may be different from those in Inner-Circle Englishes, as in:

> They insisted *to go* in spite of my advice.

And expressions and idioms may arise which are not familiar to users of other Englishes:

> *Give me chance/way* ('let me pass', 'excuse me')

Tripathi (1990) gives similar examples from Zambia: the word *boy* is used among girls with the meaning 'friend'. Sentence-fronting and repetition are used for topicalization: *A lie he told if that he told*. In Cameroon, the situation is even further complicated by the admixture of another Western language in the linguistic context, according to Simo Bobda (1994). The influence from French may alter the meanings and functions of words in Cameroon English, such as *convocation* 'a summons', *manifestation* 'a public demonstration', and *to assist at* 'to attend (a ceremony)'.

Such examples illustrate the intuitively obvious claim that, just as in the mutability over time of a language which is on its home ground, language changes when it is used in new social and cultural contexts, not forgetting that the temporal aspect is always in force as well.

In literary creativity, too, the potential of the medium is exploited to represent the reality of new situations. As Rao (1938 [1974]: v) says, 'We cannot write like the English. We should not. We can not write only as Indians. We have grown to look at the large world as part of us. Our method of expression therefore has to be a dialect which will some day prove to be as distinctive and colourful as the Irish or the American.' He goes on to say, 'The tempo of Indian life must be infused into our English, even as the tempo of American or Irish life has gone into the making of theirs.' Referring to the epics of ancient India, the *Mahabharata* (214,778 verses) and the *Ramayana* (48,000 verses) he characterizes storytelling in India as the telling of 'an interminable tale' and says, '[T]his was and still is the ordinary style of our story telling' (p. vi).

Chinua Achebe (1965: 29–30) expresses similar feelings: '[M]y answer to the question, Can an African ever learn English well enough to be able to use it effectively in creative writing?, is certainly yes. If on the other hand you ask: Can he ever learn to use it like a native speaker? I should say, I hope not. It is neither necessary nor desirable for him to be able to do so. The price a world language must be prepared to pay is submission to many different kinds of use.'

More recently, Rushdie (1982: 7) has echoed the sentiment: '[The English] language needs to be decolonized, to be made in other images, if those of us who use it from positions outside Anglo-Saxon cultures are to be more than artistic "Uncle Toms". And it is this endeavor that gives the new literatures of Africa, the Caribbean and India much of their present vitality and excitement.'

It should be mentioned, regarding the notion of monocultural bases of Inner-Circle literature, that a wide variety of writers who are not exactly in the line of 'Hellenic-Roman descent' have gained audiences and recognition. In the US, for example, Native American authors such as Leslie Marmon Silko and William Least Heat Moon have written in English, but from their experiences and cultural backgrounds, as well as African-American authors such as Maya Angelou, James Baldwin, Langston Hughes and many others, who would at one time have been considered outside the canon because of previously widely held ethnic/racial prejudices.

Multilinguals' language use

The examples above make it clear that multilingual people's grammars are best thought of in terms of 'verbal repertoires', as has been said before; and that they use 'a formally and functionally determined range of languages ... as part of their competence for linguistic interaction' (B. Kachru, 1986b: 164). In other words, they have many expressive resources with which to present complex situational contexts.

One of the salient devices available to such users is the ability and effortlessness of mixing and switching, and the adoption of stylistic and discoursal strategies from the total available verbal and cultural repertoire. Texts are nativized — given their regional, national and local characters — by the appeal to such 'multinorms of styles and strategies' in each 'distinct context of situation' (p. 164). This distinctiveness is both formal and contextual, and can be seen as 'limiting' or 'extending' the text, depending on how one looks at linguistic experimentation. The readers from outside the cultural context of situation of a text must do their active parts in making the text speak intelligibly and cohesively; if they do not, or to the extent that they cannot, the text is 'limited' for them, in terms of what they as readers can get from it. On the other hand, attention to the reading is rewarded with improved understandings of context, characterizations, 'motivation for innovations, and the formal and functional implications of such language use' (p. 164). In these senses, the text is 'extended', and, by the acceptance of such creativity into the world-wide circle of 'English', the concept of world Englishes is further extended.

Contextual nativization is illustrated by the passage cited below. Any text must bring into account its context of setting — place, time and participants. Cohesive devices are also nativizing characteristics of texts, having to do with lexical choices and grammar. The following passage, from Narayan (1990: 22), is set in India, and refers to the opening of a *sari* shop which the character Coomar owns. Coomar has become successful to this point in his business career, following a crucial financial stake from Nagaraj earlier in the story:

> When Raman, the painter, had finally fixed the sign board on the arch at the gate, they stood away in the middle of Grove Street and surveyed it with satisfaction. Raman had imparted colour and design to COOMAR'S BOEING SARI CENTRE. Coomar took Raman in and seated him on the carpet and offered him five hundred rupees tucked amidst green betel leaves, two coconuts and a bunch of bananas on a tray. Raman accepted it gratefully and took his leave. Nagaraj said, 'Good style ... I mean your payment.'
>
> 'Goddess Lakshmi has been kind,' was all that Coomar was to say (*sic*).
>
> Now Nagaraj uttered the question that had been bothering him all along. 'Why Boeing? What is it?'
>
> Coomar himself was not clear in his mind about it. So he said, 'It's a name which I noticed on a paper wrapped round a yarn sample, and it appealed to me somehow.'

There are various features of this text that mark it and its represented situation as being from outside the monolingual Inner Circle of English. For example, the painter receives his payment, not in a 'cards-on-the-table' open way, but covered up, 'tucked amidst betel leaves', which are auspicious in their import to the Indian participants, as are the coconuts and bananas. Nagaraj comments favourably on the traditional 'style' of the completion of the transaction. Lakshmi is the Hindu goddess of prosperity, and Coomar invokes her (rather than saying, as an American might, 'Oh, I've been lucky'). And in the adoption of the 'Boeing' name for his store, Coomar has gone with sound symbolism and appearance. This use is similar to the 'decorative' motivation for English in Japan (see Chapter 12).

Rhetorical strategies are a salient feature of text-nativization, including the use of contextually appropriate figures of speech. Africa-evoking expressions, for example, are 'like a bush-fire in the harmattan' and 'like a yam tendril in the rainy season' (B. Kachru, 1986b: 167). To these could be added Philippine English expressions such as 'pythons as big as coconut trunks', and 'veins ... like the ever-reaching, growing vines of rattan' (Jose, 1968: 28).

Second, the direct reflection of 'rhetorical devices for contextualizing and authenticating speech interaction' (B. Kachru, 1986b: 167) help in nativization of a text. African-based examples of presenting the authentication lent to a discourse by cultural history and tradition are 'our people have a saying' and 'the elders have said'. These are examples of devices that show characters marking what they are about to say as worth listening to by their audiences, as well as 'preserv[ing] the "orality" of the discourse' (p. 167). Other devices include discourse markers, items that have no independent meaning but that signal solidarity with interlocutors and are therefore polite. One example is the *eh* particle in Australian and New Zealand English (Meyerhoff, 1994), especially as used by Maori speakers, and the *la(h)* particle in Malaysian-Singapore English (Pakir, 1992a; also see Chapter 17).

Third, 'transcreating proverbs and other idioms' (more than just 'translating' them) sets the text in its cultural framework. When Achebe is cited as characterizing these devices as 'the palm oil with which words are eaten', the figure is a self-defining example. The African image takes the reader outside the Inner-Circle experience. Such devices may be used to 'nativize ... abuses, curses, blessings and flattery' (B. Kachru, 1986b: 168; see further South Asian examples in Chapter 11).

Fourth, 'culturally dependent speech styles' (p. 167) are utilized, to set narrative and conversation in a particular cultural context and to depict that context authentically and convincingly to the reader. Raja Rao, as has been mentioned before, says of Indian writing in English: 'we tell one interminable tale ... and when our thoughts stop our breath stops and we move on to another thought. This ... is the ordinary style of our story telling' (Rao, 1974: vi). In employing this strategy in his novel *Kanthapura*, which explicitly takes on the form of oral storytelling, the reader finds this sort of narrative and discourse, as in the lines cited above, and in this continuation of the passage:

"What a title for a *Harikatha*!" cried out old Venkatalakshamma ... It is neither about Rama nor Krishna." — "But," said her son, who too has been to the city, "but, Mother, the Mahatma is a saint, a holy man." — "Holy man or lover of a widow, what does it matter to me? When I go to the temple I want to hear about Rama and Krishna and Mahadeva and not all this city nonsense," said she. And being an obedient son, he was silent. But the old woman came along that evening. She could never stay away from a *Harikatha*. And sitting beside us, how she wept! (Rao, 1974: 14–5)

The strings of clauses and sentence-initial conjunctions serve to make the discourse into a lively oral flow characteristic of the whole tone and style of the novel.

The Maori style of storytelling is described by Grace (1998: 28) in the following words, and her novel, *Baby No Eyes* (1998) follows the tradition:

> There is a way the older people have of telling a story, a way where the beginning is not the beginning, the end is not the end. It starts from a center and moves away from there in such widening circles that you don't know how you will finally arrive at the point of understanding, which becomes itself another core, a new center. You can only trust these tellers as they start you on a blindfold journey with a handful of words which they have seemingly clutched from nowhere: there was a hei pounamu, a green moth, a suitcase, a birdnosed man, Rebecca who was mother, a man who was a ghost, a woman good at making dresses, a teapot with a dent by its nose.

The use of selected syntactic structures may make a text culturally appropriate: the African writer 'Tutuola makes frequent use of asking direct questions or ... rhetorical questions in the narration', as does Raja Rao in *Kanthapura* (B. Kachru, 1986b: 168). Such creative adaptations heighten 'a reader's involvement' with the text and story.

A broader view of this marking of texts in the Outer Circle has to do with 'the nativized cohesive characteristics of various Englishes'. B. Kachru (1986b) cites Y. Kachru's (1983) and Pandharipande's (1983) studies on Hindi and Marathi, respectively, in saying that Indian-language texts exhibit 'spiral' or 'circular' structures, with 'a greater degree of tolerance for digressions ... provided the digressions link various episodes in discourse paragraphs in a spiral-like structure' (p. 168). The three-step Western, Aristotelian syllogism comprising *major premise, minor premise* and *conclusion* has as its Indian-cultural counterpart a five-step system (citing Basham, 1954): *proposition, reason, example, application and conclusion*. A classic example is quoted from Basham (1954: 501–12):

1. There is fire on the mountain [*proposition* = Western *conclusion*]
2. because there is smoke above it, [*reason* = Western *minor premise*]
3. and where there is smoke there is fire, as, for instance, in a kitchen [*example* = Western *major premise*]
4. such is the case with the mountain [*application*]
5. and therefore there is fire on it. [*conclusion*]

Such cultural correspondences — not identities — obtain in all sorts of texts, not only written literature (B. Kachru, 1986b: 169–70).

The Indian creative author Anita Desai comments on an early stage in her observation of Indian English fiction and her own writing in these terms:

On reading other Indian writers' work in English, I felt they often laid themselves open to charges of caricature and parody. Because of the awkwardness of their language, serious situations could appear hilarious, comical ones lost their comedy and became mysterious. (Desai, 1996: 224)

Desai writes that she tried to begin writing so that her characters spoke in natural ways to one another and to the reader. She did not, however, feel that she was immediately successful:

But the language was still neutral: it happened to be English, but it could have been Hindi, Urdu, or anything else. [Later], I ventured to use dialect and colloquialisms and found myself breaking free from descriptive prose and writing dialogue instead. (1996: 226)

This comment speaks eloquently to the concept of world English*es* in the plural; one can hear its echo in the following comment by the Singaporean poet and professor of English literature Kirpal Singh:[2]

Singlish is not — and never was — the slovenly ungrammatical English which most Singaporeans might think it is. Singlish is English spoken by educated Singaporeans, especially when they are relaxed and not under pressure to conform to any 'formal' standard set by others. It is vital, dynamic, and it gives our expressions a robustness, which, at least in my experience, the rest of the world appreciates. (cited in D'Souza, 2001: 11)

It is quite likely that if there were *a* 'world' or 'international' *English* in the singular, it would be 'neutral', echoing such usual definitions of standard BrE or AmE that it is not representative of any particular locale or social group of speakers (except, often, that of 'the educated'). The fact of the matter is that Englishes around the world always have displayed their distinctiveness, and these 'deviations' from a perceived norm have caused and continue to raise controversy and even ire across proponents of 'major' and 'traditional' Englishes such as the British and American. It is worth remembering that negative attitudes could not keep American English or Australian English from developing in their historical turns. It is not likely that they will turn back the post-colonial-era developments of English in the traditionally 'non-native' parts of the world, either.

Reading contact literatures

In view of the developments discussed above, B. Kachru argues, there are two sets of criteria which broadly encompass the adjustments one must make in order to read unfamiliar types of text in rewarding ways. Superficially, the more linguistically based criteria must be sorted out and expanded in the reader's awareness: this process involves lexicon, grammar and semantics. But '[t]he structural relationships are just the visible part of such a discoursal iceberg.' The reader has to make an 'effort to cross the barriers created by monoculturalism and monolingualism', and extend awareness of the 'sociosemantic and pragmatic system' of an Outer-Circle author (1986b: 170).

These considerations open the awareness of users of all varieties of English to the extraordinary ranges of possibilities for expression by those who can draw on multicultural and multilingual experience. Such awareness makes demands on the 'readership' abilities of monolinguals, as well as on any readers unfamiliar with the variety of English employed by an author from any unfamiliar part of the English-using world. Variations in genres, styles, and devices illustrated above have their effects on English as a whole. It is in this sense that the language in all its varieties is becoming ever more a 'universal' language, not in the sense that it is one code which can be acquired in one place and then transferred to another as a whole, unadapted structure. The literatures that reflect regional and national identities are 'specific and *context-bound*' in bringing identifying features to bear. Because the nationally identifiable literatures have their particular characters, they 'are excellent resources for culture learning through literature', if readers take on the responsibility of acquiring the necessary 'appropriate interpretive methodology and framework' (1986b: 171). See also Frenck and Min (2001).

Conclusion

It may be helpful to recall the subtitle of Pinker's (1994) *The Language Instinct: How the Mind Creates Language*. The sense of this subtitle expresses just the proper frame of mind for addressing differences across varieties of any language. If language is regarded as something to be learned and replicated from speaker to speaker, then all deviations are mistakes; the only possible stance on 'correctness' is that there are no standards across individuals which can be rationally defended, since it is patently obvious that no two people speak in exactly the same ways. If, on the other hand, each individual user's mind *creates* language, then the variation across speakers is accounted for in a reasonable way, and the successful functioning of language in a society in spite of the individual, regional and national differences is observable, and therefore not very troubling.

The evidence from world Englishes suggests that as long as traditional pedagogical or literary-critical models are applied to Outer-Circle Englishes, they will be found wanting by advocates of that approach. However, that mould has been accepted as broken for several generations now, since the first diaspora of English. It is not a matter of controversy that Irish and Scottish or

American English speakers and writers must be judged 'successful' by usual standards. It is not reasonable to assert a different criterion for success for users of English in the third diaspora into Asia, Africa and the Pacific. The creativity of a written text resides not only with the writer but also with its readers, as has been shown in various pedagogical, literary and linguistic approaches to this question. Writers have the task of making their texts accessible, but not the responsibility of making them transparent. That, after all, would take a lot of the fun out of reading.

Researchers in world Englishes argue that the diaspora view of the spread of English and a recognition of its subsequent dynamic self-sorting into three circles offer a framework within which Englishes around the world can be analysed and employed in their own terms — comparable to other Englishes when it is helpfully informative to do so, but never as a matter of judging worthiness. As the Pakistani author Bapsi Sidhwa has put it, '[T]his useful language, rich also in literature, is no longer the monopoly of the British. We the excolonized have subjugated the language, beaten it on its head and made it ours! Let the English chafe and fret and fume' (1996: 232).

Suggested activities

1. Those who claim that English is the tool and medium of creativity for people in many parts of the world, not only for the relatively few of Anglo-nationality descent, argue that the broad sociolinguistic reality of English in the post-diaspora world cannot be denied. Rather than holding onto *a priori* notions of the 'centricity' of English, the pragmatic and responsible position would seem to be to recognize such creativity on its own terms and on its own ground. Discuss what this would mean for the curricula in departments of English Language and/or Literature that you are familiar with.

2. Writing about Maori-written literature, Yunick observes:

   > MLE [Maori Literature in English] is ... characterized by its creative linguistic forms and by the social conflict encoded in the translation-dance which all the MLE authors play with Maori and English. The MLE texts reflect and recreate the social tensions of [adapting] to the cultural and linguistic pressure of being a Circle within an Inner Circle. (Yunick, 2001: 176)

Having selected a world English text (not necessarily Maori) to examine, see if you can detect linguistic signs of the conflicts that Yunick says exist. Present your evidence and interpretations for discussion.

9

Teaching and testing world Englishes

We non-natives are desperately learning English; each word pronounced by us represents our blood, sweat and tears. Our English proficiency is tangible evidence of our achievement of will, not an accident. Dear Anglo-Americans, please show us you are also taking pains to make yourselves understood in an international setting.

Mikie Kiyoi (cited in McArthur, 1998: 211)[1]

Introduction

The teaching of English in its world contexts has long since ceased to be the prerogative of a few scattered 'expert, native speakers'. Indeed, that the situation was ever such in any widespread way is called into question by current reassessments. In any case, for the present day and for the future, the view that either English-language instruction must be carried on by representatives of the Inner Circle or, at least, that one of their models must be the target of any learners of English, no matter where they are or what their intention for the uses of their English are, has been challenged definitively (see, e.g., B. Kachru, 1995b). A brief discussion of the issues involved may be useful.[2]

B. Kachru is not an apologist for either side of the attitudinal controversies, the 'Trojan horse' view or the 'universalist' view (1995b: 2). He briefly presents voices from both sides, citing Ngũgĩ (1981), who has asserted that English may well be 'the most racist of all human languages', and Rao (1978), who has equated English with Sanskrit in terms of its 'universality' and characterized English as 'a language that elevates us all'. It is obvious that English is not a neutral subject or concept, and that ELT may not be considered a 'neutral' activity, as it may have been regarded in the past. That those opposing views — and every shading of attitudes in between — exist is a salient fact of our profession. This is understandable, as, to paraphrase B. Kachru (1995b: 2), the 'linguistic arm' of the colonial powers has increased in its presence and potency, rather than the reverse, in the post-colonial decades.

Questions about English teaching and learning, what the extent of its presence and participation in curricula can and should be, are not only matters of what the instrumental aspects of knowing English may be. Major issues to be considered are matters of the 'ideological content of the language', of 'attitudinal warping', and 'complex issues of identity' (B. Kachru, 1995b: 2). These issues, however, get obscured by several myths about English that remain popular.

Myths about English

The two fundamental sets of questions that have to be dealt with by the modern world involve the shift in attitudes and methods appropriate to new contexts, and a critical appraisal of the paradigms of language study, analysis, teaching and teacher education. B. Kachru identifies and clarifies six 'myths' cluttering and confusing our thinking about these questions, and offers positive reversals of thinking which will allow the teaching and learning of English to proceed along pragmatically satisfying lines. The myths are largely unexamined beliefs which shape people's approaches to issues and situations, relate to who the interlocutors are and what the cultural identity of the 'native' speakers of English is. Other issues that people approach in an uncritical way are models of English for the world, the notion that all Outer- and Expanding-Circle Englishes are interlanguages, and the motivations for the biased projection in the Inner Circle of the insistence on internal norms by other-Circle countries.

In the earliest days of the second diaspora of English into Asia and Africa, the motivation for learning English for virtually everyone in the present Outer-Circle countries was communication with outsiders, the colonizers. The presence of English in what were then 'foreign' countries and contexts had to do with trade, proselytism, and, later, education. This is the attitude that has continued to dominate much of English education to date. However, it has been well documented that there are now many local varieties of English around the world. These localized varieties are not used to interact with Inner-Circle speakers; they are used with other multilingual English speakers for whom English is not a first language, but one among a repertoire of two or more languages. As has been demonstrated (in, for example, B. Kachru, 1988; Y. Kachru, 1997b; Thumboo, 1985), sometimes the functions of these Englishes involve genres which would not be familiar to an American or British monolingual speaker.

It may seem axiomatic to, say, an American speaker of English to have a certain cohesive set of references in mind when referring to 'English' composition, 'English' literature, 'good' English, 'non-standard' English, and notions of the US as 'an English-speaking nation'. With only a mild stretch of mental effort, one might include all Inner-Circle users of English as sharing in a broad meta-culture that is bound up with being transmitted in and by English. This was not always the case: Mencken (1936) wrote extensively and persuasively on the distinction between 'the American language' and British 'English'; and one may still find a few 'English' departments at universities in the US which are officially called 'The Department of British and American Literature'. In short, 'world Englishes imply that in the varieties of English there is culture in texts and texts embody cultures'; we can see it within the Inner Circle, and certainly across the Outer Circle, which B. Kachru refers to as 'rainbow of ethnicities, of religions, of language backgrounds, and of conceptualizations of life and living' (B. Kachru, 1995b: 6).

The notion of external norms for the Outer Circles asserts the primacy and norm-providing capacity of Inner-Circle Englishes. It would be a rare US-raised and educated person who would look to British or Canadian or Australian usage for guidance as to 'standard' word choices, practical syntax, or especially, perhaps, pronunciation. Yet, this very state is what many people continue to expect for, say, users of English in India or Nigeria or Singapore. It is worth repeating that many educators and policy-makers in the Outer Circle have bought into this myth. However, Smith (1992), for example, has demonstrated that Inner-Circle-variety Englishes are by no means most intelligible or comprehensible across the world: exposure to a number of varieties, and an open-minded attitude involving the pragmatic and affective goals of communication are much more important in fostering cross-variety functionality and appreciation than where a speaker received his pronunciation (see Chapter 5).

The first three myths discussed above may be summed up, in a way, under the idealization of native speaker, whether American or British. Inner-Circle users of English are regarded — by themselves as well as by the Outer Circle — 'as monolingual and monocultural'. In fact, US speakers probably rationally see themselves as part of a monocultural monolith when they are faced with an other — e.g., British or Canadian — or when they are deliberately setting aside subgroups in situations that make it convenient to do so, e.g., when discussing ways of bringing minority-group members into 'the main stream', economically or educationally. However, as Ferguson and Heath's (1981) volume shows, the USA is multilingual and multicultural, and so are Britain and Canada.

Related especially to the myths of external models and of the interlocutor, the 'Interlanguage Myth' has the effect of relegating any Outer-Circle users to the status of, at best, those with second-class facility for all time. Basically, the interlanguage hypotheses set the model of Inner-Circle English and the starting point of any *non*-Inner-Circle user at the opposite poles of a scale which inevitably classifies the Outer-Circle speaker as a learner for life. It has been demonstrated in the literature that this classification is trivial in the light of evidence of systematicity and creativity of Outer-Circle Englishes.

Finally, the misrepresentation of the motivations for development of World Englishes may be compared to the Cassandra myth. In Greek mythology, Cassandra was granted the gift of prophecy by Apollo. However, in consequence of her refusing his amorous advances, Apollo decreed that no one who heard Cassandra's prophecies would believe them (as, when she warned the Trojans against accepting the now metaphorical wooden horse; they did not believe her and were destroyed as a consequence). B. Kachru (1995b: 8) uses this label to characterize the codifiers' weapon against those who deviate from any of the myth-makers' codes: disregard and derision of the innovation and development in Outer-Circle Englishes, labelling them as breaking rules and breaking norms, employing veiled expressions of political or other agendas, and so on.

These 'myths' are implicit (e.g., the Cassandra myth) or explicit (e.g., the Interlanguage myth) operational guidelines for the ELT profession. They justify 'chains of control' of the language in terms of normative restrictions concerning *production, function, authentication* and *canonicity*, through agencies of codification and restraint, including not only dictionaries and textbooks, but also professional journals and organizations. It is the unquestioning acceptance of the 'axioms' of the profession that precluded positive questioning of 'a variety of teaching methods', or their 'appropriateness to our [other circles'] contexts of education … of culture, and our educational systems' (B. Kachru, 1995b: 8). Consequently, professionals from the Outer and Expanding Circles have a difficult time establishing their relevance to ELT.

Discourses of marginality

B. Kachru refers to two sorts of what he has called 'the discourse of marginality'. The first is a function of the sorts of texts and reference books that have been used across the world, which have sought to promulgate English without regard for the contexts in which it was being learned and used. The second, even more powerful because it provides the basis for the first type, is 'the *depowering* discourse strategies', which Kachru categorizes as the *derationalizing, normalizing*, and *negation* strategies (1995b: 9).

Derationalizing is a strategy of moving a discourse out of the realm of serious academic dialogue. One example of this strategy, according to Kachru, is the discussions of interlanguage, in which a representative of one side has accused the other side of over-emotionalism. Another example may be found in the Phillipson's rejoinder (1999) to Berns et al. (1998). *Normalizing* 'defines a context, or a linguistic process … in a chosen way' and then ignores differences across cultural and other contexts. This is the strategy often adopted in debates about which teaching methods may be appropriate for given situations in favour of the ones developed in the Inner Circle (B. Kachru, 1995b: 9–10). *Negation* 'is essentially a strategy of non-recognition' (B. Kachru, 1995b: 10): while failing to recognize the essential differences between types and functions of Englishes, it 'emphasizes the dichotomy between US vs. THEM, native vs. non-native, and Western vs. non-Western'. Kachru asserts that 'the foundation of English education is based on the negation strategy' (B. Kachru, 1995b: 11). This is a striking accusation, which deserves the most careful and critical consideration.

World Englishes in teacher education

In recent years a number of professionals have put forward proposals to counteract the myths that guide ELT practices. Brown (1995) explains the rationale for including the world Englishes view into formal teacher preparation. The first reason that might occur to us is that to try to teach a variety of English in a country or region where it is not used is to truly try to teach 'a foreign language'; we might think it nonsensical, for example, for a teacher training programme to insist that its American participants acquire and promulgate Australian English. This same rationalization needs to be applied to English as it is used in its various contexts. Thus, the 'theories and models the students are exposed to should explore how English is learned and taught around the world' (Brown, 1995: 235).

Second, students need to become aware of the ELT apparatus, practitioners and theorists that are current in areas around the world. Indeed, since many of the students in Inner-Circle preparatory programmes are from Outer- or Expanding-Circle countries, it would be doing a disservice to them if they were left with the erroneous idea that 'the truth' about their eventual professional situations resided in the West, with no input from their own situations. Third, a reasoned pragmatic view would lead one to believe that it is the needs and goals of the eventual recipients of English language teaching that ought to be considered in planning research agendas and curricular goals. Imposing goals from outside is mere code-centred teaching, with little if any useful application.

Finally, and by no means least in importance, insistence on an Inner-Circle model of teaching for all contexts is mere 'linguistic imperialism'. Claiming to be participating in an 'international' enterprise brings with it serious ethical considerations (Brown, 1995: 236), starting with not imposing a particular language variety on people by fiat.

It is vitally important that notions of superiority of one variety over another be weeded out of students' minds before they are turned loose to practise their profession. The former axiomatic idea that any Inner-Circle variety was 'better' in all formal and functional ways than any non-Inner-Circle variety has been empirically invalidated, but still persists. The hypotheses of fossilization and interlanguage are now presented in almost all formal ELT training programmes, as if those concepts can be shown to apply in Outer-Circle situations where English is a well-established, institutionalized language.

Even monolingual English language teachers-in-training can gain the needed global perspective, first, by simply being exposed to other varieties of English than their own. Such exposure is not as difficult to accomplish nowadays as it may at one time have been, and published research in the areas of world Englishes (descriptions, lexicons, pedagogy, creative literature, etc.) is widely available and accessible. Dimensions of English as a tool, a weapon, and a bestower and marker of power are widely discussed in the available literature. Attention to the more transparently central areas of ELT, such as methodologies and grammatical descriptions, should not obscure the necessity for awareness of these issues in producing fully prepared, ethically grounded practitioners.

Citing Vavrus (1991), Brown (1995) notes that 'very few TESL M.A. programs draw upon either the theoretical or case-study material that is available and should be integrated into ELT curricula' (p. 238). It is true that in-depth research of the sort we are concerned with began in 'the late 1970s'; anyone who passed through training programmes before that time almost certainly had no exposure to the professional stance outlined here. The profession is still undergoing a period of 'absorption', so the 'late 1970s' date can by no means be taken as some sort of clear cut-off of monolingual ways of thinking. Indeed, 'monomodelism' persists not only as lack of exposure to later thinking, but as an actively promoted school of thought, or strategy, on the part of some segments of ELT profession.

The unsettling possibility has been suggested that part of the reason for withholding the pluricentric view of ELT may be economic: it may be advantageous 'to maintain a hierarchical attitude towards English which places Inner Circle English at the top' (Brown, 1995: 239). Other, less consciously self-serving reasons may be trying to cover what is considered 'necessary' and 'basic' in the limited time available in crowded and closely structured curricula, and the relative inaccessibility in the past of information about, descriptions of, and exemplifying data from widely various Englishes.

Nevertheless, the world Englishes paradigm is beginning to have positive effects of various sorts. Acceptance of local/regional norms and models is on the increase (see, e.g., Gill, 1993). Standardized tests, especially the TOEIC, are paying more attention to getting rid of Inner-Circle-only biases in identification of 'correct' answers (Lowenberg, 1993; see below). Classroom teaching materials have begun to appear which have at least some representation of speakers from all three circles, not just the Inner Circle.

Curricular changes in teacher training

Finally, Brown (1995) offers several practical suggestions for incorporating world Englishes awareness into an 'internationalization' of curricula (p. 241). She notes that 'more than six times as many libraries' carry the *TESOL Quarterly* as carry any one of the journals *English World-Wide, World Englishes, English Today* or *World Literature Written in English* (p. 239). But those other professional journals are now readily available, and should be incorporated into libraries' holdings and programmes' resource materials. International student volunteers can serve as in-class resources and exemplars. And movies such as *Mississippi Masala, Monsoon Wedding, Bend It Like Beckham* (South Asian English) and *Mister Johnson* (African English) are productions which offer excellent instructive samples of natural conversation throughout.

Brown (1995) articulates a pragmatic view which recognizes that a living language is not like a mass of manufactured car parts — it does not travel across seas and continents and then pop out of its crate ready to be installed and run in the same ways as identical counterparts back in its production home. ELT professionals must observe the linguistic and sociolinguistic parameters of Englishes around the world, as broadly and in as much depth as they can, and then apply what they learn to viable programmes of teaching and of teaching future teachers.

Implementation of curriculum

Baumgardner (1987) presents an example of implementation of the aspects of world Englishes awareness that Brown has introduced, though he focuses mainly on teaching, reading, and lexico-grammar.

One of the fundamental concerns of teaching English in the Outer Circle, where textbooks may be hard to come by or be too expensive for general class requirements, is what materials to use to teach from. Baumgardner's thesis is that 'one of the most valuable aids today in the adult [ELT] classroom world-wide is the newspaper'. Newspapers are inexpensive and easily obtained: in Pakistan at the time of Baumgardner's writing there existed as many as a dozen English-language dailies. More importantly, newspapers are amenable to all teaching situations and levels, since the topics and styles of items vary, as 'from the relatively short, simple … news brief to the more linguistically complex editorial' (Baumgardner, 1987: 241).

From the world Englishes point of view, the regional and local character of the English used in newspapers is a positive criterion, because it teaches and reinforces practice in the variety of English which learners will continue to encounter throughout their lives. This aspect raises an objection which can naturally be anticipated, however: What about all the 'errors' that students will encounter as they read? In the first place, Baumgardner notes that 'Pakistani students [and colleagues] ... are quite surprised [to learn] ... that some of the usages found in local ... newspapers would not be found in their British or American counterparts' (1987: 241). Upon realizing this, the reaction of many users would be to label the non-corresponding Pakistani-English elements as 'errors' out of hand. Both teachers and students need reassurance on this point if they are to use newspapers as a teaching/learning device with confidence.

Baumgardner concedes the presence of errors in newspapers, but he suggests that typographical errors and 'actual errors' — unintentional slips in performance that would have been weeded out with more careful proofreading — may be set aside from consideration (1987: 241). 'Local usages', elements of Pakistani English (in the world Englishes perspective) are of legitimate interest, and it is this topic that Baumgardner speaks to in the rest of his article.

English in Pakistan is a nativized, institutionalized variety of English (see Chapter 2): it has country-internal as well as external functions, and is similar to other South Asian Englishes, which together form a larger 'pan-regional variety' (Baumgardner, 1987: 242). As a participant in and reflection of its geographical, ethnic, and cultural contexts, English in Pakistan is not like English in the US or Australia: 'it is a fact that to be able to read a local Pakistani English newspaper thoroughly and with complete understanding, it is necessary that the reader be familiar with both the Urdu (and to a lesser extent Punjabi, Sindhi, Pashtoon and Baloch) language and Islamic culture' (p. 242). As an example, Baumgardner cites part of a letter to the editor of a national newspaper and several headlines from various papers, all of which contain nativized elements, including borrowings from national first languages:

1. Why a step-motherly treatment is being meted out to the poor peons, naib qasids, chowkidars and malis of the Education Department?
2. Jirga Imposes Rs. 2,000 Fine on Air Firing
   Self-styled Obnoxious Pir Held
   5-year R. I. 10 Stripes for Committing Zina

Such lexical innovations are, says Baumgardner (1987: 243), 'a matter of pride among Pakistani speakers of English', as they highlight regional and local identities. The deviations from other varieties of English give Pakistani English its defining character. While they may be found at all levels of language, Baumgardner (p. 243) focuses for illustration of this point on the area of adjective and verb complementation, drawing his examples from newspapers, 'the most complete (and perhaps only) description of Pakistani English ... Shah (1978)', and comparative data from other sources. For comparison with the Inner-Circle complementation structures, Quirk et al. (1985) is used as the source. It should be emphasized that this is a comparison, not a claim that Pakistani English takes UK English as a starting point and then alters it.

Of the six types of adjective complementation discussed in Quirk et al. (1985), only two have no direct correspondences in Pakistani English; the first may be illustrated as follows — the sentences in (3) are Inner-Circle forms, and those in (4) are Pakistani:

3. He is *interested in learning* Urdu.
    They are *capable of doing* anything.
4. [they] were only *interested to grab* power ...
    He should be ... *capable to enforce* ... controls.

In these cases, adjectives are followed by an associated preposition and *-ing* verb form in Inner-Circle varieties, and with a *to*-infinitive structure in Pakistani usage.

In a reverse set of correspondences, adjectives that require a following *to*-infinitive in BrE as in (5) appear with an associated preposition and *-ing* verb form in Pakistani English:

5. They are not *eligible to enter* the contest.
    He is not *prepared to repay* the money.
6. Students ... are also *eligible for appearing* in the qualifying examinations.
    PIA is *prepared for filing* an insurance claim.

It would be wrong to interpret these sets of correspondences as 'confusion'. At its base, this observation of different forms across Englishes is no more (or less) remarkable than noting that British speakers *go to hospital* while Americans *go to* the *hospital.*

Baumgardner (1987: 244–6) gives examples from two of the 'four main types of verb complementation' in Quirk et al. (1985), with their various subtypes; selected examples are given here. In each pair, the (a) data items are representative of Inner-Circle standard English, the (b), of Pakistani English:

7a. He *succeeded in getting* a loan.
7b. ... the government had not *succeeded to redress* the real problems ...
8a. They announced *that there would be* another drawing ...
8b. The ... Clerks Association has *announced to take out* a procession.
9a. He *avoided seeing* her.
9b. ... the police are *avoiding to enter* the campus ...
10a. He *wants to go.*
10b. I *want that* I should get leave.
11a. He *wants her to go.*

11b. … her party *wanted that* we should not intervene in internal affairs of …

12a. They *prevented him from speaking*.

12b. The student activists … *prevented the Vice-Chancellor to take charge* of his office.

Other examples offered in Baumgardner's article are in this same relation of deviation from any other variety of English (outside of South Asia) that one would like to choose for comparison. Baumgardner concedes that not every instance of complementation in Pakistani newspapers follows this nativized pattern; a newspaper editorial will contain fewer instances or perhaps none at all of a localized form as compared their occurrences in a front-page article, which in turn will probably contain fewer than, say, a news report from the provinces found on inside pages (pp. 247–8).

Classroom procedures

Following his description of characteristics, Baumgardner suggests the kinds of activities that might be based on newspapers as text (1987: 248–9). First, students can be alerted to specific reading skills: they can be taught to vary their reading strategies according to the content of the text and their goals in reading it.

Second, 'language-focused activities' may include 'correcting' and 'translating', in which students become aware of the differences between Inner-Circle varieties and Pakistani English depending on 'the teacher's stance vis-à-vis localized varieties'. Translation involves recasting text across varieties and is a preferable way of looking at variation, i.e. from a world Englishes point of view. Students may be asked to recognize and note complementation or any structure under focus and to determine whether the usages are 'local' or general. As noted above, usages that are considered 'normal' in the variety will not be recognized as 'local' by students; they will have to be told about them, or use a source text for comparison.

Active exercises might involve rewriting a Pakistani text for Inner-Circle readers, or, the other way around, rewriting an Inner-Circle text for Pakistani readers. In this regard, it is useful and interesting to try to take into account a less easily describable criterion, which traditional English teachers might have called 'idiom' or 'usage'; we might informally term it a variety's 'style'. Baumgardner gives an example from Halverson (1966). Halverson was conversing with someone whose 'English was excellent' in order to arrange a particular activity. In spite of the functional capability of both Halverson and his conversational partner, '[a]ll [his] remarks had to be translated' by a third person. Halverson's 'If you need a place, I can get one' was incomprehensible to the other person, who perfectly understood the 'translation' into his own variety: 'Doctor says, if it is a question of accommodation, suitable quarters can be arranged' (p. 251). This is an illustration not only of national-variety context, but also more specifically of the predominance of an 'officialese' style that was quite likely an outcome of the speaker's English education.

A user who never steps outside his home variety has no way of knowing that 'English' means anything else to anyone. Having experiences such as the ones described above would give students who eventually go abroad to study 'an enlightened view' — a world Englishes point of view — and they would be equipped 'to ward off the linguistic imperialism that foreign students ... sometimes encounter in the West' (pp. 249–50).

Testing world Englishes

We can legitimately question what it can mean today to say that any broadly applied instrument is 'a test of English for speakers of other languages'. The nature of testing-and-measurement is such that the scorer or rater must have a set of norms — constituting *an English* — by which to sort responses into graded categories. The many contexts and norms of world Englishes preclude any simple limitation of 'correctness', and make professional test-writers' tasks more difficult the more they come to understand about world Englishes.

Critiques of existing tests

Lowenberg (1992) reveals and examines the biases in favour of Inner-Circle-variety 'native speaker' English in standardized testing. Tests such as the Test of English as a Foreign Language (TOEFL) and Test of English for International Communication (TOEIC) are, naturally enough, taken by many people who have had little or no contact with the variety of English used and assumed as 'standard' by the test makers. As shown in this volume, English has become institutionalized in various national and cultural contexts, and even where the norms of teaching/learning are explicitly external, as in China, Japan and Korea, adaptations of English are inevitable. The reasons are that it is impossible to have English-as-first-language modellers in every classroom across the world; most models available to learners are local; and media and creative literature produced in the Outer and Expanding Circles reflect local context with no reference to the Inner Circle.

As has been discussed before (see Chapters 1, 2, 8 and 10), the nativization of English takes place in all contexts as a result of widespread study and use. Lowenberg (1992) focuses on the norms of Malaysian English, which 'diverge' from those of British or American English in various instances and respects. The working definition of 'standard' model that Lowenberg adopts is tied to education and to functional contexts. It is the variety used by 'speakers who have received the highest level of education available in that variety', and the one used in public language functions: the accepted model for official, journalistic, and academic writing and for broadcasting (p. 109).

Morphosyntactic features in the written language are the basic matter for tests such as the TOEIC, and are good indicators of nativization for investigators, for various reasons: ease of recognition and classification; availability of good descriptions; availability of 'authoritative prescriptive norms' (e.g., in 'textbooks and newspaper style sheets'); the attention given to these elements 'in most standardized tests of English; and the productivity of such elements'. Written language is by its nature usually 'successfully monitored or edited', and so it is reasonable to try to distinguish 'between sporadic "mistakes" and systematic acquisitional "errors" ' (p. 109).

Although English is in use in many domains, there are concerns about the standards and norms for Malaysian English, as speakers can observe differences between their English and that of others. Lowenberg catalogues some categories of such 'divergences' and asks: Are these confined only to Malaysian English? He considers the case of conflation of count/mass noun categories, as in '(code) *switchings*'; 'threats and *intimidations*'; and '*a consideration* for others' from the newspaper and academic writing of Malaysian professionals. What is interesting is that just these sorts of examples are produced by British and American writers of the same social and professional standings as the Malaysians from whose writing the examples above were drawn: 'by virtue of *knowledges*'; 'the prelinguistic routine "bye bye" is *one evidence* of ...'; 'advertisements for *entertainments*' (p. 112).

'Fixed collocations of verbs with particles and prepositions' exhibit the same sorts of developments across Englishes. Malaysian examples are: '*give* your book *in*'; 'to *round up* a ... visit'; '*fill up* [a printed form]'. Standard British English examples, which 'would be deviant in Standard American English', are: '[schools,] each *catering for* ... selected pupils'; '[knowledge] *approximating to* that of the teacher', where the US form would not be likely to include 'to', or any other particle (pp. 111–2). Prepositional collocations are another illustrative category. A British English example is *have [something] to hand*, where US English would call for *at hand*, and the Singapore newspaper *Straits Times* offers *in 6th Avenue*, which is good British English, but not American (which calls for *on*), and *at Belmont Road*.

Thus, says Lowenberg, 'it is crucial to distinguish possible "innovations", which result from ... extensions of productive linguistic processes, from features that are clearly "mistakes" in any variety of Standard English, in that they do not result from these processes' (pp. 113–4). The above examples obviously are not 'mistakes'.

Similar examples and analyses are offered of stylistic differences. One straightforward example is the use of *would*, which in Malaysian and

Singaporean Englishes is felt to be both 'more polite and formal' than *will*, as in 'we hope that they *would accept* the verdict of the rest of the country' (p. 99, in a quotation attributed to the then Prime Minister of Malaysia, *The Washington Post*, 22 September 1990, p. A15). Euphemisms may be innovative with respect to Inner-Circle English, as for example in the verb-phrase *outrage modesty* for 'sexually molest/rape' in Malaysian and Singaporean usage. More complex examples involve elaboration and 'formal style', as in an example from an invitation to a professional conference in India: 'The next circular will *intimate you* about the modalities of participation, accommodation and other aspects ...' (p. 100).

While individual tokens may be difficult to classify as mistake or divergence, broad observation can offer items that seem well established in some varieties but are not regarded as acceptable in others: 'to *cope up with* something' is a widely recognized example. Given such differences across varieties, 'the international validity of certain items in the Test of English for International Communication (TOEIC)' is called into question. Offered as a test for businesses and institutions to assess candidates' or employees' command of an 'internationally' viable English, the TOEIC is supposed to be 'unbiased toward any variety of Standard English' (pp. 115–6). However, Lowenberg draws examples from 'a commercially published [TOEIC] practice book' and 'the official [Educational Testing Service] bulletin' to show that such a bias does indeed exist (or did at the time of his writing).

It is worth stressing that these sorts of observations are not the same as saying 'anything goes'. Test-makers have to be aware of the very wide variety of legitimate standards developing in English across the world. Particularly in making or using a standardized test like the TOEIC, ELT professionals have to be alert to the norms of the countries and regions they expect to serve.

In his commentary on a collection of symposium papers on testing, Davidson (1993) supports the observations exemplified by Lowenberg (1992 and 1993) in stating that 'measurement is a culturally bound process'. Not only is the material of tests different from place to place, but '[n]ations and cultures have different expectations and procedures for behavioral testing' (p. 113). Davidson calls attention to Spolsky (1993: 88), who raises concerns about 'deification of reliability' and 'the neocolonialist measurement imperialism of the spread of US standards of testing' (p. 114). This view of the topic from a testing professional takes into account the necessity for social and cultural dimensions in testing.

Tests of language proficiency inherently 'promote' some set of norms; Davidson (p. 114) notes that Lowenberg (1993) offers 'many examples of language test items which consider a linguistic form incorrect by virtue of its misfit to a given norm'. And this is exactly the ELT profession's quandary: What do we teach, and what is 'the norm'? Who decides what the norm is? If teachers world-wide 'teach to' the TOEFL, for example, then the linguistic parameters of the TOEFL become 'the norm'. As Davidson says, it is ethically 'unwise' to develop and promote 'EFL tests without attention to the linguistic norms to which those tests adhere' (p. 114).

The testing symposium papers call for ethical as well as profession-specific attention to three vital areas: 'standards and cultures for testing', 'linguistic norms promoted by EFL tests', and 'the reality of tests in situated use' (p. 115). Assessment brings out all the connections of language with the 'real worlds' of its users. First, language proficiency assessment is related to power; setting or assuming 'standards' is the same as defining 'errors', and those decisions may be made by someone who is not even aware of the imposition that is taking place. Second, 'all testing ... may result in test items of dubious localized validity' (p. 116). Third, the use of tests must be considered carefully. A test may be well designed in itself, but may not be applicable to a given situation.

Conclusion

Research and thinking on issues in ELT point to the need for increased exposure to and open-minded acceptance of variation and respect for users of English from the Outer and Expanding Circles, which is what Kiyoi, a Japanese executive of the International Energy Agency, demanded in her letter, quoted from at the beginning of this chapter. These are words easily said, but the ideas require some getting used to through active participation in investigation and application. Such expansion of awareness is a challenge for teacher-trainers and classroom ESL teachers to incorporate new ideas in their conceptual apparatus and professional practices.

Suggested activities

1. B. Kachru notes (1995b: 11) that the six myths he has outlined are only a selected few of 'many more such myths'. Examine an ESL textbook, or a professional paper from an ELT journal and formulate the myth(s) that it is based on. See if you come up with additional ones beyond the six undoubtedly fundamental ones discussed in Kachru's article.
2. On the Internet or in a printed source, examine a selected institution's ELT training programme. In a short essay, point out the positive features and/or weaknesses of the programme, in terms of (a) the model it is based on, i.e., whether it is based on a single model or multiple models; (b) its emphasis on proficiency in either American or British 'standard' English proficiency or on teaching skills; (c) its focus on one particular method (audio-lingual or communicative or ESP) or a choice of methods, including the bilingual method and translation; and (d) course materials

with the aim of presenting Anglo-American culture or representing local culture(s).

3. Another 'arm' of myth-perpetuation is research publication in the professions. Examine the contents and authorship of a selected journal or two. Report your findings about the world-wide scope of the journal(s). To what extent do the Outer and Expanding Circles seem to receive recognition and attention?

10

Teaching world English literatures

No one believes me when I say
my mistress is half-caste. Perched
on the genealogical tree somewhere
is a Muslim midwife and a Goan cook.
But she is more mixed than that.
Down the genetic lane, babus
and professors of English
also made their one-night contributions
...
No, she is not Anglo-Indian ...
She is not Goan, not Syrian Christian,
She is Indian English, the language that I use.

Daruwalla (1993: 185–6)[1]

Introduction

In most contexts of language teaching, literature is kept strictly separated from the teaching operation. The rationale for such separation is that literary works contain idiosyncratic uses of language that do not lend themselves to grading of language material, which may be considered essential from the point of view of good teaching practice. However, Widdowson (1979: 154) suggests that literary works 'can be incorporated as an integrative element into a language course, and that, properly presented, [they] can serve as an invaluable aid in the development of communicative competence'.[2] Additionally, they can lead to cross-cultural understanding by making readers familiar with the cultural contexts in which the literary works were created. Furthermore, the innovative and creative use of language may lead Inner-Circle readers to a greater appreciation of the flexibility of the familiar linguistic medium, the English language.

English literatures originating in Asia and Africa have been discussed under various labels: new literatures, commonwealth literatures, colonial and postcolonial literatures, among others.[3] B. Kachru (1986b) refers to them as 'contact literatures', as they represent the result of the contact of English with other languages and traditions of literatures in the multilingual and multicultural contexts in, for example, Asia, Africa, and the Philippines (see Chapter 8). The hybridity that has resulted from contact is what prompts Daruwalla to characterize the English he uses as 'half-caste' and 'mixed'. Contact literature is the term that will be used in this chapter for English literatures of Asia, Africa, the Caribbean, and the Philippines.

The rationale for contact literatures in the classroom

The reason for incorporating this body of literature is not its value as exotica in language teaching materials. Rather, it serves purposes that artificially created and graded text materials fail to serve.

First, contact literary works are 'authentic' in that they came into existence for purposes other than for language teaching; they illustrate a genuine use of the variety in which they were produced. Secondly, they have gained international recognition, as is evident from the awards of various prizes, including the Nobel Prize for literature (see Chapter 2 for a list of prizes and their recipients). Finally, they reflect particular cultural contexts and let readers discover the similarities and differences between what they are familiar with and the 'unfamiliar' being presented in the text. In the following excerpt from a novel by Singh (1959: 17), familiar English words present localized usages for situation- and culture-specific interpretations that are unfamiliar to readers from other circles or varieties:

> 'This heat has given me a headache,' he complained and stood up. 'I am going to bed.'
> 'Yes, you must be tired,' agreed his mother. 'Champak, press his head, he will sleep better.'
> 'I will,' replied Champak, standing up. She bent her head to receive her mother-in-law's blessing. '*Sat Sri Akal.*'
> '*Sat Sri Akal,*' replied Sabhrai lightly touching Champak's shoulder.
> '*Sat Sri Akal,*' said Sher Singh.
> 'Live in plenty. Live a long age,' replied Sabhrai taking her son's hand and kissing it. 'Sleep well.'

All the words in the above episode are from English, except for the greeting *Sat Sri Akal.*[4] The context is also familiar, a son declaring he is going to bed and uttering a greeting such as 'good night', and his mother giving an appropriate response. Other elements of the text, however, may not be as *interpretable* as this (see Chapter 5). Some of the obvious unfamiliar contextual factors may be the fact of the mother-in-law's presence in the scene, the command that the mother-in-law issues to the daughter-in-law to 'press' the son's head, and the daughter-in-law and the son receiving the elder's 'blessing' before retiring for the night.

Another not-so-obvious cultural feature is the mother's response to her son's greeting as compared to her gesture following the daughter-in-law's greeting. Indian readers of the novel with literary sensibility would immediately wonder about the relationship between the mother-in-law and the daughter-in-law. And they would be proven right: later in the novel it becomes clear that Sahbrai is not very fond of her daughter-in-law: 'Sabhrai, who had never particularly cared for Champak, stroked her head' (p. 189).

The greeting *Sat Sri Akal* identifies the family as belonging to the Sikh community, and the son's use of this phrase followed by mother's blessings 'Live in plenty' and 'Live a long age' represent the traditional pattern of such exchanges in South Asia (see Y. Kachru, 1995b). The command to her daughter-in-law, 'Press his head', is normal in that in the joint family, where married sons live with their parents, daughters-in-law are treated no differently from daughters — they are expected to obey their parents-in-law in the same way as the daughters are. Thus, the institution of 'family' as it functions in India and the patterns of interaction that are attested in that context may not be familiar to all readers.

Writers of contact literatures exploit the languages in their repertoires in a way that is rare among Inner-Circle writers (there are, of course, cases of such linguistic creativity in the initial diaspora of English in, for example, Ireland, W. B. Yates and James Joyce being two prominent examples). Thumboo's observations in this context summarize this point: the writers in, for example, India, Nigeria, and Singapore, are formed by two worlds, at times belonging to richly complicated multiliterary ecosystems (see Thumboo, 1985). They have twin perspectives, one established by English, the basic medium of their creativity, the other by their mother tongues and their associated literatures. It is worth remembering that the literary system of Europe that T. S. Eliot outlines in his 'Tradition and the Individual Talent' — especially the specific lines of descent from Homer, through Virgil and Dante, down to national literatures — has counterparts in other literary ecosystems. In India, for instance, there are Sanskrit texts and the great epics (Thumboo, 1985).

Stylistic devices

Writers are aware of the languages in their repertoire, and they try them out, 'relishing their power to describe and apprehend experience' (Lewis Nkosi, quoted in Thumboo, 1992: 269–70). As Gumperz and Cook-Gumperz observe:

'New communicative strategies are created based on the juxtaposition of the two sets of forms which symbolize not only group membership but adherence to a set of values. These communicative conventions are largely independent of the actual language.' These conventions become embedded in the other language, as they 'reflect the identity of the group itself and can act as powerful instruments of persuasion ... for participants who share its values' (1982: 6).

Thus, Raja Rao is able to render into English the narrative mode of the *sthala purāṇa* (myth with local associations) and the discourse of a Kannada-speaking grandmother in *Kanthapura* (1938) and the Sanskritic metaphysical speculations in *The Serpent and the Rope* (1963). Alberdt Wendt is able to do the same with the style of the traditional Maori storyteller, the *tusitala*, and the characteristic modes of speech in Maori in the dialogues in his works (Talib, 2002: 152–3).[5]

One set of linguistic devices that contact literatures use is that of code-mixing and code-switching (see Kamwangamalu, 1989; Bhatt, 1996; and Chapter 18). The mixing and switching may involve languages such as Yoruba, Igbo (Africa), Hindi, Punjabi, Kannada (India), Tagalog, Spanish, Pangasinan (The Philippines), Chinese, Malay (Singapore), or the entire lectal range (India, Nigeria, Singapore), where basilect or pidgin, mesolect or colloquial, and acrolect (educated 'standard') varieties may be exploited for what they connote in their sociocultural settings.

Note that language/dialect mixing and switching has always been a feature of all literary traditions. The difference is that earlier English literatures in the Inner Circles mostly switched between English dialects, and classical or (West) European languages. Now, in the Outer and Expanding Circles, the switching involves non-Indo-European languages and a number of languages that the West has not been familiar with in any serious sense.[6] An example of such mixing with a pidgin follows:

> Chief Minster: I want to see the Chairman of the Corporation.
> Security Guard: Why for?
> Chief Minister: It's private.
> Security Guard: Private, ehn?
> Chief Minister: Yes.
> Security Guard: Wetting be dis place? Not office? Dis na office. If you wan see Sherman for private you just go to his house. Dis na office time.

> (Saro-Wiwa, 1989: 76)

The use of pidgin is for characterization: the security guard is not very well-educated and does not command the acrolect.

Of course, the author's creativity does not necessarily have to rely upon mixing and switching, as is clear from the following:

During the funeral service, Rahel watched a small black bat climb up Baby Kochamma's expensive funeral sari with gently clinging curled claws. When it reached the place between her sari and her blouse, her bare midriff, Baby Kochamma screamed and hit the air with her hymnbook, the singing stopped for a 'What is it? What happened?' and for a Furrywhirring and Sariflapping.

(Roy, 1997: 8)

Compounds such as *furrywhirring* and *sariflapping* are not part of English, but in this case, they create a vivid comic image of the panic and pandemonium of the event.

Reading a text cross-culturally

Tawake (1993) is an example of reading a work by a writer from a culture with which a majority of readers of English literature are not familiar. The novel is by Keri Hulme, a Maori; its context is contemporary New Zealand, and its three main characters are all connected in some degree to traditional Maori life and values.

Figure 10.1 Keri Hulme

Background

Tawake's examination of the novel is based in reader-response theory, the concept that 'what the reader brings to the text determines the experience the reader will have of the literature' (1993: 325). This view of the reading experience assigns readers an active role in the understanding and interpretation of the work, rather than permitting them only a passive 'appreciation' role. The reader and text engage in 'a set of transactions', and it is the reader who makes the text as such into an 'imaginative experience' (p. 325).

The other-culture aspect of this sort of reading experience is important. Readers certainly may be said to do this in almost all of their experiences. That is, an American reader from a northwestern state may read a novel set in New Orleans, Louisiana: though reader, author and text may all be 'American', the reader will need to bring some interpretive apparatus to bear on the text, in order to enjoy it as 'imaginative experience'. However, the 'crossing' of two very different sets of national and ethnic experiences and values leaps out at us as an enterprise requiring special vigilance and active open-mindedness.

It is worth mentioning, as well, the trust that the reader must have in the author. If we believe that reading literatures teaches us something about peoples and cultures, then we rely on the authors to represent them in legitimate ways. In a work of pure science fiction such as Frank Herbert's novel *Dune*, the cultural contexts are completely inventions of the author's imagination, and 'no reference to actual persons living or dead should be inferred'. This is a different situation from the one which readers experience in a novel such as *The Bone People*.

Interpreting The Bone People

After a brief recounting of the basic elements of people and story, Tawake's explication of the novel is organized as sets of sections, in which she treats 'theme and character'; 'who are the Bone People?'; and 'why is Simon abused?'. Tawake's purpose is to show that 'the experience this novel provides … is relatively richer when the reader has knowledge of the times and cultural realities of Maoris living in New Zealand as well as … of other literature … out of the same social context' (p. 326). The story line involves three people; the first is the first-person narrator, Kerewin Holmes. Kerewin is part ethnic Maori, who characterizes herself as Maori (p. 326). Simon is a Caucasian boy. Joe is partly Caucasian and mostly Maori (p. 326).

Simon comes into Kerewin's life, apparently having been cast up on a beach by a storm. Kerewin first encounters Joe in a bar, before she knows him as connected to Simon; he is clearly drunk — 'he teeters back and forward' (Hulme, 1986: 12) — and is telling a story which he punctuates repetitively with a swear word. Narrator Kerewin comments:

> Why this speech filled with bitterness and contempt? You hate English, man? I can understand that but why not do your conversing in Maori and spare us this contamination? No swear words in that tongue … there he goes again. Ah, hell, the [swear] word has its place, but all the time? … aue.[7] (Hulme, 1986: 12)

Later on, Joe comes to Kerewin's place because he has learned that she has taken Simon in. Kerewin's world is disrupted as she is drawn further into her relationships with Joe and Simon (p. 327).

According to Tawake, '[t]he first way of reading the novel interprets the book as an expression of the contradictions and complexities of human nature' (p. 327). Nothing and no one in the story are what or who they appear to be.

In the second interpretation, Tawake emphasizes the theme of disconnection from family. She notes that 'family in the Maori context involves broader networks of connections than it does in typical Western contexts'. This is a social factor that is often noted in Asian and African contexts. An added dimension is that what binds people in a family is 'their attachment to the land and their common heritage'. From this point of view, the three main characters undergo disconnections, but together form a new network: 'in a meld of Maori-Caucasian blood lines, they establish a family of the future' (p. 330).

This family-oriented interpretation adds some depth to the reader's experience, by bringing up the connection of the individual to 'the life of the land and the lives of the extended family who share [it]' (p. 330). This interpretation is unavailable to the culturally limited reader, according to Tawake. In line with her feeling that wider acquaintance with contextually similar literature serves to deepen the interpretive experience, Tawake briefly recounts the story line of another novel, *Whanau* (Ihimaera, 1974), in which the protagonist 'struggle[s] against her own brother to preserve the wealth of the land for the wider village family' (pp. 330–1).

Figure 10.2 Witi Ihimaera

The first reading of 'Who are the Bone People?' yields the interpretation that '[t]he bone people may be ... those who experience the peculiar intensity or depth of feeling and perception attributed to Kerewin early on in the novel'. Simon is such a person because he 'perceives things ... not apparent to ordinary people' (p. 328). In the second reading of the 'Who?' question, Tawake introduces a poem, also by Hulme, which makes use of 'bones' both literally and metaphorically (Tawake, 1993: 329–30):

> ...Where are your bones?
> Aue! My bones are flour
> ground to make an alien bread.

Tawake then explains that '[t]he poem identifies the bone people as descendants of Maori ancestors who have continued to suffer loss at the hands of an alien people'. In this sense, the characters in the novel 'are the bone people because they are the ancestors of a new people' (p. 330).

The final pair of interpretive sections refers to the question, 'Why is Simon abused?' (p. 328 *ff.*). The first, simple interpretation is that Joe is simply repeating the brutal treatment he suffered from his grandfather. There is also some question of his punishing Simon for hints of a homosexual relationship with a 'suspected pederast', in a deeper reaction to Joe's own past ambivalent sexual relationships. Tawake characterizes this interpretation as 'persuasive but impoverished' (p. 329).

In the second reading of the abuse theme, Tawake asserts that Simon's treatment by his foster father serves to emphasize 'the rift between each character and that character's family'. Thus, each character 'embodies the estrangement Maori people have experienced from the old ways', a 'loss of humanity ... linked to their loss of cultural identity'. The resolution of the conflict seems then to lie in overcoming these disconnections, to create a future 'united people who share a symbiotic relationship' (pp. 331–2).

While each reading of the novel is valid in itself, the one that is informed by familiarity with the Maori, including a broader reading of Maori-produced literature, offers more depth, 'a more fully elaborated interpretation'. Links between a work, its context in a literature, and that literature's grounding in and reflection of a culture are essential to any meaningful degree of cross-cultural understanding of texts.

Teaching other-culture literatures

As readers encounter texts produced by authors outside their own sociocultural traditions, they need to develop new ways of engaging those texts, if they are not to be frustrated and dissatisfied with what they read. Courtright (2001) suggests one way by employing a 'think-aloud' protocol for elucidating how culturally different English literary texts are read and understood by educated readers, and what conclusions about the advisability of including such texts in ELT classes can be drawn from readers' responses.

Methodology

Courtright's selections for her study included works by Chinua Achebe from Nigeria, and Anita Desai from India, both well-known Outer-Circle writers and representatives of institutionalized varieties. She used short stories as the texts for her study because 'a short story represents a complete discoursal entity', and is 'a manageable unit for classroom instruction' (p. 41). Thus, the methods and findings of the study may have applicability to teaching world Englishes and world English literatures. The think-aloud method gave Courtright some access to how the readers (two each from India, Nigeria and the US) worked through the texts, forming hypotheses about meanings and relationships in the stories and revising their guesses on the basis of further reading.

The stories were marked into units of paragraph length, and the readers were asked to comment aloud on each unit as they read. First, they told the researcher what they had understood from the unit, then what they felt its importance was in the whole text so far, and finally, they asked questions about the text (p. 51). Courtright writes that '[t]he first two tasks correspond roughly to Smith's levels of comprehensibility and interpretability, while the third ... may involve aspects of any level of Intelligibility' (see Chapter 5). She uses an expanded definition of Intelligibility, as compared with Smith's:

> For purposes of this dissertation, I have chosen to use the term "Intelligibility" to refer to what the reader makes of a given text; what (s)he understands of a contact literary text and how (s)he understands it. While the term 'Intelligibility' has often been associated with the lower, comprehension-level aspects of meaning and meaning-making, a much broader definition is utilized here. (Courtright, 2001: 24)

(Courtright notes that she uses a capitalized spelling to denote the narrower definition given above.)

A fundamental issue addressed by the study is whether only 'proficient readers of English' will find such texts accessible. It becomes clear in the reported reader comments that considerable attention must be given to 'the codes, both linguistic and cultural, which the writer has employed' (p. 5). In such tasks, the Inner-Circle readers clearly were not at any advantage as compared to those from the Outer Circle. Two Nigerian and two Indian consultants worked with Courtright to scrutinize the texts for their '[sociocultural] representativeness, critical acceptability, and the multilingual creativity' (p. 46). The feedback of these consultants gave Courtright added confidence in her decision to use the selected stories.

In summary, the methodological set-up of the study involved exposing Inner-Circle readers, Outer-Circle readers not from the sociocultural contexts of the story texts, and Outer-Circle readers who were familiar with those contexts to two short stories by multilingual creative authors. It was expected that unfamiliar elements of lexis and, more importantly, of social and cultural features of the narratives and discourses among characters would raise questions to be resolved by the readers at the levels of comprehensibility and interpretability. Courtright concludes, '[a]ssuming that any text in English is processed similarly by all English speakers is a dangerously oversimplified assumption' (p. 181).

The texts in the study are 'The Madman' by Achebe (1971) and 'A Devoted Son' by Desai (1978). Both stories contain elements that provide local authenticity, such as personal names, titles, proverbs and discourse markers

(p. 43). In the Desai story, for example, the Hindi word *ghee* ('clarified butter') occurs repeatedly. 'Both of the Indian subject readers noted the use of "ghee" and attempted to explain it within … their responses.' This is an example of a regionally marked lexical item and referent, the sort of element that at once identifies text as being set in a given sociocultural context and raises the possibility of intelligibility and comprehensibility difficulties for readers from other contexts.

Further readers' responses included, for example, an Indian reader who related scenes in 'The Madman' such as 'a small village market' to familiar comparable scenes in India (pp. 125–6). A US reader, however, said, 'I found myself wanting to understand the story more than I was able to' (p. 127). This reader commented:

> So much was assumed concerning the cultural taboos of running naked into the occult part of the market. Granted, I can figure out that it's not a bright thing to do, but I felt like there was so much more meaning attached to it than I was able to glean. (p. 128)

However, the same reader responded to an inquiry about what he enjoyed in reading the story with: 'The challenge of trying to make sense of another culture' (p. 128). It is such openness of mind and affect that makes accessibility to texts not only possible but rewarding.

A sample comment which indicates a reaction in terms of speech-community identity is the following:

> This is just different, than most, um, American, you know, short stories. I don't think that you could get away with this if you wanted to be published in the New Yorker. Um … this uh … again, I don't know the culture, but this lack of connection, the apparent connection, between, um, the first part, and then most of, of what happens on the second, without identifying the, the protagonist here, more immediately. This is not, a, standard … American, short story, you know, writing, technique, the way stories are constructed, so this is different. (p. 129)

Courtright comments (p. 129): 'Clearly while the reader is willing to acknowledge that a different norm may be operating here, he still feels that the norm is "not standard".'

It is worth noting that not all Outer-Circle readers like and understand all Outer-Circle authors, any more than such all-or-none expectations can be fulfilled between US readers and authors. Courtright notes:

> While both Nigerian readers rated highly the literary quality and their personal enjoyment of "The Madman," the Indian readers were split on their appreciation and enjoyment of "A Devoted Son." The Indian female reader

clearly did not enjoy the story, although she found the extended language of the text interesting and "comfortable." (p. 147)

Implications

Courtright asserts the need for 'a new or expanded framework for reading and evaluating contact literary text in English' (p. 167). Not only may lexical items from the situational context of the text present difficulties, but the semantics and pragmatic uses of these items may cause even more impenetrability; for example, it is easy to apprehend the semantics of 'touching a participant's feet', but it must be worked out from the text (if the narrative does not intimate it directly) what the associated forces of demonstrating affection and respect in the Indian family and broader social structures are (p. 168). Relations as indicated by the elements of discourse may be opaque to some readers; Courtright notes, for example, that 'Western readers ... [of] the dialogue between [the father in "A Devoted Son"] and his Western-educated son, Rakesh, are confused about who is winning the argument' (p. 169).

Since the author of any given text is being read by any number of readers from various social and educational traditions, it is important that metalanguage and metaliterature awareness be raised, and that explicit training be available. If readers can be made aware of the levels of comprehension of language and texts, they can work out ways of effectually engaging them: that is, when they see an unfamiliar term, they can reasonably guess, given its spelling, that it is probably pronounced in one or a limited range of ways; given its use in the sentence or larger unit, it probably refers to a certain class of objects or phenomena; given the attention it gets in the narrative and/or the reactions to it of other participants in the text, its significance seems to be of a particular sort; and so on. Readers' experience with texts can and should improve their capacities to engage and enjoy other such texts.

Text selection

Teachers who want to broaden their students' ability to appreciate multicultural literature have to give careful consideration to their selections of texts to be studied:

> Such factors as the number of loan-words or the amount of code-mixing, the nature of the items that are represented by unintelligible words, or the type and amount of contextual cross-referencing that occurs ... can affect overall intelligibility of the text. (Courtright, 2001: 171)

Courtright points out that if the text is not very explicitly marked as being of a particular region, nation or culture (in terms of, for example, code-mixed dialogue), it may require even closer reading. The relationships among characters and a character's place within a situation may be assumed by the author in ways that are different from the assumptions of the reader. Without clues in the text, these sorts of mismatches may go unnoticed.

For example, 'the African reader, reading about the roles of fathers and sons in Africa, seems to understand the text in a way that the North American reader does not' (p. 172). 'Father' and 'son' are common kin-terms, but their 'meanings' within a culture may raise comprehensibility concerns, and the significance of such a relation within a situation in the text may be a matter of interpretability.

Assessment

The virtually infinite configurations of authored texts and readers raise important concerns about assessment (see Chapter 9). It is of course not reasonable for a researcher or teacher to assign *a* reading or *the* reading to a text, and then grade readers' responses as more or less deviant from that. We may compare Lowenberg's (1993) study of TOEIC responses that were scored as 'incorrect', even though they accorded with grammatically sound structures in terms of some varieties of English. This is not to say that just any interpretation may be valid. Useful and informative interpretations are not matters of opinion, but must be rationally based on what readers may know or can infer from a text about its sociocultural parameters.

In teacher education in world Englishes, exposing teachers-in-training to as wide a variety of English texts as possible is helpful. Familiarity will lead teachers to 'acknowledge the possibility of a different set of norms' than the ones they are used to and forestall any automatic 'labeling of [contact literary] texts as inferior ... on the part of those who are responsible for selecting and teaching' (p. 179). The same goes for trusting too much what they already are comfortable with in terms of lexis, grammar, or any level of language use, and thus regarding any difference as deficiency. Courtright notes that one of the American readers labelled the language of a pilot-study Singaporean text (p. 137) 'pseudo-British', implying 'an attempt to parrot "real" or "standard" English'. Though the attitude is not acknowledged openly, the reader's language describing the form of the text 'suggests a rather pejorative view of, at least, this particular contact literary text' (p. 179).

A further level of subtle interference may need attention: readers may recognize the difference represented in text on the text's own terms, but continue 'measuring the quality of these texts against a standard that is derived from an Inner Circle canon', and regard non-Inner-Circle features as ' "exotic", or "non-progressive" ' (p. 180). These are considerations that should be taken seriously by ELT professionals.

Conclusion

It is a common belief and token of advice that 'learning a foreign language teaches you about your own language'. Grammatical and stylistic analyses of literary texts to unpack their linguistic and cultural meaning are rewarding activities, and the vivid metaphors, images and episodes contribute to language learning by encouraging reading for enjoyment and not just for learning structural patterns. To make culturally different texts accessible and meaningful as learning experiences, 'the methods of analysis must be identified and taught'. Making students, including ELT professionals-in-training, aware of the levels of intelligibility, comprehensibility and interpretability provides a framework for their access to world English texts, and opens the possibility that not only will they be receptive of such texts, but will have 'the potential for learning more about the properties of text itself' (p. 181).

Suggested activities

1. Pick a short story by an Outer-Circle author. You might start with collections by the following authors: Chinua Achebe, R. K. Narayan, Jhumpa Lahiri, Shirley Lim, or an author from your region.
   Read the story in a group project, each one of the group members reading it by themselves and noting elements at the levels of intelligibility, comprehensibility and interpretability that catch their attention. Does the author provide context clues as to their meaning and use, and to what extent (see 'cushioning' in Chapter 14)? Compare your notes with those of classmates on the selected text; write up a summary report or presentation.
2. Individually, or as a group or class project, select a text as in (1) and present it to readers, using Courtright's methodology (division of the text into short units, listening to readers as they verbalize their working through the texts, and so on). Write up your results in a brief essay. How do your findings correlate with Courtright's? Did you find anything new or surprising?

Part III
Profiles across Cultures

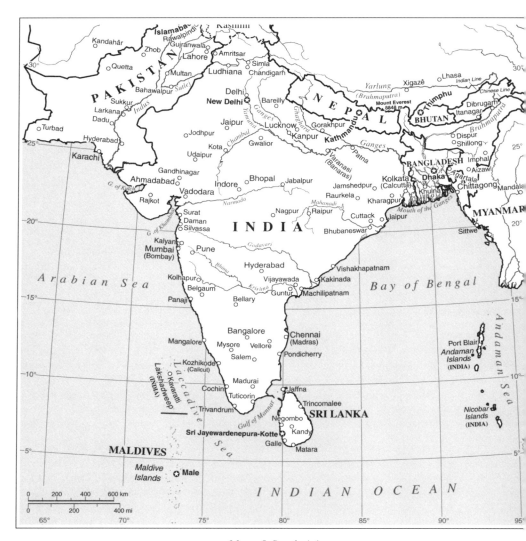

Map of South Asia

11

South Asian English

... I am an Indian, very brown, born in
Malabar, I speak three languages, write in
Two dream in one. Don't write in English, they said,
English is not your mother-tongue. Why not leave
Me alone, critics, friends, visiting cousins,
Everyone of you? Why not let me speak in
Any language I like? The language I speak
Becomes mine, its distortions, its queernesses,
All mine, mine alone ...
It is as human as I am human, don't
you see? It voices my joys, my longings, my
Hopes, and it is as useful to me as cawing
is to crows or roaring to lions, ...

Kamala Das (de Souza, 1997:10)

Introduction

South Asia is a linguistic area with one of the longest histories of contact,
influence, use, and teaching and learning of English-in-diaspora in the world.
As B. Kachru (1986a: 36) clarifies, '[the] use of the term *South Asian English*
is not to be understood as indicative of linguistic homogeneity in this variety
nor of a uniform linguistic competence. It refers to several broad regional
varieties such as Indian English, Lankan English and Pakistani English.'

Historical background

Setting aside a visitor from England to the tomb of St Thomas in South India
in 882, as reported in the *Anglo-Saxon Chronicle* (McArthur, 1992: 504), the end
of the year 1600 saw the beginnings of officially sanctioned expansion out of

Britain to India. By the end of the seventeenth century, British 'trading "factories" ' controlled virtually all international trade with India (i.e., the entire subcontinent). In 1689, with the establishment of the three 'presidencies' or administrative districts in Bengal, Bombay (now Mumbai) and Madras (now Chennai), British rule was established in the subcontinent by the East India Company. In 1773, the British government established a Governor Generalship in India and by the India Act of 1784, a department to manage Indian Affairs was created. Following the so-called 'Mutiny' of 1857, the Act for the Better Government of India in 1858 resulted in British government assuming the responsibility of governing India.

In addition to the administrative agencies, the spread of English in India and Ceylon (now Sri Lanka) is traced back to the Christian missionaries and the desire of highly placed Indian elite to use English for acquiring knowledge of modern science and technology. Christian proselytizing played its part by establishing missionary schools, beginning in 1715 in Chennai, where English was the medium of instruction and was encouraged for general interaction within certain domains. Thus, the diaspora of English into India is at least as old as that into North America, though of course under very different sociolinguistic conditions.

Just as there continue to be widely divergent interpretations and appreciations of the presence and use of English in South Asia today, in the nineteenth century there were influential Indians who believed that modern English was the way out of backwardness in terms of science and technology. An official action by Foreign Secretary William Wilberforce in 1814 gave impetus to English in India's missionary schools. Sri Lanka shares a similar history and state of affairs, where there were more than two hundred such schools by 1831.

The push came from internal sources, too. In 1823 Raja Rammohan Roy (1772–1833) spoke in strong terms against the British government's plan to '[establish] a Sanskrit school under Hindoo Pundits', and called instead for 'employing European gentlemen of talent and education to instruct the natives of India in mathematics, … and other useful sciences' (B. Kachru, 1994a: 505).

This perception of the superiority of English and the broad culture it represented was naturally the pre-eminent view among policy-makers within the British Raj. There had been a long-standing debate, often termed the Oriental-Occidental (or Anglicist-Orientalist) controversy. The culminating document of this debate is the well-known 'Minute' of Lord T. B. Macaulay (d. 1859) written in 1835. Macaulay believed that 'the learning of the East was "a little hocus-pocus about the use of cusa-grass and the modes of absorption into the Deity" ' (B. Kachru, 1994a: 506). The Minute, addressed to the Supreme Council of India, asserted that:

> … English is better worth knowing than Sanscrit [Sanskrit] or Arabic; that the natives are desirous to be taught English … we must … do our best to

form a class who may be interpreters between us and the millions whom we govern; a class of persons, Indian in blood and colour, but English in taste, in opinions, in morals, and in intellect.

It is perhaps not so often noted that Macaulay's next line presaged an aspect of the sociolinguistic reality of later South Asia:

To that class we may leave it to refine the vernacular dialects of the country, to enrich [them] with terms of science ... from the Western nomenclature, and to render them by degrees fit vehicles for conveying knowledge to the great mass of the population. (B. Kachru and McArthur, 1992: 505)

Consequent to Macaulay's recommendation, official action gave absolute primacy to teaching English and teaching in English. Three English-medium universities were established in Chennai, Calcutta (now Kolkata) and Mumbai, and two more by the end of the nineteenth century in Allahabad and Lahore in West Punjab, now a part of Pakistan (McArthur, 1992: 505). Less than fifty years after Macaulay's Minute, by the early 1800s a majority of Indian primary schools were English-medium (B. Kachru, 1994a: 507). India at that point included what are now Pakistan and Bangladesh. The foundation of the presence of English in South Asia was firmly in place.

Status of South Asian English

English remained a foreign language in India for the next several decades. As its use grew more pervasive, especially in the social and political climate following the official achievement of independence in 1947 and subsequent growth in literacy, it became a member of the South Asian repertoire of languages. B. Kachru defines modern South Asian English (SAE) as 'the educated variety of South Asian English', with, of course, 'varieties within this variety' (1994a: 508; see McArthur [1992] for brief notes on varieties of South Asian Englishes). This definition is identical to that of any major variety of English: British English means the educated variety codified in grammars and dictionaries rather than the many geographical or social dialects. Similarly, American English as a label refers to the 'educated' or 'standard' variety rather than African-American or Chicano English.

The passage of the Official Languages Act in 1967 made English co-equal with Hindi 'for all official purposes of the union, for Parliament, and for communications between the union and the states' (Ferguson, 1996a: 31). Through various ups and downs of policy and public sentiment, English has retained and strengthened its place in the South Asian linguistic landscape. Of the seven major uses of 'superposed languages in South Asia, English is a significant participant in six, namely, as a lingua franca, in government, education, literature, influence, and development' (Ferguson 1996a: 32).[1] The first four uses are transparent; by *influence* is meant its impact on the local languages in literary genres and linguistic structure and as the source for new vocabulary, and by *development* is meant its uses in areas such as management, technical access, governmental services, and so on. The only use in which it is not a participant is religion, a function performed only by Sanskrit among the four 'imperialist' languages (Ferguson, 1996: 34–5).[2] Sanskrit is the language of religion for Hinduism and Arabic for Islam in South Asia, though other regional languages play a role, too.

Ferguson notes (p. 37) that this 'relative lack of religious identification for South Asian English is clearly a regional advantage', given the significant religious differences and tensions across the subcontinent. Though English originally had and still retains some identification with Christianity, it is more neutral in its affective associations than any other possible choice. Thus, one important aspect of the value of English in South Asia is its capacity to provide *neutralization*. Choosing a given code in a multilingual context asserts one or more identities, for example, of religion, caste, and educational attainment, in addition to signalling the message. Since English is outside the traditional indigenous array of codes, it is released from these responsibilities. The same consideration makes pan-regional news and commentary in English as workable and appealing as it apparently is, thereby explaining its wide use in the Indian media.

Similar to India, in modern Pakistan English continues to have a central position in the national life. The several evolutions of Pakistan's constitution have indicated the desirability of getting rid of English in favour of Urdu, but proponents of this cause have yet to bring it to a successful conclusion (Rahman, 1990: 1–2). The position of English in science and technology, media, international communication and creative writing remains unquestionable in multilingual Pakistan as it is in India and Sri Lanka. (See Rahman [1996] for discussion related to Bangladesh and Verma [1996] for Nepal.)

The subvarieties of SAE depend on the basic criteria of geography, proficiency, and ethnicity. B. Kachru observes (1994a: 512–3): 'The recognition of varieties within [SAE] is a clear indicator of [its] institutionalisation, its range in terms of functional allocation, and its depth in terms of societal penetration … [The varieties'] shared comprehensibility and interpretability are markers of the acculturation in South Asia.'

Nativization: Characteristics of South Asian English

The acculturation of English in the subcontinent, broadly interpreted, constitutes its 'South Asianness'. As an *additional* language in the multilingual cultures of South Asia, English is necessarily described in terms of its forms and contextual and pragmatic functions within South Asia. The language is used for international purposes also, but that is not its only function. This is equally true of any recognizable variety of English, whether in the Inner or Outer Circle; if there is 'marginal interaction' between South Asian users and, say, British or American users, there is likewise marginal interaction between most British users and those from the USA or Australia. It is SAE's historical status as, initially, a foreign language and later as a learned second language that causes the question of influence of any Inner-Circle variety even to arise. As the uses of SAE are crucial for internal purposes, the medium has adapted itself to the circumstances in which communities of users of the language find themselves.

B. Kachru (1994a: 514–26) provides some salient identifying characteristics of SAE in phonology, grammar, and lexicon. There are many more features in even these generalized lists than can readily be detailed in this summary. A few selected illustrations are presented here; for others, see B. Kachru (1994a) and S. Sridhar (1996); also see Chapter 3 for discussion of characteristics of varieties in a more general context.

In phonology, as expected across any varieties of such a widespread language, there are various segmental qualities that are distinctive for SAE. It is commonly noted, for example, that retroflex stop consonants *t, d* correspond to the alveolar consonants *t, d* of Inner-Circle varieties. Initial voiceless plosives *p, t, k* are not aspirated in SAE; the fricatives *f, θ, ð* are pronounced as *pʰ, tʰ, d*, respectively; the distinction between clear and dark *l* is not maintained; no distinction is made between *v* and *w* — both are pronounced [w]; and most diphthongs are pronounced as simple vowels. In some subvarieties the distinction between tense and lax vowels (e.g., those of *deep* vs. *dip*, *seat* vs. *sit*, *boot* vs. *book*) is not made; in some, the initial vowels are preceded by a glide so that *inner* is pronounced as [yinnər] and *open* as [wopən]; in some the sibilants in *same* and *shame* are pronounced with *s*; and *j* (as in *major*), *z* (as in *razor*) and *ʒ* (as in *measure*) are all pronounced as *j*. In Punjabi-speaking areas of India and Pakistan, the initial clusters are simplified by inserting an epenthetic vowel so that *sport* is pronounced [səport]; Hindi-Urdu speakers in India and Pakistan may pronounce it as [isport]. Features of stress and rhythm give SAE its defining sound (see Chapter 2).

In grammar, the distribution of articles remains an open question discussed at least since Dustoor (1954). Reduplication is common for emphasis: *Cut it into small small pieces* (see B. Kachru, 1994a: 520 *ff.*). Tense forms are used analogous to aspectual forms of Indian languages (see Y. Kachru, 1987). The use of prepositions is different from that in BrE or AmE (see Chapter 2). The items *yes, no?*, and *isn't it?* are used as general tags, e.g., *He was angry, isn't it?* (B. Kachru, 1986a: 40). Idioms and metaphors are transferred from South Asian languages, such as Kannada, *In olden times, woman just **worked like*** *a bullock* (S. Sridhar, 1996: 58); or Hindi-Urdu-Punjabi, *we **eat their salt**, and as long as we eat it, we will remain loyal* (Singh, 1959: 78), *... you are a big man and we are but **small radishes from an unknown garden*** (Singh, 1959: 27), and *The Play had gone bad, **Like pickle in the monsoon*** (Roy, 1997: 139). S. Sridhar (1996) presents a list of grammatical characteristics in what he calls a 'low mesolectal variety' spoken in the state of Karnataka in India.

Lexicon has naturally come in for a lot of attention, since even non-linguists are aware of this level of language. South Asian lexical items have come into English through travel literature, and through items related to the legal system, revenue and administration — in short, through government-language registers — from various sources (B. Kachru, 1994a: 522). Some of these survive more or less actively in SAE: *chit* 'a note or letter', *tiffin* 'snack', *buggi* 'carriage'. Some have local currency only, though they are English formations or collocations: *upliftment* 'improving the plight of the downtrodden', *botheration* 'inconvenience', *cousin brother* or *sister, batch-mate* 'fellow student', and *head-bath* 'washing one's hair after massaging with oil' (B. Kachru, 1983; Nihalani, Tongue and Hosali, 1979). Some items are common in both British and American English, for example, *pundit* and *mantra*; they may have even acquired metaphorical or other extensions in their adoptive varieties, as in *political pundit*, referring to a media commentator-essayist. Other items have become part of English, but only specifically of SAE (e.g., *ahimsa* 'non-violence', *satyagraha* 'friendly passive resistance', *gherao* 'surrounding a person in authority to isolate him/her, as a method of protest').

Further, some items are simple words (*bungalow* 'one-storeyed house'); some are hybrids, phrases of two (or more) terms including an element from English and another language (*lathi charge* 'baton charge' [a *lathi* is a long bamboo or wooden rod used as a weapon, often by police in crowd control]). Hybrid items are themselves of several types, including register-restricted items such as *purdah woman*, literally 'a woman in a veil', used with reference to Islamic tenants of women's appearance in public, while *purdah* 'veil' itself has no register restrictions in Hindi-Urdu; and reduplicated items, such as *lathi stick*, in which the English and non-English elements are essentially synonyms (for extensive discussions and examples, see B. Kachru [1986b] and Baumgardner [1993]).

In discourse, SAE follows the conventions of conversational interaction and politeness characteristics of South Asian languages (Y. Kachru, 1987; K. Sridhar, 1991; Valentine, 1988, 1991, 1995). For instance, cases where both partial agreement-disagreements are expressed are more acceptable if the sequence of expression is *yes, but* ... . It is unexpected in other Englishes to have a sequence such as *no, ... but yeah*, which also occurs in Indian English data (Valentine, 1995: 243–4). In style of writing, the historical role of religious, administrative and legal texts and the Indian notion of 'high style' have been noted (Görlach, 1995; B. Kachru, 1983; Y. Kachru, 1987, 1998, 2003; S. Sridhar, 1996).

Bilinguals' creativity

Turning to 'bilinguals' creativity', B. Kachru (1994a: 528) notes South Asia's 'long tradition of creative uses of English in journalism, broadcasting, literary genres and advertising'. For example, only the US and UK produce more books in English than India does. Throughout South Asia, 'even in an average-sized city, there is a newspaper in English, and the local radio and/or television station ... allocates some time to English'. Four of the seven Indian dailies over a hundred years old are published in English, for example, the *Times of India* (Bombay, now Mumbai). Of 21,784 print periodicals in India, 3,691 were in English (1984 figures); only those in Hindi held a higher percentage of the total. The Indian government publishes more information in English than in any other language, including Hindi. English is the language of pan-regional newspapers, illustrated by counts of eighteen English-language dailies and thirty-five weeklies in Pakistan (Baumgardner, 1990), and the presence of English-language newspapers and periodicals in twenty-eight of the thirty-five Indian states and union territories (B. Kachru, 1994a: 529). Creativity in English is attested in all genres, from those associated with speech to popular media to high literature.

In India, particularly, creative writing in English indicates its wide acceptance as 'one of the voices in which India speaks' (B. Kachru, 1994a: 529). It is a language with an official status, and it is recognized by the literary academy of India on a par with Indian languages. Literary works published in English win awards just as those published in Indian languages do. In Pakistan and Sri Lanka, also, English creative writing is recognized as representative of the countries and cultures.

Literary creativity stems from the early nineteenth century (B. Kachru, 1994a: 530). But other sorts of creative use of English, especially in putting forward concerns and arguments to move the region towards independence, exploited 'the language of an elite culture which cut across linguistic, cultural and religious boundaries'. It is this use of English in creating awareness of historical and cultural heritage and in uniting nations for political independence by projecting a national identity that established the language as a South Asian language.

South Asian writers, whether from India, Pakistan or Sri Lanka, agree that there is 'no one answer to the question, "why write in English?" ' (B. Kachru, 1994a: 531). This is the topic of the poem by Kamala Das (1997), quoted at the beginning of this chapter (see also Chapter 10). The pragmatic reality is that many authors write in English (see Desai, 1996; Dissanayake, 1985 *ff.*; Hashmi, 1980; Sidhwa, 1996; Thumboo, 1985 *ff.*, among others), and people read their works. The literatures can be identified, at one level, as South Asian (i.e., *not* UK, Australian, etc.); and, at another level, as recognizably national: 'In these literatures a new historical and cultural backdrop is introduced to

English literature' (B. Kachru, 1994a: 523). The salient features of SAE literatures, then, involve 'contextual nativisation', 'new organisation[s] of textual structure', and 'devices ... for nativising rhetorical strategies' (B. Kachru, 1994a: 522–3). As the Indian creative writer Anita Desai asserts:

> Those purists who speak of the desirability of one language, one tradition, one culture must come from a more secluded, more elevated part of the world than I do. In my experience, Indian life has always been an amalgam of so many languages, cultures, and civilizations that they formed one very compactly woven whole, a fabric of different textures and colors, so inextricably woven together that to pull them apart would be to tear the fabric, to turn a perfectly serviceable garment into a pile of unusable rags and shreds. (Desai, 1996: 221–2).

South Asian writers, those from India, Pakistan and Sri Lanka, such as Ahmad Ali, Anita Desai, Alamgir Hashmi, R. K. Narayan, R. Parthasarathy, Raja Rao, Arundhati Roy, Bapsi Sidhwa, Khushwant Singh, Yasmin Gooneratne, and others too numerous to name here have established the canonicity of South Asian English literatures as distinct from the Anglo-American canons (B. Kachru, 2002, 2005; see also Dissanayake, 1985; Thumboo, 1985, 1992, 2001a).

Figure 11.1 Anita Desai

Englishization in South Asia

The other side of linguistic convergence concerns 'the Englishisation of South Asian languages' (B. Kachru, 1994a: 534–6), as English has been added to the preceding empire languages, Sanskrit and Persian. Persian, a foreign language, left lasting marks on South Asian languages and cultures, but has not continued in anything resembling the multidimensional currency of English. Not only has English influenced the languages of South Asia as a source of lexical borrowings and novel constructions, but it has also 'made models available for the development of [new] literary genres' and extended 'the thematic range of literatures'. Perhaps most importantly, it has become 'a resource for the transmission of literary controversies, innovations and trends' from across the world. This has had the general effect of 'releasing the South Asian languages from the rigorous constraints of the classical literary traditions'.

B. Kachru (1994a: 537 *ff.*) provides an extensive catalogue of categories and examples of the linguistic influence of English on South Asian languages at all levels. Lexical innovations, 'the greatest intrusion from a language in contact', are exemplified by loanwords, loan shifts, hybridization and parallel lexical sets. The motivations for such innovations are social and cultural; e.g., in Kashmiri English, *widow, cancer, bathroom, sex* are preferred by educated natives to the Kashmiri words. The native words have caste, class or regional connotations, which is not true of their English counterparts.

Figure 11.2 Raja Rao

Grammatical influences are represented by, for example, the increased use of impersonal constructions: 'Hindi-Urdu *suna gaya hai* "it is rumored" '; passive constructions with agents; and varied word order, e.g., 'SVO [vs. usual SOV] ... in Hindi-Urdu is used for stylistic effect' (B. Kachru, 1994a: 539).

Code-mixing, 'the use of two or more languages in a cohesive way within a stream of discourse', is a widespread phenomenon among multilingual SAE users, in all modes and virtually all registers (see Chapter 18). Code-mixing with English provides register-identification, particularly the registers of science and technology, and style-identification in that English is a marker of being highly educated, modern and Westernized. Most importantly, English has 'social value' in indicating the users' 'mobility and "outward-looking" attitude' (B. Kachru, 1994a: 540–1). Use of code-mixed varieties of South Asian languages represents the highly innovative and creative potential of multilinguals' linguistic repertoire and is pervasive in audio-visual media, on campuses of universities and colleges, and in professional contexts.

Attitudes towards English

The awareness of English as a force in South Asia is clearly emphasized by the attention paid to it by the constitutions and subsequent government policy approaches in the years of turmoil following independence in this region. Indeed, a tendency to leave language questions alone has been a prominent attitude: the controversies are so deeply rooted and complex that almost any approach seems to stir emotionally charged reactions and upsets. One thing remains clear: the functional domains of English in South Asia have actually expanded rather than shrunk. For example, the constitution of India specified 26 January 1965 as the date on which English would no longer be used as an official language of the new state. Since then, in spite of attempts to phase out English, practical difficulties in implementing the original constitutional mandate have convinced the successive governments to leave the status quo undisturbed.

The same is true of Pakistan; although the position of Urdu was officially strengthened subsequent to the 1959 constitution and later amendments, the domain of English has not by any means been overrun by Urdu. Sri Lanka paid a heavy price, and continues to do so, when it replaced English, first with the three-language policy (English, Sinhalese and Tamil) and later amended it to give Sinhalese a more prominent national and official role.

Photo 11.3 Bapsi Sidhwa

The policy has been recently modified with the reinstatement of English (Fernando, 1996).

In spite of the dominant status of English, however, B. Kachru notes that Macaulay's vision of 'a class of persons, Indian in blood and colour, but English in taste, in opinions, in morals, and in intellect' did not come true. Instead, 'English became a vehicle for national unity, and … pan-Indian cultural and political awakening' (B. Kachru, 1994a: 545). With the explosion of multinational media and the wave of globalization, English in its indigenized variety is gaining both depth and range in South Asia.

Speculations about the future of English continue, as in Graddol (1997). With changing realities of population and economic growth, it is projected that Hindi-Urdu may become a regional medium in South Asia, displacing English. Some commentators present the sorts of doubts summarized by Bailey (1996: 51): 'Is English a proper South Asian language? Is it mainly an important additional language for the region? Or is it inimical to the aspirations of the people?'

Attitudinally, South Asians are as divided about English as about indigenous languages. The attitudes of South Asians towards English amount to what Kachru (1994a: 549–50) terms a linguistic 'schizophrenia'. Three categories of opinion continue to make themselves apparent: the Westernization/technological progress view, the absolute rejection view, and 'a somewhat neutral position', in which English would be retained as 'one of the foreign languages, but not in competition with local languages'.

There are a number of schools of thought regarding how English should be situated within the multiplicity of South Asian languages (B. Kachru, 1996: 15–8). A persistent trend has been for some people to be aware of, and even focus on, the formal differences between South Asian, British and American

Englishes ('The Descriptivists and Contrastivists'). In contrast, the 'Functionalists' take into account the linguistic and cultural contextualization of English in South Asia. Beginning in the mid-1960s, their views led to close examination of the parameters of South Asian Englishes, which made possible the recognition of subvarieties and the real 'understanding of language in culturally and linguistically plural contexts' (p. 18).

Outside commentators such as Prator (1968) and Quirk (1988) have lent their weight to the push for the application of exocentric norms to South Asian Englishes as to all other Outer-Circle Englishes. Such concerns lead directly to considerations of models to be adhered to and promulgated.

Models for South Asian Englishes

A pervasive and seemingly permanent source of concern and controversy in SAE is what model should be followed in language education and other intra-national domains. There is a wide gap between the perceived norm and the performance of users (B. Kachru, 1994a: 526 *ff.*). The perceived standard was for many years British English, for the obvious historical reasons. Users of English in South Asia seem to have been caught in a double bind. There are some who use a perceptibly 'South Asian' English but regard users of SAE as uneducated and falling short of the 'perceived norm'. Then there are those who regard users who come close to the perceived British norm as putting on airs, indicating a desire to separate themselves from the community. More recently, there is a more realistic attitude towards the issue of a model in that SAE is increasingly recognized and accepted. As reported figures indicate, it is to some extent a matter of self-confidence, a question of the users admitting that they use a given variety, and identifying themselves with it and with the sociolinguistic reality it represents.

The controversies continue, with strong argument on all sides, and some light among the storms. There are debates on the ontological status of SAE, teaching of English in a multicultural context, pragmatics of the users and uses, questions of cultural identity, notions of communicative competence, and the development of SAE literatures (B. Kachru, 1994a: 550 *ff.*)

Conclusion

The observations and issues raised here in trying to account for English in the multilingual and multicultural contexts of South Asia demonstrate 'the complexity of describing an institutionalized ... variety of English' (B. Kachru, 1994a: 552). The general point is that if a language looks and sounds like English, and has multidimensional functions in the community in which it is observed, then it is a kind of English. It may be American or Indian, British or Pakistani, Australian or Sri Lankan: it is worth studying in its own terms on its own ground, as well as for comparative or diachronic reasons.

Suggested activities

1. Consider the following three excerpts from English language newspapers. Can you identify the report(s) that is/are from the region of South Asia?

A. *Hand-Held Computers to Help City Collect on Parking Tickets*

... When traffic agents write the wrong information on parking tickets, or write illegibly, car owners can challenge the tickets and get out of paying them: hundreds of thousand of such challenges each year cost the city millions of [currency] in lost revenue. But beginning next month, the city will begin using hand-held computers to scan registration stickers on vehicles' windshields, print out parking tickets and, officials say, reduce errors.

Chief X of the Police Department's Transportation Bureau said the new hand-held computers should reduce the error rate to 1 percent of all tickets issued, from 13 percent. Finance Department officials say they expect that the computers will help save the city [Numeral] million this year, as they are phased in, and more in the future.

B. *Govt. to act tough on plastic ban*

[Name of City]: Taking the anti-plastic campaign forward, [Name of State] Government on Monday warned the manufacturers of harsher steps like prosecution and snapping of power connections if they violate the ban on making carry bags of less than 20 micron thickness and of 20x30 size.

The Government has notified rules in this regard as part of efforts to check use of plastic articles, found to be posing severe environmental consequences, an official said today.

The task of enforcing the ban would be that of secretaries of local bodies. If violation of ban came to notice, it should be reported to the state pollution control board.

C. *Anti-smoking campaign targets renaming of brands*

A government-sponsored anti-smoking campaign launched today aims to target the "misleading" marketing ploys of the cigarette manufacturers who have been forced to abandon terms such as "low tar", "light" and "mild".

... The campaign, linked to a dedicated website, represents the most concerted attack yet on the industry. Previous advertisements have been more aimed at educating the public about health dangers from smoking and ways of learning to quit. But there is concern that smokers become immune to overt messages even if 70% of them say they want to quit. Tobacco products now have to carry large public warnings and from the end of this month. ... [Name of Region] law will prohibit the descriptions "low", "light" and "mild".

People who use such products are thought to be relatively brand loyal, having adopted them because they thought that they were somehow healthier than other forms of cigarette.

But the anti-smoking lobby argues that this is not the case. Smokers inhale more deeply and their fingers automatically cover the ventilation holes in the cigarettes to dilute the effects of the nicotine and other chemicals in tobacco, it says.

2. Read the following extract from a news report and identify the Indian English elements in it (extract from 'Invitation to Coke and privation to villagers', section labelled 'Open Page', *The Hindu,* 7 October 2003).

However, a key issue is the fiscal autonomy of local government. One of the ways by which the State retains control over panchayats is through the control of fiscal powers and resources. Various studies of panchayat finances suggest that their ability to mobilise funds is constrained by factors such as low local revenue base, unwillingness to tax local voters, project-tied grants, lack of political will on the part of State governments to devolve revenue powers and a 'resistant' bureaucracy. The share of its own revenue in total income of Gram Panchayat in Kerala declined continuously from 61 per cent in 1995–96 to 15 per cent in 1999–2000. This makes the local institution merely as an executive arm of the State to execute its programmes. Secondly, the presence of a very big corporate entity in a small village can at times make the village panchayat completely reliant on the company, as the company will be the highest single contributor to the panchayat finances. For example, a decision of revoking Coca-Cola plant's license cost the Perumatty Panchayat a major portion of its annual income. In such cases, the ability of the local government to control the company is inhibited.

Map of East Asia

12

East Asian Englishes

The march of civilization in Japan has already reached the heart of the nation – the English language following it suppresses the use of both Chinese and Japanese ... The absolute necessity of mastering the English language is thus forced upon us. It is a requisite of our independence in the community of nations.

Mori Arinori [d. 1899] (cited in B. Kachru, 1992d: 5)

Introduction

For a full picture of the global forms and functions of English, its presence in contexts in the Expanding Circle (see Chapter 2) must not be neglected. The Expanding Circle comprises countries where English is not an official language of government or a medium of education; it may, however, be required or strongly encouraged at a certain level of schooling. As opposed to English being an institutionalized language, as in the Outer Circle, it is used in performance varieties within restricted social domains, except in Hong Kong where creative writing in English flourishes (Bolton, 2002c).

In the People's Republic of China, Taiwan, Korea and Japan, social, cultural, economic and political factors have determined the degree and kind of English used at various periods of the history of contact with and absorption of the language. In spite of the fact that the contexts of learning and use are quite different from those in Outer-Circle countries, English has become widely spread and frequently used by some subgroups of the populations, and has had noticeable impacts on the languages and even the writing systems with which it has come into contact.

Chinese English

The arrival of English in China dates from 1637, when the first British traders reached Macau and Canton. As trade was confined to Canton by an Imperial decree after 1755, this port became the centre for world trade in tea, silk and porcelain. The first citations of Chinese Pidgin English date to 1740s, though the term Pidgin did not appear until 1859 (Bolton, 2002b: 4). After the Opium wars of 1839–42, Canton English spread northwards to Shanghai and other treaty ports of the country. Following the Treaty of Tianjin in 1862, numerous other parts of the country were opened to missionaries, merchants and colonial officials. The 'semi-colonialism' of treaty ports was a factor in the spread of English in China (Bolton, 2002b: 5).

Access to an educated variety of English grew by the early nineteenth century due to the English language education provided in missionary schools and institutions established as a result of the 'self-strengthening movement' of the 1860s (see Bolton, 2003 and Chapter 5 for details). Gradually, Pidgin English lost ground as an Anglo-Chinese culture developed in Shanghai and other centres of English education. China is regionally and linguistically a diverse country — it comprises over fifty-six ethnic groups with over eighty languages (Zhang, 2003; Cheng, 1992). Though English is not employed as an internal link language, nor does it have other characteristics of institutionalization as yet, its range and depth are growing. In 1972, under the instruction of Premier Zhou Enlai, English replaced Russian as the primary foreign language, and in 1978, it became one of the test subjects on the National College Entrance Examination (Zhang, 2003: 13). Joining the World Trade Organization has given a boost to the learning of English, and the forthcoming Olympics in 2008 is providing further incentive to the enterprise (Zhang, 2003: 14). The increasing interest in varieties of English is reflected in publications such as Zhiqiang Yan's *Introduction to World Englishes* in Chinese (Foreign Language Teaching and Research Press, Beijing, 2002).

Political and ideological concerns have played a great part in shaping English in China over the years. The early years of the twentieth century was a period when 'learning English' meant studying classical British literature; 'contemporary writings were rarely studied' (Cheng, 1992: 165). Though access to English was limited to a university-educated elite, it still managed to have an impact on written Chinese, including lexical borrowing and even some influence on syntax, for example in 'the length of [modifier] phrases and the use of passive verb forms'. English itself was not adapted, since it was intended to be learned as an intact foreign language, with norms and model coming from outside, i.e. from British English. A number of factors contributed to this acceptance of the external model, including influence of the Soviet Union, 'where British English was more or less the standard', and a dearth of opportunities for influence from the US because of Cold War politics. This, however, changed after the Revolution and its aftermath, and official policy of the People's Republic of China (PRC) underwent a dramatic change in the 1970s, as mentioned in the previous paragraph.

Zhang (2003: 17 *ff.*) lists the following earlier social functions of English in China: Christian proselytization, politicization, modernization, and internationalization. Since 1949, however, the functions have been changing gradually. As Zhao and Campbell's (1995) profile reveals, English is increasingly being used intra-nationally in certain domains such as medical and engineering professions, media and 'English corners'. In its 'invisible' function (B. Kachru, 1996), English acts as a gatekeeper and indicator of social status.

The same is true of Taiwan, where English is no longer confined to just academic subjects and limited professional domains of interaction, such as medicine, science and technology. According to Chen (1996: 267 *ff.*), English words, phrases and sentences occur quite readily in Chinese or Taiwanese dominant interactions among family and friends. It is no longer surprising to see elementary school children writing messages in both English and Chinese in their autograph books. This trend of mixing English with Chinese is due to the emergence of bilingualism in Chinese and Taiwanese following the political developments in the post-1987 period. Since then, indigenous languages of Taiwan have been given a place in non-institutional social life and the mixing and switching of codes has become quite noticeable. A policy of introducing English in the primary schools in Grade 5 in Taipei has been implemented since 1993.

Varieties of English used by native Chinese around the world (in Taiwan, Singapore, Malaysia, for example) share some features due to common linguistic and cultural background (Cheng, 1992: 162). However, in each region, English has evolved differently due to different ideologically driven policies and planning. There have been debates about what to call the variety used by the Chinese — Chinese English or China English (e.g. Kirkpatrick, et al., use the latter). Zhang (2003) draws a parallel with Indian English and uses 'Chinese English' to convey an array of functions, roles, proficiency levels and situational features. The contrasting term is Chinglish, which, like Hinglish (Hindi-English), Spanglish (Spanish-English) and Singlish (Singapore-English), has inherited a derogatory meaning denoting a pidgin-like code.

Characteristics of Chinese English

Chinese English (CE) shares many of the features of other varieties of English. Its sound system has the following features: No distinction is made between tense and lax vowels as in *heat* and *hit* or *mood* and *hood*. The fricatives θ and ð are often replaced by *s* and *z*; fricative *v* and continuant *w* are pronounced as the continuant; compounds and adjective-noun sequences are not distinguished by stress placement; and sentence level stress shifts are different in CE, which gives CE its characteristic rhythm.

In vocabulary, there are semantic shifts in single lexical items and in compounds, e.g., *intellectual* refers to a class rather than an academic or scholar or thinker, and the compound *big pot* means egalitarianism, as in *big pot wage system,* and a *running dog* indicates a 'lackey' in the PRC. In Taiwan (Chen 1996: 275–6) *everyday* means 'short and fat', as the English item sounds like the Chinese phrase *e bui de,* and a *small case* means 'an easy task'. There are many collocations with special political significance in the PRC, as pointed out by Cheng (1992). For example, growth

Photo 12.1 Agnes Lam, well-known poet of Hong Kong, see p. 357

of productive forces, strength of the socialist state and rise in living standards together are *the three favourables.* The expression *the three-no-enterprises* indicates no capital, no plant and no administrative structure.

In grammar and discourse, Zhang (2003) lists the following features: Chinese does not have an article system, so Chinese English (CE) rarely uses articles, especially the definite article. No distinction is made between adjectives and adverbs in CE. The third-singular ending with verbs does not regularly occur. CE shows a marked preference for adverbs rather than tense/aspect endings to indicate temporality. The other characteristics are avoidance of passive construction and negative questions; a question-answering system based on agreement-disagreement as in AfrE, IE, PhE, and others; rare use of the subjunctive, and use of *because … therefore* as a correlative pair.

In discourse, greeting and saying goodbye routines are expressed by the following expressions, respectively: *Have you eaten already? Walk slowly slowly ho. Slow slow walk aunty.* Use of *uncle* and *aunt* for people of an older generation is common, as in *I fell off my bike and two kind aunts* [ladies] *helped me to the hospital.* Some idiomatic expressions are distinctly Chinese, e.g., *When you have free time, come to play* [visit]; *playing away from home* 'having an extra-marital affair'; *Welcome Back to Zhuhai* (sign at the airport meaning 'Goodbye and you are welcome to visit again'). The creative aspects of idiom and metaphor construction are further illustrated by examples such as the following (Cheng, 1992: 169–70): *iron and steel and hat factories* is a phrase meaning 'wanton attack'; and *… they were like 'mayflies lightly plotting to topple the giant tree'.* Zhang (2003) also has examples of conventions of writing from the genres of personal letters and instructional texts. The former are illustrated with a letter of request and the latter with a set of instructions accompanying a herbal medicine.

In Hong Kong, the nativization of English has had more time to set in (Bolton, 2002b). Under British colonial government, there was no stated language policy, though English 'had the status of the official language of government, the official language of law, and was de facto the most widely used medium of secondary and university education'. In 1974, Chinese was designated an official language. In 1995, a policy was promulgated which called for the development of 'a civil service which is biliterate in English and Chinese and trilingual in English, Cantonese and Putonghua [the national language of the PRC]' (p. 35, citing Lau, 1995). Bolton, in his conclusion, proposes: 'the time may have finally arrived when Hong Kong can move on to create a space for its own use, and discourses, of English, with a place for the language as *one* of Hong Kong's languages in a diverse and pluralistic society' (2002c: 51, original emphasis).

The PRC, Taiwan and Hong Kong are all multilingual and exhibit the characteristic patterns of language use for such contexts, including those of code-switching and mixing with English. Chen (1996: 278) concludes that code-switching has entered the repertoire of Taiwanese people '(1) as a linguistic style appropriate in certain situations, such as in expressing group solidarity, releasing deep emotions, or uttering derogatory expressions' which sound more refined and neutral, and '(2) as a social-identity marker that connotes the prestigious educational or professional status of the speaker'.

CE represents a case of expansion of English beyond the colonies: China was never a colony of the British in the sense that India was, and yet the British controlled most of the trade to and from China. Japan presents a similar case of a semi-colony after the Second World War, as does Korea after the Korean War.

Japanese English

Although Japanese had been borrowing words from European sources since the sixteenth century, the impact of English began in earnest after the famous historical episode of Commodore Perry's entrance into Tokyo Bay in 1853 with a demand from the President of the USA for inauguration of trade relations between the two countries. The real opening of Japan, however, took place after 1868 with the arrival of American missionaries who taught English at private and government schools (Ike, 1995: 4).

The social changes under way in Japan in the Meiji period 'instigated [an] interest in learning English well enough to read Western books and to speak with these new visitors' (Stanlaw, 1992: 179 *ff.*). Reflecting the often-quoted pronouncements about the future of English by John Adams in the US, Japanese scholars and educators wrote about their predictions for the eventual triumph of English. Mori Arinori, who was to become the first minister of education, went so far as to call Japanese a 'meager language', which was 'doomed to yield to the domination of the English tongue' (Stanlaw, 2004: 65). Although Japanese was, of course, never abolished, English borrowing proceeded at a great rate, to the point that in Hepburn's 1867 dictionary, the romanization (*romaji*) system was introduced which continues in use even today.

The officially promulgated nationalism of the years preceding and during the Second World War saw governmental attempts to banish English, for example replacing such usual words as *anaunsâ* 'announcer' with 'the esoteric *hôsô-in* (literally "broadcast person")' (Stanlaw, 1992: 180). This era also saw the replacement of *besuboru* 'baseball' with the term *yakyū* 'bag ball', still in use today. As soon as the war ended, however, English made its comeback. By now, because of its intimate incorporation into spoken Japanese, English has become *nativized* in various respects and plays an important part in the communicative strategies of the Japanese.

In fact, Stanlaw (2004: 2–3) claims that:

> English has a critical place in the Japanese symbol system — both public and private, linguistic and social; ... English plays a very important role in Japanese cognitive, emotional, and perceptual processes; ... ironically, English plays a critical role in the reification of the sense of self in Japan; and the Japanese 'loanword' phenomenon is a unique and special case, defying any of the proposed sociolinguistic continuums used to describe such situations.

Characteristics of Japanese English

English in Japan has both a pragmatic function and an 'emblematic' or decorative function (Hyde, 2002). In the realm of pragmatic function, the number and scope of English borrowings in Japanese is phenomenal. A loanword dictionary gave 'over 27,000 entries' in 1977. English is of course prevalent in advertising; Stanlaw (1992: 180) cites Horiuchi (1963) in stating that a study of a month's issues of the daily newspaper *Asahi* revealed only one advertisement — for a typical Japanese food — that used no English loanwords. Stanlaw reports that loanwords have found their way into entries from members of the royal family in Imperial Court poetry contests, in which even traditional Chinese loanwords are usually avoided. This is a striking indicator of the degree to which elements of English have been made an integral part of the Japanese language.

Stanlaw, citing Higa (1973) and a National Language Research Institute study, observes that almost 81 percent of borrowed words in Japanese are from English, so that 'approximately 8 percent of the total Japanese vocabulary is derived from English'. The borrowings, however, have been assimilated to conform to the phonological structure of the Japanese language. Stanlaw (2004: 74) lists the major processes of segmental modification in English loan words:

i.   insertion of a vowel to simplify consonant clusters,
ii. addition of –*o* and –*i* as a final
iii. syllabic after words ending in *t,d* and *č, ǰ*, respectively;

iv. addition of –*u* as a final syllabic in all other cases;
v.   The realization of θ as *s, z, š, t or ts,* ð as *z* or *ǰ, l* as *r,* final *r* as *a:,* and *v* as *b.*

The following items show some examples of (i)–(iv) above: the examples of (i) and (iv) are from Hayashi and Hayashi (1995), the others are from Stanlaw (2004: 74):

stool	sutuuru
gray zone	gureezoon
seven-eleven	sebunirebun
thought	sooto
this	zisu
colour	karaa

The only consonant-final syllables are those ending in *-n.* In the case of a word's being a salient loan, some grammatical accommodations are made, such as deriving adverbs with the postpositional particle *ni* ('in, at') instead of the derivational affix *ku* which is used with native words: *naisu ni* 'nicely' (all the examples in the subsequent paragraphs are from Stanlaw [1992], except where identified as from a different source). Verbs are usually constructed by adding *suru* 'do', as *appu-suru* 'to improve (go up)' and *gorofu o suru* 'to play golf' ('golf + *object-marker* + do'). Other affixes or compounded elements may be added freely according to function, as *amerika* + *jin* 'American person', *shin* + *kanto* + *ha* 'neo-Kantianism ["new + Kant + -ism"]'. English words may be shortened, as *depāto* '*department* store' and *sukī* '*skī*ng'. Kay (1995: 70) notes that while usually the ends of words are truncated, there are examples such as *nisu* 'var*nish*' and *hon* 'plat*form*' in which the beginnings of words are lost.

Marginal but noteworthy influences of English on Japanese are a claimed increase in use of personal pronouns (*kare* 'he', *kanojo* 'she', *anata* 'you') and 'a few — but very popular — phrases' that utilize *mai* 'my', as *mai hōmu* '(my) home', *mai puraibasî* '(my) privacy'.

Compounding is a productive process applied to or involving loans, and may take several forms. Hybrids (Stanlaw's 'blendings') are phrases containing an element from each language, as *meriken ko* literally 'American powder', i.e. 'flour'; *denki sutando*, literally 'electric stand', for 'standing desk lamp'; *haburashi* (literally) 'tooth brush' (Kay, 1995: 70). Some compounds are 'a phrase or a fixed collocation', as *ofu dei* 'off day'; *tēburu supīchi*, literally 'table speech', i.e. 'after-dinner speech'. Kay (p. 71) notes that some borrowings occur only in phrases, as *kyaria ūman* 'career woman' and *fāsuto fūdo* 'fast food': Japanese words would be used for any individual item's meaning or function, such as *onna* 'woman'.

As would be expected, the semantics of borrowed items runs the gamut, from more or less literal transfer (*gorofu, tenisu*) to various sorts of changes in meaning. Restriction of meaning is exemplified by *mishin*, used only for 'sewing machine', *rikuesto* 'only in asking [requesting] a band to play a ... song'. Kay (p. 71) offers examples of terms which are applied only to 'Western-style versions' of the referents: *resutoran* for a (Western-style) 'restaurant'; *ringo* 'apple' is used ordinarily, but *appuru pai* 'apple pie', a dessert of foreign origin. Another common element of this type is *gohan* '(cooked) rice', but *kare raisu* 'curry [with] rice'. Stanlaw (2004: 14–5) notes that it is not the case that a borrowing will always be applied to a perception or indication of foreignness.

Semantic shifting is exemplified by items such as *furonto* '[hotel] reception desk', *baikingu* (literally 'Viking') 'buffet', as in an 'eat-all-you-like' restaurant, and *ekō* ('echo') 'acoustics' (Kay 1995: 71). An often-cited example is *manshon* ['mansion'] for '[upscale] apartment, condominium', but the term has this meaning in other Englishes also. Shifting may range from changes of sense to redefinition: *sabisu* ('service') is used for 'on the house/complimentary'. Stanlaw notes *chīku dansu* ('cheek dance') 'ballroom dancing'; *madamu* 'proprietress of a bar'; and Kay (p. 71) cites *potto* ('pot') 'thermos [insulated] flask'.

Kay says further that some phrases may have meanings different from what their elements in combination would have in other Englishes, 'possibly because the component words were taken in separately, and recombined by chance', thus creating the apparent ambiguity, as *shōto katto* (literally 'short cut') 'short haircut' and *torēningu pantsu* 'sweat pants', athletic wear (in, for example, US English, 'training pants' are underwear for very young children, a developmental step up from diapers).

Though Stanlaw presents some evidence to support 'a tendency for men to use more loanwords in academic discussions than in everyday speech', he concludes that data so far do not clearly support such topic- or gender-based interpretations. Rather, individuals' personal styles and topics seem to be the criteria for frequency of use of borrowings (see Hayashi and Hayashi, 1995: 195). Loans seem to be relatively frequent in discussions of originally Western sports such as baseball and golf, and in 'romantic' topics. Kay (1995: 72–3) compares this to the choices of lifestyle available to Japanese, who may live in homes with various combinations of Western and Japanese-style rooms. This 'compartmentalization' may apply to word-choices, also, and depend on integral or ephemeral criteria, such as the mood of the moment.

Advertising is the usually first-cited reason for or source of borrowings, but Stanlaw (1992: 197) points out that 'as yet no one has offered any evidence that advertising is the cause (rather than a reflection) of the use of English loanwords'. While criteria of some sort of 'outward-looking' style may favour use of loans, denigration of their over-use may militate against them. Thus, it is not at all clear how the sources of loans may be identified or classified. Stanlaw concludes:

> We cannot yet predict where and when an English loanword will be used, who will use it, and what strategies he intends to implement while doing so ... So far, all that is really understood is that the use of English is widespread and is apparently affected by situational and social factors, and that these variables are terribly conflated. (p. 197)

In spite of phonological assimilation, borrowed items are separated by employing a different set of symbols in writing (the Katakana script derived from Chinese characters). They are also different from the native vocabulary in their syllable structure and in being polysyllabic. As a result, the borrowings have had little impact on the structure of the native sound system or lexical structure.

The phonological assimilation of a large number of English items has had an impact on Japanese English. The Japanese pronunciation of these items is transferred to pronunciation of English, which results in Japanese English sounding very different from other varieties. English has also been nativized to signal specific Japanese meaning and create specific cultural effects for the Japanese audience with no regard for intelligibility with non-Japanese. In the area of decorative function, for instance, collocations such as *coffee and kitchen*, or *sandwiches and cafe*, and real estate slogans such as *We create a bright and affluent life* appeal to the Japanese sensibility, however odd others may consider them. When Japanese Railway advertising uses an item such as *traing*, it is defended by correspondents writing letters to the newspaper *Daily Yomiuri* in following words: '... when using English, they usually want to create a vivid image in viewers' minds in a way that cannot be achieved through the usual worn-out word order or usage. When they use "traing", they are constructing an image from material — English words in this case — even if they are not linguistically correct in doing so ... They probably thought everyday Japanese words would not evoke the same freshness' (Hyde, 2002: 14).

This 'decorative' function has been used in fictional portrayals of Japan for national and cultural 'colour', as in the following descriptions in a Japanese city by a Westerner in a novel:

> ... he passed a coffee shop with the name, written in English over the door, *Persistent Pursuit of Dainty*. Waiting for a light, he found himself beside a businessman carrying a GROOVY CAT shopping bag:
>
> GROOVY CAT: let's call a groovy guy a 'Groovy Cat.' Guys tough, check out the scene, love to dancing with Funky Babes. Let's all strive to be Groovy Cats. (McInerney, 1985: 105–6)

As noted previously, English in Japan has no internal reason for its promulgation; the medium of instruction in all public institutions and of all government business is Japanese. Stanlaw (1992: 181, 191) notes the existence of a cline of proficiency in English in Japan, from people who 'know a few words' to a relatively small segment who are fluent in the language.

The situation is about to change, however, with the new government policy of empowering learners with the ability to use the language in the global context, that is, 'cultivating "Japanese with English Abilities" ' as defined by the Ministry of Education, Culture, Sports, Science and Technology or MEXT. It includes '[a] Strategic Plan to Cultivate "Japanese with English Abilities" ', formulated in July 2002, as a comprehensive plan to be implemented for the purpose of drastically reforming English education in Japan. The current Action Plan announced in March 2003 establishes a system for cultivating 'Japanese with English abilities' in five years, based on measures included in the strategic plan and the budget for 2003. The goal of English education is to make certain learners achieve certain levels of competence in spoken English at each stage of their schooling and tertiary education. The goals are defined in terms of STEP (Society for Testing English Proficiency) and the Universities are expected to set their proficiency levels according to the professional requirements of the graduating population. It is specified that the goals are to be achieved by 2008.

It is worth noting that as a pervasive (or invasive, depending on one's point of view) component of the natural lexicon, and to some extent a reflection of changing, including Western-imported, social norms and values, English has become a part of 'various Japanese cognitive schemas' (Stanlaw, 2004: 300). At the pragmatic level, according to Baxter (1980: 49), 'English in Japan is not English as a foreign language. It is English as a language tied to Japan's present needs and future goals. It is a language with a definite status in the country, a status which rests upon history and upon present realities.'

The title of Baxter's paper is in the form of a question: 'How should I speak English? American-ly, Japanese-ly or internationally?' The criteria of 'speaking Japanese-ly' have to do with phonology, lexis, and syntax. Lexical innovation includes outright coinage, e.g. *base-up*, 'an increase in ... salary level', as well as less drastic shifts of meaning or sense, e.g. *pick up* 'choose', *wet* 'sentimental'. At the discourse level of semantics and pragmatics, '[d]irect propositional statements are often avoided', with higher frequencies of qualifiers such as 'perhaps' and 'I think' which are intended to make assertions less intrusive of one's own views (Baxter, 1980: 51).

Baxter points out (1980: 52), '... [S]peaking English Japanese-ly goes beyond strictly linguistic elements; it is a manner of speaking English that does not threaten the speaker nor come into conflict with this person's identity as a Japanese. It is also the means by which a Japanese can say, "I'm an English speaker." '

Korean English

Korea came into contact with English towards the end of the nineteenth century, but during the Japanese occupation, the link was weakened. English regained and strengthened its position after the Second World War. At the end of the Korean War (1950–53), English language learning and teaching became widespread in South Korea, while North Korea came under Russian influence. The current education system in South Korea is based on the Education Law promulgated in 1948. It was revised in 1998 and, with added amendments, now governs all matters relating to schools and higher education in South Korea.

The major structural characteristics of the South Korean education system are based on six years of elementary (primary) school, three years of middle (lower secondary) school, three years of high school (upper secondary) school, and four years of college (university). The medium of instruction is Korean, but English is a compulsory subject from middle school onward. With the emphasis on globalization, English was introduced as a subject in the third year of elementary schools in 1997 and is taught for two hours a week.

In North Korea, Russian was the only foreign language taught until the mid-1960s. In 1964 English was given the status of a first foreign language along with Russian. Its status was strengthened in the 1970s, and the language was introduced in the fourth grade of primary school in 1985 (Baik and Shim, 1995). Very few studies are available on the status, characteristics and functions of English in South Korea, and they are practically non-existent on North Korea. The rest of this section, therefore, will primarily present material on South Korea (Korea, henceforth).

Characteristics of Korean English

According to Shim (1999), the English textbooks being used in middle and high schools already exemplify the results of spontaneous codification of Korean English. Although the professed objective of ELT in Korea is based on the American English model, the language embodied in the English textbook and reference material examined by Shim differs from the model in three important respects.

Under the category of lexico-semantic differences (Shim, 1999: 250 *ff.*) are listed items such as the following: *growth* as a count noun (*hills and valleys ... covered with fresh green growths*); *after all* to mean 'finally'; *do with* to indicate 'endure' (*Do you think I can do with an insolent man like him?*); and *make at* to denote 'attack' (*The wolf made straight at the travellers*).

Under morpho-syntactic differences, items such as the following occur (Shim, 1999: 252 *ff.*): definite article *the* is presented as an obligatory marker of specificity that must precede the head noun of a relative clause or a noun in a prepositional phrase, thus rendering a grammatical sentence such as *he is a man who can help the police* ungrammatical for Korean English users. Non-count nouns are used as count nouns, as in *a hard work, a great patience*, etc. No distinction is made between simple present and present progressive or simple past and past perfect verb tenses. See also Jung and Min (1999).

Pragmatic differences (Shim, 1999: 254 *ff.*) are exemplified by the use of expressions such as *Why don't you ... ?* as a suggestion or direction in polite conversation, and questions such as: *What are you?* to ask 'What profession do you belong to?'

Englishization of Korean

English has affected the sole official national language, Korean, at all levels of language from phonetics to style choice, and has even become noticeable in users' choices of scripts. The history of this development reflects the history of scripts in Korea. According to Jung (2001: 259 *ff.*), Chinese-derived 'characters' or *Hancha* were current and prestigious among educated Koreans from the inception of their use in the fifth century AD through the 1920s. The invention of an alphabet, *Hangul*, in the fifteenth century provided an alternative writing system; but *Hancha* remained the preferred form of writing, with Hangul being 'associated with the uneducated — women and children'. However, the movement to replace the Chinese characters with Hangul by purists in favour of preserving the Korean identity of the language and the writing system unwittingly made it possible for English as a dominant language in the post-Korean War era to make inroads into Korean. The Englishization thus introduced had effects at the levels of script and phonology and beyond.

Citing Shim (1994), Baik notes (2001: 182–3) that word-final fricatives, disallowed by Korean phonology, are increasingly produced in English loanwords, so that *pos* 'bus' now occurs in preference to the more traditional [besu]. Baik supports his point by noting that, while final-vowel ellipsis in Korean words may occur in ordinary conversational speech, they always appear in 'deliberate speech', while with borrowed forms such as *pos*, the final vowel that would conform to the Korean phonological rule does not appear. Thus, the phonological constraints of Korean have been expanded under the apparent influence of English.

Further, the number of English loanwords used by Koreans is increasing steadily, and the script used for these loanwords has changed from Hangul to the Roman script. In morphology and syntax, Baik (2001: 185–6) discusses a development in the function of the plural marker *dul*, such that while it was formerly used with an object nominal to indicate that the pro-dropped subject was plural, it may now also be used to mark object plurals in a way that would be regarded as redundant according to the pre-English-influence Korean grammar. Baik writes that this use of *dul* is still prescriptively considered incorrect, though it is coming into increasing use. A similar linguistic occurrence shows the expansion of the use of the indefinite determiner *han*. Code-switching with English is also becoming more common, for example: ilgopsimyen *not bad*-ya '7 o'clock is not bad'.

Jung (2001: 265–73) discusses the history of advertising copy in Korea, specifically in a periodical, *Sin-Dong-A*. The connotations of tradition, 'high quality, reliability, [and] being highly prized' were conveyed by Hancha in advertisements through the 1970s. Beginning in the seventies, Hangul began to take over some of these functions, and now they have to some extent been taken over by English (p. 270). Since the 1990s, some advertisements contain entire paragraphs in English which are not transliterated or translated, as in the following:

> Crown super dry will take you into the new world with the taste of cleanness
> ....

Jung concludes that English in Korean advertising 'is now a major medium of expression in product names as well as attention-getters' (p. 274).

Conclusion

Studies such as the ones drawn on in this chapter show that the Englishes in Expanding-Circle situations exhibit various kinds of absorption into their respective societies. While in all such cases English is an in-country 'foreign' language, it is manipulated by its users in certain clearly goal-oriented ways and rather naturally absorbed by the host language and culture. Examination of English in other Expanding-Circle nations and regions will reveal still other configurations of relationships between the first language(s) and this additional language.

Suggested activities

1. T'sou (1983) joined the chorus about falling standards in Chinese and English and characterized the education system in Hong Kong thus:

   > The end result of the educational system ... is very often a product which can be generally described as 'cultural eunuch' — someone who knows what things could be or might be like in cultural terms but who is not able to take part. This product is brought about by the encrustation of a light veneer of

Western culture, glimpsed through exposure to the English language in schools and the media, on to a less than wholesome body of Chinese values and culture. (T'sou, 1983; cited in Bolton and Lim, 2000: 431)

In the following decade, the Philippine poet Germino Abad was delighted to assert that 'English is now ours, we have colonized it' (*Philippine Daily Inquirer*, 12 August 1996: 13, from Bolton and Lim, 2000: 431), an assertion which marks a completely different attitude towards the spread of English.

What position would you and your classmates take with regard to the desirability of wider English education in your region and how English is changing in your cultural context? Give arguments to support your position on both educational practices and context-dependent variation in the language.

2. Examine the employment advertisements in East Asian newspapers and see what sorts of positions specify that applicants must or should have some degree of proficiency in English. Do you find any where you are surprised that English would be a requirement? See what you can find out about English as a desirable addition to one's curriculum vitae in East Asia, 'just because'. What do you believe are the explanations for this sort and degree of attention to English?

13

Southeast Asian Englishes

We can appropriate and reinvent the language to our own ends. ... The rhythm of things — you have to get that ... If the Indians can do it in Indian English, I don't see why we can't do it in Malaysian English. It is all a matter of confidence ... It is rather like an artificial limb which you turn to your own advantage. We should not be so constrained by the fact that it was the language of our oppressors. If we want to think of it as the language of our oppressors, then it will oppress us.

Raslan (2000: 188–9)

Introduction

English plays a major role in many spheres of life in Southeast Asia, including those that involve academic, diplomatic, and economic pursuits. However, the Southeast Asian region presents a more diverse picture as compared to South Asia in that some parts of it have institutionalized Englishes (e.g., Singapore, the Philippines), whereas others fall into the Expanding Circle of English along with China, Japan and Korea (e.g., Indonesia, Malaysia, Thailand). In this chapter, we will focus on some aspects of English in Indonesia, Malaysia, the Philippines, Singapore, and Thailand. In some sense, these countries share some common cultural traits and developments in the acculturation of English to their native contexts.

Photo 13.1 Edwin Thumboo

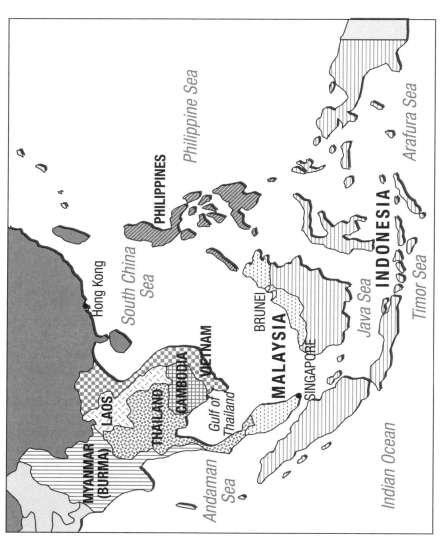

Map of Southeast Asia

Historical background

English was introduced as a result of colonialism in all these Southeast Asian countries except Thailand, which was never a colony of any European power. Nevertheless, each country in the region presents a slightly different profile.

The colonial history of Peninsular Malaysia begins with the acquisition of Penang by the East India Company in 1786. Subsequently, Stamford Raffles established a trading settlement in Singapore on behalf of the Company in 1819, and the Straits Settlements became established by 1826. Thus began the colonial rule that lasted almost 140 years, with the brief interlude of the Japanese occupation (1942–45). In 1946 the Malaya Federation was set up, while Singapore remained a separate Crown colony. The Malaya Federation gained independence in 1957, and Singapore gained self-government in 1959. It merged with the Malaya Federation in 1963, but later became an independent republic in 1965.

Education in English was introduced into the Straits Settlements from the early nineteenth century. But the British experience in India, where the spread of English education led to the rise of nationalism, resulted in the British being cautious in introducing English education widely in Malaysia. The policy resulted in four types of schools: Chinese in the Chinese-majority regions, Traditional Arabic (for religious instruction only) and Malay schools in the Malay areas, Tamil in the South Asian majority areas, and English-medium schools for the rich and the elite of the Malaysian society. After independence, Malay or Bahasa Malaysia emerged as the national language of the new nation.

According to the National Education Policy implemented in 1982, Malay is the medium of education up to the secondary level in all national schools (earlier English- and Malay-medium schools), and Malay is taught obligatorily in national-type primary schools (earlier Chinese- and Tamil-medium schools). At the secondary level, all schools employ Malay as the medium of instruction so that all students completing high school can move to the university level. Ethnic language schools are required to provide for instruction in pupils' own languages also (Chinese, Tamil, etc.). English is taught obligatorily in all schools. There are private English-medium schools with links to universities in the UK, USA, Australia and Canada. At the university level, most courses are taught in the national language, i.e., Malay, except for some courses in medicine, engineering, and various courses at the Institute of Advanced Studies and postgraduate (i.e., graduate) courses in various faculties and centres (Asmah Haji Omar, 1992).

At independence in 1965, Singapore adopted a policy of education in which all four official languages — English, Malay, Mandarin and Tamil — were given equal status in the education system. All four were used as media of education at the primary and secondary levels; in addition, all four languages were made available as second languages in all schools (Tay, 1993b).

This policy was revised in 1987, when English was made the sole medium of instruction at the primary and secondary levels for the purposes of national integration and international competitiveness in the economic sphere, while instruction in the other three languages also continued for the maintenance of cultural identities.

In 1521, Magellan led a Spanish expedition to make the official European 'discovery' of the archipelago that was later named the 'Filipinas'; this laid the foundation for European colonization of the Philippines. Spain's conquest of the Philippines was followed by four hundred years of Spanish rule. The majority of native people became landless peasant sharecroppers, while the Catholic Church owned vast tracts of land and controlled the education system. An independence movement against the Spanish rule, started in 1896 by the Filipinos, finally resulted in American intervention culminating in the defeat of the Spanish at the hands of the American forces in 1898. Thus began the American colonization of the Philippines. There was resistance to occupation, but after a prolonged war between the American forces and the Philippines (1899–1902), US rule was established. Thirty years later, the Philippines became self-governing. During the Second World War, the country was briefly occupied by the Japanese, but at the end of the war, the USA re-established its control. The nation was granted independence in 1946 and became the Republic of the Philippines.

The first person to think of English, rather than Spanish, as the medium of instruction in schools in the Philippines was Apolinario Mabini (nineteenth century). In 1901, English became the sole medium of instruction (Gonzalez, 1997: 26). Thomasite English teachers came from the USA, and by 1921 about two thousand English teachers from the USA had come and gone. Initially, Americans constituted a third of the English teachers, but by 1921, they represented only 9 percent, so it is safe to say that from the beginning, most Filipinos learned English from other Filipinos (Gonzalez, 1997: 26–7). In 1901, nobody in the Philippines spoke English; in the 1918 census, about 47.3 percent of Filipinos above ten years of age were reported to be able to speak English, and 55.6 percent able to read and write it (p. 27).

Filipino and English were declared official languages of the Philippines in 1973 in the second constitution, as opposed to Spanish and English in the first constitution, in 1935 (Llamzon, 1997: 43). English, however, was the language of the public schools (from fourth grade through college until recently) and is the de facto national language of business, commerce, law and government, and often of the mass media and popular entertainment. The Presidential Commission on Education Reform (PCER, 2000) recommendation on making more options available for medium of instruction for the first grade allows for more flexibility in adopting English or Filipino as a medium, and for adopting regional languages as media in Grade 1, with Filipino and English as subjects. Beginning with Grade 2, the recommendation is for mathematics and science to be taught through the medium of English and all other subjects in Filipino, though Filipino is not ruled out for mathematics and science if suitable teaching materials and qualified teachers are available (Bernardo, 2004).

Indonesia was a colony of The Netherlands for four centuries before it declared its independence in 1945. During the colonial period, Dutch was the main language of education, but for practical reasons, since The Netherlands was a small country surrounded by powerful countries such as Britain, France and Germany, English, French and German were also taught at the high school level. European-style education, however, was confined to a small minority of Indonesians, so that the people of the 16,000 islands, speaking more than 500 languages, had no common language. Malay, as the *lingua franca* in the domain of commerce, was used widely in Southeast Asia. Though only about ten million Indonesians were familiar with Malay, it was known all over the islands, as opposed to Javanese, which has more numerous speakers as a first language, but is confined to Java. In 1928 the Indonesians rallied around the slogan of *one country, one nation and one language* and adopted Malay as an Indonesian language. During the occupation by the Japanese (1942–45), the use of Dutch was forbidden, and as the Japanese could not introduce their language immediately, the national Indonesian language, Malay, gained ground. After independence, Bahasa Indonesia or the Indonesian language became the sole national and official language of the country. English was introduced as a compulsory second language at the junior and senior high school levels in place of Dutch, which is still taught as a foreign language, as are French, German, etc.

Thailand was the only country in Southeast Asia that escaped colonization by the Europeans. King Rama IV (ruled 1851–68) concluded treaties with European countries, mostly in the form of a Treaty of Friendship and Commerce, thus avoiding colonization and establishing modern Thailand. He made many social and economic reforms during his reign. Since English became the *lingua franca* of the Far East, Rama IV realized that the kind of education provided by the monasteries and the court was not adequate for producing future government officials. He therefore commanded that measures be taken to modernize the education of the country. Accordingly, a good knowledge of English formed a part of the new educational requirements for the officials, as it had become a necessary key to further knowledge and a medium of communication with foreigners.

English was introduced into the public school curriculum in 1913 and remained a required subject until 1977, with instruction in the language beginning in the fifth school year. Since then, several policy revisions have taken place; the latest one introduces English at the lower primary level and continues instruction through the completion of high school (Pongtongchareon, 1999: 60).

Status and function of English

Asmah Haji Omar (1992: 9) describes the multilingual situation in Malaysia in terms of three layers of multilinguality in the country. The primary layer consists of Austronesian languages (Malay, and the languages of Sabah and Sarawak) and the Austroasiatic languages of the aborigines of Malaysia (there are nineteen such groups in Malaysia). The secondary layer consists of Germanic and Romance (English, Kristang), Indo-Aryan (Bengali, Hindi, Punjabi), Dravidian (Tamil, Telugu, Malayalam), Sino-Tibetan (Chinese, Thai), Semitic (Arabic) and Austronesian (Javanese, Achehnese).

Malay and, to some extent, English, run across communities; other languages are confined to their own communities. Asmah Haji Omar goes on to characterize the multilingual situation in terms of a batik pattern: 'The batik has a basic motif which is surrounded by secondary ones. In batik printing, the first to appear on the white cloth is the basic motif; then come the secondary ones. Batik patterns get modified over the ages; certain motifs get bigger, and others smaller. Certain motifs run through the space provided by the cloth, while others are confined to certain corners only' (1992: 9).

Bahasa Malaysia has expanded its range as the sole official language of the nation and is the medium of instruction from primary to university level. It is designated the sole language of administration, and since 1990, the High Courts have been required to use Malay. However, English continues to be used in official domains because of what Asmah Haji Omar calls the 'comfortability' factor experienced by most middle-aged administrators as a result of their own educational backgrounds, and the awareness of the sociolinguistic constraints on using Malay (1992: 44). In the big business houses and commercial firms, and to some extent in the legal system, English still dominates. English thus occupies a status much higher than other ethnic languages, such as Achehnese, Chinese, Javanese, Tamil and Thai. Arabic is confined to the religious domain of Islam and does not overlap with Malay or English in any domain.

The New Education Policy designates English the 'second most important language' after Bahasa Malaysia. This has resulted in a great impact of English on academic life. All university students take English as a requirement for graduation. University of Malaya students have to take eight credits of English — four for general English and four for English for specific purposes. There is freedom of choice for the language used for writing dissertations. However, the statistics for the years 1995–97 show that over two-thirds of MA and PhD dissertations were written in English. Only in Islamic Studies, the Faculty of Arts and the Social Sciences, and the Faculty of Education were a majority of dissertations written in the national language, Bahasa Malaysia (Asmah Haji Omar, 2000: 16–7).

In the Philippines, English replaced Spanish as the official language with the establishment of the American rule. English continued to be the official language of the schools and government after the Philippines gained independence from the USA in July 1946, along with the teaching of the national language in colleges of education for future teachers and at each grade level beginning in Grade 1. According to Gonzalez (1997: 29–30), between 1939–80 the number of speakers of English grew from 26.6 percent (over 4 million 264,000) to 64.5 percent (25 million). Since the 1990 census did not include information on the number of speakers of English, the Linguistic Society of the Philippines conducted a study and reported on the basis of a sample of 1,200 respondents that 56 percent of Filipinos are able to speak English, 73 percent are able to read, and 59 percent are able to write it (Social Weather Stations, 1994).

Indonesia proclaimed itself independent from four centuries of Dutch rule on 17 August 1945, but gained recognition as an independent nation only in December 1949. During the colonial period, Dutch was the official language, which at independence was replaced by Bahasa Indonesia. Instead of Dutch, English became the second most important language in the school curriculum at the high school level (Alisjahbana, 1990). For additional information on teaching and learning English in the world, see Britton et al. (1991).

Sociolinguistic profile

As English becomes the language of school and higher education and plays a dominant role in the professions and the economic life of the nations of Southeast Asia, its social roles undergo a change, too. Even though the perception of English remains that of a foreign language in multilingual and ethnically plural countries such as Indonesia, Malaysia and Thailand, it is gradually becoming the language of social interaction, as it does not carry the load of the sociolinguistic connotations of the indigenous languages.

Such use of English is exemplified by the conversation between the two Malaysian teachers cited at the beginning of Chapter 19. Note that educated citizens of Malaysia are proficient in the national language and do not have to resort to English for inter-ethnic communication. However, code-mixed English is very common in informal conversations in public domains, and sometimes even in intimate domains.

The Malay items in the conversation have the following meaning: *Eh* 'particle', *ah* 'particle', *pun* 'also', *makan* 'food, to eat', *susah* 'difficult', *lah* 'a particle conveying various affective meanings', used in Malaysia and Singapore in informal contexts to show solidarity among interactants (see the discussion of *la* in Chapter 17), *kari paps* 'English item, curry puffs, assimilated to the sound system of Malay'. Note also the grammatical differences; lack of inversion in the question (*where on earth you went ah?, You were makaning where?*), use of sentence fragments (*no sign till one o'clock, so susah one*), lack of subject (*just nibbled, so not really hungry, got plenty of, so not bad*); also the use of *one* (*so susah one*). This is not the acrolect or standard variety that Malaysians would use on formal occasions, but this mesolectal or colloquial variety serves the purpose of establishing a shared social space in non-formal domains.

Characteristics of Southeast Asian Englishes

The grammatical characteristics of Southeast Asian Englishes have been described in a number of publications, including those by Bautista (1997b), Crewe (1977), Gonzalez (1983), Llamzon (1969), Platt and Weber (1980), Said and Ng (2000), Tay (1993b), and Tongue (1979), in addition to scores of unpublished papers and dissertations. The following is a brief account of some phonological, lexical, syntactic and discoursal features of Southeast Asian Englishes.

Phonology

Many of the phonological features are shared with South Asian and African Englishes. According to Llamzon (1997: 41–8), in Philippine English stops are not aspirated initially and not released finally; [s] is used for both [s] and [z] as in *sink* and *zinc*, and also for [š] as in *shame* and [ž] as in *treasure*; dental [t] is used for the initial sound in *thin*, and [d] for initial sound in *this*. Sometimes [h] is not pronounced. Delivery is syllable-timed, not stress-timed.

Zuraidah Mohd Don (2000: 35–46) reports on an empirical study and asserts that most of the contrasts in vowel sounds of British English are lost in Malaysian English (ME, henceforth). For instance, ME does not maintain the contrast between tense and lax vowel sounds, so that the pairs *seat* and *sit*, *pool* and *pull* are pronounced in the same way. Similarly, the following pairs, distinct in BrE and AmE, are pronounced identically: *met* and *mat* [e]; *cot* and *caught* [o], *cut* and *cart* [a]. The second vowel sound in words such as *forward* and the vowel in *bird* are both pronounced with [ə]. The diphthongs are simplified so that *make* is pronounced with [e] and *coat* with [o]. Vowel reduction in unstressed syllables is absent, and nouns and verbs are not distinguished by the placement of stress, as in BrE or AmE *'import* vs. *im'port*. In polysyllabic words the initial syllable is stressed, e.g., *'develop, 'tradition*, etc. Many of these features are shared by Singapore English also (see Low and Brown, 2003).

The shared phonological features of Outer- and Expanding-Circle Englishes in Asia are the following (these are similar to features in other regions, for example, Africa; see Chapter 14): lack of tense and lax contrast in high front and back vowels (*i, u* type sounds) in some varieties (e.g., Singapore, see Brown, 1992) or subvarieties (e.g., Indian English as spoken in the state of Orissa), substitution of simple vowels for diphthongs, and lack of reduction of vowels in unstressed syllables. The properties of mid vowels and low vowels may differ from variety to variety, but the contrasts are usually maintained. In consonants lack of aspiration in initial plosive or stops (*p, t, k*), substitution of alveolar (*t, d*) by their dental counterparts, lack of distinction between sibilants (*s, z, š, ž*) and substitution of labio-dental (*f, v*) with labial (*p, w* or *b*) and interdental fricatives (θ, ð) by stops or sibilants (*t, d* or *s, z*) are attested in many varieties, so is the substitution of *w* and *v* by either *w* or labio-dental continuant *v*. Some Southeast Asian varieties exhibit merging of *r* and *l* in non-initial position (Hong Kong, Singapore), and some simplify final consonant clusters.

The rhythmic features of Southeast Asian Englishes are very different from those of Inner-Circle Englishes, as has been mentioned before. Word stress is not distinctive, that is, it does not distinguish between nouns and verbs, for example, *'excuse* and *ex'cuse*, or between compounds and phrases, for example, *'White House* and *white' house*. Sentence stress also shows characteristics different from Inner-Circle Englishes, which may lead to difficulties in communicating across varieties (Gumperz, 1982a, b). In fact, Gumperz (1982b: 189–93) describes how prosodic features of Philippine English (and some grammatical and discoursal features) contributed to perjury charges against a Philippine doctor in a US court. Ultimately, the charges were dropped after 'expert' testimony from a linguist.

Vocabulary

Similar to their East Asian and South Asian counterparts, Southeast Asian Englishes also have lexical resources that extend the range of the American or British English of their historical inheritance. These fall into several categories, such as neologisms, borrowing, new compounds, etc. Examples include:

(1) Singapore English: *actsy* 'show off', *missy* 'nurse', *chop* 'rubber stamp', *Marina kids* 'youngsters who spend their leisure time at or around Marina Square, a shopping centre', *graduate mothers* 'graduate (well-educated) married women, encouraged to have more children and accorded certain privileges in Singapore, as compared to *non-graduate mothers*' (cited in Pakir, 1992b);

(2) Philippine English: *deep* 'puristic or hard to understand' as an attribute of language, *stick* 'cigarette', *high blood* 'tense, upset', *blow-out* 'treating someone with a snack or meal', *motel* 'a hotel used for pre-marital or extramarital affairs',

manualize 'to prepare manuals', *go ahead* 'leave before others with host's permission', *studentry* 'student body', *Amboy* 'a Filipino perceived to be too pro-American', *promdi* 'from the province', *behest loan* 'unguaranteed bank loan given to presidential cronies', *pulot boy* 'boy who picks up tennis balls in a game', *balikbayan box* 'box in which Filipinos returning from abroad put all their shopping' (Bautista, 1997b), *bedspacer* 'anyone who stays in a dormitory or shared room in a boarding house but does not take meals there', *comfort room* 'a room equipped with toilet, washing facilities, etc.', *fiscal* 'an official having the function of a public prosecutor', *watch-your-car* 'an unlicensed attendant who guards and sometimes cleans parked cars in return for tips' (Bolton and Butler, 2004);

Photo 13.2 Tish Bautista

(3) Malaysian English: *antilog* 'a male hated by a girl', *popcorn* 'a loquacious person', *kachang* 'peanuts, easy', *slambar* 'relax', *red spot, open shelf* 'girls who are popular and those who are not', *day bugs* 'those who come to attend school but do not live in residence halls' (Said and Ng, 2000).

The borrowings from local languages make English more relevant to local contexts; they also serve ideological purposes. For instance, Lowenberg (1999: 161–2) discusses how 'Malay elites are institutionalizing their dominance through English, which is the native language of very few Malaysians but is still the principal code for communication among Malaysia's multi-ethnic elites' by utilizing the linguistic device of replacing 'English words with denotatively equivalent terms from Malay, resulting in what Clyne (1999: 111) has termed the "covert" expression of racism and the institutionalization of inequality'. The following advertisement and news item make a clear distinction between Malay citizens based on their ethnic origin, and privileges Malays (*bumiputera*) over those of Chinese or Indian origin:

> OFFICE COORDINATOR wanted. Varsity/college graduate (any discipline). Male/female. *Bumiputera*. Sociable, able to mix well with people, fluent English. (*New Straits Times*, 20 March 1989)

> Foreign ownership decreased from 61.7 per cent to 25.5 per cent while non-*Bumiputera's* increased from 34 per cent to 56.7. (*New Straits Times*, 22 March 1989)

Even innocuous English compounds such as *Chinese-educated* and *English-educated* may bear a great deal of baggage in a specific context. Ho (1992: 207

ff.) discusses how the terms designate two separate groups of people in Singapore, the former in the majority and politically more active, the latter a minority, elitist, and less political; opinions exchanged in newspapers indicate that the two terms have a divisive effect on the society. Similar observations can be made about compounds such as *communal dining* and *intercaste marriage* in South Asian English.

Grammar

Southeast Asian Englishes share many characteristics of other Outer- and Expanding-Circle Englishes in their grammars. Some of the salient features are listed here.

The distinction between count and non-count nouns is not as institutionalized as in Inner-Circle Englishes. Therefore, it is quite common to observe forms such as *furnitures, equipments, a research,* and *one evidence.* Some count nouns are preceded by redundant partitives and show agreement in number with the head nouns, as in *sticks of cigarettes, stalks of roses,* and *units of 3-bedroom flats* (examples from Singapore English, see Low and Brown, 2003).

The gender distinctions among pronouns are not always maintained; for example, in Thai English and also in Singapore, *he* and *she* may be used interchangeably to refer to male and female referents.

Verbs tenses are not marked consistently, as most Southeast Asian languages mark aspects rather than tenses. Adverbs may be used to mark tenses, as in the following narrative (Singapore English, Tay, 1993b: 99):

> Her fiancé at that time *brought over* some canned ribs, pork ribs, yes, about ... twenty eight (of) cans of them. And then we *return* about fourteen of them. ... he *came over* with (a) ... a basket of fruits which we *retain* half and return the other ...

Here, the tenses of *brought over* vs. *return* and *came over* vs. *retain* vary where the speaker first uses the past and then the non-past in the very next clause. See also A. Tickoo (2002) for the use of *then/after that* in Vietnamese English.

Many Southeast Asian languages do not have a copula construction comparable to *she is a student* or *he is tall.* Simple juxtaposition of the subject and the complement yields the meaning of identification or attribution. This feature is attested in Southeast Asian Englishes also. According to Ho (1993) and Ho and Platt (1993), in Singapore English *be* may be left out in the progressive as in *she singing,* in the passive construction as in *he hurt,* as a linking verb as in *she Mary Jo, we hungry,* or *The wedding at 7 pm.*

Reduplication is common in all Southeast Asian Englishes and may be used to indicate the following meanings (Low and Brown, 2003: 59–60):

diminution, as in *no traffic police, stop stop a while* ('stop a little'); double reduplication to signal continuity, e.g., *Take a bus no good. Always stop, stop, stop* ('keeps on stopping'); reduplicated adjectives express intensified meaning, as in *Don't always eat sweet sweet things* ('very sweet') or *Ei, hotter, hotter* ('much hotter').

Adjectives that are at the extreme ends of a scale do not co-occur with intensifiers in many varieties of English; phrases such as *very gigantic* and *extremely microscopic* are odd. In some Southeast Asian varieties (e.g., in Singapore), however, expressions such as *very huge* and *more immense* are not uncommon (Low and Brown, 2003: 61).

Many other features shared with other Outer- and Expanding-Circle Englishes, such as reversal of the word order of object and adverb in sentences (*interpret orally the selection*), reversal of subject and verb in embedded questions (*Ask what are boys fond of playing*), coordination of clauses in different moods (*Tell us who your friends are and what do you do when you're with them*); distinctive usage patterns of prepositions (*Call Ø some students to answer* and *Review on pronouns ...*) have also been described as part of Philippine English (Peña, 1997).

Discourse

Southeast Asian Englishes have certain distinct conventions of language use, some of which have been discussed in literature. A few of them are listed here.

Terms of address: the convention in Southeast Asia, as in East Asia, is to use a title and the given name of the person to address the interlocutor. Therefore, someone named Susan M. Lightfoot can usually expect to be addressed as Ms Susan.

Topics which are off limits in Inner-Circle casual conversations may not be so in Southeast Asian English, for instance, one's salary, age, weight, marital status, number of children, cost of personal items, and rent of one's apartment (Malaysian English, Gaudart, 2000). Questions about these matters are considered polite as they indicate that the speaker is genuinely interested in the addressee. This is true in South Asia, also.

One topic of Singapore-Malaysian English that has attracted a great deal of research effort is the use of the pragmatic particles *la(h), what, ma,* etc. These particles have no semantic content in isolation; they are used in informal contexts to express interactional meanings. Wee (2003) describes these meanings as follows (see also Chapter 17 for the discussion in Pakir, 1992a): *lah* = intimacy, disapproval, highlighting of items, pointing out the obvious and contradiction; *what* = contradiction, strong assertion; and *ma* = justifying one's belief or assertion, stating the obvious. The meanings of such particles are discussed in a number of studies, including Platt (1987), Platt and Ho (1989), Wong (2004) and Ler (2001).

Code-mixing and code-switching with local languages is a common strategy, for example, *I just simply choose one because I'm in need of it so I just er chin chai take one only* [*chin chai* 'without being fastidious' from Hokkien] (Nair-Venugopal, 2000: 80).

Figures of speech, similes, metaphors, and so on, are drawn from local contexts: *The leaves of the tree rustled like a new sarong* (Tay, 1993b: 101); *mango green, chico brown* (Jose, 1997: 168).

The literary canon of Southeast Asia is not exclusively based on the Anglo-American tradition. Instead, it draws upon the rich legacy of earlier literary creativity from several sources. To quote Thumboo:

> For the Malay sub-ecosystem alone we would have to list the *hikayats, syairs, matras, pantuns, keroncong, wayang kulit, makyong, menora, bangsawan,* and these apart from a 'modern' literature. The outsider will find some of the genres unusual in what they bring together. The *keroncong,* for example, rests on feelings of sweet-sadness, not something momentary as in the 'Ode to Melancholy', but as an appropriate state of being, inspired and annotated by a sense of the brevity of life. (Thumboo, 1985: 216)

The same is true of other countries of Southeast Asia where traditions of indigenous languages mingle with Chinese, Sanskrit, and Tamil traditions to create a tapestry of many colours and hues. In fact, writers from Southeast Asian countries have been aware of their physical and sociocultural contexts and how these affect creativity in English. Martin cites the Filipino writer and critic Casiano Calalang, who in his essay 'On Story Telling' (1928) says:

> … it will profit us to pay particular attention to our surroundings, to the peculiarities that make them different from others, to the atmosphere of our villages which can not be confounded with the metropolitanism of the cities. And when in our mind the differences are clear, let us start with enthusiasm and vigor to write stories that will breathe the heat and passion of the tropics, and bear the distinctive stamp FILIPINO. (Martin, 2004: 136)

Conclusion

Just as in South Asia, there is a tradition of literary creativity in Southeast Asian countries also. This is especially true of the Philippines, Malaysia and Singapore and has been discussed in several critical works. As Ashcroft, Griffiths and Tiffin (1989: 8) observe, '[post-colonial contexts such as Africa, South Asia and Southeast Asia] have been the site of some of the most exciting and innovative literatures of the modern period and this has, at least in part, been the result of the energies uncovered by the political tension between the idea of a normative code and a variety of regional usages'. The Philippine writer Jose (1997: 168) emphasizes using material that writers know 'firsthand' and asserts,

'I have expunged the word "summer" from my writing unless it is in the context of four seasons ... Because there is no summer in this country. We have a dry season, wet season, rainy season, dusty season, but never, never "summer".' The attitudes towards English are undergoing a change, even in areas where English was formerly perceived as a colonial language incapable of expressive local cultural identities. This is reflected in the remarks by Malaysian writer Karim Raslan (Said and Ng, 2000: 189), quoted at the beginning of this chapter. Southeast Asia thus represents another centre of development of English.

Suggested activities

1. The Malaysian writer Karim Raslan compares the English language in Malaysia to 'an artificial limb' and says, 'It is like an artificial limb that you turn to your own advantage' in the quote at the beginning of this chapter. Do you agree with this characterization of English in Southeast Asia? If not, can you give some arguments to show it is another organic part of the multilinguals' repertoire, vital to their proper functioning?

2. Amara Prasithrathsint (1999: 68–9) has the following to say about 'good English' in the Thai context: 'The first component of "good English" is knowledge of the conceptual world of English.' The 'culturally significant' conceptual categories are the grammatical notions of singular vs. plural, mass vs. count, tense vs. lax distinctions, subject-verb agreement, finite and non-finite verbs, and voice distinction between active and passive. Lexicon and idioms may vary, but not these grammatical features, as they represent the 'cognitive world of English-speaking people'. The second component is the 'knowledge of dialects', for example, Thais must be able to understand 'English spoken by a Malay, an Indian, a Singaporean, a Texan, a Scot, a New Yorker, and so on'. Additionally, 'ability to switch between his/her vernacular English and standard English should be encouraged because it is socially beneficial or even necessary'. The third component is 'registers of English'. Thais must have knowledge of registers at the 'operative level'. They should be able to use the informal style, the formal style of business letters and reports, and English for special purposes.

    a. Do you agree with the characterization of grammatical categories as representing cognitive categories? Think about the following questions:
    i. if grammatical number, gender, count vs. mass and other such distinctions represent 'cognitive categories', does that mean if a language does not encode these distinctions, the speakers of such a language have no knowledge of one vs. many, male vs. female,

things that can be counted and things that cannot be counted, and so on?

ii. English marks number three times, first in a number expression, second in a plural marker on a noun, and third in agreement on a verb, e.g., '*one dog is* barking' vs. '*two dogs are* barking'. Is that logically or universally necessary for expressing the meaning of one vs. two entities?

b. The second and third components of Prasithrathsint's 'good English' identify specific capabilities. Is it necessary for all users of English to acquire these, and in the same ways? Look at the papers in Newbrook (1999) and form your arguments about Thai English.

14

African Englishes

Why shouldn't there be a Nigerian or West African English which we can use to express our own ideas, thinking and philosophy in our own way?

Gabriel Okara (cited in Ngũgĩ, 1986: 9)

Introduction

English in Africa, as in other Outer-Circle situations, is very much in the character of a naturalized citizen: it retains its heritage, and also takes on features of its newer social and functional contexts. The colonial powers left their marks on the African continent in linguistic ways, as in others. Along with French and Portuguese, English is a continuing presence in the government, education and commerce of African countries including Ghana, Kenya, Nigeria, South Africa and Tanzania (McArthur, 1992: 20; Bokamba, 1992: 126). Functions of English include its use in high courts, parliaments, print and broadcast media, road signs and business (Crystal, 1995: 103).

The sorts of adaptations that English has continued to undergo are of the types of nativization that we expect to find in multilingual, multicultural contexts. The innovations occur in all levels of the language, from phonemic inventory through semantics and discourse, and may be classified in ways that are familiar in the sociolinguistics of language change. The multilingual nature of the African context gives rise to complexities far beyond those in data from monolingual situations.

Given the great number of languages — perhaps a thousand (Bokamba, 1992: 125) — spoken within the finite, albeit very large, geographical space that is Africa, the advantages of having available a code that works across groups, regions and even nations are obvious. Upon examination, however, many issues come to light, such as those involving educational opportunities and concerns of personal identity.

Historical background

As McArthur (1992: 20) points out, the phrase 'African English' could apply to English anywhere on the continent, 'including English as used in Egypt by speakers of Arabic'; as generally used, though, the term usually refers to English as used by Black Africans, 'especially to [those in] ex-British colonies', and in Liberia, with its historical ties to the US, where English is the official language. The traditional division of the sub-Saharan continent and of the African Englishes spoken in the corresponding countries comprises West Africa (Ghana, Nigeria, and Liberia), East Africa (Kenya, Tanzania) and Southern Africa (Botswana, Namibia, and Zambia). South Africa represents a different case, with its English-speaking immigrant population and now the spread of English among the Afrikaners, other European groups, and the original inhabitants of the region.

The status of English and its range and depth of distribution in modern Africa differ from context to context. In some cases, the situation of English might appear odd to an Inner-Circle citizen and English user. For example, English is the official language in Namibia, but it is used by only 7 percent of the population, while Afrikaans is the most commonly shared language, especially among Whites (World Factbook). In fact, Bokamba (1992: 140) asserts that 'it is ... inaccurate to refer to African nations as Anglophone' if only very small percentages of their populations actually use English, even though it may be the official language. Liberia, South Africa (see the discussion of Gough [1996a] below), and Zimbabwe do not fall into this category.

Bokamba notes that the period of colonial contact between English and African languages was shorter than in the comparable situation in India; he gives a generalized figure of 'about eighty-five years', as opposed to approximately 250 in India. Of course, some contacts with English in Africa have been going on for longer than Bokamba's figure indicates. The oldest republic in Africa, Liberia, was established as a site of repatriation of freed US slaves in 1822, and Sierra Leone was designated a Crown Colony of Britain in 1808.

Issues of attitude readily arise when the idea of an 'African English' is discussed: some people in both the Outer and Inner Circles would argue that it is a misnomer to speak of, for example, 'Nigerian English' (see Chapter 7). However, an often-quoted assertion by Bamgboṣe begins:

> The question whether there is a 'Nigerian English' should, at this point, have become a non-issue. For one thing, it is generally known that in a language contact situation ... the second language is bound to be influenced by its linguistic and cultural environment. (Bamgboṣe, 1992: 148)

The relatively shorter time that colonizers spent in control of governments, educational systems, and so on, in Africa generally speaking has not been a decisive factor in determining the degree of influence that English has exerted, the power and prestige that have accrued to it, or the controversies that its presence and use produce. In spite of all the debates about educational policies, standards and sociocultural consequences of adopting an alien language, English continues to spread and is being acculturated with the same vigour as is noticeable in Asia and other regions. Examples that Bokamba (1992: 126) cites demonstrate 'certain [shared] properties' from various nations, which 'can be identified as *Africanisms*, in that they reflect structural characteristics of African languages'. Bokamba's treatment and those of Simo Bobda (1994), Gyasi (1991) and Tripathi (1990) are limited to mostly lexical, semantic and syntactic features of examples drawn from Cameroon, Ghana, Kenya, Nigeria, Tanzania and Zambia. Regarding first-language influence in general, Bokamba (1992: 127) notes that often 'the embedding of an African language structure into English is accomplished with such sophistication that it becomes difficult ... to detect it unless one is familiar with the speaker's native language'.

Grammatical and idiomatic innovations

There are various broad categories of syntactic characteristics that may mark a text as 'African'. Some of them, such as variations in uses of function words, particularly articles, are common across Outer-Circle Englishes.

The most salient and frequent feature of African English, according to Bokamba, is 'omission of function words such as ... articles'; he offers examples drawn from Kirk-Greene (1971, based on Nigerian speakers' language use) and Sey (1973, based on Ghanaian speakers' language use) such as:

1. Let strong ... team be organized.
2. He gave me tough time.
3. I am going to cinema. (p. 128)

African languages typically lack an overt syntactic category corresponding to English articles, and this is usually cited as a major reason for their 'sporadic' appearance in African English. Such grammatical differences from Inner-Circle Englishes occur in the English of all users from all educational levels in Africa. This gives credence to the notion that it is an African feature, not merely a matter of some sort of educational failure. Of course, there are differences in article usage within and across Inner-Circle varieties; Americans generally say 'going *to church*' but '... to *the hospital*', while British speakers normally use no article in either phrase (see Chapter 3). Such considerations have to be taken into account before any judgement is made about the phenomenon in African Englishes.

A second type of property is exemplified by sentences such as (3) and (4) below, which use generic nouns or pronouns in regionally characteristic ways:

4. He is a real/whole person [i.e. an adult].
5. You are a sociable somebody [i.e. a sociable person]. (Bokamba, 1992)

Such items are attributed to first-language influence, from Swahili and Hausa, among others. Other examples include the use of *boy* by girls for their friends and *footing* to mean 'walking' in Zambia (Tripathi, 1990).

A third type of characteristically African English structure exhibits plurals of nouns which in Inner-Circle varieties are in the mass or non-count category. Drawing from Kirk-Greene (1971) and Sey (1973), Bokamba offers examples such as 'all my *furnitures* and ... *properties*'; '*noises* of laughter and *chats*'; 'the *respects* they deserve'. He attributes this category of differences to first-language influence and to the 'semantic inconsistencies of English itself' (1992: 131). African languages do distinguish count and mass nouns, but the membership in the categories is not the same as in Inner-Circle English. Correspondents of *furniture*, *property* and *chat* 'are countable in most African languages', and noise 'generally occurs only in the plural'. Thus, from the users' point of view, the 'logic' of the semantics of these categories may be different from that of the Inner Circle.

Other putative features of African Englishes include redundant insertion of pronouns to 'echo' expressed subjects (Bokamba, 1992: 131); such structuring 'is often observed in the English speech of Bantu language speakers (e.g., Kenyans, Tanzanians, Zambians)'. This phenomenon, certainly not unknown in informal registers in Inner-Circle varieties, is exemplified in (6–8) below:

6. My daughter *she* is attending ...
7. Robert *he* is currently employed by ...
8. *Me* I am going to sleep. (Tripathi, 1990)

While Bokamba characterizes this echo-subject structure as a reflection of 'the subject-verb agreement system of Bantu languages, whereby a subject prefix obligatorily occurs with a finite verb', Tripathi states that its function is to topicalize the antecedent noun or pronoun.

The resumptive pronouns may occur in non-subject positions, specifically in relative clauses, as a reflection of that obligatory structure in various West African languages (Bokamba, 1992: 131–2):

9. ... in a country where you have never been *there* before.
10. The guests whom I invited *them* have arrived.
11. Thank you for the letter which you wrote *it*. (Gyasi, 1991)

It is worth noting that Semitic languages, Persian, and some varieties of Indian English (S. Sridhar, 1996), among others, share this feature with African languages, including the Englishes of Africa.

Another observable feature of African Englishes is the comparative construction without the two-element structure preferred by Inner-Circle varieties ('more *adjective* than *standard*'). African English users typically rely on using a single terms such as *more* or *than* to indicate the comparison, as in (12) below.

12. It is the youths who are skillful ... *than* the adults.

An often remarked-on structure of African Englishes is the polarity of responses to negative questions (see Chapter 3). While an American would be likely to reply to (13) with one of the choices in (14a) as appropriate, an African speaker would pick one from (14b):

13. Hasn't the President left?
14a. No (not yet) [if he has not left].
     Yes (he has) [if he has left].
14b. Yes (he hasn't left yet).
     No (he has left). (Bokamba, 1992: 132)

Bokamba shows that this 'logical' phenomenon is not limited to question-answer exchanges; number (16) as a response to (15) would seem anomalous to an Inner-Circle user:

15. I hope you won't have any difficulty ... next term.
16. I hope so [i.e., ... that what you have said will indeed be true].

Membership in parts of speech or word classes is different in African Englishes, for example, in Ghanaian English, sentences such as the following with adjectives used as verbs are grammatical and acceptable (Gyasi, 1991):

17. Your behaviour *tantamounts* to insubordination.
18. It *doesn't worth* the price.

Semantic concerns are 'perhaps the most interesting and dynamic area' of African markedness. Bokamba (1992) offers four categories of such deviations from Inner-Circle varieties. Again, these will be familiar in any diachronic examination of language, that is, they are natural processes, in no way indicative of 'degradation' or 'simplification'. The first category, *semantic extension*, adds meanings to broadly established English lexical items: 'Some *amount*' means 'money' or 'cash'; 'an *arrangement* man' is someone who usually gets his way. The phrase 'a *benchman*' is 'a crony or intimate friend'; and someone who *bluffs* may be dressed 'ornately or fashionably'. Simo Bobda

(1994) lists *to escort* in the sense of 'to accompany', *ground* to mean 'top soil' and *temporal* to denote 'temporary'.

Semantic shifts change meanings and functions of words such that their 'central contexts become marginal, and vice versa' (Bokamba, 1992; citing Sey, 1973). Thus, *machine* may mean specifically sewing machine, *minerals* — soft drinks, *serviceable* — 'willing to serve', s*cholarise* 'have a high rate of school attendance', *installmental* 'by installment', and *guested* 'to have a guest' (Simo Bobda, 1994). *Transfer* involves 'complete reassignment of the meaning of a word'. Thus, to *see red*, Inner-Circle 'become very angry', is Ghanaian English for 'a threat to harm or punish a person'; *steer* is a 'steering wheel', as in 'he lost control of the *steer* ...' (Bokamba, 1992).

Coinage is an important agent of Africanization of English: 'It is in *coinage* that African English exhibits the rich derivational morphology that is so characteristic of African languages' (Bokamba, 1992). He gives various examples, including the following:

19. [They] had pre-knowledge of one another's *wheretos* of going and *whereabouts*.
20. ... facing a lot of *hardcap* ['hardship'].
21. ... he has given nothing *coinable* ['no money'].

Compounding is very productive in all African Englishes: 'These *been-to* boys' (those who have travelled abroad, specifically to Britain or America); 'a *me-and-my-darling*' (a small sofa or love seat); 'your *my dear* girl-/boyfriend'. Some of these are loan translations, while others are formed analogically. Simo Bobda (1994) lists *chicken-parlour* 'commercial place where chicken, fish and drinks are sold', and *job side/site* 'work place'. Tripathi (1990) notes a process of 'Reverse compounding: *knife bread, sheet bed* for "bread knife" and "bed sheet", respectively'. Examples involving verbs may exemplify all the categories reviewed, extensions, shifts, transfers, and coinages (Bokamba, 1992):

22. Are you *nauseating* ['homesick'] for Nigeria yet?
23. ... he had been illegally *destooled* ['had power taken away, been removed from office']

Functionally, English is restricted to public domains of use, such as education and broadcasting. That, however, has not discouraged African creative writers in their concerted efforts to mark their English as decidedly African as they can (see Chapters 8 and 10). Bokamba comments on the fashioning of African English in the following terms:

> All these factors — interference from mother tongues, adaptations necessitated by the language learning and contact situation ... and the deliberate attempts by Africans to preserve and transmit African cultural

thought in English — conspire ... to form what I have termed African English. (Bokamba , 1992: 142)

It is interesting to note the partially negative cast of Bokamba's evaluation, in his appeal to '*interference* from mother tongues'. It is legitimate to ask whether this is the proper way to think of the formations of African Englishes, and to wonder whether this is the term that Bokamba himself would choose today, thinking in a broader context. While *transfer(ence)* is certainly evident, this is not to say that all non-Inner-Circle Englishes are 'tainted' in some inevitable way by detrimental psychological forces.

Oṣundare (1995) cites explicitly the language-culture connections explored and exploited by African English-using writers: 'the African writer today (like most other Africans) is not only bilingual but also bicultural'. The problem, then, as the Nigerian English writer Chinua Achebe and Indian English writer Raja Rao have pointed out in often-cited works, is how to transmit the various cultures in English, a language not historically tied to them. Translation is, obviously, one means of using English for such purposes, including 'well-translated ... idioms and collocations' and 'experimental translation' (Oṣundare, 1995: 345). Examples include the following:

24. His name lived in proverbs (i.e., 'He is immortal'; from *Danda*, N. Nwankwo [1964: 63])
25. What this new religion will bring ... wears a hat on its head (i.e., 'This new religion portends danger'; from *Arrow of God*, Chinua Achebe [1969: 45])

Oyelẹyẹ (1995) notes that 'one of the greatest problems of the bilingual African writers is the rendering in English of the speech of monolingual characters'. The writers' art resides in bringing in enough 'local colour' to texts to make them authentic but not artificially or mechanically 'exotic', and to give readers at least a sense of background relationships and other cultural necessities. As Oyelẹyẹ notes, 'It is not in the speech of semi-literate elders alone that the local colour is observable, even the highly educated will exhibit it in appropriate situations' (1995: 369).

With this overview of Africanization generally in mind, it will be instructive to turn to the more specific situation in South Africa outlined by Gough (1996a).

Figure 14.1 Chinua Achebe

Black South African English

According to Gough (1996a: 54): 'The acquisitional context and domains of use of English for typical black learners reveal broad similarities to those described for new Englishes elsewhere.'; thus, we would expect the criteria and processes outlined in Bokamba (1992) to apply in this more specific situation. The effects of apartheid in South Africa, especially in education, have shaped South African English in its bases and on-going development, and given it its identifiable character.

Figure 14.2 Ngũgĩ wa Thiong'o

Bokamba (1992) gave an upper estimate of 10 percent of the African population as proficient in English; however, Gough (1996a: 53) offers a wide range of estimates for the number of black South African users of English: an upper-end number, 61 percent taken from a 1993 survey, 32 percent taken from 1991 census data, to a figure 'considerably lower' than 29 percent taken from de Kadt (1993: 314). Comparison with the figures from the 1960 census reveals that 'knowledge of English as a second language has increased twice as rapidly as knowledge of Afrikaans' (Gough, 1996a: 53). In his introduction to Silva et al. (1996), however, Gough (1996b) writes, 'Recent estimates based on the 1991 census (Schuring, 1993) indicate that approximately 45% of the South African population have a speaking knowledge of English ...'. Whatever the figure may be, there seems to be a growing realization that a variety of English is in the making, which may be labelled Black South African English (BSAE).

The Black South African English education context

One of the most important criteria related to knowledge of English in South Africa is education; English is a language learned in school for virtually all black users. Gough (1996a: 53, citing Schuring, 1993:1), writes that 'less than 1/4% of blacks indicate[d] English as being their first language in 1991'. The first four years of elementary education are carried on in a first language for most blacks. Then the school language becomes English. Appropriate text materials are not available, and instruction is carried on by teachers who are 'overwhelmingly non-native speakers and products of Bantu education themselves' (p. 54). This echoes the often-cited remark of Bamgboṣe (1992:

149) which notes that Nigerian English teachers can only teach 'the standard' when they 'have their textbooks open before them'. The pupils' input, as one would expect, is black English. English is largely a language of public domains, with 'the vernacular or vernacular mixed with English … generally used in everyday encounters'. Thus, English for black South Africans represents one option in a wide-ranging repertoire of languages. Following the desegregation of education in 1991, 'an alternative educational context has emerged', one in which 'there is a far greater pressure to speak English and to change one's accent'.

Figure 14.3 Wole Soyinka

In media, '[c]ode switching and the use of black urban slang' occur in writing that has local identity, while standard English is the medium for other types of topics. Gough (1996a: 55–6) provides an example from a column (with the non-English title *Sondela Wena Ndabazantu*) from an English-language magazine, *Pace* (1994):

> Hola Magents! I know that all along the male species had to have a lot of *njori* (money) and a flashy *s'lahla* (car) to be able to attract the following sex. Get what I mean? But now things have changed. Some dudes reckon themselves to be the best offer ever given to women …

Some elements, e.g. *njori*, are in italics — some even with parenthetical translations — while some, e.g. 'Hola Magents' ('Hey, gents') are in ordinary type. Writers such as the columnist cited above must have their own sense of the degree to which given elements are likely to be fully comprehensible to their readers (p. 56). Such use of local language items is true of other African English varieties, too. Dako (2002: 53) gives several examples from print media, e.g., 'But what is all this *huhudious* media coverage, which tells only one side of the story?' (*Mirror*, 19 February 1994). The item *huhudious* is made up of Akan *huhu* 'blow hot air' and the English adjectivizing suffix *-ous*. In TV broadcasting, code-switching is common and desirable according to a cited 1993 survey of viewers. The preference is for use of vernaculars, not English, in radio broadcasting generally, but a 1993 report showed 'an English-medium music programme oriented to urban blacks has one of the highest listenerships of all stations amongst blacks'. Variation within BSAE has yet to be investigated in useful ways, and Gough suggests that recognition of nativization and plurality is appropriate, in keeping with a world Englishes approach (Gough, 1996a: 56).

Ideological issues

While English may be seen as the language of an historic oppressor, it has also been and continues to be 'the language of liberation and resistance and … an instrument of black unity' (Gough, 1996a). In addition to this attitudinal ambiguity, there is also the concern of what is 'English', so that 'its institutionalised existence [is] often denied by its speakers'. Such rather contradictory perspectives have been seen to obtain across the Outer Circle (see Chapter 7).

Pressures towards or perceptions in favour of 'standard English', especially where that means standard British English, gives rise to oppositional attitudes, even among those who may already have access to the language. There is a recognition that English is not a neutral instrument, but in fact tends to privilege a few (those who have had positive educational opportunities) among the many. The alternatives for a solution are to reject English or to adopt more open-minded attitudes towards accepting nativized varieties of it (Gough, 1996a). In spite of the ambivalence of attitudes, 'an enormous stock of English words has been adopted into Afrikaans and the African languages'. This fact and the frequency of code-switching with English indicate the widespread and deep effect of English in South Africa (Gough, 1996b).

Characteristics of Black South African English

The accent, grammar and semantics of BSAE exhibit the sorts of adaptations that we have come to recognize as representative of English in its Outer-Circle contexts, and more particularly to accord with most of the general characterizations of African Englishes in Bokamba (1992) and other writers cited above.

In phonology, vowels are the usual basis of discussion of claimed pronunciation differences from other Englishes. Vowels that in Inner-Circle Englishes are pronounced distinctly are conflated in BSAE, under the influence of first-language five- or seven-vowel systems, and this fusion results in regionally identifiable pronunciations. For example, the three vowels of *strut, bath* and *palm* may all be pronounced /a/, and those of *foot* and *goose,* /u/ (Gough, 1996a: 60, his examples). Since southern African languages tend to have a lot of consonants, there is less difference from other Englishes in this aspect of phonology. 'Some features can be attributed to specific native language influences', as the *ch* of *church* being pronounced *sh* by Zulu speakers for whom '/tʃ/ is a marginal phoneme'.

The lexical-stress system of Inner-Circle Englishes is largely absent. The only regularity is that stress may be assigned 'very often on the penultimate syllable', which is the one that is lengthened according to a regular rule in Bantu languages. Given this unavailability of stress as a suprasegmentals criterion, stress-timing is also not available, and vowels that are unstressed — and thus reduced to [ə] (schwa) in Inner-Circle varieties — are pronounced as full vowels in BSAE.

Gough presents a list of twenty-three morphological and syntactic features which characterize BSAE; some of these are noted by Bokamba as indicative of African Englishes generally, such as count/non-count noun differences ('she was carrying *a luggage*') and resumptive pronoun insertions ('the man who I saw *him* was ...'; see Mesthrie [1997] for a description of this phenomenon, labelled topicalization, in BSAE). Some of the features cataloged by Gough are not mentioned by Bokamba, for example: lack of morphological marking of number on nouns ('We did all our *subject* in English'), 'extension of the progressive' ('racism *is still existing*'), and 'idiosyncratic' verb-complement structures ('That thing made me *to know* God'; I tried *that I might see her*'). Some are obviously similar to those in Englishes of other regions, such as various preposition choices ('... *explained about* the situation'; '... *refusing with* my book'; '... difficult to *cope up with* my work'). Others may be readily found in Inner-Circle varieties, although sometimes in more marked uses; for example, 'Question order retained in indirect question'. Questions such as 'I asked him *why did he go*' are common in spoken US English, with some 'extra' pragmatic load. Green (1989: 135–6) shows that subject-verb inversion in embedded questions in US English indicates that the addressee does not, in fact, know the answer to the question. It is easy to imagine that such interpretive differences could require extra attention from participants in cross-variety English exchanges.

In any case, whether 'through native-language transfer ... [or] universal features', various characteristics of BSAE in some aggregate distinguish it as a regional and ethnic variety. In vocabulary, extensive borrowing is the norm (e.g., *kwela-kwela* 'taxi or police ... van'). Gough notes that borrowings may vary with region, so that, for example, *skebenga* 'criminal' is used in Xhosa-speaking areas. Semantic extension is common, for example:

26. He *proposed* love to her — 'He told her he loved her.'
27. You are *scarce* — 'I haven't seen you for a while.'
28. Jane is pretty.
    Thandive is *worse* [i.e., '... prettier than Jane.']

Discourse markers exhibit differences from Inner-Circle varieties, apparently 'strongly influenced by the mother tongue' (p. 66): *in fact* 'is used in conversation as a topic-change or topic-initiating marker', as '*In fact*, I want to talk to you ...'. Gough says that this use is likely based on 'Xhosa *kanene* (lit. "truthfully")', which is used in this way.

Focus in utterances is exhibited via manipulation of word order, since stress and intonation as used in Inner-Circle varieties are not available, as mentioned above. An element under focus in a sentence tends to occur initially; this manipulation may also involve concomitant features such as resumptive pronoun insertion, as in:

29. The best education, I need to get it.
30. A student, if he cheats, he will be expelled.

Code-switching 'is a common feature of black South African discourse, as it is more generally in the new English-speaking world' (see Chapter 18). Code-switching in South Africa, as in the Outer circle generally, is common to the point of being 'the norm' among 'elite, educated and powerful' people. The ability to use English and an indigenous language makes it clear to participants that the speaker is maintaining ethnic and cultural identity while demonstrating access to modernity and to economic and technological advantages; Gough asserts that code-switching is 'particularly common' on university campuses. Another aspect of the efficacy of code-switching lies in its social-group-maintenance functions, in 'certain urban varieties, such as Soweto Zulu Slang' (p. 69); Gough provides examples such as:

31. I-Chiefs isidle nge-*referees optional time, otherwise* ngabe ihambe **sleg**. **Maar** *why* benga*stophi this system* ye-*injury time*? ('Chiefs [a local soccer team] have won owing to referee's optional time, otherwise they could have lost. But why is this system of injury time not phased out?') [Non-italicized elements are Zulu, italicized are English, boldface are Afrikaans]

In his conclusion, Gough reiterates the functions and features of BASE that include it in the category of institutionalized Outer-Circle Englishes: 'Amongst black South Africans, [BASE] has increasingly gained an extended range of communicative uses, an extended register and stylistic range and exhibits the nativisation of registers and styles and also ... is developing a body of nativised English literature.' Gough notes that the schizophrenic attitude that divides real from perceived use and standards still exists, as, indeed, it does to some degree among users of all English varieties. He emphasizes educational reforms that will lead to 'the meaningful participation in society of the majority of the country's citizens' (Gough, 1996a: 70).

Conclusion

The studies discussed above provide introductory information and insights into the situation and nature of Englishes in Africa, in broad outline and in more specific exemplification and interpretations. One sees that examples of difference from some selected norm may be expanded virtually without limit the more specifically one looks at varieties within varieties, eventually coming to the usage of an individual if the investigation is taken that far. At that level, broader comparisons may not be very useful; what is important is to see the processes that constitute an identifiable variety. Once one recognizes that value judgements depend on where we decide to start from, it is easier to overcome the attitudinal baggage that is so much of an impediment to solving important questions of language-use policies and access to education.

Suggested activities

1. Consider the following passage by Ngũgĩ wa Thiong'o (1986) *Decolonising the Mind: The Politics of Language in African Literature* (Nairobi: Heinemann Kenya, p. 3):

    > The oppressed and the exploited of the earth maintain their defiance: liberty from theft. But the biggest weapon wielded and actually daily unleashed by imperialism against that collective defiance is the cultural bomb. The effect of a cultural bomb is to annihilate a people's belief in their names, in their languages, in their environment, in their heritage of struggle, in their unity, in their capacities and ultimately in themselves. It makes them see their past as one wasteland of non-achievement and it makes them want to distance themselves from that wasteland. It makes them want to identify with that which is furthest removed from themselves; for instance, with other peoples' languages rather than their own.

    a. Do you agree with Ngũgĩ's characterization of English as a cultural bomb? If yes, give arguments in support of your position. If no, what evidence can you provide to argue against Ngũgĩ's views?

    b. Does the history of English in your own country conform to what Ngũgĩ says about the use of English 'annihilating peoples' belief in their names, in their languages, [and] in their environment'? Marshal facts and arguments to support your position.

2. Read the following excerpt from the Kenyan newspaper *Daily Nation* (8 October 2003), and identify the African features of the text. You may just list the borrowed items. However, some explanation of the observed differences in grammar, including use of English words, will be more interesting and telling.

    > Sitting in the doorway of her *manyatta* (traditional homestead), Josephine Lesootia strings beads together to make necklaces, bracelets and other handicrafts …

Her *manyatta*, only 500 metres away from the Ewaso Nyiro River, which divides Samburu and Isiolo districts, is one of many settlements in the area.

...

Since she came here, Lesootia's roles have changed dramatically. While her children go to school, she has little time to impart in them the traditional knowledge, erstwhile a role performed by parents. ... She is ... making beaded bracelets and necklaces commercially. ...

Traditionally, the Samburu people are a pastoral, hunter-gatherer community. ... They are also livestock keepers — cattle, camels, sheep and goats. ...

Now, Lesootia and her colleagues are taking to small-scale agriculture and trade. ... They sell their beadwork to tourists. ...

To lure them, they use song and dance, which always does the trick. ...

Although the women play the main role in luring the tourists into the homestead, they have six Samburu warriors and three girls who perform dances and songs to attract the guests.

The price of one *ngerepa*, a necklace, could go for up to Sh5,000 during peak season, usually in December, while bracelets retail at Sh500. The women spend about Sh100 buying raw material for each piece.

3. Oṣundare (1995) labels tactics such as following a non-English lexical item or phrase with an English equivalent in a text 'cushioning'. He says that 'Achebe, who is the most remarkable practitioner of ... [such] lexical equivocation ... literally abandons it in his later novels, probably because he felt that some of the items cushioned in his earlier works have now become established and need no further explaining' (p. 352). Browse through the much-cited *Things Fall Apart* (1958) and a later novel such as *Anthills of the Savanna* (1988) to see if you find identical or similar elements that are 'cushioned' in the one but not in the other. Is cushioning entirely absent in the later work? How does cushioning work for you as a reader of such text?

15

African-American Vernacular English

A: See what y'all did now, I told y'all 'bout messin' with stuff don't (be)long to y'all.

B: I ain't do it. He did.

C: No I didn't! You always sayin' I do stuff. You did it.

Whatley (1981: 96)

Introduction

In a country with a wide diversity of social groups, it is a given that there will be various dialects or varieties of speech. Wolfram (1981: 50) lists eighteen major dialect areas in the US, for example, Northeastern New England, the Virginia Piedmont, and Western Carolina and Eastern Tennessee. In a nation as geographically large and socially diverse as the US, most people are at least informally aware of many kinds of English. There are some types that may have a higher level of general visibility, such as 'New York (City) English', 'California English', 'Chicano English', and so on. Such stereotypes may be exploited for characterizations in situational TV shows and in movies, for example.

General geographical associations often involve an urban-rural dimension. For 'getting ahead', i.e. having social and economic opportunities and options, people typically think that it is 'better' to be perceived as an urban rather than as a rural person and speaker. Being urban implies having better educational opportunities, for one thing, and better education is associated with various sorts of status and power in terms of access to society's resources.

In people's minds, the existence of speech variation is associated with all such factors — even though there may not be observational and analytical foundations for their beliefs. For instance, it is still a widely held belief in the US that using 'ain't' automatically marks a speaker as uneducated and socially unsophisticated. The literature of English geographical and social dialectology is full of comments on whether particular speakers or regional groups pronounce post-vocalic /r/; at some times and in some places, 'r-lessness' is considered prestigious, and sometimes not. Such examples show the effects of people's attitudes towards others, not linguistic 'goodness/badness' as such, in interpreting and applying observations of language behaviour.

African-American Vernacular English: Basic considerations

It is not an exaggeration to say that Americans of African descent (not all of whom speak the variety of English commonly associated with people of their apparent ethnicity) are the most salient minority in the US, and that African-American Vernacular English (AAVE) has more visibility than any other commonly recognized US variety. Wolfram (2000: 39) notes: 'In fact, Schneider's (1996: 3) survey of published research on dialects of American English from 1965 through 1993 alone indicates that AAVE has had more than five times as many publications devoted to it than any other variety of English and more publications than all other varieties of English combined.' Various labels have been applied to this variety, including Vernacular Black English and simply Black English; following various current writers' usage, 'AAVE' is chosen here. When language attitudes like those touched on above become associated in people's minds with ethnicity, then the potential for tension increases dramatically; sometimes the labelling of a dialect in a particular way may be considered offensive.

Debates in the media and in academic literature about the nature, structure, legitimacy and uses of AAVE are frequent and long-term, and are often heated. Mufwene and Rickford refer to the 'fury of polemics … following the Oakland [California] School Board's decision in December 1996 to make its teachers sensitive to the vernacular of African-American students' (1998: 1). Arguments rage about how similar or different AAVE is with respect to other varieties of English, and whether it should be used in schools or whether it should be taught. Wolfram (1991: 106) calls AAVE 'the paradigm case for examining the role of ethnicity in dialects … The sociolinguistic scrutiny of this variety dwarfs other ethnic varieties by comparison.'

Whatley (1981: 92) outlines the history of AAVE from the forced removal of people to the US from the earliest colonial days through the 'great exodus of Blacks from the Southeast to the Northeast and other parts of the country in the early twentieth century'. The variety-contact situations that came about under de facto as well as officially enforced segregation policies worked to produce variety maintenance for the African-American group, leading naturally to the development of a distinctive variety (p. 93). Whatley cites Dillard's *Black*

English: Its History and Usage in the United States (1972) as '[bringing] to the attention of the American public a major question regarding the system of language used by Black Americans. Was [AAVE] a separate system or was it part of the same system as other Englishes?' (p. 99; one can note, by the way, this early use of the plural form 'Englishes' to refer to 'varieties of English').

Origins and development of African-American Vernacular English

Data, as opposed to reconstruction and inference, which can directly indicate the characteristics of the precursors of modern AAVE are available in ex-slave narratives and what are termed 'hoodoo' texts (Green, 2002). According to Green, work carried on by the Depression-era Federal Writer's Project collected 'over 2,000 interviews (from 1936–38) with ex-slaves from seventeen states'. In addition, hoodoo texts, i.e. materials on 'witchcraft and magic', comprise over 1,600 interviews recorded between the years 1936–40 and a few more in 1970 (Green, 2002: 8; see Ewers [1996] for discussion of the hoodoo texts). Although these data are quite late, they represent the best extant approximations of actual Black speech of the slave era.

There are, generally speaking, three theories or sets of hypotheses which seek to account for the origins and early development of AAVE. As summarized by L. Green (2002: 9), the first, the *substratist hypothesis*, turns on the facts of the West African Niger-Congo languages spoken by the first slaves brought into America (i.e., before the appearance of second and later generations of speakers), and asserts that grammatical and phonological characteristics of AAVE evolved from that unusual forced and multilingual contact situation. According to this hypothesis, AAVE is a derivative of West African languages and is only superficially similar to English (for discussion of this position, see Dalby, 1972; Dunn, 1976; DeBose and Faraclas, 1993; this is approximately the position adopted by the Oakland School Board in 1996 regarding the status of Ebonics in public schools).

The second view, the *creolist hypothesis*, argues from similarities of features and processes of development between AAVE and, for example, Jamaican Creole and Gullah that there is a strong possibility that slaves from Africa and from the Caribbean brought creoles which they already spoke into America (see Rickford [1998] for elaboration of this view).

Finally, the *Anglicist* view holds that more usual adaptive processes of dialect formation were involved in Black slaves' acquisition of English, so that 'the characteristic patterns of AAVE are actually found in other varieties of English, especially in Southern varieties and earlier stages of English' (L. Green, 2002: 9; see Poplack, 2000; Mufwene, 2001a; Winford, 1997, 1998; Wolfram, 2000, for discussions of this approach).

Characteristics of African-American Vernacular English

While uninformed opinion or outright stereotyping may hold that one or another feature of speech is definitively representative of AAVE, Wolfram (1991: 111) notes that, rather than any particular feature or set of features, the variety is defined by its collection and configuration of various features. He asserts: 'On the whole, phonological variables are more apt to show regionally-restricted social significance than are grammatical variables' (Wolfram, 1991: 99). Mufwene (2001a) includes a detailed discussion of the issue of what constitutes AAVE.

Examples of phonological features distinguishing AAVE may include the relative frequency and patterning of consonant cluster simplification. Consonant cluster simplification is a rule in all varieties of English, but in many varieties it only applies when the cluster is followed by a consonant. In the speech of some speakers of AAVE, for example, the third person singular verb morpheme is absent from 80–95 percent of its possible occurrences, 'while comparable white speakers show a range of 1–15 percent at the most' (Wolfram, 1991: 109).

Hinton and Pollock (2000) examine regional variations in the phonological characteristics of AAVE, particularly the distribution of /r/, because, they say, such investigations bear on 'the convergence-divergence controversy' concerning AAVE and general American. Further, their study highlights the fact that there is no one 'AAVE' that constitutes the specific speech variety for all AAVE users, any more than such uniformity can be ascribed to any other variety of English. For instance: 'The adult participants in [Hinton and Pollock's] study expressed their negative opinions of the southern AAVE dialect of their relatives living in the south. They referred to [the southern] way of speaking as "country talk" and made disparaging statements concerning their dialect ... "They got it bad down there" ' (p. 69).

Bailey and Thomas (1998: 88–9) list a number of 'frequently cited features of AAVE phonology' in a table and categorize them into (a) those that are part of GE, but are more frequent in AAVE, (b) those that are part of old-fashioned Southern White speech, and (c) those that are unique to AAVE. For instance, deletion of the last of a word-final sequence of consonants, as in *hand* → *han'*, deletion of an unstressed syllable, as in *about* → *'bout* and *government* → *gov'ment*, deletion of one of two identical syllables, as in *Mississippi* → *Missi'ppi*, 'labialization of interdental fricatives', as in *bath* → *baf*, and a few others listed by Bailey and Thomas are exhibited in other dialects of US English also. Reversal of word-final *s* + a stop consonant, as in *desk* → *deks*, vocalization of *r* as in *four* → [foə], glide reduction, as in *tied* → [ta:d], and 'merger of /E/ and [I] before nasals', as in *pen* → *pin*, and a number of other features are also found in Southern White speech. Possibly unique AAVE features include the following: 'reduction of final nasal to vowel nasality', as in *man* → *mǣ*, loss of final consonants, principally affecting nasals, as in *five* → [fa:], *fine* → [fa:], and devoicing of word-final stop, as in *bad* → *bat*. (Examples all from Bailey and Thomas, 1998: 88–9; see also pp. 86–92 for other features and details of occurrence.)

Labov (1998) addresses these questions of the origins and on-going development of modern AAVE with regard to similarities and systematic differences between General American English (GE) and AAVE. Citing Baugh (1983), Labov (1998: 116) defines AAVE as '[T]he uniform grammar used by African Americans who have minimal contact with other dialects typically in contexts where only speakers of that vernacular are present.'

Labov's treatment compares the tense and aspect systems of AAVE and other varieties of American English in terms of their morphosyntactic structures and the semantics associated with them, for example, 'contrasts in AAVE between *He be tired* vs. *He tired*. There has never been any reason to believe that this [difference] is the result of a low-level rule of phonological deletion of *be*' (1998: 114).

If AAVE is a separate language from what Labov terms General English (GE), then the questions an investigator must address are quite different from those which are aimed at bringing out dialect relationships and distinctions. Labov asserts that AAVE comprises '*co-existent* systems' (emphasis added). In his view, AAVE contains distinct GE and African-American components. It is 'the AA component [which] allows speakers … to construct sentence types that are not available in [other varieties of English]' (Labov, 1998: 117–8).

Labov further categorizes grammatical elements in AAVE into three sets: 'common', 'negative', and 'positive' (pp. 116–8). *Common* features are those found in AAVE and other varieties, including most basic structures and rules, such as uses of modal auxiliaries, required participial forms of verbs following auxiliaries, and many others. *Negative* morphosyntactic features are so named because of their absence in AAVE; examples include the absence of the attributive possessive *-s* morpheme ('this volume*'s* readership') and third-person present singular *-s* ('she go*es*').

The *positive* category comprises features that AAVE exploits which are not, generally speaking, available in other varieties of American English. There are some overlaps with the usage of other varieties, such as use of perfect-form *done* in Southern white varieties, but the semantics and pragmatics of the forms are more extensive in AAVE. This category is exhibited mainly in aspectual elements such as *be, done,* and *be done*. To support his thesis, Labov presents a detailed explication of three indicative features of AAVE morpho-syntax: non-finite *be*, two subcategories involving *done*, and non-recent perfective *been*.

Non-finite BE

Non-finite *be* is a social marker for AAVE. As opposed to its use in other varieties, AAVE *be* has three defining properties: it requires *do*-support (**ben't* is unacceptable, *don't be* is grammatical); it cannot be used to make tag questions; and it does not invert with a subject, as auxiliaries such as 'do' and 'have' do. Non-finite *be* has usually been interpreted as an indicator of habitual state or activity. Like other elements in this category, it carries no tense information; this is shown by examples involving future and past real time (Labov's examples; p. 120):

1. When June come, I *be* outta school … .
2. When my son was young, the women *be* givin' him money.

In addition to the apparent 'habitual' semantics of *be*, it is also used with 'durative' and 'intensive' senses, as in (3), which Labov characterizes as an assertion of 'the attribution of blame for a particular incident' (p. 122):

3. So you know it all *don't be* on her; it *be* half on me … .

Such examples indicate that the form is used 'to refer to extended steady states, usually indicating a higher state of reality than normally predicated' (p. 122).

Further, Labov notes research, e.g. Bailey (1993), which clearly shows that the use of *be* in modern AAVE is an urban and later-twentieth-century development: 'use of invariant *be + ing* to mark habitual aspect is found among *all* urban speakers born after 1944 … while … none of the speakers born before 1944 uses this feature' (1998: 123). See also Smitherman (1997).

Perfect DONE

AAVE *done* works with content verbs to indicate completion (perfectivity), possibly but not necessarily in the recent past (p. 124 *ff.*). Examples (4) and (5) below illustrate these functions (p. 124):

4. You don't have it 'cause you *done* used it.
5. They *done* used all the good ones by now.

However, *done* is also used with 'punctual' verbs, in which case it corresponds to a sense of 'already', which may occur in utterances with *done*:

6. I *done* told you already.

Done may be used with 'iterative adverbs like *twice*', while *be* (above) cannot (p. 125):

7. I *done* got wet twice goin' to the store.

Completion may also be 'backgrounded' in favour of an 'intensive' sense, as in (8) and (9):

8. If Pop'd catch us, he say, 'Boy — you *done* done it now.'
9. After I *done* won all that money.

And further, *done* has developed a third set of semantic functions, which indicate a 'sense of moral indignation', corresponding to GE 'had the nerve to [do X]' (p. 126), as exemplified in (10) and (11):

10. He *done* slept with … Darlene … and he supposed to be a good friend of Henry. (Darlene's husband …)
11. So he … got the nerve to lie to me … talking 'bout he *done* went to work.

Sequential *BE DONE*

AAVE *be done* may be used in a sense corresponding to GE 'will have done [X]', as shown by its 'prototypical' occurrence with the time-adverb phrase *by the time [that]*, as in (12) and (13) (p. 130):

12. My ice cream's gonna *be done* melted by the time we get there.
13. So they can *be done* ate their lunch by the time they get there.

Again, the AAVE component's *be done* is not the same as the GE component's; the examples offered indicate that the time-sequencing constraint of the GE structure is not what is in effect here. The analysis of examples such as those below indicate that the AAVE structure 'combines relative location in time with "inevitable result" '; Labov characterizes this interpretation as 'a *future resultative*'; this is shown in examples (14–17) (pp. 131–2):

14. You *be done* slapped me by now ('you would have usually walked away from me by now')
15. I'll *be done* killed [him] if he tries to lay a hand on my kid again.
16. Don't do that 'cause you *be done* messed up your clothes! (to [children] running up and down steps)
17. Stop it dammit before I *be done* lay down my religion.

According to Labov, '[17] is plainly a threat that the speaker will abandon his usual peaceful conduct … The aspect marker *be done* is assigned to the second of [the] two events' (p. 132). Plainly, a 'translation' using GE *will have* will not work here. Other examples make it clear that *be done* is not dependent on future tense, but occurs in general statements as well:

18. I don't pay them no attention … If you pay them attention, you *be done* went batty …
19. If you love your enemy, they *be done* eat you alive in this society …

Labov notes that the determining factor in using these two senses of *be done* is which of two successive events it governs. A sequence of events is a common factor, hence the characterization as 'sequential'. These observations show that this variety has structures and uses of morphosyntactic elements that are not present in the GE component of the overall AAVE system (p. 134).

Non-recent perfective BEEN

This 'non-recent perfective' particle is shown to be a complex element, which is stressed, low in pitch, precedes a past-tense verb, and refers to a condition that 'was true in the past … has been true for a comparatively long time' and that continues to be true, as in (20) (p. 135):

20. They *been* called the cops, and they're still not here.

A telling example is drawn from Rickford (1973), who gathered responses of AAVE and non-AAVE speakers who were presented with the statement 'She *been* married' and were then asked 'Is she still married?' The typical non-AAVE answer was 'No', while most AAVE speakers replied 'Yes', bearing out the analysis that this use of *been* indicates a condition that continues to be true (Labov, 1998: 135).

The non-GE nature of this element is also emphasized by example (21), where *been* precedes a *be + ing* structure (p. 135):

21. I *been* been knowing Russell … .

This sentence indicates the speaker's assertion that he has known the person for a long time. Other examples indicate that the 'non-recent' sense is to be interpreted 'psychologically', not necessarily temporally as such; in such cases, it indicates that the speaker has stopped participating in an event (p. 136):

22. A: You gonna quit?
    B: I *been* quit …

Discourse in AAVE

Labov, Whatley and others have described the differences between GE and AAVE texts, whether narratives, sermons, political speeches, or special genres or verbal play such as *fussing, signifying* and *instigating*. Signifying is also known as *sounding, the dozens, snapping, capping,* etc. (Morgan, 1998). In signifying, the *Your Mother* or *Yo Mama* statements are 'a device to practice and perfect verbal skills' (Morgan, 1998: 269). These statements have specific grammatical forms, such as the 'That's why' in this example cited from Morgan:

23. That's why your mother is so dumb: she was filling out a job application and it said, 'sign here.' And she put, 'Aquarius.'

Two co-existing systems

Labov observes and interprets the behaviours of a set of particles (*be, done,* etc.) which do not behave like their superficially (e.g., phonologically) similar GE auxiliaries. In presenting these two sets of features, here motivated as *systems,* Labov notes the 'intuitive' self-characterization of an AAVE/other-English speaker: 'I can speak Black English or I can speak Standard English.' This perception, according to Labov, fails to account for the 'continuum of styles and an intimate mixing of different values of the variants' (p. 140). If one takes the view that different features or speech styles represent different variants or dialects, it is tantamount to a claim that speakers are *code-switching* (see Chapter 18).

Labov's approach, however, motivates the recognition of a new category of elements which 'is not … different in kind from the recognition of a category of factive or stative verbs [for English generally]'. That is, the availability in AAVE of this category of lexical items, which do not have equivalents in Standard English or GE, distinguishes AAVE from other varieties (p. 141). Labov points out:

> If a speaker of AAVE selects an AA element as the first member of the auxiliary … , then a wide range of syntactic options (i.e., in GE) are excluded. On the other hand, if the first element of the auxiliary contains a finite tense marker, then those syntactic possibilities are activated. (p. 142)

It is important as a consideration of investigative methodology to observe Labov's approach to these questions. Rather than simply describing AAVE on its own terms, with respect to no other dialect of English, he connects it historically and socially, while asserting its reality and viability as a recognizable variety of American English. At the same time, rather than simply listing differences, Labov relates the elements in question to one another and to other varieties of AmE, uncovering and supporting their systematic character.

Labov points out the richness of these developments in the syntax, semantics and pragmatics of AAVE, which should be recognized as positive and creative, not characterized as 'imperfect learning of (Standard) English'. In positing the co-existent systems, he presents an interpretation in which the grammatical categories of tense and aspect are handled by the GE system:

> The optional AA component can then be said to be freed from the drudgery of every-day grammatical work, and can be specialized to develop the highly colored semantics of social interaction that we have reviewed. This process is the opposite of the semantic bleaching that is typical of grammaticalization: it may be thought of as grammatical colorization' (Labov, 1998: 147)

It cannot be denied that social factors impede cross-varietal influences in the case of AAVE vis-à-vis GE. Labov writes that white US speakers live in a segregated world — linguistically, as well as in other respects — while AAVE speakers live in two worlds. He notes, as an illustration, that in the dialogue presented in television shows featuring African-American families, the characters' speech 'capture[s] many aspects of phonological and grammatical style-shifting within the GE component, but there appears to be an unconscious barrier against the ... recognition of the AA component'; basic uses of *be* and *done* are the only apparent exceptions (p. 147). This hint from popular culture may be taken to reflect an unfortunate situation of separation of two major segments of US society, to the cultural and social-political detriment of both (Kochman 1981).

Conclusion

It is unlikely that the social and political issues associated with AAVE will be set into the background any time soon. As Baron (2000: 17) puts it, the 1996 Oakland, California, attempt to have AAVE declared and treated as another language in a bilingual relationship with general English was defeated in part because, 'despite their revolutionary sloganeering, the teachers and administrators of the Oakland schools share with the public a conservative view of language that focuses, in the end, not on the language students bring to school, but on vague, idealized, and poorly understood standards of correctness that students are told to acquire'.

Pandey (2000: 1) writes in her introduction to a symposium on the Ebonics debate: 'One thing the current ... debate has made clear is that language — whether viewed as a dialect, a "Standard", or as an "adulterated corruption" — is a social construct, and socially owned and judged. It is clearly not the sole property of linguists.' This is not to say that the linguistic aspects should not be pursued and promulgated; these sorts of interactions are, after all, what is taken to be within the purview of and the motivation for 'sociolinguistics'.

Suggested activities

1. Watch the movie *Daughters of the Dust* (1998), *The Color Purple* (1987), or another film that not only includes but incorporates African-American

characters and cultures in a thorough-going way. Observe and comment on the sociolinguistic character of the dialogues and interactions in the film. Compare your observations and interpretations with those of the other members of your class or group.

2. Use the internet to get copies of the original Oakland School Board resolution concerning the nature and status of AAVE in December 1996 and the revised version of January 1997 (a place to start: *linguistlist.org/ topics/ebonics/ebonics-res2.html*). Compare the texts; what modifications and alterations were made? Research the statements that were made concerning the changes, and/or speculate on the basis of sociolinguistics criteria as to why the changes were made.

3. Such debates as the one in Oakland (which quickly became nation-wide) turn on the question of whether AAVE, or Ebonics, is a language or a variety of English (Pandey, 2000: 12). Choose sides in a group or your class as a whole and debate this issue. What conclusions or compromises can you reach?

4. How different is AAVE from General American English, compared to, say, geographically isolated dialects (about which no 'language or dialect' controversy rages), such as the mesolect of Singapore/Malaysia, Cockney of the UK, or Appalachian speech or the language of communities of the Outer Banks of the US? (For source material, you may see, for example, relevant parts of the video *American Tongues* [1987], Wolfram and Schilling-Estes' *Hoi Toide on the Outer Banks* [1997], and Wolfram and Christian's *Appalachian Speech* [1976].) Accumulate some data on points of comparison, and write up an argument presenting your view of whether AAVE is different in substantive ways from other varieties of American English, or only in some degrees and in some characteristics.

Part IV
Applied Theory and World Englishes

16

Researching grammar

Language is one of the forms of expression of the universal human intellectual power, and it is continuously dynamic. [1]

von Humboldt (1936)

Introduction

Grammarians and historical linguists have always been aware of the fact that language is 'continuously dynamic'; grammatical rules of languages are not static. They are neither resistant to change nor without exceptions. Furthermore, it is not the case that speakers, however well educated, are always sure about their judgements regarding grammatical rules, especially if the rules themselves have several subparts. Researchers in world Englishes are interested in observing the ongoing changes and variations in grammar in all the Circles of English. They investigate how rules work by observation, and by collecting large-scale corpora to analyse. It will be instructive to look at a few studies to see how such research is conducted and whether the results provide any insight into the continuing developments in world Englishes.

The study reported in Taylor (1993) explores the state of the subject-verb agreement rule, which is not clear in all its details and seems to be undergoing spontaneous change in AmE and BrE, the two varieties with long traditions of codification and standardization. Bao and Wee (1998) account for the variation in the use of the item *until* in Singapore English in terms of substratum influence. Both these studies are based on personal observations of spoken and written data. The other two studies presented here are based on corpora: Collins (1991) on a relatively large corpus of Australian English collected and made machine-readable in institutional settings, and Baker and Eggington (1999) on a smaller corpus of texts from five regional Englishes.

Grammatical agreement

Quirk et al. (1985: 757) state the general rule of concord or agreement in English and then go on to say, 'English speakers are often rather uncertain about the rules of concord'. It is not difficult to see the grounds for uncertainty. First, there is the general *grammatical* rule that the verb agrees with the subject in number and person. However, there are also other general rules, those of *notional* and *proximity* agreement (Quirk et al., 1985: 757), which overrule the grammatical rule. Notional concord specifies that the verb agrees with the subject even when there are no markers of number present if the subject notionally belongs to a certain category. Thus, collective nouns such as *team*, *government* and *people* are used with verbs showing plural concord as they signal plurality in meaning. The proximity rule operates in sentences such as *A number of options were considered*, where the plural agreement follows the plurality of *options*, the noun closest to the verb, though the head noun (*a number*) is singular. Quirk et al. (1985: 757) asserts that proximity concord is more acceptable when it is reinforced by notional concord, and that it 'occurs mainly in unplanned discourse'. The other factors that play a role in determining agreement features are coordination and disjunction (Quirk et al., 1985).

Taylor (1993) examines a small data set of fifty-two examples collected from published sources to see if they can be accounted for by the rules and the factors that play a role in determining agreement according to Quirk et al. (1985). All the data are from writings by well-known scholars, including linguists, and published by reputable publishers in Britain and the USA. It is, therefore, reasonable to assume that they went through rigorous processes of reviewing, editing, and copy-editing before publication. Taylor's paper first presents and discusses a number of clear cases of notional and proximity concord of both types: singular subject with plural verb (Type A), and plural subject with singular verb (Type B), some of which are reproduced below (the page numbers are from Taylor, 1993; the numbering of examples is ours; the noun phrase with which the verb agrees has been italicized where necessary to make the point clear).

Notional concord

1. Again, *the New Swan series* aim to do this.
2. My own recollection of *school visits* amply bear out these differences.
3. Perhaps it will be claimed that *the convention of arranging lines* neatly on a page one below another, as distinct from the rambling continuity of prose, *together with accompanying difference* in the use of capital letters, are clearly conventions of writing. (Taylor, 1993: 11–5)

The expression *together with* in (3) is treated as a conjunction; therefore, the coordinate subject justifies the plural concord. The pronoun and verb agreement pattern in the following example is interesting:

4. Although *the British Ability Scales* have been developed after many years of research *it has failed* to tackle some of the crucial issues concerning the nature of intelligence and its measurement.

The plural agreement in *have been developed*, singular reference in *it*, and the subsequent singular agreement in *has failed* are noteworthy. The main clause takes the notional subject, the instrument or test as a unit, representing the subject, leading to the pronoun and verb agreement pattern observed in the sentence.

Proximity concord

5. Likewise, it is simply not true that the traditions of *qualitative research* from which case-study research draws inspiration *eschews* generalizations. (Taylor, 1993: 16)

Here, the verb *eschews* agrees with the closest singular noun within the subject, *qualitative research*. There are, however, occurrences which the rules do not account for in a straightforward manner, e.g., examples (6–8) below:

6. Prices of equipment have risen dramatically since 1974: government subsidies and parental power *has* not, on the whole, kept pace with it. (p. 16)

The conjoined noun phrase subject *government subsidies and parental power* requires plural agreement, but the verb displays singular agreement. One explanation may be in terms of the proximity of the *parental power* to the verb; the other may be in terms of a unitary concept of a necessary condition to meet the challenge of rising prices: *government subsidies and parental power.*

7. I rather suspect that these speculations about the otherwise quite surprising appeal of environmentalist views has more than a little truth to it. (p. 17)

The only singular noun in the sentence, *appeal*, occurs between two plural nouns, *speculations* and *views*, and yet seems to trigger singular agreement. Thus, this is not a case of proximity concord. The same is true of the following, where the verbal agreement does not seem to follow any of the rules:

8. Kleiman's research suggests that personality factors, such as anxiety, confidence, and willingness to take risks, provides information on which students are likely to avoid various structures.

All of the examples cited are from written texts, which presumably went through careful review and editing. Taylor, therefore, concludes that these examples suggest that in spite of codification and spread of education, speakers and writers of AmE and BrE are becoming less sensitive to traditional grammatical rules of concord. If the requirement of subject-verb agreement seems to be on its way out, the following questions arise (1993: 17): 'If mature native speakers are so uncertain about concord, what should our attitude towards learners' difficulties with concord be? What do we teach? What is standard usage? In the absence of help from standard grammars where do we turn for help?'

Variation study

The ongoing change in grammatical rules is one area that demands attention from the ELT profession. The other is variation in grammar, exemplified in Bao and Wee (1998), which focuses on one particular item in a variety with a more recent history of attempts at codification, Singapore English (SgE). It demonstrates that the uses of *until* in SgE are different from those in BrE. It compares the SgE uses with the use of a comparable item, *dao*, in Chinese, and claims that the range of *until* in SgE has been extended to some of the functions of *dao*, leading to the observed differences from BrE. Thus, such grammatical variation is explainable in terms of nativization under substratum influence from Chinese, one of the languages in the repertoire of SgE speakers.

The item *until* in English grammar has two functions: it is both a conjunction and a preposition (Quirk et al., 1985). As a conjunction, *until* has two meanings: it can either indicate a point in time, or it can signal a result, as in:

1. We will guard the building *until* the statue is safely shipped back. (point in time)
2. Dad will be busy *until* the book is out. (result)

The prepositional use is illustrated in sentences such as the following:

3. The delegates will remain in town *until* next month.

A sentence with an *until*-clause or phrase (*until*-phrase, henceforth) is well-formed if the action or process signalled by the main clause ceases the moment the action or process signalled by the *until*-clause or phrase occurs. That is, the sentences in (1)–(3) signal that the 'guarding', 'being busy' and 'remaining in town' will come to an end the moment the statue is gone, the book is out and the next month arrives, respectively. All the main-clause verbs above (*guard, be busy* and *remain*) are durative. If, however, the main-clause verb is non-durative, the *until*-phrase can only be used in the negative, e.g.,

4. The game couldn't begin *until* the coach gave the signal.

The item *until* in SgE shares these properties with BrE, but has additional features, as in the following (p. 33; the numbering of examples is ours):

5. I waited *until* I (was) angry. [The linking verb is optional in SgE.]
6. I ate *until* I (was) sick.

The *until*-phrase functions as an adjunct of result in (6), being angry is a result of waiting in (7) below, and in (8), being sick results from eating too much. Additionally, the situation described by the main clause verbs, *waited* and *ate*, can continue to exist even after the result has been obtained. Thus, (7) might be used to signal that the speaker is waiting in a government office, gets angry because of the long wait, but has no choice except to keep on waiting.

7. I waited *until* I (was) angry; luckily my turn came ten minutes later.
8. I ate *until* I (was) sick, but I didn't want to stop because I already paid for the food.

This means that in SgE, the action or process of the main verb does not cease at the point where the action or process denoted by the *until*-phrase occurs. The two actions/processes continue concurrently, or overlap to some extent. This semantic extension makes it possible for SgE to exploit certain syntactic possibilities which are ruled out in Inner-Circle Englishes in general. The syntactic innovations in SgE are illustrated below (p. 34):

9. Why you paint the wall *until* like that?
10. Yesterday Patricia talked *until* very happy.
11. Don't talk *until* (your) saliva flies all over.
12. Look at you, laugh *until* (your) face (is) red.

Examples (9)–(12) are possible in SgE, unlike in BrE. All the above have a 'result' or 'to the extent' meaning.

The extended semantic range of *until* in SgE parallels the meaning of the aspectual *dao* in Chinese, which also functions as a verb. The item has the following meanings: a destination marker analogous to the English directional preposition *to*, as in *go to the library*; a temporal limit analogous to English *until*, except that *dao* does not signal an end point and, therefore, does not indicate the cessation of the action of the main verb; success in action, as in *find many shells*; degree or result, as in *confused to the extent that one forgets one's name* (p. 35).

In summary, use of *until* in SgE shares one feature with Inner-Circle Englishes and differs in two. It shares the feature of post-main clause positioning of an *until* phrase with BrE. However, it differs from BrE in its temporal and degree/result meanings. SgE thus provides evidence for nativization in the functions of *until* which combine two features of *dao*: its semantics (degree/result meaning) and the subtle difference in indicating non-terminal temporality.

Corpus analysis: Grammatical and style variation

The grammatical description of languages based on large corpora of real spoken and written texts is a relatively recent development in linguistic research, although linguists have always based their generalizations on written, and to some extent oral, texts. Two events contributed directly to the emergence of corpus-based linguistic research: the compilation of a survey of linguistic usage in Great Britain initiated by Quirk in the 1960s that resulted in a comprehensive grammar of contemporary English (Quirk et al., 1985), and the rapid strides in computer technology which made it possible to carry out research on corpora containing millions of words. The latter gave impetus to the collection of a number of corpora in machine-readable form with sophisticated tagging, parsing and other programs to process large data sets (see, e.g., Biber et al., 1998; Greenbaum and Nelson, 1996; Kennedy, 1998; Lawler and Dry, 1998; Nelson, 2004, among others). The two papers discussed here give a glimpse of the range of possibilities in this area of research on varieties of English.

Modals of obligation and necessity

The meaning of modality is expressed by several categories in English grammar, including nouns (*ability, possibility, necessity*), adjectives (*possible, necessary*), adverbs (*perhaps, surely*), and verbs (*be able, be imperative*). The category of modals, however, expresses modality in a distinct way. Modals are items such as *can, may, must, should, ought, have (got) to, need to*, which systematically differ from other modal expressions (Quirk et al., 1985).

Collins (1991) focuses on a select subset of modals, those of 'obligation' and 'necessity', e.g., *must, should, ought, need* and *have (got) to*, and explores their behaviour in Australian English (AusE) as compared to AmE and BrE. Each of these modals has two primary meanings: 'epistemic', signalling the speaker's certainty and suppositions, and 'root', indicating obligation, compulsion, requirement, etc. In their epistemic meanings, *must* and *have (got) to* express a greater degree of conviction as compared to *should* and *ought*. The item *have (got) to* is the main exponent of root obligation in informal speech in AusE (p. 153).

The database for the study comprises a quarter of a million words from the following genres (pp. 150–1): press reportage from the AusE corpus, a smaller sample of formal writing from a textbook on linguistics, a relatively larger data set of transcripts of luncheon and dinner party conversations by Horvath (1985), and a smaller sample of relatively formal speech from Senate Questions without Notice. The formal genres represent 56,000 words. All the texts are from the 1980s. The choice of these data is justified because informal/ semi-formal use of language is what we come across most frequently. Most people use language for casual conversation more often than any other genre, and newspapers are read more widely than any other type of published material.

For comparison with AusE, Collins (1991) uses the study of modals in AmE by Hermerén (1978) and BrE by Coates (1983), though comparing the three varieties is difficult due to the following factors: (1) there is 'selective presentation of frequencies' in both the AmE and BrE studies; (2) the data sets used in the three studies do not exactly match; and (3) Hermerén (1978) uses 'a different form of semantic classification' which makes it necessary to combine 'figures for separate categories' to make comparison possible. There is also 'a chronological gap' across the AmE (early 1960s), BrE (late 1950s) and AusE (1980s) corpora.

The conclusions that can be drawn from the frequency distribution of *must, should, ought, need, have to* and *have got to* are as follows:

a. If *have to* and *have got to* are considered variants of the same item, this item is the most frequent (11 per 10,000 words), and markedly so in conversation (22 per 10,000 words).

b. Similarly, the frequency of *should* in parliamentary speech is quite high (16.1 per 10,000 words), as it is useful in 'offering advice, making recommendations and encoding expressions of propriety'.

c. Numbers for *ought* and *need* are extremely small (0.5 and 0.2 per 10,000 words, respectively). However, the claim that *ought* is obsolete needs to be revaluated in view of its occurrence in speech rather than in writing in BrE (Coates, 1983).

d. Press reportage makes the least use of modals (15.9 per 10,000 words) as compared to conversation (37.9), parliamentary debate (32.9), and learned prose (21.8). This is consistent with the purpose of this genre: to report news factually without expressing personal assumptions and speculations.

Comparative figures for AusE, BrE and AmE (p. 153) show that there are substantial differences between AusE and the other two varieties in the use of modals, which may be due to the time factor, or the difference in the genres represented in the three corpora. The figures for *must, should* and *ought* are higher in BrE and AmE; the AmE corpus does not have any occurrence of *need, have to* and *have got to*. The modal *need* has a frequency of 0.3 in BrE speech and 0.7 in written data; *have to* has a frequency of 7.0 in writing only; and *have got to* does not occur at all. Since the modal *ought* has a relatively low frequency in all the three corpora and *need* is not attested in the AmE corpus, the three modals selected for further discussion are *must, should* and *have (got) to*.

The modal must

The epistemic use of *must* is five times as frequent as the root use in AusE (Collins, 1991: 154, Table 10.5), whereas in BrE it is almost equal: the figures for AusE are 9.1 percent for the root meaning and 50 percent for the epistemic, while the comparable figures for BrE are 24.3 percent and 21.1 percent. In writing, all the varieties show a greater frequency for the root use as compared to the epistemic. In AusE conversation the modal *have got to* seems to have taken over the root meaning slot of *must*: the frequency of *have got to* in speech is 99 percent compared to 1 percent in writing (p. 157, Table 10.6). There are no occurrences of the item in the epistemic meaning in the AusE data that the study is based on.

Root *must* has a range of meanings beginning from a strong, subjective, almost imperative-like use (Lyons, 1977: 792; Coates, 1983: 32), to a weak requirement, as in examples (1)–(3) below:

1. You *must* come over for dinner one night.
2. We *must* remember this when transcribing words like 'bútter'.
3. It is clear that anyone who wants to discuss how language works *must* have an easy and reliable way of referring to the basic units of language, the phoneme.

Epistemic *must* signals the speaker's certainty about the truth of the proposition and may be preceded or followed by co-text detailing the basis of speaker assumption, as in *you must be tired after your 6-mile run*. In the AusE data, epistemic *must* more often 'refers to states or activities in the present' and 'exhibits a strong tendency to occur with the perfect' and progressive aspects (Collins, 1991: 155).

The AusE data supports Quirk et al.'s claim (1985: 225 note b) that '*must* [logical necessity] cannot normally be used in interrogative and negative clauses' and that *mustn't* in the sense of *can't* is more common in AmE (BrE uses *can't*). The six occurrences of *mustn't* attested in the corpus are all in the conversational data; the distribution of *can't* across genres is almost even.

The modal have (got) to

It has already been pointed out that the root meaning of *must* has been taken over by *have got to* in AusE. The latter may also express epistemic meaning (not attested in Collins' database). Root *have got to* has a range of meaning similar to *must*, as in the following examples (pp. 157–8):

4. Well, this old lady, they'd tuck her into bed ... and 'You stop there' the nurse'd say, 'You *gotta* stop there, love, don't you get out ...'
5. She's brought a nice peanut brittle bar there and well I'*ve got to* keep my mind above that.
6. Well she'*s got to* be able to do all that before they'll let her go back.

It is also used to convey habitual meaning, as in *You've got to be on their backs all the time, haven't you?*

The phonological realization of *have got to* may also vary in AusE between *be got to* and *have got and*, as in the following:

7. Cause you'*re gotta* come back in again.
8. Yes, that's the trouble. You'*ve got and* ask.

The modal should

The modal *should* functions as a quasi-subjunctive in addition to functioning as a modal of necessity (epistemic) and obligation (root). Its use for hypothetical *would* with first-person subject is rare in AusE. In both speech and writing, *should* in the root sense is dominant as compared to its epistemic sense (84 percent vs. 10 percent; p. 161). The comparable figures for BrE are 54.9 percent vs. 17.5 percent. The percentages are based on tokens per 10,000 words (p. 152).

Root *should* has a range of meaning encompassing strongly subjective, with moral or legal implications, to weakly objective, suggesting 'correct' behaviour. The examples are not transparent; they need background information to be interpreted as strong subjective, and are therefore not cited here. Epistemic *should* expresses likelihood or a less certain assumption on the part of the speaker, as in the following (p. 162):

9. 'It *should* be a fantastic race for the public with three drivers fighting for the title,' said Prost.

The modal *ought* also expresses both root and epistemic meanings in AusE as opposed to BrE; root *ought* has more of a meaning of 'a recommendation' or 'asserting the desirability of an activity or state of affairs' (p. 163).

Relevance of corpora to research

It is clear from the study that while *must, have (got) to, should* and *ought* all express both root and epistemic meanings, *must* is the only modal in which the epistemic meaning is dominant, while *have (got) to* is the primary exponent of root obligation.

Collins' study illustrates the following advantages of using corpora for linguistic research: (a) real data forces researchers to deal with the entire range of use of the modals, no matter how resistant to generalization the data are; and (b) it makes comparison across varieties and within varieties among genres possible, which is useful for a number of applications.

Analysing literatures in five Englishes

An article by Baker and Eggington (1999) examines literatures written in five Englishes: Indian (IE), West African (AfrE), BrE, Anglo-American (AmE) and Mexican American (MexE).[2] The paper is based on the methodology developed in Biber (1988), which used multidimensional factor analysis to identify differences across genres and varieties in American English. The authors randomly chose twenty short stories from each of the five varieties, ten written by male and ten by female authors — a total of 100 stories, all originally written in English and published between 1970 and 1994.

To ensure comparability, the following five criteria were applied in the choice of texts (Purves, 1988): (1) all texts must be written in settings as similar as possible, i.e., both the audience and the purpose of the writings should be similar; (2) they must be consistent in their function and cognitive demands as well as in the specific subject matter; (3) the language must be defined. Since all texts are written in English and the entire text was used for each short story, this criterion is met; (4) the occupations of the writers should be similar. Most of the writers in this study are professional writers and university professors, and so the occupations are relatively similar; and (5) the educational level of all the writers must be similar.

Methodology

The corpus of approximately 300,000 words was scanned by Baker and Eggington into computer-readable format, checked for accuracy, tagged using

Biber's tagging program, and rechecked. A multidimensional factor analysis was conducted on the tagging count, as was a General Linear Models procedure with 'variety' as an independent variable and individual factors as dependent variables.

The purpose of the study was to ascertain whether the same differences in themes and constructions among the varieties as noted by linguists and literary scholars were maintained in the tagged corpus. One way to measure differences is to determine whether literary texts exhibit typical characteristics of oral communication. Biber's database consisted of several genres of both written and spoken English. The texts used in the study were compared to the results of Biber (1988) to determine whether the texts had more of the characteristics of written or spoken discourse. The program used linguistic tagging and factor analysis in order to find the frequency of select linguistic features associated with certain types of texts. The factors, based on constellations of linguistic features such as first-person pronoun or suasive verbs, are significant in that they are exponents of the following five dimensions within which texts can be located:

1. Involved vs. informational discourse
2. Narrative vs. non-narrative concerns
3. Explicit vs. situation-dependent reference
4. Overt expression of persuasion
5. Abstract vs. non-abstract information

Each dimension is on a continuum, so that a text is assigned a particular characteristic to different degrees. A personal letter scores high on Dimension 1, nearer to the 'involved side' of the continuum, because it usually employs first-person pronouns, active verbs and other relevant linguistic forms. By contrast, a scientific article scores closer to the 'informational' end of the continuum because it usually contains passive verbs and other indicative features. The analysis gave a score to each text for each dimension.

Hypotheses of the study

Baker and Eggington's first hypothesis was that the texts from the three non-Inner-Circle varieties of English — AfrE, IE and MexE — would be similar to each other on the five dimensions and would differ from the two 'standard' varieties, AmE and BrE.

Since Dimensions 1, 3 and 5 play crucial roles in determining the oral/literate dimensions of a text, the first hypothesis predicted that AfrE authors, from predominantly oral cultures, would score most closely to oral texts, followed by IE writers familiar with both oral and literary traditions, and the next would be MexE writers with formal training in English and an oral tradition in Spanish. On Dimensions 2 and 4, Baker and Eggington hypothesized that the AfrE, IE and MexE would score closer to texts written in the standard varieties on which they were based: MexE texts would score closer to AmE texts, whereas IE and AfrE texts would score closer to BrE texts.

Their second hypothesis was that texts from AmE and BrE would score very similarly to each other, as both are 'standard' and have relatively recently diverged from the same writing tradition.

Results

The five varieties and their mean scores on each of the dimensions are shown in a table, which is summarized below, where Dimensions 3 and 5 show statistical significance. This suggests that the texts differ in their use of linguistic characteristics related to spoken and written discourse.

The scores characterize the text type. Since the database consisted of short stories, high positive scores would be expected on Dimensions 1 and 2 (Involved vs. Informational, Narrative vs. Non-narrative) signalling a position towards the 'involved' and 'narrative' ends of the continua, and high negative scores on Dimensions 3–5 (Explicit vs. Situation-dependent, Overt Expression of Persuasion, Abstract vs. Non-abstract), indicating a position far from the 'explicit', 'persuasive' and 'abstract' ends.

The Dimension 1 trait 'involved' is attributable to conversational interaction in which interpersonal relations and more immediate ideas predominate. 'Informational', on the other hand, is a characteristic of scientific and technical texts in which precise information is conveyed succinctly. AfrE texts scored closer to AmE texts; both were more towards the 'involved' end of the continuum than the BrE, IE or MexE. In fact, MexE was the most 'informational' of the five Englishes.

Dimension 2 indicates conforming to a narrative style with select grammatical features, e.g., third-person pronouns, past-tense verbs that move events forward, devices such as reported speech that recreate scenes, etc., used in telling stories. Non-narrative texts, on the other hand, describe states with present-tense verbs and adjectives.[3] On this dimension, AfrE displayed the most narrative features as compared to the others. Dimension 3 demonstrates how much the writer takes for granted the readers' familiarity with the immediate context of the text. Oral texts typically score closer to the 'situation dependent' end, and would therefore have more negative scores for 'explicit reference'. AmE texts scored closest to the situation-dependent end of the scale.

The figures in Dimension 4 show 'how much the texts attempt to persuade the reader or how much they reveal the speaker's attitude and point of view' (p. 351). Modals, conditionals, suasive verbs such as *command, demand,* and *instruct,* and adjective and verb complements, e.g., *sad to have left, wanted to do right*, signal persuasion. BrE and IE texts scored very close to each other on this dimension. Scores on Dimension 5 are based on how technical, formal, and abstract the texts are, determined by the occurrence of passives (with or without agent), cohesive devices such as conjunctions, participial clauses, etc. Scores on Dimension 5 are low for fiction.

The authors' first hypothesis was supported by the scores of the AfrE texts: AfrE literary texts exhibit more traditional characteristics of oral texts than BrE texts do. AfrE texts ranked closer to the AmE text scores than to any other group. The results of this study confirm earlier research that examines AfrE language and literature. The prediction that MexE texts would also show typical characteristics of oral texts is falsified; their scores are closer to the written texts than even the BrE.

Explanations for findings

The authors speculate that the reason IE and BrE are so close may be either that IE writers are treating BrE writing as their model or that they are combining the features of two literary traditions (indigenous and BrE), or that they are expressing their creativity in metaphors and other literary devices rather than in grammar. AfrE writers, on the other hand, may be consciously trying to write their languages in English (see Chapter 10). They may also see the function of literature differently and view it as a political tool with a persuasive function, as the relatively high score on Dimension 4 suggests.

As for hypothesis 2, texts written in AmE differed greatly from those in BrE, contrary to the author's predictions about the two 'standard' varieties. In fact, AmE texts score closer to traditional oral texts than all other varieties of English. These results confirm Biber's (1987) earliest finding that American texts tend to be more informal than British texts, and that the reason bilingual texts differ from monolingual texts is the cultural and oral traditions of other languages in the writers' repertoires.

The authors suggest that methodologies and typologies that set monolingual writing as the norm need to be revised to include multi-norms of bilingual creativity. 'If the two established varieties of English (AmE and BrE) have differences between them, then we cannot assume that there is some sort of "standard" English writing style ... even in the traditional literary canon' (p. 355).

Conclusion

Research has established that not only the varieties in the Outer and Expanding Circles exhibit variation: Inner-Circle varieties are also subject to the same forces that result in change and difference. This has consequences for the description and codification of world Englishes, and for the ELT profession when considering norms, standards, models, and canonicity of English literatures.

Suggested activities

1. Look up the items *unless* and *anymore* in three regional dictionaries (e.g., The *Macquarie Dictionary, American Heritage Dictionary, Oxford Advanced Learner's Dictionary*). Discuss your findings in class.
2. This is an exercise in carrying out a small project in corpus analysis. A classification of the uses of the English definite article *the* is given in (I) below. Examine the Data in (II), and assign each occurrence of the article *the* in the data to a proposed class. List the exceptions, if any, and explain why they do not belong to any of the proposed classes.

    (I) Classification of Definite *the*

    A. Anaphoric (definite NPs that refer to a previous discourse entity).
        John bought a car. **The car/vehicle** *turned out to be a lemon.*

    B. Immediate Situation (definite NP used to refer to an object in the situation of utterance; it may be visible or inferred)
        At the dining table: *Please pass* **the salt!**
        Sign at the zoo: *Don't feed* **the bears!**

    C. Larger Situation (in which the speaker appeals to shared knowledge)
        Talking about lunch on a campus: *Shall we meet in* **the faculty dining room?**

    D. Associative Anaphoric (speaker and hearer may share knowledge of the relations between certain objects (the triggers) and their components and attributes (the associates):
        There was an accident at the intersection. **The car** *was smashed, but* **the driver** *escaped.*

    E. Unfamiliar (definite NPs that are not anaphoric, do not rely on information about the situation of utterance, and are not associates of some triggers in the previous discourse)

        a. NP Complements
            the fact/suggestion *that* ... , **the place** *where* ...

        b. Nominal Modifiers
            the colour *maroon,* **the number** *three*

c.   Referential Relative
     The book *that you were reading ...*

d.   Associative Clause (definite NPs that specify both the trigger and the associate)
     The OP ED page *of the NY Times ...*

e.   Unexplanatory Modifiers
     The Last person *to leave the party was an old woman.*

F.   Institutional ('sporadic reference' in Quirk et al.)
     The USA, The UN

G.   Fixed Collocations ('the logical use of *the*' in Quirk et al.)
     the first flight *to Denver,* ... *catch* **the last bus,** ...

H.   Generic
     the musk ox, the tiger ...

I.   Idioms
     a shot in **the arm**

(II) Data

Text 1:   This study examines the pragmatics of refusals among speakers of English and Arabic. It compares (a) the English language refusal strategies of samples of native English speakers, both in the United States and Egypt; (b) the English language refusal strategies of samples of Arab students of English, in the same two countries; and (c) the Arabic language refusal strategies of a sample of Arabic speakers in Egypt.

Data were elicited through a discourse-completion task modelled after Blum-Kulka and Olshtain (1984), designed to elicit various types of refusals, offers and invitations.

Analysis focuses on strategies expected to lead to either pragmalinguistic or sociopragmatic failure (Thomas, 1983) in the Arabic-speaking learners' refusals.
[Paul S. Stevens, The pragmatics of 'No!': Some strategies in English and Arabic. In *IDEAL* 6, 1993.]

Text 2:   ... Why does the developed world worry so much about sustainability? Because we constantly hear a litany of how the environment is in poor shape. Natural resources are running out. Population is growing, leaving less and less to eat. Species are becoming extinct in vast numbers. Forests are disappearing. The planet's air and water are getting ever more polluted. Human activity is, in short, defiling the earth — and as it does so, humanity may end up killing itself.

There is, however, one problem: this litany is not supported by the evidence. Energy and other natural resources have become more abundant, not less so. More food is now produced per capita than at any time in the world's history. Fewer people are starving. Species are, it is true, becoming extinct. But only about 0.7 percent of them are expected to disappear in the next 50 years, not the 20 percent to 50 percent that some have predicted. Most forms of environmental pollution look as though they have either been exaggerated or are transient — associated with the early phases of industrialization. They are best cured not by restricting economic growth but by accelerating it.

[Bjorn Lomborg, The environmentalists are wrong. *The New York Times*, 26 August 2002.]

17

Dictionaries of world Englishes

A. Abdul here has to go to the bank to get some cash, but he can't take a taxi unless he has some cash; it's a *vicious cycle*. I don't have my car ...

B. Let me *pick* him and take him to the bank. I guess he is in the library.

A. Yes, he is. *Goodbye* then.

B. *Thank you.*

Skandera (1999)

Introduction

The items in italics in the above constructed dialogue are difficult to understand for speakers of English not used to this variety. The word *pick* for the phrasal verb *pick up*, the idiomatic expression *vicious cycle* for *vicious circle*, and the response *Thank you* to *Goodbye* are all common in Kenyan English (Skandera, 1999), though they are not listed with these meanings in any dictionary familiar to most users of English (e.g., Oxford, Cambridge, Random House, Webster's, Longman's).

The role that dictionaries play in standardizing a language has been demonstrated effectively by the compilation of dictionaries of British English by Samuel Johnson, American English by Noah Webster, and more recently, the *Macquarie Dictionary* of Australian English (1981; see Butler [1992] for a historical overview of this project).

Sometimes we see titles that explicitly mention one or another world variety, but sometimes such a limitation or focus is only implied, requiring the association of the title with a specific publisher. As the varieties of world Englishes gain cohesion and visibility, we are beginning to see more regionally and nationally identifiable lexicographic material on the market. This chapter illustrates how readers can use existing dictionary entries (or other English-language sources, such as newspapers) from various countries (e.g., Australia, India, and Korea, from the Inner, Outer and Expanding Circles) to identify regional items. It also leads them to think about whether and how to include such items in language teaching materials.

Butler (1997) gives an overview of important considerations in collecting and deciding about the inclusion of items in a regional dictionary. Leitner and Sieloff (1998) offer a more focused example of how to go about discovering the current state of recognition of a historically important subset of a national variety's lexicon. The papers by Bautista (1997a) and Pakir (1992a), discussed here in some detail, represent the attempts at dictionary making in two national varieties: Philippine English (PhE) and Singaporean English (SE). Other national varieties will be referred to as pertinent, but not discussed in detail, although they have a long tradition of lexicography, e.g., Indian English (IE; see B. Kachru, 1980, 1983, 2005b, for details) and Caribbean English (CbE; for details, see Cassidy and LePage, 2003).

The Asian context

Butler (1997) explicitly articulates some of the things that people may think dictionaries can do, what they in fact can do, and what they might be able to do in the evolving world of Englishes. She notes in passing that some people believe that including or excluding a word in or from a dictionary will have some directly linked effect on the real world. She reports, for example, that someone wanted the word *cancer* removed as a means of eradicating the disease. Slightly less irrationally, some people wanted racist terms to be deleted, since they are offensive to one or another community. Butler, however, takes the position (pp. 90–1) that a dictionary is supposed to mirror the usage of a community in some broad sense, and if words are in widespread current use in some segment(s) of that community, it is not reasonable to leave them out.

Butler points out that in a more routine sense, the real effect of a dictionary is to provide support and assurance to people who may appeal to it for spelling or usage. Such general community agreement tells dictionary users, for example, that the Australian pronunciation 'filum', for *film*, will not be accepted as legitimate any time soon. This is an observation, as Butler emphasizes, not a fiat which establishes rightness or wrongness:

> [T]he dictionary appears to control these notions of standardness and non-standardness, acceptability and non-acceptability, desirability and non-desirability. Fortunately dictionary editors don't let this illusion go to their heads … We have no power to eradicate cancer, not even really to improve spellings. All we can do is describe the way things are to the best of our ability. (Butler, 1997: 91)

It is in a situation where standards compete that the 'right' of a word to be in the dictionary or not assumes huge importance. If a dictionary is a faithful recording of the usage of a community, then that right is assigned by the range and depth of occurrence of a given word: the dictionary has no control over the common usage; all it does is record the decision general use has made. However, once something is recorded in a dictionary, it assumes a degree of power and control over common usage. In situations such as those involving English in the Outer Circle, there can be conflicting demands from two standards — a well-documented, prestigious, outside standard and a poorly documented, de facto, internal standard. In such situations, the de facto forms are not recognized as legitimate by the sorts of people who might be expected to use a dictionary, i.e., the educated and highly literate. This is the sort of situation that obtained historically in Australia. Butler reports that in dealing with this situation, *The Macquarie Dictionary* (1981) presented in a very real form an image of the wholeness of Australian English, and as a direct consequence the false dichotomy between 'the Queen's English' and 'Aussie slang' quickly disappeared.

The impetus for publishing a dictionary naturally lies to a great extent in its projected marketing, of course. The audience for a dictionary which will serve the Southeast and South Asian regions are people who Butler refers to as 'cultivated' users of English, i.e., those who write and publish texts, use reference books, travel and encounter other Englishes, negotiate, and are involved in politics, tourism, teaching, the media, and commerce. These are the kinds of people who buy books and dictionaries.

A proposed Regional Dictionary for world Englishes in the Southeast Asian and South Asian context will include current lexical items in categories such as the following (p. 93 *ff.*; selected examples presented here):

New words and expressions; the examples include new definitions for old words, i.e., semantic shifting:

Aircon	*noun SE Asian English Colloquial* 1. airconditioning ... (96)
cyberspace	*noun* 1. a communications network ...
good call	*Colloquial* (an exclamation expressing approval for ... a good decision, analysis, etc.) (94)
rojak	*noun Singaporean and Malaysian English* ... 2. an ethnic or cultural mixture, expecially [*sic*] one that is unassimilated and crude ...
wannabe	*noun Colloquial* one who aspires to be something or someone specified: *a Madonna wannabe*... (95)

Localisms; this category includes borrowings and semantically shifted usages:

ABC *noun*	Australian- ... or American-born (usually in Hong Kong) Chinese [Malay a(ir) b(atu) c(ampur) mixed ice]
actsy	*adjective* conceited; proud ...
agak-agak	*verb* 1. to estimate (a quantity); guess ...

Collocations; drawing on the corpus (see below), 'common combinations of words' are presented:

Dance band, ~hall, ~floor, ~party ...; ballroom dance, bush ~, war ~, tribal
~. (eight items are listed with *dance* as the attributive element, and
fifteen with it as the head.)

Butler addresses the major categories of considerations that went into the conceptualization of the Regional Dictionary (see B. Kachru, 1983: 165–89 and Görlach, 1991a). With regard to aims and intended users, the work is expected to serve 'the average educated speaker of English in a range of countries in South-East Asia and South Asia' (p. 99).

In compiling the Regional Dictionary, the task is to 'present all the material, not just the new entries, from a regional point of view', without any Australian or other national bias. A phonemic pronunciation system will be used, so that users can read entry words as their varieties lead them to. The dictionary will be restricted to standard forms, including some informal forms, because to cover all spoken forms of all varieties would not be practical (p. 97).

The sources for items to be included are published materials, including fiction, non-fiction and newspaper writing, and selections of entries are moderated by the intuitions of a 'native' speaker of each variety of English in the region. The collected items go into a corpus, ASIACORP. The crucial criterion is that all the entry items be genuinely representative of the varieties of the authors from which they are drawn, not modifications made with broader international consumption in mind.

Frequency of occurrence of an item is an important consideration. If words occur only in specific texts or in the work of a particular author, then their listing would be a matter of how inclusive the dictionary is intended to be. The decision to use published materials and require confirmation of familiarity by native speakers of the given variety tends to weed out infrequent items. Butler speaks of 'boundaries' separating standard from nonstandard usage (pp. 103–4), and says that cultivated speakers would resist crossing this divide; they would only do so in particular contexts or for particular effect. The intended range of inclusion of items in the Regional Dictionary is such that it includes all of the standard written lexicon and pushes some way into the standard spoken form, depending on frequency in the corpus.

The result of such filtering is the determination of a central area of overlap, comprising those items that speakers of all varieties find acceptable, with a wide range of variety-specific items, regional or national, around the core. One clear concern is that restricting the corpus may seem to indicate a degree of prescriptivism; but the attempt at a non-prescriptive descriptivism rests on the combined resources of the collected items and the judgements solicited from speakers of the relevant varieties. The dictionary is intended to be neither 'a glossary of exceptions to an external norm' nor 'a complete account of any one variety' (p. 111).

It does not seem to be possible yet to do away completely with some degree of reference to external norms. Taking into account judgements about the market for the dictionary, Butler observes, '[t]he region distinguishes between British and American Englishes but varieties such as Scottish English or Jamaican English are not important to the region' (p. 113). An interesting consideration in this regard is that the usage of AmE or BrE may be a record of the stereotyping of the early twentieth century and not of current usage in these varieties. She notes that in some cases a British dictionary labels an item as American, and an American dictionary labels it British. This sort of observation bears strongly on the need for a real attempt to collect representative data from identifiably variety-specific sources. Butler refers to AusE in its relation to BrE and AmE as 'our position as a language community and a dictionary wedged between the two main players'. Like 'native speaker', people seem reluctant to give up the notion that any given English needs to be, if not identical to one of the two, then at least British-like or US-like.

Returning to questions of market and of British/US dominance, Butler says that the recognized validity of the dictionary as a representative resource for the Englishes of the region lies in 'the authority of the English language communities in the region as reflected in the corpus of English in Asia' (p. 113). Users in the countries represented should be able to acknowledge and have confidence in their language — the English that they actually use, not that they think they use, that they would like to use, or that they believe they should use. It is clear from observation that neither BrE nor AmE nor yet 'some bland creature called International English' is the English used in the countries of the region. This dictionary, like all such resource and teaching materials, should be recognizable and accepted as representative of each region's and nation's English. As Butler puts it, the power of a dictionary is 'to reveal to people what they already know, but haven't for a variety of reasons been able to acknowledge, that is, that they have an English all their own' (p. 123).

The Australian context

Related to the issues of inclusion of items and differentiation of varieties raised by Butler, Leitner and Sieloff (1998) address nativization of lexicon and 'homogenization' of varieties. Their study focuses on 'the vitality of lexical effects of language contact amongst selected Australian speakers [of English]' (p. 154).

Citing Dixon et al. (1990), Leitner and Sieloff (1998: 154) say that Aboriginal lexical items borrowed into 'Mainstream Australian English' (mAE) have been said to give the variety its clearest distinction as opposed to British or other varieties. A few of these words have spread beyond Australia and are familiar to virtually any British or American speaker, and to speakers of many other Englishes as well, for example, *boomerang, dingo, kangaroo, koala* and *walkabout,* while others are more likely to be considered unusual by speakers of other Englishes, e.g. *yabber* ('to talk incessantly') and *gunyah* ('a temporary shelter').

Similar to a point raised by Butler concerning the possible 'stereotyping' of British and US labels for given items, Leitner and Sieloff note that decisions to label items in mAE dictionaries as etymologically 'Aboriginal' are still loosely based on historical evidence. Various questions then arise, including the following:

* Are the items in current use?
* How restricted are they in terms of regions, styles or registers?
* Do they participate in the language at large, for example in acquiring 'extended or figurative meanings'? (p. 158)

To investigate the currency of lexical items of Aboriginal-language origin in mAE, the authors used a questionnaire, despite various problems that might arise with such a methodology, largely because of their lacking actual communicative intent. To elicit their responses, the researchers used the context of a foreigner's asking for help; for example:

> One of the most popular Australian songs is 'Waltzing Matilda.' And, yet, even foreigners with a quite good knowledge of English find it pretty hard to understand.
> What, for instance, do the following words mean to you?
> a billabong: . . .
> matilda . . .

Scoring of responses into three categories, *known, known to some extent* and *not known* was somewhat complex. Dixon et al. (1990), *The Macquarie Dictionary* and *The Australian National Dictionary* were used as the arbiters of correctness of responses. Answers that were not 'fully correct' might, for example, be too broad or not exactly fit the item, for instance 'tree' for *paddymelon*, where 'plant' would have been more appropriate (p. 158).

The researchers' overall conclusion about their list of eighty-eight lexical items (including some phrases, such as *point the bone at*) was that most of the Aboriginal expressions are not widely known among mAE speakers. Yet these are words characterized as giving Australian English a large measure of its distinctive character. Only twenty-one of the eighty-eight items were assigned to the 'known' category for more than 50 percent of respondents (p. 160); those items with the higher levels of recognition were from the subcategories of 'fauna, culture, and people' (p. 167); few of the words were found to be easily recalled by the speakers; and many of the older expressions are part of an archaic, much romanticized, layer of mAE lexis (p. 167).

These findings and considerations tell us that caution must be used when consulting dictionaries as 'codifying' resources. Both Butler's and Leitner and Sieloff's observations indicate the historical tendencies in such attempts to provide a holistic 'snapshot' of a language. In terms of their idea of 'homogenization', Leitner and Sieloff say: 'As such expressions fall into oblivion or are replaced by more transparent loan translations, hybrids, etc., the process of nativization may partly be reversed. AmE appears to be becoming more similar again to other varieties of English world-wide' (1998: 167).

This may be somewhat overstated. That this particular lexical set of words from Aboriginal-language sources may be diminishing in currency seems clear from the reported research; however, there are so many other features of Australian English that lend it its distinctiveness, including other lexical sets, that there seems little likelihood of its becoming 'homogenized' with, say, British or American.

Philippine English

Bautista (1997a) lists the sources from which items could be drawn for inclusion in a PhE dictionary. The starting point was the Macquarie Asian Corpus — a database of published works of fiction and non-fiction, and English language newspapers from Hong Kong, the Philippines, Malaysia and Singapore. Macquarie aimed at identifying items that did not appear in the headwords of the Australian English dictionary and sending them to experts of the respective national varieties. These respondents provided definitions and recommended inclusion in or exclusion from the Asian dictionary and provided the definition of selected items. The lists were then sent to larger groups of speakers of the national varieties for their feedback.

The Asian Corpus database provides attestations, numbers of occurrences of specific items, and their sources. However, it is based on printed sources and captures only the more formal uses of English in the communities' repertoire. Therefore, Bautista includes in her discussion items that occur in works on Philippine English by scholars such as Alberca, Cruz, Llamzon, Gonzalez, Tabor, and her own work (pp. 49–50; all page references henceforth are to Bautista [1997a], unless otherwise specified). The focus is still on the educated speech at the acrolectal end of the repertoire; the less educated varieties, such as *yaya* English and *bargirl* English are not included in the discussion.

Bautista cites the general lexicographers' belief that a lexicon develops by (a) normal expansion of the range of items, (b) retention of older items that may have dropped out of the source language, (c) making up of new items, and (d) borrowing from other languages. Expansion of range may involve extending the semantic range of items or changing their grammatical category for use in novel ways. Familiar examples are 'kleenex' for 'facial tissue', and 'to xerox' for 'to copy' in general. An example of extension in PhE from the Asian Corpus is: *band-aid* [a brand name for a self-adhesive patch to cover small wounds] to mean 'a self-adhesive patch' in general. The citation in the Asian Corpus reads (p. 51):

> There are anti sea-sickness tablets, and even a circular "band-aid" to place behind the ear about an hour before departure.

Other lexical items, not brand names, whose semantic range is different in PhE include: *brown-out* to mean failure of electricity; *open* to mean switch on and *close* to mean switch off electricity, and *bath* to mean shower, too (this use is shared by many other varieties, including SAE). One item which has an opposite meaning in PhE when compared with other varieties is the word *salvage*. In PhE *salvage* means 'to kill in cold blood, usually used when police or soldiers kill suspects before trial, i.e., summary execution — a meaning that came into existence only during the Marcos years, and found resonance because of its Spanish overtones, *salvaje* meaning bad; *sinalbahe siya*→ *na-salvage siya*→ he was salvaged' (p. 53).

Change in grammatical category, often accomplished by derivational affixes, is seen in items such as *fiscalize* 'to call attention to abuse'. According to Bautista, *The Macquarie Dictionary* has an entry for *fiscal* meaning a public prosecutor, but no listing of *fiscalize* as a verb. Use of mass nouns as count nouns (such as *equipment* and *research*, not only in the plural but also with the article *a* in singular) is attested frequently in PhE, as it is in other varieties (see Chapter 3). Use of new verb-preposition constructions, such as *based from*, *result to*, *cope up with*, *fill up* (*a form*; the latter two in SAE also), are attested. One new collocation is *all what* meaning 'all that' or 'everything', as in *Let's do all what we can to make the Conference a success* (p. 56).

The second category, retention of archaisms, is seen in items such as a widened use of the term *solon* meaning a lawmaker, *viand* meaning an item of food, *folk* collocating with *barrio, Quiapo,* etc. and *nary* ('no/none'), which is rarely used in other varieties (pp. 56–57).

Neologisms, the third category, based on analogy, clipping, compounding, abbreviations and complete innovations, are all attested in PhE. Some examples are: *carnapper* [AmE 'carjacker'], *jubilarian, reelectionist,* and *studentry* [student body], as in the following (p. 59):

> Your alma mater may be having a homecoming soon. Why wait till you're a *jubilarian?*

> A *Non-reelectionist* in fact is a Stronger Leader than a *Reelectionist.*

> On the face of it, however, the school's official should be commended for seeking to teach a "culture of peace" among the *studentry,* an effort that could have far-reaching effects ...

Clippings in PhE are represented by items such as *ball pen* [ball point], *aircon* [also in SME, and Hong Kong Varieties], *Amboy* [too pro-American], *kinder* [kindergarten], and *sem* [semester]. These are comparable to items such as *funda* for *fundamental,* and *disco* for *disciplinary committee* (note the witticism in the latter), commonly used on university and college campuses in IE. Abbreviations such as NGO are common in all varieties of English, but the following are characteristic of PhE (p. 61): *DH* (domestic help), *KJ* (kill joy), KKB (*kanya-kanyang bayad* or go Dutch), TNT (*tago-ng-tago,* illegal immigrant Filipinos in hiding in the host country) and TY (thank you).

Total neologisms, a common process shared by many varieties, are items made up of parts of words, such as *Imeldific* (anything exaggeratedly ostentatious or in bad taste), *Taglish* (Tagalog-English code-switching), *eat-and-run* (going to a party, eating and leaving without any socializing), *presidentiable* (likely presidential candidate), and *trapo* (traditional politician, same as a Tagalog word for dirty rag).

Compounding is very productive process in all varieties and PhE is no exception. Some examples of variety-specific compounds are: *blue-seal* (imported cigarettes, later transferred to foreign girl-friends), *dirty kitchen* (a kitchen where real cooking is done in affluent households rather than the kitchen for show that the owner may use sometimes), *captain ball* (captain of a basketball or baseball team), and *whistle bomb* (firecracker that makes a whistling sound). Hybrid compounding, with one item from a language of the Philippines is also a productive process (for the same process in IE, see B. Kachru, 1983). Examples are *bakya crowd* (lower-class crowd), *common tao* (ordinary Filipino), and *turo-turo restaurant* (fast-food place where one points to the dishes one wants to order) (pp. 63–67).

The last category, borrowings from substrate or contact languages, have enriched all varieties of English. PhE has also added to its lexicon from a number of languages, including Spanish, Chinese, Japanese English, and Tagalog. The semantic fields where such borrowings have occurred are flora and fauna, food, national identity or culture, politics, general items including kinship and address terms, and certain discourse markers such as *daw* or *kuno* 'it is said', 'according to the grapevine', *sayang!* 'what a pity, what a waste, how unfortunate', and *no?* (combining *no* of English and *ano* 'what' of Tagalog).

Singaporean English

Discourse markers or particles in SE are the topic of Pakir (1992a). This study is narrower in scope than Bautista (1997a), but raises important issues regarding inclusion of items that have three characteristics not shared by ordinary lexical items and idioms: they occur in speech and not in formal writing; they are not strictly lexical items with meaning(s); and they are borrowed into English and are multifunctional. These features make it difficult to provide concise and accurate dictionary definitions.

Pakir (1992a) chooses as examples two items that occur in Singaporean and Malaysian English speech in a variety of contexts: *la* and *what*. Like discourse markers in English (e.g., *oh, well, now, y'know,* etc.), they do not add to the propositional content of utterances, but do add communicative meaning to them. They modify the meaning of utterances by signalling the attitude of the speaker, thereby adding affective meaning. Thus, they play pragmatic roles in Singaporean and Malaysian English (SME). Pakir, referring to earlier work on these particles (p. 144; all page references from here onward are to Pakir [1992a], unless otherwise specified), lists their formal characteristics as follows: they are not obligatory; they do not occur independently; their positions of occurrence are sentence-final, clause-final or phrase-final; they have multiple meanings; and their meanings are tied to intonation and tonicity.

Both *la* and *what* have two forms: short and long. Both forms of *la* occur with falling intonation, and the short *la* seems to occur more frequently. Their occurrence is exemplified in the following utterances (p. 144):

Short *la*

    A. Well, you might be going end of this year, right?
    B. Ya, possibly, hopefully. If everything is together *la.*

Long *la*

    A. They're picky, right? They want Honors Grads.
    B. No *la.*
    C. Ya *la.*

According to Pakir, the long *la* may be accompanied by high pitch, signalling speaker impatience or annoyance (p. 144).

Examples of short and long *what* are given in the following examples (p. 145):

Short *what*

1. I am your friend *what* (indicates: 'isn't it obvious?')

Long *what*

2. Friend friend only *what* (expresses: objection; indignation)

According to Pakir, most occurrences of *what* are with falling tone, and when they do occur with rising tone, they coincide with the ordinary function of the question word *what* (p. 145).

The difficulty of establishing the source, uses and functions of the particles *la* has been recognized in earlier literature as well. Sources of *la* have been many: from Malay, Mandarin, Hokkien, and Cantonese. Platt and Ho (1989: 221) suggest that the diverse population of Malaysia and Singapore, speaking Malay and several dialects of Chinese, displays differing levels of competence in English. It is thus quite likely that the particle in some speakers' English reflects its functions in Chinese, whereas in others' English, it is just a carrier of pitch movement. Chan (1991: 213) argues that the particle serves two functions: one of signalling a shared feature of SME, therefore of camaraderie with other SME speakers, and the other of playing a role in the tonicity of the tone unit. Other researchers have identified the functions of *la* as one of a code-marker, an affective item, and a marker of emphasis and contrastive focus (Pakir 1992a: 146–7). Wilma (1987) lists the following pragmatic meanings of *la* (cited by Pakir, 1992a: 146): pointing out the obviousness of some phenomenon, softening the effect of an utterance so that it sounds like a suggestion rather than a command, softening an explanation so that it does not sound harsh, dismissing an unimportant part of a long utterance, deflecting compliments, and conveying a lack of enthusiasm for something.

The particle *what* presents equal complexity. According to Smith (1985), cited by Pakir (1992a: 147), *what* signals that the speaker is objecting to something as unjustified or unimportant and the co-text usually makes it obvious what the grounds for such objections are. The following utterances exemplify this use. X and Y are discussing a student who is going overseas and will miss classes for one month:

> X: He'll never pass the third year.
> Y: It's only for one month *what*.

X has been rebuked for spitting on the floor and A is telling about it:

> A: He also spits *what*. (p. 147)

Having discussed the source and function of *la* and *what*, Pakir (1992a: 147–8) takes up the question of whether the particles are a feature of substandard MSE or colloquial educated SME. According to Platt and Ho (1989: 220), only three particles occur along the whole lectal continuum, except in formal situations where considerable self-monitoring takes place. These are *a*, *la* and *what*. They also note that *la* and *what* occur in the informal speech of educated speakers of English more frequently than other discourse markers.

The suggested sample dictionary entries have the following headings: Head Word, Part of Speech, Pronunciation, Language Label (informal, spoken, etc.), Definition and Etymology:

> Usage note:
>
> You use *what*
> 1.1 In a retort to convey disapproval or to register objection to a suggestion, complaint.
> 1.2 In a retort to convey annoyance, impatience, irritation.
> 1.3 In reference to an action/viewpoint attributed to a third party.
> 1.4 To share information.
> 1.5 To express indignation, protecting oneself or one's point of view.
> 1.6 To show up what is obviously so, etc.
>
> *What* functions (objection with a challenging note, expression of obviousness with impatience and irritation, expression of indignation, expression of boldness or definite opinions, etc.) would indicate that only individuals whose solidarity and familiarity levels are high would use it among themselves, and never at the formal level. However, for uneducated speakers of the English language formality level does not seem to matter much. All speakers of Singapore English use the *what* particle in their informal conversations, with friends and family members. A feature of informal Singapore English (Pakir, 1992a: 150–1).

Pakir concludes by saying that the suggested entries are tentative at this point and need further research on the functions and stylistic variation on the one hand and the phonological aspects of pitch and tonicity on the other hand.

Conclusion

The papers discussed above raise various important considerations for study and appreciation of the lexicons of world Englishes. It seems clear that there is a 'core' of common vocabulary items across world Englishes which is very large, in terms of absolute numbers. The uses that are made of these items and how they combine and extend themselves add a great deal of the identifiable character to any given variety, bringing out the broad reaches of the intuitive nature of people's use of language. How one learns or acquires English, in what circumstances of a given circle and to what degree of educational formality, may determine the amount of a user's reliance on a dictionary. Observations from these papers indicate that, far from being some sort of 'holy writ' for language learners and users, dictionaries are human-made tools, which must be used with a good deal of rational awareness and attention.

Suggested activities

1. Look in newspapers aimed at 'a local market', e.g., small-city or town newspapers from your area, as opposed to nationally distributed ones (e.g., in the US, *The New York Times*, or in Britain, *The Times*). Scan 'breaking news' stories from the area, the editorial pages and readers' letters to the editor. What lexical items, phrases, or idioms can you identify that are not parts of the broader standard language for your nation or region? Are they in the dictionary? (What dictionary?) Under what circumstances and for what purposes might you include them in ELT materials?

2. Using internet resources, compare editorials and nationally/regionally relevant news stories (vs. international ones) in major newspapers from Britain, Australia, the US, India, Nigeria, Singapore, or any other country you are interested in. What distinctive features of lexis and style do you detect? Do you see signs in the data you examined that English is becoming 'homogenized' in its lexis?

18

Code-mixing and code-switching

mɛ̃ to PURE hindī bolnā LIKE kartī hū̃. MIX karne kā to QUESTION hī nahī̃ uṭhtā. apnī DAUGHTER aur SONS ko bhī PURE hindī bolne ko ENCOURAGE kartī hū̃.

"I like to speak pure Hindi. The question of mixing Hindi and English does not arise. I also encourage my daughter and sons to speak pure Hindi."

K. Sridhar (personal communication)

Introduction

A well-recognized phenomenon in the speech of bilingual or multilingual people (hereafter, the inclusive term 'multilingual' will be generally used) is the appearance of items, phrases and longer strings of speech in two or more languages or codes in the utterances of individual participants. South Asian English speakers quite typically will employ, for example, Hindi and English in their conversations, in blocks of speech that have not proven easy to identify in terms of the linguistic structures involved. The points in sentences or discourse which seem to allow or to cause speakers to switch from language A to B and back again have likewise defied straightforward categorization. For users of this volume who have access to multilingual speakers, observed and/ or recorded conversations will serve as sources of data for investigation of this topic; for those not so fortunately situated, media broadcasts, newspapers and literature will provide examples of how codes are mixed to achieve certain communicative goals.

The phenomenon of code-mixing

Tay (1993a: 125) seeks to show how code-mixing works 'as a communicative strategy in multilingual communities among proficient bilingual speakers'; that is, code-mixing is itself a communicative act that has significance for the participants in a verbal exchange. While speakers sometimes may make a conscious choice to code-mix, perhaps in much the same way that a monolingual speaker would consider 'just the right words' for a special purpose, the example from Sridhar at the beginning of this chapter indicates that speakers may engage in code-mixing as a natural and unconscious language act.

The following example from Tay's data provides a sample of this sort of discourse, especially for users of this volume who have not experienced code-mixing first-hand (1993a: 139; format somewhat edited; Mandarin and Hokkien transcriptions in italics):

> Oh I see, *guài bú dè* ('no wonder' [Mandarin])...*wŏ xíe yīng wén bī jiào kuài* ('I write faster in English' [Mandarin]), *gùa sìa eng bóon lūan jú tu lūan jú sìa* ('when I write English, I simply scribble and write, carelessly' [Hokkien]), *jĭarú* ('if' [Mandarin]) move *dè* (particle [Mandarin]) fast, *bŏ tèk khàk o* ('not sure' [Hokkien]) *Dùi bú qĭ* ('sorry' [Mandarin]). I got to go.

It is easy to see from even such a small bit of conversation, with *nine switches* among *three languages*, that a monolingual English speaker is at a serious disadvantage in a conversation with a multilingual Singaporean. Put less dramatically, multilingual speakers have at their disposal shades of sense and 'texture' that may not be easy for monolinguals to have any feeling for, though they can understand the phenomenon.

Another such extended example is provided by an e-mail message to Yamuna Kachru in which Hindi is embedded in English. The writer was reacting to the death of a family member:

> ... I think she knew that the end was near as she gave ... all kinds of instructions. She was very lucky as she went the way as we all would like to go — almost *chalte phirte*. She was absolutely free of any obligation from anyone — no one had the time to do *sewa* for her — she was really lucky.
>
> The tenth day and the 11th day functions went well ... They are planning to go to Hardwar on Monday. I will tell you *pucca* tomorrow.
>
> Love to all, I had better sleep and rest my legs as I am the only young *buddhi* here or my legs will *jawab denge.*

In this very intimate text, it is clear that the writer assumed that the recipient would understand the Hindi elements: *chalte-phirte* 'walking and moving', i.e., all one's limbs in perfect working order; *sewa* 'service', i.e., loving care of someone; *pucca* 'definitely'; *buddhi* 'old woman'; 'legs will *jawab denge*', 'legs will buckle' (literally 'give up'). While at least one of the elements, *sewa*, may be a necessary choice because it represents cultural elements of the situation, there seems to be no 'reason' for the other choices, such as *pucca*, which is no obvious improvement on or refinement of its English equivalent 'definitely'.

Indeed, sometimes the 'switched-to' elements constitute a majority of the mass of the text, as in the following Indian English newspaper headline (*Indian Express*, New Delhi, 18 August 2002):

> James Lyngdoh *ko gussa kyon ata hai?*
> 'What makes James Lyngdoh angry?'

The reference is to Chief Election Commissioner James Michael Lyngdoh of India; the item is about the timing of state elections in Gujarat following the communal riots in which thousands of people were killed. Although the paper is an English-medium publication, this entire headline except for the personal names is in Hindi.

It is significant that Tay's title intimates directly that switching and mixing are 'a' strategy: indeed, one of her first points of discussion concerns the plausibility of distinguishing them from one another. Usual working definitions assign *switching* to alternations of codes across sentences, and *mixing* within sentences. Tay appeals to the example cited above to show that her Singaporean data do not support making the distinction. The first sentence, which contains English and Mandarin, would be considered mixing under the working definitions, while the next two sentences, which are in Mandarin and Hokkien, would be representative of switching, since they are alternations across sentences, and are both complete sentences. 'Yet to classify the entire exchange in this way, as an alternation between code switching and code mixing, seems counter-intuitive. It breaks up the discourse in a way which does not reflect the total communicative impact' (p. 127).

Further, Tay asserts that the difficulty of distinguishing between grammatical systems and the uncertainty of which language the various often-used particles of Singaporeans' conversation should be assigned to also blur the putative distinction between the two related phenomena. Throughout the rest of her paper, she uses the two terms interchangeably. Chan (2003: 3) supports this view; he assumes that it is unnecessary to make the various distinctions found in the literature, such as *switching* as opposed to *mixing* and *intra-sentential* as opposed to *inter-sentential* switching.

For Inner-Circle speakers of English who have studied other languages in classroom settings, code-mixing is likely to be a new, even startling phenomenon. Using an English word in French as a foreign language class constitutes going outside the code under focus, and is a 'mistake'. In such cases, the motivation for using the 'foreign' word would be the simple pragmatic goal of substituting for an unknown element in what one is trying to say. This is a plausible but incorrect first assumption about the nature of code-switching: one might think that speakers are filling gaps in their linguistic repertoires by employing a familiar term from another language. Tay stresses that the speakers from whom she gathered the data for her study, representing typical Singaporean speakers, were all well-educated and comfortably multilingual in the languages they used (p. 126). This is the general observation to be made of spontaneous code-switching in conversation.

Unlike mixing, *borrowing* does function to provide necessary elements that do not exist in the matrix language. Further, borrowed items often undergo phonological and morphological assimilation, as in US English *latte* or *frappé*, which are pronounced by many people as 'la-te' and 'frapp', in accordance with some sorts of 'nativization' criteria. In contrast, code-mixing may utilize the whole range of the elements of the languages available to the speaker. These codes undergo mergers of various sorts: Tay speaks to 'the use of particles, and common categories of tense and aspect, number and concord', which characterize informal exchanges among Singaporeans. For example, particles such as /le/ and /á/ 'with a rising intonation' occur not only in patently mixed speech, but also in utterances which are otherwise all in English. This shows that, although the particles originate in Chinese languages, 'they have taken on a wide range of ... meanings when used in Singaporean English. *Non*-Chinese Singaporeans ... seem familiar with the meanings conveyed by their use' (p. 128, emphasis added).

The pragmatics of code-switching

A great deal of attention has been given to trying to determine the junctures in speech at which natural code-mixing may occur, and why they allow this flexibility. Two of the most studied criteria have been the *equivalence constraint* and the *free morpheme constraint*. Citing Sridhar and Sridhar (1980), who proposed a 'dual structure principle', Tay notes that constraints relating to 'equivalence' have to do with the structures of constituents or whether constituents from language A may occur in particular positions in B. The Singaporean data do not support these attempts at formulated constraints, however. For instance, in one item from her data, a code-mixed example follows neither the word order of constituents in Teochew nor in English (p. 131).

The free morpheme constraint, cited from Poplack (1980), refers to the putative impossibility of switching across free-bound morphemes. However, Tay offers such examples as Singaporean *kuning*, where the English bound morpheme *–ing* is attached to the Hokkien word *kun* meaning 'sleep' (p. 131). Thus, appeals that focus on linguistic structure of constituents or elements seem not to account for the Singaporean data.

Chan (2003: 1) asserts as his major thesis that '[t]here are no specific syntactic constraints on code-switching. Code-switching utterances are constrained by the same grammar, the same set of mechanisms which constrains monolingual utterances.' He also dismisses the concept of any 'third grammar' that serves to combine or coordinate the two grammars involved in the simple cases of code-switching, i.e. those involving just two languages. (Obviously, an extra-grammar proposal becomes a more complex issue when more languages are involved, as with Tay's Mandarin-Hokkien-English data.) Chan points out that a proposal that appeals to a third grammar when the data can be accounted for without it is theoretically uneconomical (pp. 57–8). In addition, a claim to cognitive economy says that there is no need to postulate a *latent* ' "code-switching grammar" or a set of "code-switching constraints' " in the language competences of *monolingual* speakers, which would be a consequence of proposing such a facility for any speaker who might at some time become multilingual.

Chan also refers to Sridhar and Sridhar (1980), which he characterizes as a 'pioneering' attempt to move explanations of code-switching away from ties to any third grammar (p. 49). Sridhar and Sridhar proposed 'two stages' in the construction of a code-switched utterance, one of which forms the 'guest' components in accordance with the grammar of that language, and a second one which introduces that construction into the sentence frame in more or less the same way as the speaker would insert corresponding 'host' language constituents, without any appeal to an external grammar.

As Chan summarizes the situation regarding the rules that govern code-switching, 'research on syntactic constraints in code-switching has brought about a state of indecision' (p. 56). While code-switching does not seem to be random (without constraints of any sort), proposals about those constraints have thus far been refuted by counter-examples from live data. For example, Chan cites Belazi, Rubin and Toribio's (1994: 228) Functional Head Constraint. 'Functional head' refers to the governing syntactic element in a phrase, such as the preposition in a prepositional phrase – *to* is the functional head in *to the movies*, and the complementizer *that* is the functional head of a *that*-clause (e.g., *He said **that he was sick***). The proposed Functional Head Constraint, then, asserts that the language that is used for the head element must be used for the elements that it governs: for example, don't mix English and Hindi within a prepositional phrase, or don't use English for the main verb in a verb phrase such as '*enjoy* going to the movies' and Hindi for the complement verb *going*.

However, Chan (2003: 35–6) notes that Bhatt (1995) and Mahootian and Santorini (1996: 471) provide counter-data, as in an example involving auxiliary verb in Italian and main verb in French (cited from Di Sciullo, Muysken and Singh 1986: 15), which is ruled out by the FH Constraint:

> No *parce que*   hanno *donné des cours*
> No because have given   of the lectures
> 'No, because they gave lectures'

In this example, the Italian auxiliary *hanno* is followed by the French content verb *donné*.

Chan also provides a counter-example (pp. 36–7) which involves switching between a negative (NEG) and verb phrase VP in a Cantonese-English switched utterance:

> ngo5 [m4 [$_{VP}$ *quantify my life in hours*]]
> I   NEG   quantify my life in hours
> 'I don't quantify my life in hours.'

Since the Cantonese negative element is the Functional Head of the constituent, it should be followed by a Cantonese verb phrase; however, the phrase occurs in English.

Another such counter-example is provided by the following, in which English is embedded in Hindi [TV programme, *Glimpses of India*, 30 July 2003]:

> Gopalpur ek choṭā sā *fishing village* hɛ, *famous for its beaches*. Yah *lake* itnā baṛā hɛ ki *you can't tell* ki kahā *lake* khatam hotā hɛ aur ākāsh shurū.
>
> 'Gopalpur is a fishing village, famous for its beaches. This lake is so big that you can't tell where the lake ends and the sky begins.'

There are two complementizers *ki* from Hindi in the above example, one of which is followed by a complement clause in English, in violation of the FH Constraint. Thus, it seems that seeking constraints of grammatical utterances in accounting for code-mixing or switching may lead researchers down a blind alley.

Azuma (1996b: 366) proposes a 'stand alone principle' to account for data that are recalcitrant to any account in terms of free morpheme or syntactic constraints. He suggests that the following principle may account for code-switching: 'A "chunk", any segment that can meaningfully stand alone in the speaker's mind, may be code-switched.' It is hard to reconcile this claim with examples such as the following in Hindi-English code-mixed utterances (from a conversation between two young friends):

> You take a small bit of *āṭā* and *belo*fy it and then *talo* it to make *puri*s.
> 'You take a small bit of the dough and roll it out and then fry it to make *puris*.'

One could perhaps say that the plural ending –*s* has a semantic content and therefore it can 'stand alone meaningfully' and that makes *puri*-s a viable expression. But that does not account for *belo*-fy where 'fy' has no semantic content; it is merely a derivational morpheme that changes substantives or nominals into verbals. The really interesting fact is that Hindi *bel-nā* 'to roll out (dough)' is a verb and does not need to be verbalized; *belo* is the familiar imperative form. Examples such as these show that structural or formal explanations do not go very far in accounting for the data in code-switching or -mixing.

Code-switching/mixing as communication

Another category of explanations for code-switching focuses on its functions. Tay discusses six categories. *Quotations* or reports of quotations (e.g., 'She said, "I'm going to study tomorrow" '/ 'She told me [that] she was going to study tomorrow') tend to occur in the language that the original speaker used. This intuitively appealing claim is supported by Tay's data (p. 132). Chan, however, while acknowledging the plausibility of this proposal and the frequency of data which supports it, calls such a categorical claim 'simplistic' (p. 290). Another 'natural' category would seem to be *Addressee specification*, mixing which directs 'the message to one of several possible addressees', supported by an example in Tay's data (p. 132).

Interjections are said to resist switching, but Tay's examples do not support the claim. She points out that her Singapore data illustrate the numerous and frequently used particles which occur no matter which language is dominant. The particles cannot be regarded 'as mere interjections or sentence fillers' since they convey a lot of speakers' attitudinal information which cannot be inferred from the rest of the utterance, thus are pragmatically important. *Reiteration* of information in a second code may 'clarify', 'amplify' or 'emphasize' a part of a message. This is a function that Tay's examples do seem to support.

According to Tay, *Personalization versus Objectivization*, which has to do with the degree of speaker involvement or distance from a message, is a usefully explanatory criterion. Tay says that this function has to do with the communicative aspect which she wishes to propose as the real impetus of code-mixing. In regard to a particular example, she observes:

> ... the varying degrees of personal involvement in the same topic ... probably explains the frequent switches between English and the other languages. Typically, the more involved the speaker became and the more determined she was about making her comments and criticisms known, the more Teochew and Hokkien appeared in the discourse. (Tay, 1993a: 134)

Code-mixing seems, then, to rest on a bilingual's competence in creative use of language and is a communicative choice which necessarily draws on linguistic structure as such, but also on the message and the speaker's intentions (p. 135).

Chan writes that code-switching operates pragmatically in just the same ways as non-code-switched speech. That is, speakers make choices that will serve immediate needs of politeness, face-saving, increasing or decreasing distance from conversational participants, and so on; it is just that multilingual speakers have greater ranges of options than do monolinguals. Further, Chan suggests that 'code-switching is also *a textualization cue* which gives hints to the listeners about how the forthcoming discourse is to be interpreted differently from the preceding utterances' (as in a reported quotation indicating a change of speaker). Such an interpretation is supported by the following examples involving English in Japanese bank ads (from Azuma, 1996a). According to Azuma, in addition to the prestige factor, core borrowing (i.e., borrowing of an item equivalent to an already existing item in Japanese) can function as face-saving strategy in interaction between Japanese speakers. This assertion is supported by examples such as the following:

1. **Roon** de   kuruma wo katta no?
   loan   by   car   acc. bought Q
   Did you take a loan to buy the car?

2. *Kyassinngu wa anshin dekiru*   *kyooki*   *kamee*   *no   mise   de.*
   cashing   topic feel secured can organization member   Gen shop at
   Please get a loan from the member shops of the organization.

The use of straight Japanese *shakkin-site* 'loan-did' in place of *roon de* 'loan by' in (1) would be more face-threatening to the addressee since it would imply that the person taking the loan has no control over his/her finances. The borrowed item *roon* 'loan' has no such implication; instead, it probably has the flavour of a usual transaction, as in the West, where car-buying is usually 'financed' by the seller or a bank. Similarly, the use of the item *kyassinngu* 'cash' in (2), also a bank advertisement, conveys the image of a modern customer instead of the image of a financially encumbered loan-seeker.

A notable aspect of the multilingual situation in Singapore is that the nation's languages — English, Hokkien, Mandarin, etc. — exist in such proximity and frequency of use that there has developed 'a common core vocabulary' which is available even to those who do not speak the source languages of the lexical items: 'An important part of the vocabulary used in code ... mixing will consist of this common core vocabulary' (Tay, 1993a: 135). Tay claims that a common grammatical system involving tense, aspect, number and concord also serves to make the use of spoken English, Malay and Chinese languages similar in Singapore.

As has been mentioned before, the communicative intent imparted to an utterance may involve creating rapport or distance between the speaker and other participants, and establishing group identity or distance. Tay comments on three strategies which are used to convey these various aspects of intent.

Particles such as /la/, /ha/ and /a/ seem to be used to establish rapport, but, says Tay, these have received little study relative to how important they seem to be for informal Singaporean conversation (see, however, Chapter 13). The meaning or depth of attitudinal richness is apparently tied to the ethnicity or language facility of the conversational participants.

Second, the choice of code seems to rest upon the speaker's sense of 'colourfulness', 'expressiveness' and 'economy'; if saying something in English requires a longer phrase than the Mandarin equivalent, then the latter will be chosen. Lexical items have acquired new connotations, and these derivations and uses are areas calling for further research. Third, in conveying attitudes, 'the use of particles seems to take the place of intonation patterns' used for the same sorts of purposes in other situations. The data raise questions of what shared assumptions are appealed to in participants' utterances and reactions to others' speech, and this area also calls for more study.

The expressive use of two languages from a repertoire is exploited in popular media such as newspapers, songs and films. An example from an Indian popular song about the conditions that are conducive to experiencing love in the contemporary Indian metropolis is illustrative (lyrics by Sameer, music by Anu Malik; the Hindi items are in italics, the English items are in their regular spelling, and a line-by-line translation is on the right):

disco *mẽ* dance *honā cāhiye*	'There should be disco dancing'
kabhī kabhī chance *honā cāhiye*	'Sometimes there should be a chance'
coke popcorn wafer *honā cāhiye*	'There should be coke, popcorn, wafers'
khālī khālī theater *honā cāhiye*	'There should be an empty theater'
motor bike *par jānā cāhiye*	'(One) should go on a motor bike'
are bār bār break *lagānā cāhiye*	'(One) should apply the break frequently'
hameshā alert *honā cāhiye*	'(One) should always be alert'
thoṛā thoṛā flirt *honā cāhiye*	'(One) should flirt a little'

The lyric has very little semantic content; the English items create an impact that is humorous and the song makes fun of Westernized youth culture in big cities.

Conclusion

It is clear that limiting the study of code-mixing to a linguistic or functional point of view per se will fail to capture the ways in which English (and other languages) have been adapted in the Singaporean and other speech communities. Because of the obvious involvement and creative adaptation on the part of the users of languages, they must be studied 'as independent systems'; trying to discover and interpret phenomena as incorrect deviations from one or another standard language will not produce cogent analyses (Tay, 1993a: 137):

> Much of the meaning potential that is contained, for example, in the particles, and in the use of English in code-mixed … utterances would have been lost if Singaporean English were considered merely a deviant form of British English.

Tay notes as well that the obvious well-established uses of and speakers' fluency in Singaporean English rule out considering it a 'learner variety'; those who use the language in the speech community are not learners. Code-mixing among Singaporean English speakers is 'motivated by the desire to communicate as effectively and expressively as possible', utilizing the codes available in their repertoire. This 'expressiveness', or bilingual creativity, has resulted in a situation in which 'Singaporean English has become far richer than, for example, British English, because of its contact with other languages spoken in Singapore; Singaporean Mandarin is also … richer than … Peking Mandarin for the same reason' (p. 138).

Code-mixing is shown above to be a matter of communicative choices on the parts of conversational participants who have more than one language available to them (see also the studies in Bhatia and Ritchie, 1989; Bhatt, 1996; Kamwangamalu, 1989, 1996; Myers-Scotton, 1996; Sridhar and Sridhar, 1980, among others, for contexts other than that of Singapore). The data and interpretations indicate that a concept of bilingualism as comprising various discrete language entities does not serve to describe what goes on in comfortable code-mixed exchanges (Sridhar and Sridhar, 1980). As Tay puts it (p. 138), 'form is to be perceived as the outcome of communication rather than as the focus of bilingual speech.'

Suggested activities

1. If the community in which you are studying or your circle of acquaintances includes multilingual people, observe them in informal conversation (with their permission) and make notes about your impressions of what is going on when they switch from language to language. If you can be an active participant, so much the better: you can try to 'manipulate' the conversation to see if your mixing or other sorts of choices elicit mixing from your conversational partners. How many languages are involved? Can you get any sense of what 'causes' or 'allows' the alternations of languages?

2. Engage your partners in a metalanguage examination about their mixing of languages. Do they seem to have some sense of why they mix, and when? Tay's study indicates that mixing among fluent code-mixers is unconscious. Unless your participants are fellow linguistics students, you may expect initially to get some facile answers, such as 'It's just easier for me to say it this way' or even 'I can't say it in [English]'. In such cases, try to probe and see if you can alert your partners to the sorts of considerations that Tay has raised, and record their responses. Write up your observations and analyses.

3. If you cannot find live code-mixers to observe, look at newspapers from English-using countries on the internet and creative literature by Outer-Circle authors (see Chapters 4 and 8). You are quite likely to find at least short segments of code-mixed discourse, particularly in the dialogues in short stories and novels. In a short essay, report on what you have found and comment on the communicative effects of the mixing you observe.

19

Culture and conventions of speaking

Two teachers outside a shopping complex in Kuala Lumpur, Malaysia

Khadijah: Eh Mala, where on earth you went ah? I searching, searching all over the place for you — no sign till one o'clock, so I *pun* got hungry, I went for *makan*.

Mala: You were *makaning* where? My sister, she said she saw you near Globes — when we were searching for parking space. So *susah* one, you know? Went roun(d) and roun(d) nearly six times *pun* [also], no place. That's why so late *lah*!

Khadijah: So you ate or not?

Mala: Not yet *lah* — just nibbled some 'kari paps' [curry puffs] at about eleven, so not really hungry.

Khadijah: Okay then, come we go into Mum Loong — it seems got plenty of sales for house wares and costume jewelleries especially.

Baskaran (1994: 28)

Introduction

English is used differently in interpersonal interaction throughout the three Circles. In multilinguals' language use, there is much mixing and switching of different codes, as is illustrated by the excerpt above from a Malaysian conversation among two school teachers. There are a number of solidarity and attitude markers in the above conversation, e.g., *ah, you know,* and two instances of *lah*. This use of such markers seems to be a feature of East Asian and Southeast Asian Englishes such as SME more than of, say, South Asian or Inner-Circle Englishes.

In addition to linguistic and interactional features, conventions of speaking in terms of turn, floor, and other components differ along several parameters:

societies and cultures, ethnic groups, and groups defined by age, gender, social status, educational background, etc. (see Chapter 5). There has been a great deal of research on male and female styles of speaking (e.g., Tannen, 1993), and it has been established that the two genders follow quite different systems of conversational interaction. In this chapter, the focus is on differences related to age, gender and ethnicity in interaction. The examples are drawn from Australia, India and New Zealand. Mitchell and Delbridge (1965), Shopen (1978) and Horvath (1985) identify gender as an important variable in Australian English. The following summary of a study illustrates how adolescent boys and girls in Australia, as they grow older, use language to construct their separate gender identities (Eisikovits, 1989: 35–54).

Gender and age in language use

The data consist of over fifty hours of conversation recorded on tape. The subjects were twenty males and twenty females born in Australia and of Australia-born parents. They were equally divided into two age groups, those in Year 8 of secondary school (average age a month less than fourteen years) and an older group in Year 10 (average age just past sixteen years). They lived in working-class neighbourhoods of inner Sydney and were interviewed in pairs. Members of the younger group were interviewed again in Year 10 to get comparative data for observing development over time (Eisikovits, 1989: 36–7).

The focus of the study was on how grammar was exploited differently by the two gender groups; therefore, three highly stigmatized variables were chosen for examination out of the twelve variables of Inner Sydney English in a previous larger study (Eisikovits, 1981). The choice of the use of non-standard features was motivated by the observation (e.g., in Labov, 1966; Milroy, 1980; and others) that females are more sensitive to prestige forms in speech and use fewer non-standard forms as compared to males.

The three variables selected for the study were (p. 37):

1. Non-shared past tense forms such as *seen* and *done*, as in: *He woke up an seen something.*
2. multiple negation as in: *They don't say nothing.*
3. invariable *don't* as in: *Mum don't have to do nothing.*

The occurrence of these forms in the speech of the groups was as follows (p. 37; each group consisted of ten subjects):

Younger girls:	134/313 or 42.8%
Older girls:	86/307 or 28%
Younger boys:	139/481 or 28.9%
Older boys:	137/411 or 33.3%

The data make it clear that whereas there is a significant decline in the use of non-standard forms with age among female adolescents (p<0.001), there is no such decline in the males. In some cases, there is over a 40 percent decline in the use of non-standard forms among female subjects (from 94.4 percent to 45.2 percent in the use of *done*, and from 93.3 percent to 52.9 percent in the use of *come*). In contrast, the use of *done* declines slightly among male subjects (from 65.5 percent to 61.3 percent), but the use of non-standard *come* shows an impressive increase (from 55.8 percent to 75.9 percent).

The use of multiple negation shows a similar pattern (p. 40): among the young girls, it goes from 48.7 percent to 21.7 percent between grades 8 and 10 (p<0.001); among males the decline is not significant (50.5 percent to 44.1 percent). In fact, male subjects who did not use multiple negation at grade 8 level (subjects 5B and 6B) seem to have acquired it by grade 10 level.

The use of invariable *don't* in all grammatical contexts shows an interesting pattern. First of all, it is very infrequent among young girls (only 4.8 percent use it, as opposed to 16.7 percent young boys). The use of this form increases as the young boys grow up: it climbs sharply from 16.7 percent to 51.7 percent among the boys. The pattern suggests that this grammatical variable is heavily sex-marked.

Explanation for the difference

The question that arises is: why is there such a difference across the two groups as they grow older? Why should there be a decrease in the use of non-standard forms among the adolescent girls and an increase in such use among the adolescent boys? As Eisikovits observes (1989: 41), '[c]learly at least two separate but intersecting factors [are] involved here: one developmental and the other relating to sex differences.'

It has already been mentioned that women are believed to be more sensitive to prestige forms of speech. Additionally, they show more stylistic variation than men in more formal speech situations (Labov, 1972c; Wolfram, 1969; Trudgill, 1972). The awareness that different social situations call for different codes develops gradually as people acquire language. Labov (1964) suggests that six markers along the continuum of change in language use can be identified in this developmental sequence: (i) basic grammar, (ii) the vernacular, (iii) social perception, (iv) stylistic variation, (v) consistent standard, and (vi) the acquisition of full range (Eisikovits, 1989: 41). According to this conceptualization, the subjects of Eisikovits' study could be said to be at stages (iii) and (iv), i.e., gradually perceiving the social significance of speech and gradually learning to modify their own speech accordingly.

The difficulty, however, arises with the lack of such change, or rather, change in the opposite direction in some cases, in the speech of the male subjects. One possible explanation for this anomaly may be that adolescent boys and girls do not share the same perception of prestige forms (Eisikovits, 1989: 42). As Smith (1985) observes, given the fact that men and women live in two quite different social slots and are often treated differently even in those that are identical, it is reasonable to find that they will be accustomed to different sets of contextually defined norms of interaction, and those will form the basis of their own speech and their judgement of others' speech.

The subjects of Eisikovits' study were interviewed towards the end of their schooling, when they were about to enter the adult world of work and social responsibilities. The world-views of the young males and females were found to be quite different at this point. The older girls show a realization of the responsibilities of adulthood and are aware of the need to fit in rather than being in conflict with social norms. This change is reflected in one subject's remark: 'I think I've settled down a lot. It's better not being in trouble anyway' (Subject 1E, p. 42).

Another subject replied to a question about whether she felt a lot older in the following words (Subject IC, pp. 42–3):

> That was funny you said that because, see I keep a diary an I was reading over what I'd written before and just from the beginning of the year you can see that what you've written, how stupid you must've been then to do that sort of thing, you know, 'cause whatever you've said or done or something you wrote, I've written it down, you know, the fights I've had with Mum an that. Then, like when you read it through you think, "Yeah, that was ridiculous. Mum was right all the time," or summat like that, you know. Yeah, you notice how you do change an that. You realise your mistakes.

This attitude encompasses language use, as is clear from 1E's response to a question about what her fights with her boyfriend are about (p. 43): 'Ph, petty things. Like, oh, sometimes he swears at me and I don't like swearing any more … we have a fight about that.' She goes on to comment: ' … Sometimes, like, sometimes I'll be in the mood for it an other times I'll think, you know, "I don't wanna say that." Cause when you listen t'other people it sounds terrible.'

The male subjects, however, seem to have quite a different perception. They see themselves as 'grown up', too. However, the implication is not to 'settle down' or to conform to social norms, but to move towards 'self-assertion', 'toughness' and 'an unwillingness to be dictated to'. Some typical comments quoted in the study are:

> Subject 9D: 'They said juniors are definitely not allowed to drink. We still drink though. They can't stop us really.'
> Subject 1D: 'I was pulled up by the police about 20 yards from me front door. They said, "Where do ya live?" That made me feel real good. I said, "Right there." You know you can give'em cheek, bit a cheek back an they can't say nothing.' (p. 43)

When the interviewer asked if his parents tried to push him into any job, 5F replied: 'No, if they did, I'd push 'em back.'

Subjects told stories of conflicts with police, the school authorities, and to a lesser extent with parents 'with defiance and bravado'. Narratives of outmaneuvering the authorities were presented as 'evidence of toughness and skill'. The lessening of family conflict was less due to boys conforming with their parents' behavioural norms and more because of reduced parental control. When asked what the causes of conflict with parents were, 2D says (p. 44):

> Oh, we useta have rows. That was before I was 16. Useta have rows about coming home too late, early in the morning an that. But now, it's just when I get in trouble off the police or something, you know.

When asked what happens when he comes home drunk, he says, 'I do every week. But Dad doesn't mind.' About homework, 1D says, 'If I wanna do it, I do it. If I don't Mum don't care.' 2D adds, 'They make me sisters an that do their homework.'

The same parental lack of control is in evidence in language use, too. When asked if they were punished for swearing, this is what the boys say (p. 44); 6D said, 'Oh, swore once when I was about five an I was belted off me mother. Tried to wash me mouth out with soap.' 5D has this to say, 'Oh, they just took me inside an smacked me.' He adds, 'If I swear in front of me mother now she don't say nothing.' The prestige value attached to non-standard language forms is such that boys correct themselves towards them if they happen to use standard forms in their speech (p. 45). For instance, 6F says, 'I didn't know what I did — what I done.' And 1F says, 'He's my family doctor … An 'e gave — give it to me an 'e said …'

The sensitivity to context-dependent style variation shows up in elicitation versus free speech situations and discourse types, e.g., narration, conversation and opinion (in response to interview questions). Among girls, the use of non-standard forms goes down in the context of elicitation of responses and also as they grow older. Among boys, the use of non-standard forms increases under the same conditions. In discourse types, the girls use the most non-standard forms in narration, fewer in conversation, and the fewest in opinion. As they grow older, the frequency of non-standard forms in all these contexts decreases. The boys show exactly the reverse pattern.

There is interesting variation in the use of multiple negation: rather unexpectedly, this feature occurs more frequently among older girls in conversation (25.3 percent) as well as opinion (18.9 percent) as opposed to narration (16.4 percent).The explanation for the variation is that whereas the younger girls, like the younger boys, tell stories with a linear sequence of events, older girls frequently add interpretive and evaluative commentary that interrupts the narration. Secondly, the younger girls' stories were frequently about conflict with parents, school and friends, whereas the older girls' stories displayed more harmony.

The data presented in the study suggests that the norms that the girls develop are in consonance with the external social expectations in their environment. The boys, on the other hand, use non-standard forms 'to affirm their own masculinity and toughness and their working class anti-establishment values' (p. 52). The conclusion is unavoidable that there are age- and sex-related differences in the variety of Australian English which adolescents in this Sidney working-class neighbourhood use.

Gender in Indian English

This section is concerned primarily with two parameters: the code, i.e., the variety of English that is being used for conversational interaction, and gender, i.e., the strategies that men and women use differently in interaction. The focus is on a specific topic: how agreement-disagreement is indicated in the speech of users of Indian English (IE). Close attention is paid to the theoretical framework and the methodology of the study of agreement-disagreement patterns in IE in Valentine (1995).

Valentine's study is broadly situated within the framework of pragmatics, i.e., speech acts, politeness and the cooperative principle (see Chapter 4). One way of engaging in polite interaction is to create an ambiance of solidarity by signalling mutual agreement, or when necessary, indicating disagreement in a manner that does not cause offence. Research has shown that in Burundi (Albert, 1972), the addressee may say 'Yes, I definitely agree', and then proceed to state their opinion which is contradictory to what the first speaker had said. In American English, women say 'yeah' to mean they are following what the speaker is saying, whereas men say 'yeah' to mean they agree with the speaker (Maltz and Borker, 1982). In Japanese conversation, the addressee's 'yes' does not mean he/she accepts whatever is being said; it simply means 'I am paying attention to what you are saying'.

Since the conventions of speaking seem to differ across cultures, it is reasonable to investigate whether varieties of English developed in different cultural contexts differ in the use of agreement-disagreement strategies. If they do, this will create opportunities for raising awareness of differences to achieve intelligibility across varieties.

Strategies of agreement-disagreement

According to Valentine (1995), female speakers of IE use strategies to signal agreement-disagreement in ways that are unfamiliar to speakers of other varieties of English. The data came from taped conversations among subjects that ranged from nineteen-year-old college students to sixtyish-year-old working and non-working men and women.

Agreement strategies

The data shows four agreement strategies: direct expressions of agreement, building upon the previous speaker's turn, partial or complete repetition of components in the previous speaker's turn, and delaying or hedging.

◆ Direct expressions of agreement

Items such as the ones in boldface below exemplify this strategy (Valentine, 1995: 230–1; the 'f' and 'm' preceding the designations of the speakers, A, B and C, denote female and male speakers, respectively):

1. fA: it sounds wonderful when you talk about it. it's very difficult ...
   fB: **Yeah, ma'am it's like she was saying** she would like to be a spinster. It's something. It takes a lot of guts to say that in public.

2. mA: There is a vast difference between the relations in the urban areas and the rural areas of India ...
   mB: **absolutely true**. In fact Venketeswara College, New Delhi is certainly not India ...

Certain features of the above exchanges are worth noting. In example 1, speaker A's utterance sets up the expectation for speaker B's positive response. Example 2 exemplifies upgraded agreement (p. 231) in that an intensifier, *absolutely true*, is used to show enthusiastic agreement with the previous speaker.

Building upon the previous speaker's turn:

Female speakers adopt this strategy of building collaborative agreement frequently, as in the following (pp. 232–3):

3. fA: Why do men like to talk to women so much and why do women like to talk to women so much? And does that happen in India do you think as well?
   fB: **Yeah, it does** I think the main reason for this is because women are very good listeners **like you said** they will always listen to you, ...
   fC: **Probably another thing** would be that women try to keep themselves in that position and view things from other person's point of view. ...

Both B and C are building in a number of turns collaboratively on what A said previously, using the expressions *like you said*, and *another thing*.

Repetition:

One of the preferred strategies of politeness is to repeat a component of the previous speaker's turn, or a complete turn, to show agreement, as in the following (pp. 233–4):

4.   mA: It's going to be **very difficult** to find somebody who thinks exactly the way I do.
     fB: It's **very difficult** to say
     mA: **very difficult** since we come to a co-ed school, a co-ed college ...

Female speakers utilize this strategy in a number of turns to indicate emphatic agreement:

5.   fA: So dating is **common** nowadays.
     fB: Yeah. This is **very common**.
     fC: **Very common**.
     fB: **Really common**. And in this level well we are doing research. ...

◆ Delaying and hedging agreement:

The utterance of mB in excerpt 6 below is a good example of hedging before indicating agreement.

6.   fA: So if you had a problem you would go to your male friend?
     mB: Actually it would depend on the kind of problem I might even go and consult my father ... **but yeah certainly if I have something a problem of a kind** which I can discuss with my best friend ... **yeah sure I would certainly seek his help** ...

Strategies of disagreement

Unlike agreement, which is not face-threatening to one's partner in conversation, disagreement or argument is more likely to be perceived as face-threatening. Participants use various strategies to express disagreement depending upon their perception of how the interaction is likely to be affected by it. Indian English speakers use the following strategies to indicate disagreement: explicit statements of disagreement or stated disagreement components; softened negative statements, honorifics, apologies, etc.; delaying; and hedging. A few examples of disagreement strategies follow.

◆ Direct disagreement

The direct disagreement expressions, frequently prefaced by mitigating items such as *I think*, address terms such as *ma'am*, seeking agreement by using an interrogative, etc, exhibited in the data are (pp. 236–7): *I think I hold a different view here, no, I won't say, Wrong, ne* ('no' in Hindi), *[s]o don't you think that's hypocritical?* The topic below is male domination in Indian society:

7.   fA: Were you treated differently?
     fB: **Well ma'am I won't say I was treated differently but yeah** in spite of saying that I have very broad-minded parents and all there are certain areas in the house … when my mother's cooking you lay down the table you wind it up okay my brother will probably go down and keep the car back and his bike back. But dusting and all is it comes to me.

The subject first disagrees with the suggestion that she was treated differently, softening the disagreement with *Well ma'am I won't say*, but then agrees with *but yeah* and elaborates what the 'difference' in treatment involved.

◆ Delayed disagreement with negative statement

In discussing how often a male subject would offer to help his wife in household chores, the following exchange takes place (p. 240); note the delayed negative response towards the end:

8:   fA: But if she [your wife] doesn't need your assistance would you offer?
     mB: [after a long preface about his other responsibilities] … five-six years ago, I would volunteer like I would just go in and say "can I do this for you?" and things like that. Now I don't think … if she asks me "can you just come in? gimme a hand"? well, I do it. **But not readily forthcoming**.

A common strategy among female speakers is of first supporting what the previous speaker has said and then continuing on, and disagreeing (p. 240):

9:   fA: my family. Of course they wants [*sic*] me to get married, they pressurize me, but I think they've got to know by now, that when I am adamant at some point, nothing can budge me.
     fB: Well, ma'am to be very frank … I find that I definitely would want to pursue a career … but definitely I would like to have a family, too. … I could have a problem with my husband on that issue. I'm prepared for that. **But, then I would definitely like to have a family, too.**

◆ Co-existent agreement-disagreement

Cases where both partial agreement-disagreement are expressed are more acceptable in other Englishes if the sequence of expression is *yes, but* ... It is unexpected to have a sequence such as *no, ... but yeah*, which also occurs in Indian English data (pp. 243–4):

10. fA: Do you think it (wife abuse) is common?
    fB: In India? In rural families this is common.
    fC: **No, it's common**. Very much common even in very literate families.

There are cases where direct disagreement is expressed and is followed by backing down in the speech of both male and female speakers:

11. fA: So in your family were you treated differently from your brothers in other ways?
    fB: **No, not in other ways, but yeah yes I was**. They didn't allow me.

In light of her findings, Valentine (1995) emphasizes the following points relevant to the teaching of English in the three circles: (a) research on how people learn languages needs to take into account the properties of extended discourse in specific contexts instead of merely concentrating on sentence-level properties of language; (b) teachers have to be educated to consider the interdependence of grammar of language and grammar of culture, i.e., the conventions of culture that determine context-dependent language use; (c) the English language teaching profession has to aim at raising awareness of shared and non-shared features of world Englishes to tailor language teaching materials for maximizing international intelligibility and success in cross-cultural interaction in various domains of contact; and (d) finally, teachers of English in all Circles have to be aware of their own attitudes and recognize the status and depth of institutionalization of various world Englishes and how ethnic, gender, national and other identities are projected through them.

Ethnic variation in discourse

Ethnic differences in language use are illustrated by a study in New Zealand (Stubbe and Holmes, 1999). Although there is a standard New Zealand variety of English, there are distinct linguistic and discourse-related features that mark the different styles of interaction of the two ethnic groups: Maori and Pakeha (people of European origin); there are gender distinctions in interaction in addition to the two ethnic styles; and both Pakeha and Maori participants are familiar with each other's styles and manipulate them to signal various types of accommodation in interaction with each other. Thus, ethnic differences not only co-exist, they are used to co-construct meaning in interpersonal interactions.

The authors provide evidence to show that there are distinct styles of interaction among Maori speakers of New Zealand English (NZE), who, unlike the Pakeha, are bicultural. On the basis of earlier research and work in progress, they establish that the discourse patterns of Maori NZE speakers are distinctive in the use of the following linguistic devices: (a) tag questions and expressions like *eh, you know*, (b) high-rise terminal intonation, (c) back-channel cues, pauses and silence, (d) humour; (e) structure of narratives in conversation, and (f) patterns of code-switching and shifting of styles (p. 251). Some of these are discussed with examples in the following sections. The data for NZE interactions in the study are drawn from the Wellington Corpus of Spoken New Zealand English (WCSNZE) and several interactions from the Language in Workplace Project (LWP) to identify the features of Maori NZE related to the coding of ethnic identity and characteristics of NZE that signal aspects of Maori and Pakeha social and professional identities (pp. 251–2).

Pragmatic devices

According to Stubbe and Holmes, the addressee-oriented pragmatic devices that signal solidarity between speakers and addressees correlate systematically with a range of social and contextual variables. One such device is the use of the particle *eh*, more frequent in the speech of Maori young men as compared to the Pakeha. This was confirmed by analyses of several corpora. The frequency index for all Maori speakers in the conversation section of WCSNZE is 38; it is 13 for the Pakeha; however, the index for the young Maori men is 120, which is very high.[1] In another study by Stubbe (in press) of 84 conversations and radio interviews involving middle-class Maori and Pakeha dyads from WCSNZE, *eh* was used nine times more frequently overall by Maori speakers, and even more frequently by young Maori working-class men.

Borrowing from Maori

Borrowing of words and meanings from Maori serves as a strategy for indicating Maori identity (p. 255). The borrowings and long segments of code-switching function as: (a) solidarity markers; they make it possible for the speakers/writers to distance themselves from standard NZE; (b) markers of shared ethnic identity and supportive attitude towards the language; and (c) markers of supportive attitude towards the goal of reviving the Maori language and culture. In the following fragment, the Maori items are in boldface; note the use of *eh* to further emphasize the solidarity between the two interactants, who lived in the same area of the country as children (pp. 255–6):[2]

Rewi:	Tikitiki//well we're\across the river from there and
Ngata:	/**ae** ['yes']\\
Rewi:	if we wanted to go to Tikitiki we had to go right around to Ruatoria and back out again
Ngata:	that's right ... we didn't cross across ++ **te awa rere haere te- too koutou taniwha i teeraa waa** ['the river flowed over the taniwha (a legendary monster which resides in deep water) there']
Rewi:	in winter eh
Ngata:	**mo te wai- tino hohonu te wai** ['because of the water—the water was very deep']

Maori speakers also transfer features of the Maori address system, e.g., use of *mate, bro, sis, cuz, nanny, aunty* and *uncle*, to shift the interaction towards the solidarity end of the affective scale. The use of the pronoun *yous* in Maori NZE reflects the tripartite number system of the Maori language, i.e., the singular/dual/plural system.

Silence

The favoured positive politeness strategy in interactions is more silence and less back channel or feedback to the speaker (see Tannen and Saville-Troike [1985] on the role of silence in interaction). Maori listeners are apt to be careful in interfering with the speaker's floor, especially during informal narratives in conversation. On average, they use one-third less verbal feedback than their Pakeha counterparts:

> From a Pakeha perspective, ideas often appear to be introduced in a fairly sketchy fashion, and are left undeveloped, at least initially. Speakers leave a great deal unstated, relying on implicit contextualization to convey their intended meaning. ... Sometimes in a conversation between Maori, a narrative or discussion point will initially receive little or no verbal response, but will instead be picked up and extended much later in the conversation. From the perspective of a Pakeha listener, it may not obviously seem to 'fit' there, as there are no explicit signals marking it as a previously mentioned topic, but this nevertheless serves as a type of non-localized feedback. (p. 256)

Narrative structure

Maori narratives differ from Pakeha narratives in that the former may leave out certain structural components of narratives. Labov (1972a: 354–96) proposes six components of a narrative: abstract, orientation, complicating action, evaluation, resolution, and coda. Most Pakeha and Maori in general conform to this structure, though few contain all six components. In some of the Maori stories, evaluation is not expressed explicitly; evaluation and coda are left out when the interlocutors are steeped in Maori culture and know each other well. This sort of omission is attested more among Maori males and older Maori women.

Humour

The use of humour for creating solidarity also exhibits differing patterns. Young Maori males use humour as ethnic boundary markers in addition to using it to relieve tensions between group members as Pakeha males do. One motivation for this may be the fact that ethnic differences are much more salient for the minority Maori as compared to the dominant Pakeha. The following illustrates this use of humour in Maori male conversation (p. 259):

> Two Maori young men wondering why the film Geronimo had a short run in New Zealand:
>
> Mike: yeah it's good I don't know why they stopped it eh — I suppose people just didn't like Geronimo big deal
>
> Kingi: well—apparently it didn't have enough whities in it// [laughs]\
>
> Mike: /[laughs]\\
>
> Kingi: no lead role eh
>
> Mike: [laughs] [drawls]: yeah:
>
> Kingi: what can you do
>
> Mike: well that's true

The characteristic discourse features of Maori NZE together with distinctive linguistic features of Maori NZE form the basis for variation along a style continuum. Maori speakers draw on identifiable Maori features in their NZE discourse, depending on factors such as social and ethnic background of the participants, setting, relative importance of indicating ethnic identity in a given context, etc.

Professional discourse

Discourse in NZE differs along ethnic lines in the professional context just as it does in purely social contexts. The Pakeha style of interaction among males is different from the Maori style, but members of the emerging Maori middle class have the ability and desire to shift back and forth along a continuum between Maori and Pakeha NZE. Maori males adopt an informal and supportive tone by means of sardonic remarks and laughter, facilitate feedback with elements such as *yeah* and *right*, and, through the use of Maori features such as *eh* and high rise tone, affirm their Maori identity. The use of non-standard grammar (e.g., *you got, I ain't got*) and syllable-timed rhythm are also indicative of a distinct Maori-accented English.

Pakeha men express their opinions and suggestions very directly and explicitly. Expressions like *definitely, basically, clearly* are common. The pronouns *I* and *you* occur relatively frequently, accompanied by speaker-oriented devices like *I think*. All these features function to reduce the degree of informality, and suggest a greater degree of social distance, even though the men are of equal status (p. 272). In addition, the sequence of topics is linear, there are no informal, addressee-oriented features, and there is explicit expression of opinions. All these have the effect of projecting the two participants' identities as 'efficient, task-focused professionals who are "in charge", and know where they stand in relation to one another' (pp. 272–3).

Professional interaction among Pakeha females exhibits different properties, signalling a gender difference in interaction. The authors present data to show that female interaction contains many solidarity markers together with a high number of epistemic forms which function to mitigate potential face threats. There are more uses of expressions such as *let's* and *we* instead of pronouns *I* and *you*, supportive minimal responses like *yeah, mm, all right, good* and more extended expressions such as *I think that's a good idea, that's great.* There are longer unfilled pauses as women work, read and write together, and co-construct a shared floor.

Pakeha-Maori interaction

When the Pakeha interact with the Maori, they show the same capacity to switch styles that is evident among the Maori. This is exemplified in the following excerpt, where a senior manager, Jan, is meeting with one of her team leaders, Heke, a Maori man, to resolve a number of misunderstandings and differing work expectations (pp. 273–4):

> Jan: I think that's the best thing it hasn't been signed by Philip because he wanted that information included
>
> Heke: all right okay [sighs]: oh look: I'm dreadfully sorry about that
>
> Jan: oh well just check out to see what happened +'cause there was clearly some miscommunication somewhere

Heke continues (although the authors do not say so, the items in bold letters seem to signal the interpersonal dimension of the interaction here):

> Heke: but I'm keeping the pressure on **[laughs]** + **actually** I – I wanted to – get your advice about that I want to do **a bit of a wee sort of ra ra** speech at the beginning of **like** of planning day tomorrow we ARE stretched people ARE starting to feel the pressure + but it's **just the kind of thing you know** it's – if if we want to be in the business you're gonna have to live with it **you know that kind of thing** …

Jan breaks into Heke's speech after some time:

> Jan: **although I mean I can appreciate the that sort of message but on the other hand** um + don't **sort of** + **sort of** say that as something that sh- that should be the norm //**like**\ that's
>
> Heke: /mm\\\\
>
> …
>
> Jan: that they need **you know** it's **the old** work smarter **sort of stuff**
> Heke: yeah
> Jan: and we need to- to **sort of** be aware of we being a (friend-) family friendly working place

According to the authors, 'Jan takes great care not to sound too critical' (p. 274). She suggests, rather than prescribes. Her speech is full of hedges like *sort of, like, sort of stuff* and the echo of addressee-oriented *you know* that mirrors Heke's style — all indicate a conciliatory tone. She also adopts a higher pitch, signalling a 'feminine' ameliorative position, and echoes Heke's *from time to time*. Her speech rhythms become more syllable-timed to accommodate her perception of the Maori style, and this is reciprocated by Heke's *ae*, a Maori expression. Jan's reference to 'family friendly working place' is also an appeal to the Maori value system which accords the extended family high priority.

The excerpt above points to the complexities of discourse styles where the same utterance may contribute simultaneously to the construction of more than one aspect of an individual's social and professional identity. On the one hand, Jan is the senior manager and needs to establish her authority and get things done by her subordinates such as Heke; on the other hand, she has to project friendliness and sensitivity to cultural and gender-difference between her addressee and herself, and take care not to offend him.

Conclusion

Researching speaking conventions by looking at interactional data illuminates the similarities and differences between varieties and provides useful input for

English education. It is obvious that a great many studies such as the ones reported here are needed to get a more complete picture of how users of world Englishes communicate with each other.

Suggested activities

1. View and record an episode (approximately fifteen minutes) of your favourite TV programme, e.g., soap opera, movie, an interview, a discussion with a number of participants on some current issue. Analyse the conversation to see how agreement or disagreement is expressed in your data.

2. Analyse the following piece of conversation between an aunt and a nephew:

    K: My life is fixed now, Lung. But you have your future ahead ... You can not afford not to save up. (Pause) Tell me, how much do you earn?

    L: I made a thousand eight last month.

    K: All right, now listen to me, Lung. Every month, you must set aside. Whatever you do, you must not touch this sum. It'll be for emergency use only. (Pause) And your marriage.

    L: I don't intend to marry, Aunty. I've told you before. I'm not a masochist.

    K: (Bowing her head) You're going to keep drifting all your life?

    L: I'm not drifting ... I'm doing OK ... Look, just don't worry about me, O.K.? I can take care of myself.

    K: Sometime, I fear for you, Lung.

    L: (Laughs) What? You're worried for me? What is it? You're afraid the family name will die out or some'um?

    a. How will you characterize the above exchanges in terms of politeness?

    b. Is the interaction cordial, exhibiting solidarity between the two participants?

    c. Are the strategies K and L using persuasive and effective?

    d. What can you infer about the relationship between K and L on the basis of the exchanges cited above?

20

Culture and conventions of writing

> But reason is only reason,
> and it only satisfies man's rational requirement.

> Fyodor Dostoevsky, *Notes from Underground*

Introduction

It was pointed out in Chapter 5 that writing conventions vary significantly across varieties of English. It is a myth that Inner-Circle Englishes follow the same conventions of writing for a particular genre (Baker and Eggington, 1999; see Chapter 16). It is even more of an imaginative feat to assert that registers and genres are uniform across the circles, notwithstanding Widdowson's assertion that

> Registers relate to domains of use, to areas of knowledge and expertise which cross national boundaries and are global of their very nature ... Registers as the varieties used by ... expert communities ... do indeed, and necessarily, change over time. But the change is naturally and endonormatively controlled from within by requirements of communication across the international community of its specialist users. (1997: 143)

In reality, the multilingual writers from Asia and Africa have to cast the linguistic medium to convey messages which may contain cultural concepts not embodied in the genetic inheritance of the language (see Chapter 10). At the same time, they have to refashion the rules of writing in accordance with their cultural norms for persuasion, narration, reporting and other purposes so that these kinds of texts can serve their needs in the areas of academia, business, news reporting, etc. As the chapters of this book make clear, the medium, 'English', is hardly a unitary concept; it has become various and pluricentric to reflect the sociocultural realities of the 'various' world.

Similarly, text types and genres are not universal across societies and cultures and establishing their comparability is not easy (see Y. Kachru, 1997a, 1997b). This becomes obvious if we try to trace even one text type across languages and cultures, whether in world Englishes or in English and other languages of the Three Circles.

Argumentation and persuasion

English as used for academic purposes includes the genre of argumentative or persuasive writing. It has been noted that writers from different parts of the world do not follow the conventions of presenting arguments or structuring their texts according to the norms of the Inner Circle (see Connor, 1996; Kaplan, 1972; among others). Researchers in world Englishes examine the cultural bases of argumentative/persuasive writing in English in contexts where English is used for scholarly presentation to see if these underlie the observed difference. The relevance of scholarly activities to the study of the use of English is obvious: if any use of English might lend itself to a priori notions of homogeneity, it would be in such professional contexts. One might readily believe that logic is logic, and that presentation of information and a cogent interpretation of it should 'naturally' be the most straightforward activity in the world. Y. Kachru's (1997b) analysis, however, makes it clear that written discourse follows the same parameters of diversity that we have seen in other aspects of world Englishes.

Argumentation across cultures

According to Y. Kachru (1997b: 48), 'judgements regarding what is or is not acceptable as academic writing are not universal, and are not free from historical and sociocultural contexts of literacy practices'. Writing is even more explicitly influenced by historical and (contemporary) societal norms by virtue of its being explicitly learned and practised with guidance, in contrast to speaking, which people are inherently able and driven to do. Not only are the fact and forms of writing themselves explicitly and conventionally determined by a society or group, but 'notions of appropriacy of written communication in a given context' are also transmitted in these ways. Thus, '[j]udging the process of writing, the cultural context of the product, and the cultural value assigned to the process and the product in other cultures from one' own perspective can be misleading and harmful to the future knowledge base of the world' (1997b: 48).

The terms and concepts of *culture, society, argumentation* and *persuasion* are all defined explicitly (1997b: 49–51). *Culture* has historical and present bases, and it 'is manifest in symbolic forms, including language'. Since language is a manifestation of culture, it follows that it has historical and contemporary aspects. *Society* is essentially a term defined by those concerned: people conceive of and refer to themselves as a population holding certain definitive views and beliefs in common, and who exhibit various kinds of organizational forms to provide cohesiveness. Within a society are groups, which have definitive memberships, organizational structures, purposes, appropriate functions, and so on. The groups have their internal functions and relations among their memberships and external functions in relating to other groups; examples are teachers and students, employers and employees, etc. Likewise, societies exhibit relations among their groups ('internal relations') and external ones, as in any given society being different from any other.

Within societies, many rules of language use develop, among which are code-mixing, in multilingual societies. In other, non-multilingual societies, Y. Kachru notes, such 'mixing and switching would be unacceptable since it would hamper intelligibility and cause consternation'. Part of societal linguistic competence — communicative competence — is the ability to write (in 'literate societies', those in which writing is practised and expected, with its appropriate domains, organizations, and styles). The exemplars which Y. Kachru (1997b) draws on are 'Anglo-American, Chinese, Indian and Japanese cultures'.

Argumentation and *persuasion* are used interchangeably by many writers on the subject, with the former usually focusing on calls to change readers' behaviour, while the latter may seek only to engender agreement with the author's view, to be convincing. Y. Kachru refers to both 'argumentative/ persuasive writing' (1997b: 52). While the usual approach to an examination of cross-cultural writing is a comparison of the 'linguistic realization of argumentation' across languages and societies, Y. Kachru examines 'cultural factors as they define argumentation' (p. 53). In general, argumentative text in the Western academic contexts has a 'schematic form that organizes the global meaning of a text; it is a problem-solving process; and its goal is to convince the audience of the points made in the text' (Tirkkonen-Condit, 1985).

First, the Anglo-American tradition of argumentative writing sets the work within its topic-context in the introduction, typically makes explicit the kind of text that will be employed (e.g., comparison-contrast), and states the topic and thesis for the work: the point of view to be presented, and/or how the problem presented is to be resolved. The body of the text treats major points needed to fulfil the promise of the thesis, typically in deductively structured paragraphs, with little tolerance for digression. The conclusion draws the points of discussion together and reasserts the thesis, often with extension or generalization of applicability. This format follows a historically induced notion of what it means to make 'an argument' — a point of view and directly relevant evidence to support it.

In the Chinese culture of persuasive essays, the major cultural influences are 'the historical method, and attention to language' (Y. Kachru, 1997b: 54–5). Following this tradition, Chinese writing exhibits a so-called *double-harness* organization in which '(a) a critique ... of communicated meaning and (b) a checking of this critique by a critique of history' offers 'a double angle of vision' for viewing the topic or proposition (Hughes, 1977). Another style, termed *linked pearl*, employs two general statements to arrive at a third one, in order to lead 'the audience to reconsider the nexus of the two initial propositions and the conclusion [drawn] from them', as a way of 'stirring criticism of accepted knowledge' in readers. Thus, the Chinese tradition is based in historicity and inference.

A good example of this sort of structure is Liu (1996), which states its topic in the title, and does not mention it in the text proper until the concluding paragraph, where it is followed by explicit identification of the three main issues of the text. As compared to the outline of an Anglo-American-style essay sketched above, Liu's opening paragraphs treat the historical background of the study of his topic, 'the paradigm shift in the study of early Chinese discourse'. This is followed by 'the notion of text as a site for ideological struggle, the rhetorical dimension of ... pre-Han discourse, and the politics of argumentation' (pp. 55–6). The structural elements of introduction-elaboration-conclusion expected in the Anglo-American model are not clearly attested in the paper.

In India, historically, the method of investigating truth was not just the inductive method, but also recognized *perception, inference, authority* and *postulation* as 'valid sources of knowledge'. Thus, the emphasis is not only on replicability and falsifiability, but on observation, inference, what has been said before by one's reputable predecessors in the field, and what one can reasonably deduce from available evidence.

The structure of the texts is also different from those outlined above — arguments may be deductively constructed or inductively built (Y. Kachru, 1988, 1992). Garapati (1991) provides an illustration of the structure of one type of Indian argumentative text. The introduction to the study does not refer to the purpose of the essay; rather, the author starts with the beginnings of Gondi dialectology and proceeds to a discussion of various works on the topic. Subsequently, problems with ethnically based names of dialects are listed, followed by a list of ten geographically based dialect names, but there is no explicit statement that these represent the author's proposals for an improved grouping or more rational names. The next sections list phonological, morphological, and lexical forms of the ten dialects. Only in the concluding section does the author explicitly state his proposal and claim, corresponding to the Western purpose and thesis, that he has identified these certain dialects, which form groups according to his lexical and other evidence. Y. Kachru further comments (p. 58):

[O]f the fifteen papers written by Indian scholars in the volume [in which Garapati's essay appears], only one introduction explicitly states what the paper is arguing about, eight others make only the purpose of the paper clear, but six introductions do not provide any information at all.

The last tradition that Y. Kachru examines is the Japanese. She quotes Moore (1967b [1981]) in saying that 'the Japanese stress harmony and tolerance — and try to minimize both practical and intellectual cleavages and confrontation' (p. 58). While American argumentative texts tend to be assertive, comparable Japanese texts contain more affective appeals. Evidence for this claim comes from Kamimura (1995), which shows that Japanese college students write deductively organized essays but use far more affective appeals as compared to American high school subjects in the study who use far more rational appeals (pp. 58–9). The American presentations in Kamimura's study tended to be more forcefully written, employing 'clauses such as *I am sure, I believe,* modals such as *should, must* and adverbs such as *totally, absolutely, strongly, no doubt,* whereas Japanese essays had clauses such as *I think, I wonder, I can't say, [subject] may, might, perhaps, may be'* (p. 59). Thus, Japanese writers in the study tended to leave more allowance for others' views, and were less straightforward in expressing the writers' own opinions and beliefs.

The three contexts discussed make it clear that in the Asian traditions of China, India and Japan, being rational is not enough; attention is paid to conventional notions of regard for history, societal harmony and style of presentation. While Y. Kachru cautions against accepting 'sweeping generalizations' about Western and non-Western writing forms and strategies, she emphasizes that (p. 60):

> What cannot ... be disputed is that the model of argumentation/persuasion developed in each culture has its own historical justification and has to be seen in the context of the literacy practices of its own place and time.

The Outer and Expanding Circles

Having observed the bases of writing in the representative traditions, the discussion in Y. Kachru (1997b) turns to argumentative/persuasive writing in English in the Outer and Expanding Circles. One thing to keep in mind is that writing styles may vary with academic discipline, as well as with cultural tradition. A study by Taylor and Chen (1991) found that, in introductions of papers by three sets of physical scientists — Anglo-American and Chinese writing in English, and Chinese writing in Chinese — the Chinese writers of both groups wrote introductions that were shorter and less 'elaborated' and also did not contain critical reviews of preceding literature. Y. Kachru identifies four features of non-Inner-Circle writing (pp. 61–2). The first is indirectness.

As, in the study of writing just mentioned, the Chinese scholars seemed unwilling to list works which they might have to critique.

Secondly, non-Western writers are said to tend towards a ' "high" style', employing 'stylistic embellishments, quotations, idioms and metaphors'. Thirdly, extensive quotation from preceding work is highly valued, whereas mere 'appeal to authority' is not considered strong argumentation in the West. Y. Kachru notes that such citations are used not only for the purposes of the argument directly, but that '[i]t is considered good manners to acknowledge one's gratitude and display one's respect for predecessors'.

Finally, Y. Kachru observes that, while a cliché Western evaluation of non-Western work is to label it derivative and un-original, 'it is a misconception to think that originality necessarily lies in novelty'. She cites the Indian tradition of written commentaries on previous philosophical and literary works, which form traditions in their own right and are valued as 'original' works (p. 62). In fact, the best of the commentaries use the earlier work as a point of departure and propose their own original ideas and arguments to augment, elucidate or critique aspects of the original. As Moore (1967a: 8) observes, the rich commentary literature of ancient India 'produces, in the guise of mere commentaries, a wide variety of points of view — at times virtually new systems — that reveal the originality and creativity of mind and thought possessed by these commentators, many of whom are commentators only in what might be called the polite sense of the word'.

The final observation focuses on the need for 'reorientation' of comparative studies of academic writing: it is the context in which the works are produced that is of fundamental interest (Y. Kachru, 1997b: 63):

> The questions that are important are the meaning of written texts in the culture, the purposes for which written texts are produced and disseminated, the functions that written texts serve, the value that is attached to written texts, and the conditions under which reading and writing skills are acquired and practiced.

The Outer- and Expanding-Circle writers are multilingual language users — a point brought out again and again in the various aspects of world Englishes examined in this book. They come from traditions that require more overt consideration for community, and are 'creative' in using all their cultural and linguistic resources, not just 'English' in some sort of mental compartment separated from all the other elements of their repertoires. In view of this ground reality, it is not obvious that there is or should or even could be a model of writing which would serve all writers, genres, disciplines and purposes, 'especially when there is no evidence that the idealized notion is a reality in all domains of argumentation and persuasion even in the Anglo-American tradition' (p. 64).

Contrastive rhetoric illustrated

Kamimura and Oi (1998) present a specific and thoroughly worked-out analysis in terms of contrastive rhetoric to see how culturally sensitive the writing task is. The authors note (p. 308) that previous studies of this sort have focused mainly on organizational criteria, such as 'placement of claims or justification'. In their study, the authors examine three other, 'extra-organizational aspects … : rhetorical appeals, diction, and cultural influences.'

The study

The researchers collected essays on the stimulus question 'What do you think of capital punishment?' from 'twenty-two New York high school seniors' and 'thirty second-year Japanese college students', whose 'intermediate' facility in English came from their average 7.2 years of formal study of the language. The topic was selected as being both familiar and controversial for both groups of students.

The organization analysis was carried out by looking at the 'main idea' and development of each essay. It was found that the American student writers generally offered a thesis statement at the beginning of their essays, supported it with details, and summarized their position and support at the end. This general-to-specific pattern (the one typically taught in US rhetoric textbooks) is not surprising to Anglo-American writers. The Japanese writers typically used one of two other patterns, either specific-to-general, with a thesis statement at the end of the essay, or an 'Omission' style, with no thesis offered. The US writers took a position and 'stuck with it', while the Japanese writers tended to 'try to incorporate both sides … with their position fluctuating throughout the essay' (p. 311).

Kamimura and Oi assigned constituents of each essay to one of seven organizational categories (pp. 309–10): Thesis Statement, Background Information, Reservation, Hesitation, Rational Appeals, Affective Appeals, Conclusion. Thesis, Background and Conclusion are self-evident categories. Reservation and Hesitation are distinguished in that a Reservation includes the writer's position, while a Hesitation does not.

Appeals are 'sentences that reflect the writer's opinions' (p. 310; see Kamimura, 1995), and are subdivided into Rational (appealing to 'logic') and Affective (appealing to 'emotion'). For example, stating that society bears an unwarranted financial burden by housing felons instead of executing them is a Rational Appeal; writing about the effects of execution on a felon's family is an Affective Appeal.

Kamimura and Oi's analysis of *organization* revealed no significant differences in the occurrence of Thesis Statements, Conclusions or Hesitations:

'both the American and Japanese students in general stated their opinions ... explicitly in the Thesis Statement and Conclusion, without hesitation'. The groups of writers differed in that the Japanese students used fifteen Reservations, compared to only three among the American essays; that is, the Japanese writers tended to express both sides of the argument as opposed to the 'linear' character of the US essays (pp. 313–4).

The frequencies of the two sorts of *Appeals* under examination were statistically significant (p. 314): forty-six of fifty-five Appeals by US writers (83.6 percent) were identified as Rational, compared with thirty-six of fifty-five (65.5 percent) used by the Japanese. Only nine US Appeals (16.4 percent) were Affective, compared with nineteen (34.6 percent) of the Japanese Appeals. The Japanese writers showed a stronger tendency to 'evoke empathy in the reader's mind', in contrast to the Americans' 'assertive stance' and use of 'reasoning'.

Diction in the essays was examined by looking at predicates (including modals), adverbs, adjectives and nouns. The US writers tended towards 'emphatic' or 'upgrading' expressions of emphasis and importance of their arguments by using, e.g., *should/must*; *totally*; *no doubt*; *the* + superlative structures. 'None of the Japanese ... used such phrases as "I am sure", "no doubt", and "no way".' The Japanese writers used 'softening' or 'downgrading' devices, such as *I think; perhaps; sad; sorrow*. This part of the analysis directly supports that in the Appeals section.

Cultural influences were expressed by the US writers in references to 'counselling', Biblical references, and financial considerations (as, taxpayers' support of prisoners). None of these elements appeared in the writing of the Japanese students, according to Kamimura and Oi. In contrast to the American writers, the Japanese referred explicitly to personal relationships ('if I were parents of person who was killed ...'), and a majority used subjunctive forms to put the writer (as in the example just above) or the reader ('If one of your family is killed, can you permit ...') in the place of someone involved in some hypothetical situation relevant to the topic. This reflects a Japanese value of empathy. In addition, these sorts of appeals to concrete situations 'might suggest the Japanese cultural tendency to ... prefer the tangible' over the abstract (pp. 317–8).

This cross-cultural examination of writing samples indicates that the social-cultural backgrounds of writers are very salient in their use of written language. Kamimura and Oi write (p. 307) that the characteristics of their Japanese subjects' writing 'all come from Japanese "high-context" culture (Hall 1976), where a message is deeply embedded in shared assumptions and human relationships ... (Okabe 1987)'. These influences are contrasted with the view of US culture as 'low-context', in which the 'social ties among individuals' have much less influence, and the importance of verbalized information is consequently heightened (p. 318).

Conclusion

Y. Kachru's discussion of the cultural bases for argumentation and Kamimura and Oi's observations and analysis should serve to motivate users of this volume to examine cross-cultural texts of various sorts in some detail, and from different points of view. This chapter supports others in this book in indicating that a text may look like 'English', but that is only the beginning. The claim in Widdowson (1997), cited earlier, that scientific and technical registers are culture-neutral and controlled only by the discourse communities of scientists and experts is just a claim at this time; there is little empirical research to support it. In fact, expert researchers in English for Special Purposes (ESP) recommend that material prepared for teaching genres within the legal register:

> could direct themselves at the *professional legal community in their particular country, region, or legal system* — or on the system being studied — on the assumption that these contexts of use will evidence their own unique linguistic and rhetorical preferences, analytical paradigms, registers, and genres. Including materials that discuss discourse community at this level would ensure that they are locally relevant and appropriate. (Candlin, Bhatia and Jensen, 2002; emphasis in the original).

Except for highly mathematical and formulaic language in certain contexts (equations in physics, formulae in chemistry, etc.), there seems no basis for claiming that interactional language use among professionals does not reflect their own sociocultural backgrounds. A great deal more research is needed to establish the reality behind any facile assumption that we may entertain in this regard.

Suggested activities

1. Examine letters to editors of newspapers in at least two Englishes. What can you observe in terms of Kamimura and Oi's criteria? In a short essay, compare samples from two different writers in terms of their assertiveness, effectiveness, etc. What other analytical criteria occur to you?
2. Read an 'op-ed' or similar in-depth presentation of a topic of some complexity in a newspaper. In an outline sketch or short essay, analyse it from one of the perspectives discussed in the chapter.
3. Use the various sections of a newspaper to identify sub-genres within the genre of 'newspaper writing', e.g., news reports, editorial, op-ed comments, letters to editors, obituaries, etc. Look at newspapers in two different Englishes: do you find the same genres in both? Are there similar genres with different characteristics?

21 *Genre analysis across cultures*

Sikh family seeks turbaned Gursikh professional for v. pretty daughter 5'6"
33. US citizen, physician at Elite Hospital. [contact information]

Jat Sikh parents seeking professional 25/28 clean shaven match for their 23
5'3" US born daughter, BS accounting working for Fortune 500 company as
auditor. [contact information]

News India Times (18 July 2003, pp. 46–7 [classified; matrimonial])

Introduction

Indian English newspapers and magazines, including the ones published in
the USA, as *News India Times* is, usually have classified advertisements for
arranged marriages, a genre peculiar to South Asia, though a comparable
genre, Personal advertisements, exists in the West, too. A cursory glance at
the above excerpt, however, is enough to convince a reader of the differences
between the genres of Personals in the West and the Matrimonials in South
Asia. First, the ads are placed by the family, not by the young woman who is
seeking a marital partner (the same is true of ads on behalf of males). Second,
the community and sub-community are mentioned — *Gursikh* vs. *Jat Sikh.*
Third, it is made clear whether the groom is to be traditional or non-traditional
— *turbaned* or *clean shaven.* Traditional Sikh men have long hair and wear a
turban; they also keep a beard. Non-traditional Sikh men cut their hair and
shave. Finally, the crucial pieces of information for the desirability of the
woman are given — citizenship status (important in a new immigrant group),
educational and professional qualifications, and age and height. Matrimonials
may also mention the parents' professional and financial status to add to the
attractiveness of the match for the prospective grooms and their families. This
genre occupies many pages in almost all newspapers in India and in Indian
ethnic newspapers in the West.

Genre analysis as a sub-field of applied linguistic research relevant to ELT may be said to have gained prominence towards the beginning of the 1980s. It is said to differ from other types of analyses of texts in that it focuses on a highly structured and conventionalized text type with a definite communicative purpose, a genre, which is recognized as such by a specific professional or academic community. Although a genre is highly constrained, the constraints are often exploited by the expert members of the community to achieve private intentions within the framework of socially recognized purposes. There are a number of factors, such as content, form, intended audience, medium or channel, that influence the nature and construction of a genre. However, it is primarily characterized by the communicative purposes that it is intended to fulfil. Any major changes in the communicative purposes are likely to result in a different genre, though minor changes or modifications are helpful in distinguishing sub-genres.

Genre most often is a highly structured and conventionalized communicative event. Various genres display constraints on allowable contributions in terms of their intent, positioning, form and functional value. This means that writers have freedom to use linguistic resources in any way they like; however, they must conform to certain standard practices within the boundaries of a particular genre. That is why it is possible to distinguish a personal letter from a business letter or a newspaper editorial from a news report. Any mismatch in the use of generic resources is noticed as odd not only by the specialist but also by proficient users of the language; most readers intuitively recognize which genre a text belongs to.

Members of a given professional or academic community have greater knowledge of the conventional purpose(s), construction and use of specific genres than do non-specialists. Greater knowledge makes it possible for specialists to exploit the conventions for private intents, e.g., experienced newspaper reporters often succeed in imposing desired perspectives on otherwise objective news reports.

Definition of genre

Bhatia (1993) modifies the definition of genre suggested in Swales (1981, 1985, 1990) to include 'the psychological, particularly the cognitive, level of genre construction' (1993: 16). He believes that ignoring the psychological factor undermines 'the importance of tactical aspects of genre construction, which play a significant role in the concept of genre as a dynamic social process' rather than a static one (p. 16). This reorientation makes it possible to highlight the fact that writers make use of two types of strategies: non-discriminative and discriminative. 'Non-discriminative strategies are concerned with the exploitation of the conventional rules of the genre' (p. 20), whereas discriminative strategies tend to vary the nature of the genre significantly, 'often introducing new or additional considerations in the communicative purposes of the text' (p. 21). This helps one to distinguish genres from sub-genres, e.g., survey articles, review articles, state-of-the-art articles are sub-genres of the genre called 'research article'.

The generic structure with its typical regularities, which is a part of the knowledge of the relevant discourse community, necessarily reflects the communicative purpose of the text type. Thus, readers are aware of the difference between a news report and a news commentary on the same topic, though both may call for activating the same background knowledge. In this sense it is different from the organization of presupposed encyclopedic knowledge in an individual, which is primarily the case in schema theory, frames or scripts.

Seven steps of analysis

Bhatia (1993: 23–34) describes the following seven steps for a comprehensive analysis, 'depending upon the purpose of the analysis, the aspect of genre one wants to focus upon, and the background knowledge one already has of the nature of the genre in question'.

1. *Placing the given text in a situational context:* First, one intuitively identifies a genre-text (a typical example of the genre) in a situational context by calling upon prior experience, the internal clues in the text, and encyclopedic knowledge. The non-specialist may have to acquire the necessary knowledge by surveying available literature in the field.
2. *Surveying existing literature:* This may involve surveying pertinent literature in the areas of linguistic, sociocultural, genre and other types of analyses and acquiring knowledge of the related speech community.
3. *Refining the situational/contextual analysis:* The intuitive placement of a text in a situational context needs to be refined by (a) defining the participant roles and relationships, (b) defining the historical, social, cultural, philosophic and/or occupational placement of the relevant community, (c) identifying the surrounding texts and linguistic traditions that form the background of the text, and (d) 'identifying the topic/subject/extra-textual reality which the text is trying to represent, change or use and the relationship of the text to that reality' (p. 23).
4. *Selecting the corpus:* Selection of the right kind and size of corpus requires (a) defining the genre/sub-genre according to its communicative purposes, situational context, and distinctive textual characteristics, and (b) an explicit statement of the criteria which allow the text to be assigned to the genre/sub-genre.
5. *Studying the institutional context:* The institutional context of the use of the

genre is important, since 'rules and conventions (linguistic, social, cultural, academic, professional) that govern the use of language in such institutional settings ... are most often implicitly understood and unconsciously followed by the participants in the communication situation' (p. 24).

6. *Levels of linguistic analysis:* Analysts have to decide at which level of analysis the most characteristic or significant linguistic features occur. The levels are those of lexico-grammatical features, text-patterning or textualization (the way a linguistic device is used in a restricted sense, e.g., past participles in a scientific article), and structural interpretation of the text genre (e.g., the four-move cognitive structure of a research article introduction discussed by Swales (1981): establishing the research field, summarizing pervious research, preparing for present research and introducing the present research, cited by Bhatia.

7. *Specialist information in genre analysis:* Finally, analysts need to establish their findings against reactions from one or more expert informants. The expert reactions confirm the findings, bring validity to the insights gained, and add psychological reality to the analysis.

Bhatia cautions that the steps are not necessarily to be followed strictly in order. Also, the analysis may reveal patterns, but they are not to be taken as prescriptive norms. Genre analysis is pattern-seeking rather than pattern-imposing.

Application of the model

A set of examples may make the process of analysis clear. Research article abstract is a well-established genre and familiar to academics in general, irrespective of their disciplinary affiliations. To quote Bhatia (1993: 78), '[t]he American National Standards Institute defines abstract as follows: "an abstract is an abbreviated, accurate representation of the contents of a document, preferably prepared by its author(s) for publication with it" (ANSI 1979: 1).' Thus, an abstract answers four questions for the readers of the article: the purpose of the research, what was done, what the findings were, and what is to be concluded from the findings. Bhatia proposes four *moves* to correspond with the four elements identified above (1993: 78–9): Introducing Purpose, Describing Methodology, Summarizing Results and Presenting Conclusions.

We will examine two abstracts here and identify the four *moves* Bhatia (1993) proposes for analysing research article abstracts. It is worth keeping in mind that some abstracts may not have all four moves discretely present in the body of the abstract, or they may have more than one move included in the same sentence.

Example 1. One aspect of the relationship between meaning and interaction is explored here by taking the English particle *actually*, which is characterized by flexibility of syntactic position, and investigating its use in a range of interactional contexts. Syntactic alternatives in the form of clause-initial or clause-final placement are found to be selected by reference to interactional exigencies. The temporally situated, contingent accomplishment of utterances in turns and their component turn-constructional units shows the emergence of meaning across a conversational sequence; it reveals syntactic flexibility as both a resource to be exploited for interactional ends and a constraint on that interaction.
[From Clift, Rebecca (2001) Meaning in interaction: The case of *actually*. *Language* 77(2), 245]

Analysis into moves:

Move 1: One aspect of the relationship between meaning and interaction is explored here by taking the English particle *actually*, which is characterized by flexibility of syntactic position, and investigating its use in a range of interactional contexts.

Move 2: Syntactic alternatives in the form of clause-initial or clause-final placement are found to be selected by reference to interactional exigencies.

Move 3: The temporally situated, contingent accomplishment of utterances in turns and their component turn-constructional units shows the emergence of meaning across a conversational sequence;

Move 4: it reveals syntactic flexibility as both a resource to be exploited for interactional ends and a constraint on that interaction.

That is, the first sentence of the abstract informs the reader what the purpose of the article is: the exploration of the relationship between linguistic meaning of syntactic positional choices and their use in interaction by focusing on the use of a single particle, *actually*. The second sentence indicates that the method of analysis adopted was to examine the sentence initial and sentence final position of *actually* in real interactions to identify the interactional factors that influenced the syntactic position. The first clause of the third sentence summarizes the results: the choice of the syntactic position signals what the participants accomplish in their turns during the conversation. The second clause presents the conclusion: the syntactic flexibility of the item in focus — the fact that it can occur sentence initially or sentence finally — is a resource that is exploited for the certain interactional ends. At the same time, it places constraints on the interaction in that the choice of a syntactic position to signal a certain meaning by one participant may preclude the other participants' pursuing their own conversational purposes.

It may be helpful to look at another example and go through the same exercise of analysing the abstract into its constituent moves.

Example 2. We explore the predictors of early mastery versus error in children's acquisition of American Sign Language. We hypothesize that the most frequent values for a particular parameter in prelinguistic gestures will be the most in early signs and the most likely sources of substitution when signing children make errors. Analyses of data from a longitudinal study of the prelinguistic gestures of five deaf and five hearing children and a longitudinal study of four deaf children's early signs have revealed evidence of significant commonalities between prelinguistic gestures and early signs. This apparent continuity between prelinguistic gesture and early sign reflects constraints operating on the infant — in all likelihood, motoric constraints — that seem to persist into the first-word period in both major language modalities. In sign, as in speech, the products of first sign use building blocks that are available to prelinguistic child.

[From Cheek, Adrianne, Kearsy Cormier, Ann Repp and Richard P. Meier (2001) Prelinguistic gesture predicts mastery and error in production of early signs. *Language* 77(2), 292]

Analysis into moves:

Move 1: We explore the predictors of early mastery versus error in children's acquisition of American Sign Language. We hypothesize that the most frequent values for a particular parameter in prelinguistic gestures will be the most in early signs and the most likely sources of substitution when signing children make errors.

Moves 2 and 3: Analyses of data from a longitudinal study of the prelinguistic gestures of five deaf and five hearing children and a longitudinal study of four deaf children's early signs have revealed evidence of significant commonalities between prelinguistic gestures and early signs.

Move 4: This apparent continuity between prelinguistic gesture and early sign reflects constraints operating on the infant — in all likelihood, motoric constraints — that seem to persist into the first-word period in both major language modalities. In sign, as in speech, the products of first sign uses building blocks that are available to prelinguistic child.

Note the inclusion of moves 2 and 3 in the same sentence in the abstract. The phrase, '[a]nalyses of data from a longitudinal study of the prelinguistic gestures of five deaf and five hearing children and a longitudinal study of four deaf children's early signs' is a description of the methodology followed in the study; the rest of the sentence, 'have revealed evidence of significant commonalities between prelinguistic gestures and early signs', sums up the results of the study. The last sentence presents some conclusions from the study.

It has already been established that a genre is a highly structured text type with a great number of sociocultural, institutional and organizational constraints and expectations. It is a recognizable communicative event characterized by a set of communicative purposes identified and mutually understood by the members of the professional or academic community in which it regularly occurs. The communicative purpose is inevitably reflected in the interpretative cognitive structuring of the genre, which reflects accumulated and conventionalized social knowledge available to a particular discourse community. For example, one has only to read scientific reports on, say, global warming or use of a particular drug to treat a medical condition to see how the positions of the writers are expressed.

Although a genre is highly structured and conventionalized, it displays constraints on allowable contributions in terms of its intent, positioning, form and functional value. Consequently writers are somewhat free to exploit the available linguistic resources according to their preferences within the boundaries of generic conventions, as has been said before. This privilege to exploit generic conventions to create new forms to suit particular contexts and express specific intents, however, is available only to those few who have achieved a certain degree of visibility in the relevant professional or academic community. For the others, as Bhatia (1997: 359) observes, 'it is more of a matter of apprenticeship in accommodating the expectations of disciplinary cultures'.

Ideology of genre

Bhatia (1997: 359) asserts that genres, 'like most institutional forms of discourse ... are socially constructed, interpreted and used'. Quoting Goodrich (1987) and Foucault (1981), he suggests that this form of discourse requires two concepts: first, the concept of 'social authorship' as opposed to the more familiar notion of 'subjective authorship', i.e., who has the right to offer such a discourse. Second, it requires the concept of 'institutional sites from which the authorized speaker makes his discourse and from which the discourse derives its "legitimate source and point of application" (Foucault 1981)'.

Bhatia further points out (360) that '[T]ypical realizations of these institutionalized forms [generic forms] are often characterized by their generic integrity, on the one hand, and their propensity for innovation on the other.' He cautions that innovations are successful only if the innovator and the intended audience are both familiar with the original.

In order to assure the maintenance of generic integrity, then, professions and disciplines have 'gatekeepers', whose function it is to preserve the generic structures. Academic communities do it by insisting that 'for the construction and dissemination of knowledge "textual activity" is as important as the "scientific activity" ' (Bhatia, 1997: 363). Swales (1981) pointed out the significance of the citation of previous research for knowledge dissemination before presenting the current findings to create new knowledge. The juxtaposition of the old and the new is significant on two counts: it establishes the justification for the new in view of the old findings and the further explorations they suggest. Furthermore, it integrates the new into the tradition of 'old' texts and the body of established knowledge they represent.

Generic conventions give apt expression to the communicative intent of the genre's producers and create a bond among the community of participants. They, however, create a social distance between those who share the generic knowledge and can manipulate it for their purposes and those who are outside the generic community. This has serious implications for society at large, as is clear from the movements for simplification of legal language, the language of insurance forms, etc. As Bhatia concludes:

> The power and politics of genre are the two sides of the same coin. In one context, it can be seen as a legitimate force often used to maintain solidarity within a disciplinary community, whereas, on the other hand, it is used to keep outsiders at a distance. On the one hand, it empowers some people, the insiders, while, at the same time, it tends to silence others, especially the outsiders. (Bhatia, 1997: 366–7)

Gatekeeping

Bhatia (1997) cites an example of this silencing of the 'others' from the context of selection of papers for conventions of two professional organizations. One of them, from the field of linguistics, presents an interesting case of gatekeeping in the 1950s and early 1960s. Papers by N. Chomsky, R. B. Lees and others of the transformational-generative 'revolution' were systematically rejected by journals of the profession such as *Language*. Bhatia (1997: 368) cites a fragment of a letter Chomsky wrote to the then editor of *Language* that explains why the eminent linguist never published any of his works in that journal. The fragment comes from a talk given by William Bright at the City University of Hong Kong in 1996 and is as follows; Chomsky wrote about:

> the level of rumor-mongering and of personal hostility ... outright falsification so scandalous that they raise serious questions about the integrity of the field ... I do not want to be associated with a journal ... which publishes flat lies ... couched in rhetoric of a sort that might be appropriate to some criminal, but that one is surprised to find in a scholarly journal.

Implications for world Englishes

The implications of generic gatekeeping are profound for world Englishes since much of contemporary discourse and genre studies is dominated and determined by Western conventions. In some areas, however, especially in advertising and business, genre writers are increasingly becoming sensitive to local traditions. Local knowledge is increasingly exploited in constructing, interpreting and using genres in these contexts. Academic and professional fields, on the other hand, have yet to deal with the issues of marginalization and exclusion of Outer- and Expanding-Circle expert knowledge. One example of this exclusion is the number of reviews published in the professional journals of applied linguistics and ELT. Hardly any book published outside the western hemisphere gets even a Short Notice in such journals (see B. Kachru, 1995b).

Genres across cultures

Another dimension of genre studies is represented by cross-cultural variation in genres. There are some studies of this aspect of genre analysis (e.g., Clyne, 1987; Frederickson, 1996; Y. Kachru, 1997b, 2001b); a great deal more research is needed to determine what role the cultural context plays in determining generic structures and innovations. As has been mentioned before, it may be that not all cultures share identical genres or generic structures.

Book blurbs across cultures

Kathpalia (1997) is an attempt to determine if there are culture-specific differences in how patrons are encouraged to buy books in book blurbs on dust jackets. She examines this genre in books published by 'international publishers' and those published in Singapore by local publishers.

According to Kathpalia (1997: 417), in order to realize the purpose of the genre, to promote the book, blurbs comprise six basic moves: *Headlines>Justifying the book> Appraising the book>Establishing credentials>Endorsement(s)>Targeting the market* (where > means 'is followed by'). Each of the moves has a specific function. The opening moves of *headlines* and *justifying the book* attract readers and convince them that the book is conforming to the conventions of the discipline but at the same time is innovative. The third move, *appraising the book*, provides a brief synopsis and evaluation of the book. The next two moves, *establishing credentials* and *endorsements*, validate the book by displaying the writer's authority to write the book, and citing supporting evidence from well-known reviewers. Finally, *targeting the market* specifies the market for which the book is suitable.

Kathpalia's study found two major sorts of differences between the books published by international publishers and those published by publishers in Singapore, or local books. First, both sets of blurb writers follow the general conventions of book blurbs. However, there are differences in the favoured moves and the distribution of moves across scholarly and popular books. For instance, *justifying the book, appraising the book* and *targeting the market* are favored both in scholarly and non-fictional local trade book blurbs, whereas *establishing credentials* and *endorsements* are rare, even in scholarly book blurbs. In contrast, in the international context, *justifying the book* is more popular in non-fiction trade-book blurbs.

Local book blurbs follow the sequence of moves faithfully, and often consist of one-, two- or three-move structures, with *appraising the book* as the central or criterial move. Thus, the moves are *justifying the book>appraising the book>targeting the market* or *establishing credentials* or *endorsements*. Among the few structural deviations to be found is one in which *targeting the market* appears as the initial move.

As regards textual patterns, there are differences between non-fiction and fiction. Blurbs of non-fiction books use a range of expository patterns such as *elaboration, expansion* and *enhancement.* These terms are further explained below.

Elaboration: The meaning of a clause is elaborated by exposition, exemplification, or clarification. The linguistic exponents for these functions are expressions such as *in other words, namely, for example, for instance, to be precise, to be explicit,* etc.

Extension: A clause extends the meaning of another by using the grammatical devices of coordination (*A and B*), alternation (*A or B*) and variation (*not A but B*).

Enhancement: A clause's meaning is enhanced by an adjoining reference to time, place, manner, cause or condition.

Fiction book blurbs use the elements of narrative to appraise the book: *Abstract>Orientation>Complication>Evaluation>Resolution>Coda.* These elements characterize the progression of the narrative. *Abstract* answers the question 'What is the story about?'. *Orientation* tells the reader/listener who did what, where, and when. *Complication* brings in what happened next. *Evaluation* establishes why the story was recounted. *Resolution* provides information about what finally happened; and *Coda* enlightens readers/listeners as to the point of the story.

Differences in book blurbs

Local book blurbs neither use all the resources of the patterns given above nor try to be innovative in using the rhetorical or grammatical patterns. For instance, local blurbs are marked by excessive use of the chronological sequencing pattern and of the cohesive devices of spatial markers that realize them; e.g., *The book has four chapters. Chapter One ... In Chapter Two ... Chapter Three ... Finally, Chapter Four... .* In contrast, international book blurbs may ignore sequencing completely.

Secondly, international book blurbs do not adhere to full clauses with strict SVO patterns; they use an elliptical VO pattern just as readily: e.g., *Covers all aspects of ... ; Provides a concise guide to ... ; Includes information on ...* . International narrative book blurbs often just hint at the *Complication,* in order to raise the level of suspense; local blurbs tend to conform to grammatical correctness at the expense of heightening uncertainty and curiosity.

There are other differences in the use of linguistic devices. In international book blurbs, for example, evaluation of the book is ubiquitous and not confined to the *Evaluation* move. This is achieved by choosing appropriate lexical items and expressions. Local book blurbs focus on the *Evaluation* move and concentrate all such expressions in the sub-move that specifies the caliber of the book.

Conclusion

The two papers drawn on here bring to attention two different dimensions of genre analysis that are not only important from the point of view of stimulating research, but also of significance from the standpoint of applied relevance in the contexts of learning and teaching. Bhatia's seven steps allow genres to be defined and discussed in terms applicable across varieties. Kathpalia's moves analysis demonstrates convincingly that cultural variables influence the form and content of genres across varieties of English.

Suggested activities

1. Consider the following book blurbs (A and B). Are you able to determine, based on your analysis according to the model presented by Kathpalia, which blurb comes from a book published by an international publisher and which one from a local publisher? Discuss the linguistic features that make it possible for you to do so, or are responsible for your inability to do so.

    A. This book is a guide to the various frameworks, concepts and methods available for the analysis of discourse within linguistics. It compares six dominant approaches to discourse analysis: speech act theory, pragmatics, ethnomethodology, interactional sociolinguistics, ethnography of communication and variation theory. The author not only considers each approach from several standpoints but she also illustrates each approach through extensive applications to a variety of concrete social and linguistic problems facing discourse analysts. Exercises pose problems to which each approach can be applied.

B. [Title of the book] brings together in a single volume, views and perspectives on the English language in the Singaporean cultural context.

Issues related to the description and documentation of English in Singapore are discussed by lexicographers, sociolinguists, phoneticians, phonologists, computational linguists and other professionals.

The papers range from practical concerns such as achievable goals in English language dictionary publishing in Singapore to theoretical ones such as how to characterize Singapore English and its sounds.

2. Look at five abstracts of research papers published in a journal devoted to your field of interest. Describe their generic structure according to the models presented in the readings.
3. The following news report is from *The Manila Times*, 17 July 2003. In what respects does it conform or not to what you expect a news report to be like in the English-language newspapers you are familiar with?

Ma, son nabbed for selling 200 grams of shabu

By Jun Elias, *Northern Luzon Bureau*

SAN FERNANDO CITY, La Union – A mother and her son were arrested here Wednesday by the police while allegedly selling 200 grams of shabu worth P200,000 to an undercover agent.

Insp. Manuel Batoon, of the Ilocos Regional Anti-Illegal Drug Task Force, identified the suspects as Noemi Masangcay and her son Rommel, both residents of Barangay Pagdaraoan in this city.

Batoon said they seized 200 grams of shabu, also known as the "poor man's cocaine," from the suspects during a buy-bust in front of the Philippine National Bank branch here at 10:30 a.m. Wednesday.

According to Batoon, they received earlier information that the Masangcays were supplying illegal drugs, particularly shabu, to users not only in San Fernando but also in the big towns and cities of the Ilocos and the Cordillera Administrative Region.

Based on the information, Batoon said he organized a team to conduct the entrapment of the suspects who did not resist arrest.

He said they filed also on Wednesday charges against the suspects for alleged violation of Republic Act 9165 or the Amended Antidrug Act of 2002.

22
Power, ideology and attitudes

> Truth is a thing of this world: it is produced only by virtue of multiple forms of constraint. And it induces regular effects of power. Each society has its régime of truth, its 'general politics' of truth: that is, the types of discourse which it accepts and makes function as true; the mechanisms and instances which enable one to distinguish true and false statements, the means by which each is sanctioned; the techniques and procedures accorded value in the acquisition of truth; the status of those who are charged with saying what counts as true.
>
> Foucault (1980: 131)

Introduction

As preceding discussions have shown (see Chapter 7), English as a language with trans-national presences in various configurations of institutionalization, ranges of functions, and depths of penetration in societies lends obvious advantages to its users. On the other hand, it is not surprising that such access to a global language comes with costs of various sorts. English is the paradigm modern language of political and economic power; as such, it is claimed by some observers to be the factor responsible for disenfranchisement of a vast majority of populations in the third world, and a major cause of the 'deaths' of hundreds of minority languages. The spread of English for these commentators represents 'linguistic imperialism'. And they see support for linguistic dominance of English as sanctioning cultural, economic, and socio-political hegemony of Anglo- and Eurocentric views over the rest of the world.

On the other hand, some views from the Outer and Expanding Circles — from those who have undergone the experience of linguistic imperialism and hegemonic discourse — offer a different response to the projection of English as a vehicle of exploitation and destruction of other cultures and languages. They see it as a window to the world, a tool that empowers them.

It is true that this window is not open to everyone in all parts of the world to the same extent — and for some, it is still firmly shut; still, the demand for more access to English is as widespread as the voices against English by those who see themselves as champions of linguistic human rights.

This chapter draws on several recent publications to discuss the issues of linguistic imperialism, hegemonic discourse and responses to the imperial design and hegemony from the Outer and Expanding Circles.

Formulation of linguistic imperialism

Phillipson (1992: 17) asserts his thesis: '[T]he advance of English, whether in Britain, North America, South Africa, Australia or New Zealand has invariably been at the expense of other languages.' He notes various examples of 'successful challenges' to this dominance of English, as in Canada, where government policy mandates bilingualism with French (p. 18). He notes the overwhelming importance of educational systems, however, and asserts that 'the monolingualism of the Anglo-American establishment blinds its representatives to the realities of multilingualism in the contemporary world and gives them a … false perspective' (p. 23).

Phillipson divides the English-using world into two collectives: the *core* and *periphery* (p. 17). The core, according to his characterization and listing, matches 'the Inner Circle' (B. Kachru, 1985), the term used throughout this volume. The periphery is subdivided into two categories: those countries that use English primarily as an international link language, such as Japan and Korea, and those that use English for various intranational purposes in a wide range of domains, such as India and Singapore, i.e., the former colonial countries. In these periphery countries, English is a desirable medium, and access to it is actively sought by many people; Phillipson supports B. Kachru's (1986a) observation that '[t]hose in possession of English benefit from an alchemy which transmutes [language] into material and social … advantage. Not surprisingly, attitudes to the language tend to be very favourable.' However, Phillipson asserts that English replaces and 'displaces' other languages, in both core and periphery countries. Displacement occurs when 'English takes over in specific domains', such as education or government (p. 27).

It is education that plays the dominant role in suppressing local languages and forcing alien languages and cultural values onto people, according to Phillipson. Though university-level educational opportunities might seem to be a good thing to some people, and may be facilitated by making English the language of instruction and research in multilingual situations, Phillipson's argument is that this 'phasing out' of vernacular languages cuts away important parts of the fabric of social and cultural life. This is said to be going on in Singapore, Hong Kong, and India (pp. 28–30). The media play important roles in this 'privileging' of English. These expansions of English, Phillipson asserts, occupy space that other languages could possibly fill, and make English the only viable choice for international enterprises.

Language as a means of unifying has long been recognized, says Phillipson. In modern countries where the national language has been seen as a visible and saleable asset, such as France and Germany (not to mention Britain and the US), promotion of the language and the culture it represents have received varying degrees of support, via missionary, nationalistic and political enterprises. Phillipson lists some examples of people and agencies that have shared an awareness of evidence of linguistic imperialism and dominance, and a desire to combat it: Gandhi in India, who held English responsible for distorting education; Ngũgĩ wa Thiong'o, whose fictional and philosophical writings show how English serves to uphold the domination of a small elite and of the foreign interests that they are allied with; and even denunciations of cultural imperialism in a Nazi critique of the British Council, which identified the advance of English with the destruction of Western civilization.

Phillipson's earlier observations have been supported by more recent studies such as Phillipson (1998, 1999, 2003), and Skutnaab-Kangas (2000, 2001) that have derived support from United Nations Resolutions on linguistic human rights and preservation of cultural and linguistic diversity. These documents advocate promotion of multilingualism instead of the focus on ELT all over the world. Their concern is that the single-minded promotion of a 'global language' is 'killing' minority languages in all parts of the world at an alarming rate, which is as destructive as the obliteration of planet earth's bio-diversity. Other scholars, for example, Canagarajah (1999) and Pennycook (1994), have drawn attention to the cultural politics of promotion of English and its consequences for populations who use other languages.

Formulation of cultural politics

Pennycook (1994) explores the origins and the disciplining of the discourse of English as an International Language (EIL); he defines discourse as a place in which 'power and knowledge are joined together'. It represents 'a constellation of power/knowledge relationships which organize texts and produce and reflect different subject positions' (Pennycook, 1994: 104, citing Foucault). Discourse in Pennycook's terms seems, then, to be about knowledge as power, and about who controls any body of knowledge, thus not only accruing power to themselves, but also controlling who will be acknowledged as having a share in that power.

Pennycook's thesis is that the power and prestige of EIL came about largely because of what he terms 'a will to description' (p. 73). That is, the colonizers were also in part linguistic codifiers, who were able to act as gatekeepers for those who wished to share in the economic and other benefits of becoming English users. They assigned to themselves the task of defining what true knowledge was and who could impart it. Underlying this thesis, Pennycook's interpretation of historical events involves the ideas of Orientalism and Anglicism in the former British colonies in Asia and Africa: the former, a policy or policies to encourage indigenous languages, and the latter, to substitute English as the medium of acquiring knowledge at the expense of other languages. While a common view is that Anglicism displaced Orientalism at a given point in colonial history in each continental context, in fact the two philosophies continued as co-existing systems, but both were promulgated and manipulated by the colonial powers in order to control access to the perceived benefits of using English, and of being an English user (pp. 73–4).

Pennycook supports his case by recounting in some detail the history of language and education policies in, for example, India, Malaya, and Singapore. His interpretation is that 'the moral imperative to imperialize came to include a moral imperative to teach English' (p. 77). The access to English, however, was to be limited. For instance, Macaulay's much commented-on Minute of 1835, in which he strongly advocated English education, also pointed out the impossibility, given the limited resources at the disposal of the British for such projects, of educating more than a small (and select) minority of Indians in English (see Chapter 11). Those few would be the 'interpreters' between the colonizers and colonized; for the rest, education in local languages would have to do. Indeed, the latter strategy was more suitable to British policies and goals, according to Pennycook.

Colonial education policy aimed at producing 'an English-educated elite and a vernacular-educated population better able to participate in a colonial economy' (p. 82). There was explicit concern about the difficulties that would arise if too many people learned English: an 1884 report by the Inspector of Schools for Malaya contains this clause:

> … as pupils who acquire a knowledge of English are invariably unwilling to earn their livelihood by manual labour, the immediate result of affording an English education to any large number of Malays would be the creation of a discontented class who might become a source of anxiety to the community. A certain number of Malays educated in English are of course required to fill clerical appointments and situations of the kind which do not include manual labour. (pp. 85–6)

Such an attitude, codified in policy, provides evidence for controlling access to English. There was a good deal of interest in acquiring an English education on the part of the colonized populations, but such enthusiasm was dealt with cautiously by the British. The language was treated as a commodity, whose value would be reduced by making it too widely available (pp. 93–4). An important aspect of this division of the local peoples into English *haves* and *have-nots* was an exacerbation of any already existing social divisions. The English-educated elite 'were, by and large, cut off both culturally and economically from their own backgrounds' (p. 94).

The emphasis on English as a controlled commodity in the colonies in turn 'occasioned a massive expansion of studies on English, and thus the birth of the discourse of EIL'. A better understanding of English, including the literary canon which was produced in it, would, according to Pennycook, 'become part of the means of governance over meanings available to the English-learning colonial subjects' (p. 98). Unlike the governmental agencies, however, missionary agents had other ideas about English education. As their goal was to spread 'light' and 'civilize' the 'savage' populations of Asia and Africa, they started missionary schools that developed into sites for proselytizing the population. Thus, not only was English connected directly with education, and by extension with politics and economics, but also with Christianity: 'The connection between English and Christianity ... suggested ultimately that English was in itself Christian' (p. 100). It came to represent the 'superior' Western civilization — and embodiment of the 'superior' religion and culture of the Anglo-/Eurocentric world.

Pennycook emphasizes that what is important about the colonial period is that it 'witnessed not so much the expansion of English as the expansion of the discourse of English as an international language' (p. 102). English was regulated by its colonial 'owners' by using the discipline of linguistics and the discourse of EIL. The two major issues are standardization and 'the extent to which linguistics is a very particular European cultural form' as it sanctions description and standardization of language (p. 109). Pennycook observes that from the cultural politics of linguistics has emerged a view of language as a homogeneous unity, as objectively describable, as an isolated structural entity; meaning is taken either to reside in a world/word correspondence that is best articulated in English or within the system itself (and typically in the brain of the native speaker); monolingualism is taken to be the norm; and speech is always given priority over writing.

Standardization became important because of:

> ... the belief that language reveals the mind and that to speak the common or 'vulgar' language demonstrated that one belonged to the vulgar classes and thus that one was morally and intellectually inferior. A clear dichotomy was constructed between the 'refined' language, in which noble sentiments and higher intellectual ideas could be expressed, and the vulgar language, in which only base passions and expression of sensations was possible. (p. 112)

Such standardization served to make it easy to tell who was who in social hierarchies. It had gender-biased elements, as well as those of geography and class: men had virtually sole access to higher education, and so the standard was de facto the English that men who had been educated in the public schools of the south of England spoke.

Linguistics as a discipline grew out of the emergence of 'nation states' and the 'myth of the "national language" ' (p. 117). One way of holding diverse groups of people in a nation-state together is to develop the notion of a homogeneous speech community that shares a language embodying the possible meanings the population shares. Such a notion of 'national language' has a particularly prescriptive and normative basis: the two dominant conceptions of meaning, that meaning is dependent on a relationship to an objective world, or that meaning is dependent on internal structural relationships in language, leave meaning not in the hands of the users, as a point of contestation, as an issue of cultural politics, but in the hands of those in the centre. This result is achieved in the former conceptualization through an assumed reciprocal connection between language and the best representation of the world, and in the latter through an assumed linguistic system from within which meanings are defined. Linguistics then is free to distance itself from questions concerning society, culture and politics — the worldliness of language — and at the same time to prescribe both a particular view of language that is monolinguistic and phonocentric (primacy of speech) and particular forms of that language, i.e., standard vs. non-standard.

Relating the developments in linguistics to the spread of English, Pennycook observes that:

> The view of the spread of English as natural, neutral and beneficial is made possible by the dominance of positivism and structuralism in linguistics and applied linguistics, since these paradigms have allowed for the concentration only on a notion of abstract system at the expense of social, cultural or political understandings of language. (p. 141)

A number of different assumptions are claimed by Pennycook to reside in the discourse of EIL (p. 120), for example, that 'language is a simple representation of reality, that the world as described by English is the world as it really is and thus to learn English is essential if anyone wants to understand the modern world'.

Ideological bases of applied linguistics

Pennycook also deals with the 'disciplining of applied linguistics' which, he writes, 'has emerged as a remarkably cohesive and powerful discourse on language education' (pp. 126–8). The years following the Second World War saw 'the start of [the field's] progress towards becoming a relatively autonomous discipline'. The development of applied linguistics as such owes a great deal to the military and political interest in teaching and learning foreign languages (p. 133 *ff.*).

Applied linguistics continued the beliefs in the primacy of spoken language. It regarded language teaching as a monolingual enterprise, in which translation into and out of a first language was to be avoided. Applied linguistics also continued to avoid any recognition of many social, cultural and political dimensions of language learning and teaching, as for example when reluctance to deal with the political contexts and implications of language planning had the effect of ignoring local or national norms for models of language. Applied linguistics involved selection and ordering of what elements of languages were to be taught, and then imposing these on classroom teachers, resulting in what Pennycook calls 'a general process of deskilling teachers' (p. 140). Linguists and applied linguists were the authorities, and teachers became only the minions of the 'discourse'.

A crucial part of earlier colonial process and later hegemonic imposition was the discursive domain of cultural definition, i.e., defining who is educated, modern, civilized, cultured, sophisticated, etc. And most of these came to be associated with English-educated elites in Asia, Africa and other parts of the world.

Views from the 'periphery'

Berns et al. (1998) and Canagarajah (2000) present arguments from the other side and ask: by looking at the entire spectrum of the spread of the English only from the perspective of the centre and ignoring the current experiential realities of the periphery, are the views expressed in Phillipson (1992) and Pennycook (1994) leading to another arc in the spiral towards the same imperialistic/hegemonic discourse?

Berns et al. (1998) report that the participants in a graduate seminar taught by Berns at Purdue University read and debated the arguments presented in Phillipson (1992) and came to some unexpected conclusions. To quote the abstract of Berns and her colleagues:

> Reading Robert Phillipson's *Linguistic Imperialism* in a graduate seminar in World Englishes at Purdue University prompted intense discussion and debate not only of the issues of language dominance and spread that the author raised, but also of the rhetorical style and strategies that he chose to present a story of linguistic oppression. This article documents the reactions of seminar participants to how Phillipson presented his argument and their conclusion that the rhetorical choices he made seriously affected their ability to find his story convincing. In particular, participants — representing English language speakers in Brazil, Greece, Hong Kong, Japan, Singapore and the USA — identified problems with the author's claims and credibility, style and tone, and terminology and coverage. They also discovered that this book, which they expected to be a narrative of hegemony, was instead an illustration of the use of narrative as a hegemonic tool. (Berns et al., 1998: 271)

The graduate students were all English language educators and as such, looked for arguments based on evidence for the claims in Phillipson (1992). They agreed that:

> The story of English language teaching and its role in contributing "constructively to greater linguistic and social equality" and how "a critical ELT [could] be committed, theoretically and practically, to combating linguicism" (319) certainly warrant extensive and critical discussion. However, from the very first chapter these issues did not command our attention. Instead, Phillipson's rhetoric and ethos dominated class discussion and reaction papers. (p. 274)

The students point out examples such as the use of the term *country* for Scandinavia, *bandwagon* for the communicative language teaching methodology, and the characterization of periphery countries as 'dominated poor ones' (Phillipson, 1992: 17) as 'potentially puzzling, even insulting, if not simply misleading' (p. 275). They are also critical of Phillipson's practice of not identifying the sources of important data and making generalizations without citing evidence for them. A cited example of the former is *This proposal is put forward in the pages of a scientific journal* ... (Phillipson, 1992: 30–1), and an instance of the latter is *Formal education in Africa and Asia in its present form tends to impede economic growth* ... (Phillipson, 1992: 239). What disturbed the graduate students a great deal was postponing discussing a crucial question to the very end: 'Are there periphery English countries where an increased use of English has been accompanied by less exploitation, more democratization, and prosperity?' (Phillipson, 1992: 314). In addition, they were concerned about the failure to separate the theoretical criticism of ELT from ascribing guilt to ELT practitioners, as they were on the way to becoming ELT professionals themselves. Consequently, by the time they read Chapter 9 of Phillipson's book, entitled 'Arguments in linguistic imperialist discourse', which they considered 'one of the more convincing chapters', they already 'were feeling increasingly hostile toward ... Phillipson's condescending and patronizing attitude toward his readers' (p. 276).

The strategies of the marginalized

Canagarajah (2000) raises questions about the major claims in Pennycook (1994). It is a well-established fact that the colonial education policy aimed at producing an English-knowing elite while maintaining a majority with local vernacular education so that the elite could act as agents of the imperial power in the colonies. There are a number of documents to support this claim, some of which Pennycook cites. In addition, there is evidence to support the claim that English education was used to establish political, economic and cultural domination over the colonized subjects. Pennycook also links the standardization of language and literary canon to the enterprise of maintaining the dichotomies between the colonizers and the colonized. All these observations, however, are from the perspective of the centre, or the colonizer. There is another side to the colonial English education, not represented in Pennycook — that is, the appropriation of the medium by the colonized and their utilization of it for projecting their own messages.

Canagarajah (2000) begins with an anecdote from Jaffna, a town in Northern Sri Lanka. The story illustrates the use of 'false compliance, parody, pretense, and mimicking' as 'strategies by which the marginalized detach themselves from the ideologies of the powerful, retain a measure of critical thinking, and gain some sense of control over their life in an oppressive situation' (p. 122). The story is about a young man being baptized into the alien religion, who is able to project his allegiance to Christian beliefs by switching to English and invoking suitable symbols for the colonizers while projecting his Hindu identity to his local community by his earlier use of Tamil, with symbols consistent with his Hindu inheritance. Canagarajah draws a parallel between such strategies and what has been termed 'fronting' in the contemporary African-American community by Kochman (1981).

The story of the young man and his use of English to 'outwit the authorities', leads Canagarajah 'to articulate a relationship between language, discourse, and ideology to explore the subtle ways in which periphery communities have negotiated the ideological potentials of English'. The article points out the strategies that the local colonized people adopted 'to construct/express their liberatory ideologies leading to their empowerment' (Canagarajah, 2000: 123).

One of the first schools for higher education, the Batticotta Seminary in Jaffna, was the site of constant debate between the missionaries and administrators, both representatives of the colonial power. While some preferred Christian discourse, others favoured English literature representing Humanist/Enlightenment discourse for its civilizing influence. The author suggests that the 'restless experimentation with the curriculum' signals the educators' doubts with regard to 'the ability of the English language to inculcate pro-colonial ideologies by itself' and their suspicion that 'nothing could guarantee that English would achieve the intended results' (p. 124).

The avoidance strategy

According to Canagarajah (p. 124), the suspicions of the colonists were later proved to be justified. Some natives passively adopted these pro-colonial discourses and their ideologies for their material advancement, which Canagarajah labels *the avoidance strategy*.

The strategy of discursive appropriation

Others resisted this influence in creative ways. They separated the abstract sign system from the ideological constructs that came with it. The Hindu revivalists started Saivaite schools — not to suppress the teaching of English, but to teach it in terms of their own Hindu discourse: they taught the English language through translated texts from Hinduism. They also popularized Hindu philosophy through parables and tracts in English, borrowing strategies used by the missionaries (p. 125). This, according to Canagarajah, is *the strategy of discursive appropriation*, which is a 'precursor to the nativized variants of postcolonial discourse that have reached a highly visible level now, as championed by those like Braj Kachru (1986)'. This is a more creative and constructive strategy compared to the avoidance strategy mentioned above.

The strategy of reinterpretation

The role that the English-educated bilinguals played in the struggle for independence and the way they utilized the code made available to them to take their own message to their fellow colonized people is evident in the words of political leaders like Gandhi and Nehru of India, and Nyerere and Banda of Africa, among others. The infusion of their own meaning in the grammar of the English language by the colonized has been termed the *strategy of reinterpretation* by Canagarajah (p. 125), while B. Kachru discusses these strategies in terms of nativization (1982 *ff.*) and the *madhyama* and the *mantra* ('the medium and the message', 2002), and Ashcroft et al. (1989) examine the transformation of the *English language of the centre* into the *Englishes of the periphery*.

The strategy of accommodation

Finally, according to Canagarajah, the English language is going through another ideological transformation in the post-colonial world. The English-educated elites of the post-colonial world are projecting the language as a medium of modernism, as a medium of scientific and technological knowledge. English thus represents empowerment of people irrespective of caste, religious or regional identities. 'The very same liberal discourses which represented progressive ideologies earlier now acquire conservative interests to prop up the power of the periphery elite' (p. 126). Canagarajah terms this manoeuvre a *strategy of accommodation*.

Contrasting ideologies

Canagarajah (2000) goes on to discuss the tension between the ideological stances that support or oppose English on nationalistic grounds in the periphery. He argues that the *linguistic appropriation* or nativization of the code makes it possible for the supporters of English to project their position as equally nationalistic. He also introduces a caveat:

> [I]t is ironic ... that my characterization of English as representing multicultural discourse in the ultra-nationalistic communities contrasts with the ideologies of the English in center communities. English represents monoculturist tendencies as reflected in the English Only bills being considered in the United States ... English can represent conflicting ideologies at the same time in different communities — i.e., militant forms of cultural homogeneity in the center and pluralism in the periphery. (Canagarajah, 2000: 129)

The article further cautions that it is possible that 'the positive ideologies represented by English in the local context will be appropriated by the international agencies of English to bring them under the ideological sway of center communities ... Therefore periphery communities have to use English critically, negotiating its use amidst the conflicting ideologies it represents in diverse historical and geographical contexts' (p. 129).

Ideologies and world Englishes

Recently, the concept of world Englishes has come under criticism in several studies. For instance, Canagarajah (1999: 180) has reproached the world Englishes paradigm for following 'the logic of the prescriptive and elitist tendencies of the center linguists'. Pennycook (2003: 517) has criticized it for operating 'with a limited and limiting conceptualization of globalization, national standards, culture and identity', focusing 'only on standardized norms of English in limited domains'. He is also unhappy with 'the location of nationally defined identities within the circles, the inability to deal with numerous contexts, and the privileging of ENL over ESL over EFL' (p. 519), and being 'insistently exclusionary, discounting creoles, so-called basilectal uses of languages, and, to a large extent, all those language forms used in the "expanding circle", since as uncodified varieties, non-standard forms still hold the status of errors' (p. 521). In addition, Parakrama (1995) has criticized the world Englishes paradigm for suggesting that in certain domains, the use of English is perceived to be more neutral than one of the local languages in the Outer and Expanding Circles. According to him, 'the pleas for the neutrality of English in the post-colonial contexts are as ubiquitous and as insistent as they are unsubstantiated and unexplained' (1995: 22).

The discussions in the chapters in this volume suggest that criticisms such as those outlined above are based on selective familiarity with the available sources on world Englishes. As Chapter 1 points out, languages and varieties do not owe their existence to codification: they are there because people use them. Any language variety is a legitimate variety; standardization and codification take place for such practical reasons as mass education, legislation, publication, inter-group communication, etc. The concept of standard language or 'cultured' language has existed since prehistoric times, as the histories of classical Chinese, Sanskrit, and other languages suggest. Human societies have used, and still use, standard languages for exercising power and control, and grammarians, lexicographers, language teachers, and publishers, among others, become gatekeepers and define who belongs and who does not belong to a 'standard' language-using community. That is, however, a matter of social organization.

Researchers in world Englishes are not the primary agents of social, political, economic, or even educational policies of nation-states. They are interested in all forms of Englishes manifested in, for example, conversations of Malaysians outside a shopping complex or high school students in Sydney, lyrics of fusion music (a recent, popular genre) in India, advertising in Korean newspapers, articles in scientific journals in China, and learned publications of the UniPress in Singapore or Oxford University Press in the UK. Pidgins, creoles, and basilectal and mesolectal forms of Englishes deserve as much attention from researchers and educators as other forms of Englishes. As has been pointed out in Chapter 9, local Englishes and teaching materials based on them are crucial in ELT based on the world Englishes approach. And multilinguals' literary creativity has been emphasized in the writing of B. Kachru (e.g., 1990b, 1995a), Thumboo (e.g., 1976, 2001a) and others, not to mention in the work of the creative authors themselves.

Conclusion

Phillipson, Pennycook, and others discussed here represent views of English and English teaching and learning which raise important questions regarding the nature of EIL, its alleged benefits, and its possible concerns and drawbacks. English is used for political bargaining and conflict-resolution to bring people together; it is also a divider of those who have access to it and those who do not, and interferes with traditional languages as links to cultures which are not easily expressed in any other codes. Thus, it is a reasonable starting-point to question to what extent English is a universal or global 'communication system'.

It is equally worth investigating how 'passively' the colonized accepted the ELT ideologies and what strategies they used to assert their own constructs of

English and its societal uses. Berns et al., Canagarajah, B. Kachru and other researchers in world Englishes point to the role of the 'periphery' in the spread of English and its present functional range. The issues of power, ideology, and politics associated with Englishes and ELT are vital and need to be discussed not only by scholars, educators and teachers but also by learners and users of Englishes (see also Hasan 2003).

Suggested activities

1. Read the following and discuss it in class. What are the stances of the reviewers towards the book under review? What are your reactions to what you read?

    Symposium on *Linguistic Imperialism* [by Robert Phillipson (1992)] *World Englishes* 12.3. Perspective 2 (pp. 342–7), Perspective 3 (pp. 347–51) and Perspective 4 (pp. 351–61).

2. Tsuda (2002) is opposed to the hegemony of English and advocates 'communication rights' and 'multilingual' communication. He says, 'in dealing with the hegemony of English, we have to overcome the functionalist view of language and communication and should come up with a more philosophical view of language and communication that transcends practical and functional constraints in communication'.

    Discuss this position in class and see if you can come up with a plan to persuade the nations of the world to agree to practise 'multilingual communication' instead of depending on English for communication across countries, regions, languages and cultures. Do you agree that people will find it to their benefit to '[transcend] practical and functional constraints in [their] communication'?

Conclusion:
Current trends and future directions

Introduction

While no book of this nature can claim to be comprehensive and exhaustive, even within a relatively limited context, the previous twenty-two chapters provide an overview of the approaches, the issues, the debates, the research findings and the cross-currents of opinions, realities and contexts of world Englishes in Asia. Before concluding this discussion, it may be instructive to recapitulate what has been realized and what needs to be kept in mind.

Aims and goals

As a research area, the sociolinguistically inspired enterprise in the study of English around the world has had to explore many related topics: grammatical descriptions of varieties, language variation, language contact and its consequences, cultural and contextual factors in the development of varieties, role of human creativity, burgeoning of different canons and canonicity, more practical problems of language policy and language education, and social and political impact of English on non-English-knowing populations in various parts of the world. The twenty-two chapters of this book have attempted to deal with almost all these facets of the phenomenon of world Englishes.

That does not mean, however, that the research on world Englishes in the past several decades has progressed to such an extent that we can claim to have reached an adequate level of understanding. For example, as regards descriptions of varieties, except for General American English and Standard British English, no other standard variety (e.g., Australian, Canadian, New Zealand in the Inner Circle, or Indian, Nigerian, Pakistani, Philippine, Singaporean or Sri Lankan in the Outer Circle, or Brazilian, Chinese, French, German, Hong Kong, Japanese, Korean, Mexican or Russian in the Expanding Circle) has a published and readily available description that is comparable to that in *A Comprehensive Grammar of the English Language* by Quirk et al. (1985). The same is true of so-called non-standard varieties, dialects, and colloquial standards such as Chicano English, Hawaiian or Jamaican Creole, Nigerian Pidgin, Singaporean basilect or mesolect, to name just a few (see, however, works such as Bautista, 2000; Bolton, 2002c; 2003; Devonish, 1991; B. Kachru, 1983; Low and Brown, 2003; Mesthrie, 1992; Rahman, 1990; Solomon, 1993).

What is true of grammatical descriptions is even more so for lexicographical compilations. Australian English has recently acquired a dictionary, *The Macquarie Dictionary*, but other varieties are still waiting for dictionaries of their own, though a number of varieties such as Indian English and Caribbean English have lexicons of varying sizes and recently, there has been a great deal of activity in compiling and publishing dictionaries (see, for example, Allsopp and Allsopp, 1996; Allsopp, 2003; Avis, 1967; Barber, 1999; Bautista and Butler, 2000; Branford, 1978; Cassidy and Le Page, 1967 [1980, 2003]; Cruz and Bautista, 1995; Dore et al., 1996; Hawkins, 1984; Lewis, 1991; Holm and Shilling, 1982; Muthiah, 1991; Orsman, 1997; G. S. Rao, 1954; Silva, 1998; Whitwoth, 1855; Yule and Burnell, 1886 [1903, 1968]).

There are a number of good studies of variation between Inner-Circle varieties and across the circles, but there is no large-scale study that provides broad insight into the parameters of variation between and among Englishes. The corpora now being compiled may lead to more and more thorough-going research, and thus result in better understanding of the phenomena of variation, but at present, all we have are glimpses of the possibilities.

The same is true of language contact and resulting changes in English in various regions, and the impact of English on the indigenous languages of the areas. We have some idea of what nativization of English in India, West Africa or Singapore brings about, and we have an equally partial picture of how Englishization affects Chinese, Hindi, Japanese, Korean or Yoruba, but more is yet to be revealed than what has come to light in these sub-fields of research.

That cultural contexts affect language use has been demonstrated in studies on speech acts, writing conventions, and so on. However, precisely how and which cultural factors manifest themselves in verbal behaviour is yet to be made explicit. One way of achieving such explicitness would be to find out if there is predictability between features of culture and linguistic routines. That is, can one guess with reasonable accuracy which linguistic elements will appropriately signal given specific cultural factors? A simple example may make this clear: given an older female addressee who is not kin to the speaker but is worthy of respect, does the cultural context demand the address term 'aunt' or 'auntie', as opposed to 'Mrs X' or 'Miss X'? In which cultural context is it more polite to utter a direct request such as 'Please turn on the AC', as opposed to giving a hint, as in 'It's boiling in here'? It is clear that correlations between cultural features and linguistic expressions lead to variety differentiation, and may cause difficulty in communicating across Englishes. As Sledd (1993: 277) observes, '[D]ifferences among the privileged [standard language speakers] are most obvious in pronunciation and vocabulary, much smaller in grammar, trickiest perhaps in areas where cultural differences cause different uses of shared linguistic forms and processes.' A more detailed understanding of the phenomenon will go a long way towards reducing the uncertainty and lead to better success in the tricky realms of cross-cultural communication.

The creative potential of Englishes in Asia and elsewhere has been highlighted in published works of noted literary critics and writers themselves (see Chapters 8 and 10). Creativity, however, is not restricted to literature; everyday language use has its own creative dimension. For instance, journalism, scholarship, advertising, print and audio-visual media all offer possibilities of exploiting language and its resources for their own purposes. There are studies that deal with the use of English in several genres of print and audio-visual media in the Asian and other contexts (see, for example, T. K. Bhatia, 2001; Hilgendorf and Martin, 2001; Jung, 2001; Moody, 2001; Moody and Matsumoto, 2003; Reyes, 2002; Reynolds, 1993; Stanlaw, 2004; Takashi, 1990; Thompson, 2002; Tsang and Wong, 2004; among others). Nevertheless, in addition to more studies on advertising and popular music and performance, other genres also deserve to be investigated. Business and financial negotiations across cultures have drawn some attention (e.g., Firth, 1995; Yamada, 1992), but a more comprehensive picture of successful negotiating strategies in Englishes across cultures has yet to emerge. There are few studies that deal with diplomacy, yet the relentless progression of globalization and internationalization demands a greater understanding of processes of diplomatic negotiations. There is no denying the fact that more diplomatic give and take at the Untied Nations, World Trade Organization and other international fora involving nation-states employ the various Englishes that participants bring with them than any other language of wider communication.

Literary creativity has resulted in a number of English literatures in addition to the well-recognized traditional canons of American and British literatures. Historical accounts and critical evaluations of these literatures is a fascinating area of research and has already inspired some theoretical and methodological approaches, debates and discussions (e.g., Ashcroft, Griffiths and Tiffin, 1989; B. Kachru, 2005). Detailed studies of English literatures of South and Southeast Asia and Africa such as the ones on American and British literatures, however, are yet to appear, though there have been impressive works on these topics (Booker, 1998; Irele and Gikandi, 2004; De La Toree, 1978; Gikandi, 1987, 2003; Griffiths, 1978; Hogan, 2000; Irele, 2001; Iyengar, 1962, 1985; King, 1980; Lim, 1994; Mukherjee, 1971; Narasimhaiah, 1978; Ngũgĩ, 1986; Rahman, 1991; among others).

No other area of world Englishes has attracted as much attention as that of language policy in language education. There are numerous contentious issues, and experts from the Inner, Outer and Expanding Circles have been vigorously arguing about ESL, EFL, EIL and ESP for decades. Gradually, the ideas of Inner Circle and other Circle experts have converged to the extent that now assertions of local approaches, methods and even local norms are not viewed as 'heresies' in any circle (see the controversy articulated in B. Kachru [1976] and Prator [1968]).

Although the teaching of English has been given a prominent place in curricula in all regions (see Chapters 11–13), ideological issues and concerns remain in almost every part of the English-using world. On the one hand are harsh pronouncements of linguistic imperialism and its discourse (see, e.g., Phillipson, 1992; Pennycook, 1994), hegemony of English and its stifling effect on other languages (Tsuda, 2002), linguistic human rights and linguicism or outright 'killing' of numerous languages (see, for example, Phillipson, 1998, 2003; Skutnabb-Kangas, 2000, 2001); on the other are more sedate voices raising questions about a variety of issues, such as language standardization, bilingual and multilingual education, teacher training programmes, materials development, etc., in language teaching, including ELT, in Asia and Africa (Bamgboṣe, 1998; Pakir, 1997). Educationists rightly worry about what will happen to the ideals of a just and equitable society where everyone should have access to same opportunities if vast majorities of pupils do not acquire adequate English and their local languages are confined to limited domains of use. On the other hand, since English has become one of the most effective means of advancement, how legitimate is it to deny people the opportunity to learn the language in the interests of preservation of mother tongue or regional language? The question of utilizing limited resources to promote local languages and at the same time provide effective instruction in English is a difficult one that all developing countries face.

Future directions

Even the necessarily limited presentations here suggest that English studies have a long way to go before all the areas of research have been explored to a level where our knowledge and understanding are significantly enhanced. There is obviously an urgent need for reasonably comprehensive grammatical descriptions and dictionaries of various Englishes, codified as well as colloquial ones. This is important for comparing the varieties and for addressing such issues as mediums of education, use in intranational administration, commerce, legal system and media, and for international diplomacy, commerce, trade, tourism, and other purposes.

It is essential for us to have more sociolinguistic information about the attitudes towards, and domains and functions of English in each context, especially as the use of English intersects with local languages. Users' and policy-makers' attitudes have impacts on the domains and functions of the language, and all three — attitudes, domains and functions — together determine the future developments in nativization and acculturation of the medium. This has been demonstrated by the studies on discourse and code-mixing and switching in different regions of the world. More detailed studies on speech acts, different genres of journalism, literature, popular culture, and societal language use is crucial for an understanding of the role of sociocultural factors in the interaction of the medium and the message.

Related to the societal use of language are the issues of standardization and codification. No matter how much controversy is generated by these issues, it is important for both learners and teachers to know what the goals of their efforts are. Even if a decision is made to use, say, Malayalee English in the state of Kerala in India, or Hong Kong English in Hong Kong, there would be a need to describe the sentence patterns, standardize spelling, select vocabulary items and idioms, and decide on the patterns of discourse that would go into textbooks, and educational policy-makers and teachers would have to adopt the standards that would determine what is acceptable and what is not in such textbooks. Along with the concerns of standardization and codification come questions of methodologies of teaching and debates about immersion in English versus bilingual teaching methods which have to be resolved. More research on the effectiveness of methodologies and the contribution of code-mixing and switching in language learning is required in order to inform teachers and learners about the practices they may be encouraged to adopt.

Related to the above issues and concerns are questions about the impact of the world-wide spread and dominance of English on the rich and varied linguistic heritages of the world. Even 'developed' and literary languages such as Arabic, Bengali (or Bangla), Chinese, French, German, Hindi, Italian, Japanese, Tamil, Telugu, Urdu and others are increasingly compelled to share their domains of use. Languages with oral traditions, those confined to smaller geographical regions, or those without a written form are increasingly losing speakers and domains of use. This is not only because of English. Other languages of wider communication have the same effects in various regions of the world. For example, in India most parents want their children to be educated in languages that ensure their mobility for future career success and local languages are not equipped to give them this. Therefore, preference for regional languages and official languages is increasing. In fact, the plea for English-medium schools is the fastest-growing demand in education in India. According to the NCERT's Fifth Educational Survey, the number of languages used in Indian schools shows a constant and accelerating rate of decline, from 81 in 1970 to 67 in 1976, 58 in 1978, and 44 in 1990. According to the same survey, the number of languages used as the medium of instruction also has decreased: in primary education, from 47 in 1978 to 24 in 1990, and in secondary education, from 43 in 1978 to 22 in 1990. The same trend is evident in most multilingual societies. This situation poses a serious challenge for the goals of multilingual and multicultural education in Asia and across the world.

Conclusion

We end this discussion of world Englishes in Asian contexts by posing a number of questions that students and scholars interested in English studies may find stimulating.

1. What was the history of spread of English in different parts of the world, and which of the historical factors still exist? (See, for example, Quirk's discussion of demographic, imperial, and econo-cultural models of the spread of English and the role of sociolinguistic realities in B. Kachru's discussion of the topic in Chapter 7.)
2. What were the agencies of diffusion and which one of those are still active in which parts of the world? (For example, imperial policies of administration and education, missionary activities, regional and international political organizations such as ASEAN, EU, UN, globalization of economies represented by multinational corporations, among others.)
3. What were the instruments through which these agencies propagated the language, and which of these instruments are still effective? ('Agencies' include official and semi-official organizations such as British Council, textbooks and language teaching methodologies, Bible translations, control of linguistic resources of scholarly publications, etc.)
4. What are the impacts of local social, cultural and linguistic heritage on English in various parts of the world and how have the local influences shaped the various Englishes?
5. What is the range and depth of penetration of English in the cognitive and sociocultural domains in various parts of the world?
6. What is the impact of English on local languages and what concerns do they raise about the survival of languages and cultures of different communities?
7. How useful is the way research in world Englishes approaches these questions? Is there a way in which inquiries in the spread, forms and functions of Englishes can be carried out while adopting neither a 'triumphalist' position nor an alarmist view that holds the spread of English responsible for the decay and death of local languages and cultures?
8. No reasonable individual disagrees with the proposition that all languages and cultures contribute uniquely to the mosaic that is the human world and are worth nurturing and strengthening. How can this best be done

in the current rapidly globalizing world? How do governments and educationists balance the demand for learning a world language that opens doors for more prosperity with the concern for preserving languages that have limited domains in geographical as well as functional terms?

These questions are not easy to answer, and the previous chapters have only provided glimpses into how researchers have attempted to deal with them. Ultimately, everyone interested in English studies has to reflect on these questions and decide which trends and directions to follow for realizing which goals. The world Englishes paradigm, as presented in this book, approaches all the questions from a position of sociolinguistic reality and investigates how this reality is shaping the Englishes and other languages in different parts of the world.

Notes

CHAPTER 3

1. The excerpt quoted from Longe (1999: 239) at the beginning of this chapter expresses advice to new students printed in a University of Benin (Nigeria) student magazine. The meaning of the items in italics are as follows: *banging* 'failing a test'; *hackeous* 'strict, mean, difficult'; *fashee* 'to regard as unwanted'; *jacker* 'reader'; *aro* 'unhinged (derived from a place name near Ibadan where a mental hospital is located); *B1* 'the mental ward at the University of Benin Hospital'; *burst* 'miss or cut', *jambite* 'a new male student admitted to the university following the Joint Admissions and Matriculation Board Examination'.
2. Although there is controversy with regard to the distinction between stress-time vs. syllable-time in phonological literature, the remarks made here about differences between varieties is a valid observation. No matter what the ultimate phonetic explanation may turn out to be for the perception of rhythmic difference, there is a perceivable dissimilarity between the Inner- and other-Circle varieties which is still being described in these terms (see, e.g., Tayao, 2004).
3. The details of sound systems in various Englishes are based on the following sources: B. Kachru (1983) for Indian English; Bao (2001), Brown (1986) and Platt and Weber (1980) for Singapore-Malaysian English; Llamzon (1997) and Bautista and Bolton (2004b) for Philippine English; Rahman (1990) for Pakistani English; and other sources listed in the references.

CHAPTER 4

1. Koyama (1992) does not indicate whether this is a recorded text of a naturally occurring conversation or a constructed dialogue.
2. The idea that an utterance may constitute an act was first articulated in the field of philosophy by Austin (1962) and subsequently elaborated in a series of works by Searle beginning with Searle (1969). For a linguistic formulation of the notion, see Sadock (1974) and other works that deal with pragmatics, such as G. Green (1989, Chapters 4 and 5).

CHAPTER 5

1. From Reid, T. R. (1998) Yobbish prat whinges on. *The Yomiuri Shimbun*. Friday, 15 May (reprinted from *The Washington Post*).
2. A cloze passage is used in testing to evaluate the test-taker's grammatical or lexical knowledge. Every nth word or item, or selected items, are deleted from a text; the test-taker is asked to read the passage and fill in the blanks in order to make the text complete in some consistent and coherent way.

CHAPTER 6

1. The parameter-setting model claims that underlying principles of linguistic structure are universal; exposure to language-specific data simply sets the parameters of applicable rules. For instance, all languages have S(ubjects), O(bjects) and V(erbs); the order in which they appear is set by the parameter of specific languages, SVO for English, SOV for Japanese, etc.
2. These observations address an outline of the major aspects of the 'models' problem in world Englishes with regard to SLA; for detailed discussions and case studies, see B. Kachru (1982b); Sridhar and Sridhar (1992); and Smith (1992). Eminently common-sense perspectives on internationally applicable notions of 'standard' English may be found in B. Kachru (1976) and Strevens (1983).
3. This may be changing in Singapore as more and more young people adopt Singaporean English as their primary language. Even Singapore, though, does not support the creolization hypothesis, as the acrolectal form has coexisted with mesolectal and basilectal forms in the past and continues to do so in the present.

CHAPTER 7

1. See B. Kachru (1995b) for more on speech community and speech fellowship.
2. The allusion in the term 'Caliban syndrome' is to Shakespeare's *The Tempest* I, ii, in which Prospero chides Caliban for being ungrateful and reminds him that it is to him, Prospero, that Caliban owes his power of speech. Caliban replies, 'You taught me language; and my profit on't / Is, I know how to curse; the red plague rid you, / For learning me your language!'

CHAPTER 8

1. This quote is from Mark Twain's 'Explanatory' note (p. xxxii) facing p. 1 of the text of *The Adventures of Huckleberry Finn* (1884/1985, Penguin Books edition, NY: Viking Penguin).
2. The interview with Kirpal Singh was published in *The Straits Times* of 15 March 1992.

CHAPTER 9

1. The excerpt from Mikie Kiyoi is from the *International Herald Tribune*, 3 November 1995.

2. This chapter draws upon B. Kachru (1995b) to a great extent, and adds other perspectives to the discussion.

CHAPTER 10

1. From Keki N. Daruwalla's poem, *The Mistress,* in Makarand Paranjape (ed.) *Indian Poetry in English,* Hyderabad: Macmillan India Limited, 1993.
2. Although Widdowson's chapter is exclusively concerned with the importance of poetry in language teaching, the arguments are equally applicable to other types of literary works.
3. The reference is to the Commonwealth of Nations, organized at the end of the British Empire to bring together the ex-colonies; the foundation of the Commonwealth as an association of truly independent sovereign states was laid in the presence of eight countries of the Commonwealth — Australia, Britain, Canada, Ceylon (Sri Lanka), India, New Zealand, Pakistan and South Africa — in April 1949 in London.
4. The major Indian languages (e.g., Hindi) do not have separate expressions for greeting and leave-taking; for instance, one may use the expression *namaste* in both situations.
5. See Resources for listings of select writers of contact literatures.
6. There is a long tradition of studying classical languages such as Arabic, Avestan, Classical Chinese, Persian and Vedic and Classical Sanskrit in certain institutions in the West. However, there is no tradition of studying modern languages of Africa, Asia and other parts of the world comparable to the study of modern European languages in Western educational institutions.
7. Hulme's glossary gives *aue* as 'exclamation of dismay, or despair' (p. 446). For references and discussion see B. Kachru (1983a).

CHAPTER 11

1. The other superposed languages were Sanskrit, Persian, and Portuguese, the latter confined to basically the west coast.
2. In the Indian diaspora in many parts of the world, however, English plays a role in religious ceremonies and rituals associated with Hinduism (see Pandharipande, 2001).

CHAPTER 16

1. Cited from *Linguistic Variability and Intellectual Development,* translated by George C. Buck and Frithjof A. Raven (1971). Philadelphia, PA: University of Pennsylvania Press.
2. The study provides brief background information and justification for the choice of these varieties of English, which are not recapitulated here.
3. Adjective as a category is predominantly stative, as opposed to verb, which is primarily dynamic in English. The use of simple present tense usually indicates static, habitual or generic properties rather than dynamic action or process.

CHAPTER 19

1. Since the overall sample size was different (50,000 word from Maori speakers and 250,000 words from Pakeha speakers) the total number of occurrences of *eh* for each group was converted to frequency index scores by calculating the rate of occurrence per 10,000 words.

2. The transcription symbols indicate the following meanings: capital letters indicate emphatic stress; square brackets indicate paralinguistic feature (such as laughter) or gloss and : : surrounding it signal its beginning and end; + indicates pause up to one second; //... \ and / ... \\ signal simultaneous speech; (word) indicates the best guess at an unclear utterance; ? signals question or rising intonation; - indicates incomplete or cut off utterance; and ... signals sections of transcript omitted from the quoted excerpt.

Glossary

abstract – a synopsis of a text (e.g., a journal article), usually written by the text author to give readers an overview of the basic features and applications of the work, such as its purpose, findings, and conclusions. (Ch. 21; V. Bhatia, 1993)

accent – the phonological features of a language or a language variety, including rhythm and intonation, distinguished from morpho-syntactic or other characteristics; also applied generally to 'the way a variety or speaker sounds', e.g., 'She has/speaks with an Australian accent.' (Chs. 3, 5; Strevens, 1983)

accommodation – adjustments that people make in their production and decoding of speech, according to the participants, situation, etc.; e.g., one may 'accommodate' one's active vocabulary to that of a conversational partner whose vocabulary is (perceived to be) limited in terms of technical familiarity, or employ usages that are (perceived to be) favourable in terms of establishing an affective connection among participants. The same is true of pronunciation. For example, Indian English typically exhibits retroflex stops where Inner-Circle varieties have alveolar stops; conversational participants across the two varieties make adjustments in their perceptions of these sets of consonants so that intelligibility is not disrupted. (Ch. 19; Stubbe and Holmes, 1999)

acculturation – the process a language undergoes in becoming adapted to a new social/cultural context; e.g., English has been acculturated by Asian speakers for functionality in their countries and regions, in genres and relationships that may be new or at least not identical to those in other circles or regions; cf. *nativization* and *accommodation*. (Ch. 2; B. Kachru, 1997)

acquisition – (language ~) as distinguished by many writers from language *learning*, the internalizing of linguistic and social competences so that a language is functional and 'natural'; often used in a general sense, as is 'learning'; cf. Second Language Acquisition. (Ch. 6; Ritchie and Bhatia, 1996) acrolect – originally used in creole studies to refer to the economically and socially most prestigious form of a language variety, now often applied to varieties of English (or other languages) that are not creoles; associated with higher levels of education and interaction with users of a 'full' form of the language. *Mesolect* and *basilect* refer to descending gradations of proficiency, completeness of lexicon, etc. (Ch. 2; Tay, 1993b)

agreement – in grammar, any relationship of 'concord' among elements or structures; English speakers may (only) be aware of 'subject-verb agreement', i.e. number concord, e.g., 'I *am*, you *are*, he/she *is*' but count/ non-count phenomena are also a kind of agreement, e.g., '*much* information, *many* books'; other languages may have various sorts of 'agreement rules' involving gender, noun-class, etc. (Ch. 3; B. Kachru, 1992)

appeals – kinds of backing or evidence that writers and speakers may use to give weight, persuasiveness, etc., to their texts; e.g., appeals may be rational or affective, and formal writing in the West makes frequent use of appeals to authority, e.g., asserting the favourable association of a well-known and respected author to bolster one's own position. (Ch. 20; Y. Kachru, 1988, 1992; Kamimura and Oi, 1998)

argumentation – the formal and functional structures and devices that make up persuasive written or spoken presentation; the criteria for 'a good argument' are largely culturally determined; cf. *appeals*. (Ch. 20; Y. Kachru 1988, 1992)

backchannel – utterances such as *yeah, mhmm, really?* which indicate that the addressee is paying attention to the speaker; a typical comparison is that Japanese speakers use a lot of backchannelling compared to US English speakers. (Ch. 4; Yamada, 1992)

borrowing – one of the most familiar ways of adding to the lexicon of a language: lexical items from language B are transferred directly into language A with greater or less nativization of pronunciation, and often with adaptations of syntactic category, semantic criteria, and pragmatic effect; a common example is the German word *delicatessen*, borrowed into English as denoting a particular sort of food shop and restaurant; the *–en* morpheme indicates German grammatical plurality, but English makes the plural *delicatessens* in accordance with its own morphological rules; compare *code-mixing*. (Ch. 18; Tay, 1993)

cleft sentence – an English syntactic structure in which the agent or topic of a sentence is demoted from its sentence-initial position to follow a topicalizing *It was …* and the VP of the sentence is moved into a subordinate *wh-* clause; e.g., *Fred stole this important book from the Bookstore* → *It was Fred who stole this important book . …* (Ch. 3; Bamgboṣe, 1992)

cloze – from 'closure', often '~ passage'; text with elements omitted according to a research or testing purpose, e.g., all articles or every nth word;

students or subjects fill in the blanks as they are led to by grammatical or other criteria under focus. (Ch. 5; Smith, 1992; Smith and Rafiqzad, 1979)

code – sometimes used for 'language', as in *code-mixing, code-switching*.

code-mixing – see *code-switching*.

code-switching – the appearance of blocks of speech in two or more languages in the utterances of multilingual conversational participants; historically, some writers have distinguished ~ *mixing* from ~ *switching* in terms of whether changes occur across clause boundaries or not, but the terms are often used interchangeably. (Ch. 18; Poplack, 1980; Tay, 1993)

codification – the act or fact of the lexicon, sound/phrase/sentence structures, etc. of a language becoming well defined in some referential sense, as in textbooks, handbooks, or dictionaries; allied with the notion of *standard(ization)*. (Ch. 7; Pakir, 1997)

coinage – inventing words (from 'making coin' – producing something new that has value); a well-known English example is the word 'googol' (the number equal to/represented by 1 followed by 100 zeros), which is attributed to the young nephew of the mathematician Edward Kasner (d. 1955); compare other means of expanding lexicons, such as *borrowing*. (Ch. 14; Bokamba, 1992)

collocation – juxtaposition of words in commonly accepted or recognized ways, e.g., 'mail a letter' is a common US English phrase corresponding to British English 'post a letter', which refers to the same activity; both are comprehensible across varieties, but 'it is said this way' in one variety or the other. (Ch. 17; Bautista, 1997a)

communicative competence – term attributed to Hymes (e.g., 1974), a speaker's capacity to use a language properly for a range of functions in various contexts with adjustments taking into account the status, attitudes, etc., of other participants; e.g., being able to construct sentences such as 'Congratulations on the newest addition to your family! My, what an adorable baby!' is a matter of *linguistic competence;* in terms of *communicative competence*, in most contexts, it is acceptable, even expected, that a speaker will congratulate new parents and make a complimentary remark about their baby, while in some cultures complimenting young women would be regarded as something not done. (Ch. 4; Hymes, 1974; K. Sridhar, 1991)

competence – capacity/ability in language or its use (see *communicative competence*) which underlies production or application. (Ch. 4; Hymes, 1974)

complementation – the 'completion' (as opposed to grammatical object) of a syntactic structure, such as the post-verbal nominal phrase in 'Professor Yamashita is *my teacher*'; very importantly used in describing and classifying verbs; e.g., 'certain causal verbs, such as *force*, require *to + verb* complements'; English differs from many languages in having a variety of forms besides full clauses available as verb-complement structures. (Ch. 3; Baumgardner, 1987)

compounding – joining two (or more) tokens of a lexical category under one instance of the category's use, commonly *compound nouns* and *~ verbs*; some compounds may be formed ad hoc, while there are innumerable stable formations, such as *lighthouse* and *table-tennis*; world varieties of English may engage in *hybrid compounding* (see), e.g., Philippine English *pulot boy* 'boy who picks up tennis balls in a game' (Chs. 13, 17; Bautista, 1997b)

comprehensibility – apprehension of semantic reference and sense in a conversation or written text (see *intelligibility*). (Ch. 5; Smith and Bisazza, 1982)

contact literature – the literature in English of Outer- or Expanding-Circle national writers, which includes strong influences from regional or national traditions. (Ch. 10; B. Kachru, 1986a)

conversation analysis – examination and interpretation of the elements and conventions of interpersonal communication, such as discourse-marking and who may nominate new topics (see *speech acts* and *cooperative principle*). (Chs. 4, 19; Sacks, Schegloff and Jefferson, 1974)

cooperative principle – taken as the basis for all natural conversation and thus a general descriptive starting-point for analysing conversation, speakers are assumed to want to 'cooperate' in making their participation as effective as possible; used by H. Grice, who asserted four basic *maxims* (see) that effect the principle, viz. Quantity, Quality, Relevance and Manner. (Ch. 4; Grice, 1975)

coordination – the joining of two structures such that neither is subordinated to the other; e.g., the nouns in *tea and coffee* are coordinate nouns in a nominal phrase, and the clauses in *JoAnn likes tea, and/but Amita prefers coffee* are coordinate clauses in a sentence; deciding what structures are coordinate may play a role in cross-variety questions of verb agreement, as in 'The newspaper, as well as the mail, *was/were* soaked by the rain.' (Ch. 16; Quirk et al., 1985)

copula (construction) – a verb, usually construed as *be* but also including words and uses such as *seem* and *appear*, that links a clause-subject with a complement (as opposed to a syntactic object); in some varieties of English, as in some languages (such as Russian), copula constructions may appear without an overt verb, e.g., *She [is] Mary Jo.* (Chs. 13, 15; Ho, 1995; Ho and Platt, 1993; Rickford, 1998)

core – in Phillipson's view, the countries corresponding exactly to B. Kachru's Inner Circle, where English is the dominant, usually only, *institutionalized* language. (Chs. 1, 22; Phillipson, 1992)

corpus – a large collection ('body') of language data which can be accessed to show not only frequency but also context of use of selected items for linguistic analysis. (Chs. 1, 17; Nelson, 2004) creativity – the use of language elements to form new structures and for new uses, and the use of language generally in new effective ways; often applied to literary production, creativity is a feature of all human language use, and is especially visible in the use of emerging varieties of English. (Ch. 8; Y. Kachru, 1992)

creole – a language emerging from a former *pidgin* (see); sometimes carried on as the name of a language, e.g., Jamaican Creole, in which case 'creole' is capitalized. (Chs. 2, 15; Siegel, 1999)

deference – a politeness feature or strategy involving covert or overt recognition of lower status relative to that of a conversational participant; e.g., *Would you mind doing this for me as soon as you can* is more deferentially phrased than *Please do this right away*, and a speaker would be presumed to know when and to whom to use either form (see *communicative competence* and *directive*). (Ch. 4; K. Sridhar, 1991)

depth – the penetration of a language, in this case English, through socioeconomic/educational strata of a society; typically, one may think of English being used by professional people in, say, Singapore, but it has a 'deeper' penetration in that it is also used by shopkeepers, street vendors, and 'working people'; see *functional domains* and *range*. (Ch. 2; B. Kachru, 1997)

description/descriptive grammar – see *prescription*.

determiner – an English syntactic/lexical category (also 'article') including *a/an* and *the* that functions with the characteristics of *countability* and *definiteness* in indicating kind of reference; source of limitless woe to generations of ESL learners. (Ch. 3; Huddleston, 1984)

dialect – neutrally, any *variety* of a language, including the standard one, but often applied derogatorily to a system used by people perceived or asserted to be of lower social status than that of the user of the term; cf. *variety*. (Ch. 1; Wolfram, 1981)

diaspora – originally more specific in reference, now applied to any sort of social spreading, in particular to the spread of English and to the out-migrations of groups of people; used to refer to the different sorts of expansions of English, beginning with the 'diaspora' of speakers into the new worlds of North America and Australia/New Zealand. (Ch. 1; B. Kachru, 1992c)

directive – (imperative) form that 'means what it says', rather than using a circumlocution that is higher in deference, e.g. *'Can I have ...?'* vs. directive *'Give me ...'* (Ch. 4; K. Sridhar, 1991)

discourse – loosely, any language use, usually construed as production (spoken or written) at levels above that of the sentence, including very lengthy productions on a topic; narration and description are common *discourse types*; also, language of specific disciplines or topics or for specified purposes, e.g. the *discourse of linguistics*; Pennycook and others use *discourse* to refer to any speech, writing, or activity having to do with a topic or an issue, as in 'the discourse of ELT' and 'colonial/hegemonic discourse'. (Ch. 19; Ch. 22; Pennycook, 1994)

discourse marker – elements in texts (spoken or written) which have no independent meaning but serve to signal such things as text-type, text-organization, speaker's attitude towards the topic, and speaker's perception of participants' attitudes; *well* is a discourse marker with many uses in English, and Singaporean/Malaysian English provide various much-discussed examples, such as *la(h)*. (Ch. 8; Pakir, 1992)

disjunction – an (instance of) an adverbial form that expresses the speaker's attitude, e.g., including *perhaps* in a sentence to show uncertainty. (Ch. 16; Quirk et al., 1985)

echo-subject structure – a duplication of a sentence-subject, perhaps as a reinforcement of subject as *topic* (see), as in '*My wife, she* prefers tea to coffee'. (Ch. 14; Bokamba, 1992)

Englishization – 'becoming more like English' or influence of English on a language with which it comes into contact, including the borrowing (and adaptation) of English lexical items and the importation of English-based or -influenced structures; the increased use of passive voice in Chinese is widely held to be an instance of Englishization (see *acculturation* and *borrowing*). (Chs. 2, 11; B. Kachru, 1994a)

epistemic – a modality having to do with the speaker's degree of confidence in what is being said; *epistemic discourse markers* (see) might include, for example, *maybe, I'm sure (that), if you agree* ...; see *modal*. (Chs. 16, 19; Stubbe and Holmes, 1999)

ethnomethodology – the investigation of what people know of their own societies and activities, and how they adjust in their interactions to achieve cooperation and effectiveness; origination attributed to H. Garfinkel; the basis for formal *conversational analysis* (see). (Ch. 4; Tannen, 1984)

exchanges – conversational turns. (Ch. 19; Valentine, 1995)

face (positive ~, negative ~, face-threatening act [FTA]) – a person's self-image, or how one perceives oneself to be perceived by others; *positive face* is involved with friendliness and wanting to be valued, while *negative face* is involved with formality and social distance in not wanting to be deterred from accomplishing goals; FTAs (impositions) *threaten* an addressee's *face*, and various politeness strategies aim at lessening the degree of threat or loss of face. (Chs. 4, 19; Brown and Levinson, 1987)

floor – (having the ~) the status of a speaker engaged in her/his conversational turn who may expect not to be interrupted, as used formally in meetings, where a speaker who is said to 'have the floor' may not, under parliamentary rules, be interrupted unless (s)he agrees to 'yield the floor' to another participant. (Ch. 4; Hayashi, 1996)

focus – the part of a proposition that gives the intended comment or information for a *theme* (see); varieties of Englishes use differing formal strategies to designate what part of an utterance is under focus; cf. *topic, theme,* and *given/new information.* (Ch. 3; Gumperz, 1982).

fossilization – a part of the Interlanguage hypotheses which speaks to the stabilization of a variety's or individual speaker's language features as 'incorrect' forms with respect to an alleged standard of success. (Ch. 6; Selinker, 1992)

functional domains – areas of life in which a language works effectively; e.g., if people use English voluntarily and 'naturally' in settings involving medical care in an Asian country, then medicine is one of the functional domains of English in that context; see *range* and *depth.* (Ch. 2; B. Kachru, 1997)

genre – a recognizably structured and conventionalized text type with an unambiguous communicative purpose, e.g., a scientific report of an experiment, or an abstract at the beginning of an academic paper, or the blurb on a book cover. (Ch. 21; V. Bhatia, 1993)

genre analysis – the investigation of *genre(s)* (see) in terms of sociolinguistic characteristics, such as appeal to audiences, specialized lexicon, etc.; Bhatia (1994) proposes that specific text-types may be analysed in terms of seven 'moves', which perform various necessary or possible functions, such as 'placing the given text in a situational context'. (Ch. 21; V. Bhatia, 1993)

Gricean Maxims – Quality ('be truthful'), Quantity ('say enough, and no more'), Relevance ('make contributions relevant to the topic and context') and Manner ('be clear and unambiguous'); see *cooperative principle.* (Ch. 4; Grice, 1975)

hegemony – domination of a language (group) by English (speakers); in the view of Phillipson, Pennycook, and others, English has an undue influence on languages with which it comes into contact, to the extent of altering their forms and functions and even causing them to pass out of use, or 'die'; often associated with colonialism and putative on-going covert colonialism or 'post-colonialism'. (Ch. 22; Phillipson, 1992)

identity – how people perceive themselves or believe that they are perceived by others; people have personal, professional, etc. identities, and language – e.g., ability to use English effectively – may be part of that identity (see *face*). (Ch. 2; Crystal, 1985)

imperative – a directive form used to get a participant-addressee to do something, e.g., *Hurry up! Start now! Please have some fruit!*; varieties of English may vary in terms of how direct a speaker may be in asking someone to do something in a given context, e.g., in a shopping situation or in giving or receiving a gift. (Ch. 4; Zhu, Li and Qian, 2000)

inflection – in phonetics/phonology, a pitch contour perceived as one of a number of grammatical or pragmatic functions, e.g., rising pitch (in English) signalling a question (whether or not a lexical question-element appears) or indicating surprise (see *intonation*); in morphology-syntax, a class of affixes which serve grammatical functions (as in English noun-pluralization or possession, e.g., 'Greg'*s* house*s*') and do not change the word-class or meaning of a stem (as opposed to *derivation*). (Ch. 3; Huddleston, 1984)

institutionalization – the official, legal assignment of functions to a language, e.g., English is *institutionalized* as a language of higher education and government in, say, Singapore. (Ch. 2; B. Kachru, 1994a)

instrumental motivations – reasons for people to learn or use an additional language that are external to themselves, e.g., for wider ranges of options for education or advancement in a job or profession; *integrative motivations*, by contrast, have to do with personal reasons involving affective or social factors, e.g., feeling drawn towards the speakers or culture of the additional language; Gardner and Lambert came to prefer the term *orientations* to motivations; compare *intrinsic/extrinsic motivations*. (Ch. 6; Gardner and Lambert, 1972)

integrative motivations – see *instrumental motivations*.

intelligibility – broadly used to mean anything in the range of 'understanding', but more usefully, the apprehension of sounds as utterances of/in a language that one knows; *comprehensibility* involves the recognition/assignment of meaning as presented by an utterance; *interpretability* has to do with catching the intention or import of an utterance. (Ch. 5; Smith, 1992)

interlanguage – the hypothesis that additional-language learners continue along a scale of closeness of approximation to a 'target' language; used also to refer to an instance of such a system, either of an individual or of a variety; widely accepted as a postulate in the inventory of SLA research and second/foreign language teaching concepts. It is suggested that the imperfect system that learners use to communicate in an additional language is an *interlanguage* as it is between the first language and the target language. The concept is arguably not valid as applied (at least) to varieties of world Englishes (see *acculturation, indigenization, institutionalization*, the *Circles* model). (Ch. 6; Y. Kachru, 1993; Selinker, 1992)

International Corpus of English (ICE) – data collected for varieties of English from fifteen countries across the three Circles, e.g., Australia, India, and Hong Kong. (Ch. 1; Nelson, 2004, http://www.ucl.ac.uk/english-usage/ice/index.htm)

interpretability – degree of success in discerning the 'meaning behind' what is overtly expressed; see *intelligibility*. (Ch. 5; Smith, 1992)

intonation – pitch contours perceived as one of a number of grammatical or pragmatic functions, e.g., rising pitch (in English) signalling a question (whether or not a lexical question-element appears) or indicating surprise; see *inflection*. (Ch. 5; Matsuura, Chiba and Fujieda, 1999) learning – becoming more proficient in a skill, including use of language, applied usually in a teaching situation; used in a general sense but also by some writers as opposed to *acquisition*. (Ch. 6; S. Sridhar, 1994)

lexicon – the 'dictionary' in the mind that comprises all the meaningful elements of language – words and morphemes – along with the lexico-grammatical information required by morphology, syntax, semantics and pragmatics; e.g., *table*, with its definitions, marked among other senses as a countable concrete noun, and the homophonic verb, marked as requiring an object of a certain sort ('table a matter/motion'); also applied to a collected/printed 'lexicon'. (Ch. 17; Bautista, 1997a)

linguistic area – a geographical space in which a number of languages have become more similar to one another over the course of many years of contact than their 'genetic' relationships would have suggested; South Asia is such a well-known area, where Indo-European, Dravidian, Austro-Asiatic and Sino-Tibetan languages have developed similarities of phonology, lexis and grammar. (Ch. 11; B. Kachru, 1986a)

linguistic imperialism – see *hegemony*.

linguistic repertoire – the aggregate of languages and their subvarieties that a speaker has available for use in the various domains of life. (Chs. 11, 18; Ferguson, 1996)

localisms – non-standard usages (morphological, lexical, syntactic, etc.) that are available and effective in the language variety of a relatively restricted geographical area; e.g., *to mommock ('annoy') someone* is a verb that is probably only known and used in a small area of coastal North Carolina, USA. (Ch. 17; Butler, 1997)

modal – any of the verb elements, such as English *will, would, shall, should*, and *can*, which indicate, e.g., logical necessity, possibility, obligation, wish, etc. In English, modals are *auxiliary* verbs in structural terms (carrying negativity and inverting with subjects to make questions) but behave more like *lexical* verbs semantically (*will* may indicate futurity but also promise or prediction, *can* may indicate capacity or permission, etc.). (Ch. 16; Collins, 1991, Quirk et al., 1985)

model – an ideal representation of a phenomenon, as in 'the standard model of pronunciation'; a theoretical or hypothetical framework, as in 'a formal linguistic model'. (Ch. 9)

monitor – a theoretically proposed aspect or 'device' of speakers' language self-awareness which keeps track of their speech as it is going on; 'monitored' speech is careful and rule-conscious, and held by some writers to actually impede or disallow *acquisition* (see *learning* and *acquisition*). (Ch. 6; Krashen, 1981)

mora – (pl. *morae* or *moras*) the duration of a syllable, often associated with Greek and Latin timing systems (the term is from Latin 'delay'), and also with modern Japanese and South Asian languages such as Hindi; while

Inner-Circle Englishes keep an approximate chronological uniformity from lexical stress to stress, mora-timed languages assign approximately the same length of time to each syllable of the same weight. (Ch. 3; Bautista, 2000)

motivations – see *instrumental, integrative ~*.

moves – the steps in or sub-parts of a text or of a textual analysis; see *genre analysis.*

native – (~ language/speaker) traditionally used for the 'first' language or 'mother tongue' of a speaker (extended to include communities and cultures), which was presumed to have been acquired within a family and close societal context without the aid (or necessity) of its having been formally taught; now largely replaced by concepts such as primary language. A native speaker is a person who acquires a language from birth in the conditions described above. (Ch. 2; Davies, 2003; Ferguson, 1992/ 1982; Paikeday, 1985)

neologism – a 'new word' that may be formed *ad hoc* but also may acquire stability in the general lexicon of a language or a variety; may include *coinage* (see), but also used to refer to any novel formation resulting from, e.g., analogy, clipping, compounding or shortening. (Ch. 17; Bautista, 1997a)

non-native – (~ language/speaker) traditionally used for a language not the 'first' language or 'mother tongue' of a speaker (extended to include communities and cultures); a non-native speaker is one who acquires or learns a second or n-th language subsequent to the first language; see *native.* (Ch. 2; Davies, 2003; Ferguson, 1992/1982; Paikeday 1985)

norm – (external ~, internal ~, ~-providing, ~-accepting) any *norm* is an expectation of participants' behaviour or beliefs based on (perceived) rules that govern a community or society; in higher education, Standard English may be asserted to be the 'norm' for professional interactions, though its actual definition may be impossible to pin down and both intentional and unconscious infractions may abound in daily use; some nations or societies may assert that the 'norm' for their English is British English, in which case Britain is the external 'norm-provider' for the variety of the adopting country, the 'norm-acceptor'; internal norms are those acceded to from within a nation or region; cf. (non-)native speakers/ varieties. (Ch. 2; B. Kachru, 1997)

particle – an invariable grammatical element; examples are *up, down, over,* which attach to verbs in English to make phrasal verbs (e.g., *look a word up, put a package down, do an assignment over*), often a source of controversy because they are homophonic/-graphic with corresponding *prepositions;* also a pragmatic element signalling speaker's attitude, such as *well, lah, what;* the latter two have received attention in the Englishes of Singapore and Malaysia (see *discourse marker*). (Ch. 17; Pakir, 1992a) performance varieties – the Englishes of Expanding-Circle countries, where the language is not *institutionalized* (see); English may be widely used and studied in such contexts, even to the extent of being a required school or university subject and necessary for obtaining employment or promotion, but it is not officially designated as a language of government, law, medium of education, etc. (Ch. 2; B. Kachru, 1994a)

periphery – in Phillipson's writings, the English-using countries not in the *core* (see), corresponding roughly to B. Kachru's Outer and Expanding Circles, where English is not the dominant national language; see *institutionalization, performance varieties*. (Chs. 1 and 22; Phillipson, 1992)

persuasion – related to (formal) argument, the attempt to bring a participant to one's own point of view or evaluation; various societies and traditions may have different methods held to be acceptable means of persuasion, e.g., appeals to logic and to emotion; cf. *suasion/-sive*. (Ch. 20; Y. Kachru, 1997b)

phonology – the component of language that produces pronunciations, drawing on phonetic inventory, constraints on allowable sound sequences, and the rules for combining sounds and morphemes (morphophonology); also the study of that component. (Ch. 3; Jenkins, 2000)

pidgin – (pidginization) a system of linguistic communication developed spontaneously in a language-contact situation; characterized by a simple (but systematic) grammar and limited lexicon; a pidgin is not a 'first language'; compare *creole*. (Ch. 22; Andersen, 1983)

pluricentric – (pluricentricity) used to refer the numerous 'centres' to which world English users may look for their *models, norms, standards* and confidence in using their varieties of English; historically, Britain was the centre; in this sense, then, with the addition of the USA, there were acknowledged (by many people) to be at least two; now, the concept encompasses *world Englishes*. Thus, English is now said to be a pluricentric language. (Ch. 1; B. Kachru, 1985)

polarity – in syntax, the positive-negative dimension in sentences, words or phrases; often used in addressing the ways in which languages and varieties of English reply to *yes/no* questions. (Ch. 3; Gumperz, 1982b, Lowenberg, 1984, Pope, 1976)

politeness – referring to strategies that maintain *face* (see) and agreeable relations for participants in language interactions; strategies may include use of honorifics, silence ('being a good listener'), *backchannelling*, and avoiding outright contradiction of another speaker's assertion. (Chs. 4 and 19; Brown and Levinson, 1987)

pragmatic particle – see *particle*.

prescription/prescriptive grammar – a model of or attitude towards a language which holds that 'correctness' is measured according to adherence to explicit rules laid down in codifying presentations such as composition handbooks, as opposed to models of and attitudes towards language(s) proposed by linguists, which are based on description drawn from observation and analysis of actual individuals' or communities' use; e.g., a prescriptive view of English holds that the 'split infinitive' structure in '... assigned someone *to closely record* phonetic differences' is unarguably wrong, while a descriptive view would take into account and refer to frequency of use, speakers' judgements of the felicity of the structure, etc. (Chs. 7, 17; Butler, 1997; Pakir, 1997)

proficiency – degree of applicable competence in using a language, thus closely tied to notions of *norms, standards,* and *intelligibility;* cf. *fluency.* (Ch. 9; Seidlhofer, 1999)

range (of functions) – the functions for which English is used by people in a society or context; typically, one may think of English being used in higher education settings in Asian nations, but it is also in wide use as a language of science, technology, tourism, and even interpersonal domains; see *functional domains* and *depth.* (Ch. 2; B. Kachru, 1997)

resumptive pronoun – a pronoun that duplicates an appositive reference in the same sentence, e.g., 'JoAnn, *she* likes to garden'; in some varieties, used for emphasis or topicalization, in others, a less marked structure. (Ch. 14; Bokamba, 1992; Gyasi, 1991; S. Sridhar, 1996)

rhetoric – broadly, any use of language, often restricted to refer to argumentative or persuasive purposes; sometimes further limited to the organization and style of writing; see also *argumentation, genre.* (Ch. 20; Y. Kachru, 1992; Kamimura and Oi, 1998)

rhythm – the timing of the flow of speech, traditionally analysed with reference to the length of time between lexical or phrase stresses, or to the time given to syllables; see *mora.* (Chs. 13 and 14; Llamzon, 1997)

root – in morphology, a base form of a word to which affixes may be added (cf. *stem*); in syntax/pragmatics, a modality indicating obligation, compulsion, requirement, etc. (see *epistemic*). (Chs. 16, 19; Collins, 1991)

RP (Received Pronunciation) – a variety of British English used by educated speakers in the southern part of English, widely accepted as the standard for speaking and as the model for teaching EFL, even though it has never been spoken by more than a tiny minority of British English speakers (it is 'received' in the sense of 'accepted'). (Ch. 1; McArthur, 1992)

semantic extension – the broadening of a lexical item's or phrase's denotation or sense, which may occur over time in a variety or across varieties of a language; e.g., in Philippine English, *open* means 'switch on [a device]'. (Ch. 17; Bautista, 1997a)

semantic shift – any change in a lexical item's or phrase's denotation or sense; words may acquire meanings/uses not normally associated with them, e.g., *destool* 'to have power taken away, to be removed from office'; see also *semantic extension.* (Chs. 14, 17; Bokamba, 1992; Butler, 1997) social marker – a language element or characteristic that correlates with social stratifications but is not in most people's awareness at the level of conscious stereotyping; a commonly cited example is the omission of final '-g' from '-ing' verb forms, e.g. *speakin(g)*, which may occur more or less frequently depending on people's perception of the need for 'being careful' in their speech in a given situation; see *social stereotype, social status*. (Ch. 4; Wolfram, 1991)

social status – an individual's or group's standing in a broader society, almost always defined with regard to economic or other power-conferring characteristics; status may vary according to the situation, including such factors as age, gender, regional identity, and so on; 'status' is not construed as a neutral term, but is always defined as a hierarchical relation; see *social stereotype, social marker*. (Ch. 4; K. Sridhar, 1991; Wolfram, 1991)

social stereotype – a language element or characteristic that people consciously associate with a (perceived) social group; a commonly cited example is the social stigma attached to any use of the word 'ain't': anyone who says 'ain't' cannot be very well educated, intelligent, etc.; see *social marker, social status*. (Ch. 4; Wolfram, 1991)

speech act (locutionary, illocutionary, perlocutionary) – any identifiable use of language; the locutionary aspect involves an utterance as such; illocutionary act refers to the action constituted by an utterance, such as asking questions, giving commands, expressing thanks, apologizing, telling jokes, etc.; perlocutionary act refers to effects of an utterance, such as eliciting information, persuading an addressee to comply with an order, showing appreciation, expressing regret, entertaining, etc. A perlocutionary act may have specific effects on participants which may or may not be the one(s) intended by the speaker. Illocutionary acts have received the most attention in the literature. (Ch. 4; Austin, 1962; Brown and Levinson, 1987)

speech community – societies which share a language, albeit one that subsumes any number of sub-varieties. The English users of the *Inner, Outer* and *Expanding Circles* (see) are all members of the broader 'English-using speech community'. A speech *fellowship* is a sub-grouping of societies within a speech community which share contextual features. (Ch. 2; B. Kachru, 1985, 1995b)

speech fellowship – see *speech community*.

standardization – bringing a language variety into focus and prominence as a body of forms and usages to be emulated, and providing or accepting necessary apparatus of codification and modeling for it, such as dictionaries, grammars, literature and media in that variety. (Chs. 1, 7; Marckwardt, 1942, McArthur, 1998)

stress – the fact or assignment of prominence, in terms primarily of pitch but also with reference to length and loudness, to phonologically or pragmatically determined syllables in an English lexical item, phrase or sentence; in Inner-Circle varieties of English, lexical stress can differentiate words (e.g., *cóntract* [n.] and *contráct* [v.]) and indicate focus or topic (e.g., 'You ate the last *cookie?*' – i.e., not the last apple or anything else); see *mora*. (Ch. 3)

stress-timed rhythm – a speech flow attained by maintaining an approximately equal time-interval between primary stresses in a phrase or sentence; this has traditionally been the characterization of Inner-Circle English speech timing; see *syllable-timed rhythm* and *mora*. (Ch. 3; Bamgboṣe, 1992, B. Kachru, 1983, Llamzon, 1997)

style – loosely, any identifiable manner of using language, e.g. formal/informal or age-based; a user's style may be affected by any aspect of the context, including participants and attitudes towards the topic. (Ch. 19; Eisikovits, 1989, Tannen, 1993)

syllable – a vowel or vocalic element such as a liquid or nasal and the consonantal elements associated with it under the sequential constraints of a particular language; e.g., the word *table* comprises two syllables; *ta, fa, sta* are possible English syllables, but *fsta* is not; see *stress-timed* and *syllable-timed rhythm* and *mora*. (Ch. 3)

syllable-timed rhythm – a speech flow maintained by assigning approximately equal time to syllables of the same weight in a phrase or sentence; this timing has traditionally been contrasted with the characterization of Inner-Circle English speech flow; see *stress-timed* and *mora*. (Ch. 3)

tag – (often '~ question') in syntax/pragmatics, a structure at the end of a sentence that invites agreement or indicates that the preceding assertion is to be assumed, from the speaker's point of view, e.g., 'You're the new ESL instructor, *aren't you?*' The syntaxes of Inner-Circle varieties include complex rules for forming different sorts of tags (e.g., '..., *are you?*' has a quite different pragmatic effect than does '..., *aren't you?*' attached to the same statement, while '..., *are you not?*' is much more formal); other varieties may have a more or less fixed form such as South and Southeast Asian Englishes ' ... , *is it?*' (Ch. 3; Platt and Weber, 1980)

textualization – (also 'text-patterning') the way a linguistic device is used in a restricted context, e.g., past participles in scientific articles. (Ch. 21; V. Bhatia, 1993, Swales, 1990)

theme – in Inner-Circle varieties, usually the initial syntactic element in an unmarked sentence, contrasted with the *focus* (see); e.g., in the sentence '*Sue* went to **the beach**', *Sue* is the theme, while **the beach** is the focus, in the context of the question 'Where did Sue go?'; compare *topic*. (Ch. 3; Gumperz, 1982b)

Three Circles (Inner, Outer, Expanding) – a historical and socially descriptive division of the varieties of world Englishes; the Inner Circle comprises countries populated by English users, the Outer-Circle Englishes were imported into already multilingual populations in the age of colonialism, and the Expanding Circle varieties stem from later developments. (Chs. 1, 2; B. Kachru, 1985)

topic – in syntax, what a sentence is about, in contrast to the predicate or comment; there are various phonological and syntactic processes for indicating topicality vs. grammatical subject in English, such as front-shifting. (Ch. 3; Mesthrie, 1997)

transfer – the application of language features or rules from a language into another language that one is learning, traditionally divided into negative ('interference') and positive, the latter those that have a 'correct' application in the host language; e.g., South Asian speakers (stereo)typically exhibit retroflex stops where other varieties have alveolar stops, possibly because such speakers perceive those stops as post-dental, contrasting with the distinctive dental stops in South Asian languages such as Hindi. (Ch. 6; Sa'adeddin, 1989)

validity – the degree to which a test draws on and measures proficiency in the (language) features that it claims to. (Ch. 9; Lowenberg, 1993)

variety – the identifiable language of a speech community, traditionally *dialect* (now usually avoided as being too negatively loaded); varieties may be defined with regard to any social or linguistic characteristic, such as gender, age, region or nation; see *circles, dialect*. (Ch. 1; B. Kachru, 1985; Wolfram, 1981)

verbal repertoires – see *linguistic repertoires*.

Annotated bibliography

Bailey, Richard W. and **Görlach**, Manfred (eds.) (1982) *English as a World Language*. Ann Arbor, MI: U. of Michigan Press. 496 pp.

Among the first generation of collections of papers on world Englishes, this work comprises 14 articles and an introduction by the editors. The chapters treat English as observed in Britain, the US, Africa (East, West, and South), South Asia and the Pacific in terms of its history, functions, examples and discussion of 'pronunciations, vocabulary, and the processes of word formation and syntax' (p. vii). Suggested Readings (pp. 467–79) are listed under topic-areas, including English as geographically characterized, e.g. Pidgin and Creole Linguistics (p. 471 *ff.*) and Canada (p. 476 *ff.*). The editors recognized the complexity and breadth of the field: 'While the essays … reflect the diverse circumstances in which English is used, we cannot claim that our contributors have exhausted the complexity of the separate histories and present varieties of English' (p. vii). Now necessarily somewhat dated, this extensive volume is still a useful resource for data and informative commentary at all levels of forms and functions.

Baumgardner, Robert J. (ed.) (1996) *South Asian English: Structure, Use, and Users.* Urbana: University of Illinois Press. 286 pp.

This volume in the series *English in the Global Context* concentrates on a subcontinent where English was introduced in the sixteenth century and has by now developed into distinct institutionalized varieties. South Asia is an extremely important part of the English-using world in various respects, not the least of which is the sheer numbers of speakers and degree to which English is used. At the time of writing, the projected number of English bilinguals for the year 2000 was 'over 84 million' (p. xiii). In India alone, books published in English constituted 45 percent of the total (pp. xiii–xiv) — a remarkable proportion, considering the large number of other South Asian languages. India also ranks in English-language publications in the world just behind the UK and the USA. Thus, this is a region calling for a good deal of attention, and in return providing sociolinguists many diverse contexts for investigation and analysis for understanding how English functions and adapts in intense contact situations. The volume is drawn from the presentations at the first International Conference on English in South Asia, Islamabad, Pakistan, January 1989. Following an introduction by the editor (pp. 1–5), sixteen chapters are presented in five parts: 1. Contexts and Issues; 2. Structure and Contact; 3. Functions and Innovations; 4. The Curriculum; and 5. English and the Multilingual's Creativity. To call this area 'interesting' is either a strict technical usage or a quiet understatement on the editor's part. In either interpretation, this volume presents a broad view of data, concerns and issues, and the treatments are focused and in depth.

Bolton, Kingsley (ed.) (2002) *Hong Kong English: Autonomy and Creativity.* Hong Kong: Hong Kong University Press. viii + 324 pp.

Following an introduction (pp. 1–25), this work comprises five parts: Language in Context, Language Form, Dimensions of Creativity, Resources, and Future Directions. A thorough index (pp. 315–24) locates topics and information. Fifteen of the sixteen articles in this collection previously appeared in *World Englishes* (vol. 19[3], 2000). Their presentation in this volume makes them more readily available to a larger readership.

Bolton's introduction presents an overview of the history, development, and status of English in Hong Kong. In addition to educational institutions, English is being spread by other agents also. For instance, school students and undergraduate university students not only study English but also teach it to family members or in tutorial arrangements. Further, a large number of 'Filipina domestic helpers or "amahs" … often mainly use English and … function as unofficial tutors with children' (p. 12).

This is an important resource, presenting aspects of a variety of English which has grown in a locale whose major immigrants have been from other areas of China (p. 1). Thus, it is of interest in tracing the mechanisms of increasing range and depth of penetration of English in an Outer-Circle setting.

Burchfield, Robert (ed.) (1994) *The Cambridge History of the English Language. Vol. V. English in Britain and Overseas: Origins and Development.* Cambridge: Cambridge University Press. xxiii + 656 pp.

The front matter of this substantial volume includes prefaces by the series editor and the volume editor, and a list of the contributors and their affiliations. Five unnumbered pages at the end list titles, editors, chapters and authors of the other volumes in the series, I–IV and VI. Burchfield provides a general introduction. The ten chapters are divided across two parts, Regional Varieties of English in Great Britain and Ireland (pp. 21–274), and English Overseas (pp. 275–553). Each chapter provides a list of references for further reading.

Part I comprises chapters on English in Scotland, Wales, and Ireland, and The Dialects of English since 1776. Part II's topics are Australia, the Caribbean, New Zealand, South Africa and South Asia. The South Asia chapter by B. Kachru is referred to *passim* in the present work. In the introduction, editor Burchfield devotes three paragraphs to a synopsis of the topic and commentary on this chapter. Specifically, he notes that '… [Kachru] has run into controversy in a way that no one foresaw' (p. 7), in regard to the legitimacy in a position that speakers outside the Inner Circle should (or can) attain Inner-Circle-like competence and performance in English. As Burchfield succinctly says, 'The debate, which has far-reaching implications, continues' (p. 7). In the last section of his introduction, Burchfield observes that 'there has not been any agreed definition of the term *standard* (or *Standard*) English among linguistic scholars in the twentieth century' (p. 15). The openness of such discussion and the comprehensive coverage and eminent contributors in this volume make it an indispensable background resource for scholars and advanced students of world varieties of English.

Görlach, Manfred, 4 volumes in the series *Varieties of English around the World* (General Editor Edgar W. Schneider), published between 1991–2002. Amsterdam/Philadelphia: John Benjamins:
Englishes. Studies in Varieties of English 1984–1988. (1991) 8 papers, 211 pp.
More Englishes: New Studies in Varieties of English 1988–1994. (1995) 8 papers, 276 pp.
Even More Englishes. Studies 1996–1997. (1998) 11 papers, x + 260 pp.
Still More Englishes. (2002) 9 papers, xiv + 240 pp.

The four volumes comprise a collection of Görlach's work spanning the years 1984–2002. Not all the items are previous publications, and in some the author 'combined papers delivered at various conferences' (Görlach, 2002: xiii). Topics range widely, from the general '… forms and functions of English around the world [1988]' (1995: 10–28) and 'English as a world language — the state of the art [1988]' (1991: 10–35) to topics drawn more specifically from regions and varieties, such as Australian English (1991: 144–73), Irish English (1995: 164–91), 'Nigerian English: broken, pidgin, creole and regional standard? [1997]' (1998: 119–51), and 'English in Singapore, Malaysia, Hong Kong, Indonesia, The Philippines … [*sic*] a second or foreign language?' (2002: 99–117).

The author provides a great range of data which readers may be able to use in addressing their interpretations of conditions and issues. In the foreword to *Still More Englishes*, Bailey wrote (2002: xii): 'Above all, Görlach's vast scholarship is grounded in fact. In the papers that are collected here, he dashes the triumphalist claims by some Anglophones that a billion or more people use the language with some degree of competence and mutual intelligibility. In place of these wild-eyed views, he gives the facts.' (See, however, the preface; according to Crystal, the number of English users is one and a half billion.)

Formats vary somewhat across the volumes, but all contain references and various indexes. The 2002 volume contains 'An annotated bibliography of EWL' (pp. 184–227).

Jenkins, Jennifer (2000) *The Phonology of English as an International Language.* Oxford: Oxford University Press. vii + 258 pp.

In her introduction (pp. 1–4), Jenkins decries the fact that, although speakers of English as an additional language now outnumber its first-language speakers, ELT pedagogy has not 'adjust[ed] its methodologies'. She then claims that linguistically, the existing and emerging second language varieties diverge most from each other in pronunciation; therefore, phonology deserves the most attention from the profession (p. 1).

Chapter 1 is a historical survey of the 'Changing patterns in the use of English' (pp. 5–23). Chapters 2 and 3 address 'Inter-' and 'Intra-speaker variation' (pp. 25–67). Chapter 4, 'Intelligibility in interlanguage talk' (pp. 69–97), emphasizes the non-primacy of the native speaker and asserts the importance of an 'active role for the receiver [hearer]', implying non-applicability of the 'interlanguage' label to non-native varieties. She concludes by stating the need for some sort of international core of phonological intelligibility.

Chapter 5 treats 'The role of transfer in determining the phonological core'. Chapters 6 and 7 (pp. 123–94), 'Pedagogic priorities' 1 and 2, aim at 'identifying the phonological core', beginning with a section on 'Establishing the Lingua Franca Core' (pp. 124–31), and 'Negotiating intelligibility in the ELT classroom'. The latter draws heavily on 'accommodation theory', a complex way of explaining how interlocutors adjust their speech, and perceptions of others' speech, to facilitate communication (pp. 167–71). Chapter 8, 'Proposals for pronunciation teaching for EIL' (pp. 195–231), recommends an overhaul of English language teacher education in pronunciation teaching and testing.

In the 'Afterword: the future of the phonology of EIL' (pp. 233–5), Jenkins speculates that the future of English as 'international language' will depend on its ability to reconcile the opposing forces of intelligibility and identity.

Jenkins, Jennifer (2003) *World Englishes: A Resource Book for Students*. London: Routledge, xvi + pp. 233.

The volume is presented as a comprehensive introduction to the subject, with a range of topics on major historical and socio-political developments from the beginning of the seventeenth century to the present.

The book is divided into four parts: A. Introduction, B. Development, C. Exploration and D. Extension; each part consists of eight units such that each unit in each part is linked to a corresponding unit in the other part. Thus, the first unit in A, 'The historical, social, and political context', continues with a discussion of colonialism in B, postcolonial America and Africa in C, and a selection to read in D: 'The discourses of postcolonialism', an extract from Pennycook's *English and the Discourses of Colonialism* (London: Routledge, 1998).

The other units deal with pidgins and creoles, the ownership of English, variation across Englishes, Standard English versus emerging Standards in the Outer Circle, the internationalization of English, the role of English in Asia and Europe, and the future of world Englishes. Other experts selected for readings in D are: Charles A. d'Epie, Henry G. Widdowson, Chinua Achebe, Ngũgĩ wa Thiong'o, Leslie Milroy, Alfred Lee, Dennis Bloodworth, Marko Modiano, Loreto Todd, Alan S. Kaye, David Li, Ulrich Ammon, and David Graddol. The book concludes with 'further reading' on each topic, references, and a 'glossarial index'. The capitalization of 'World Englishes' throughout is disconcerting; it gives the impression that there is a linguistic entity called *World Englishes*. Varieties of English in the literature are conventionally labelled *world Englishes*.

A good introduction to world Englishes in the Western context, this volume has to be supplemented with more information from non-Western contexts. (See also B. Kachru 2005a: 211–20.)

Kachru, Braj B. (ed.) (1982, 1992) *The Other Tongue: English across Cultures*. Urbana, IL: University of Illinois Press. 1st ed.: xv + 358 pp., 2nd ed.: xxv + 384 pp.

The purpose of the volume was 'to integrate and address provocative issues relevant to a deeper understanding of the forms and functions of English' (B. Kachru, 1982: 6). These aims were carried on through the second, revised and enlarged edition. Ferguson's foreword (1982: vii–xii) is a realistic appraisal of the changing status of Englishes across the globe and of attitudes towards them; he rationally dispenses with the traditional view that English is only 'a European language'. The twenty papers in the first edition are presented in five parts: I. English in Non-Native Contexts: Directions and Issues; II. Nativization: Formal and Functional; III. Contact and Change: Question of a Standard; IV. New English Literatures: Themes and Styles; and V. Contextualization: Text in Context. In the foreword to the second edition,

Peter Strevens observed that the volume was a response to the explosive spread of English among those for whom it is not the 'mother tongue' but 'the other tongue' and that this 'explosion' called for 'a particular kind of enlightenment' (1992: xi). In working towards that illumination, the second edition contains eight new chapters, some of the papers from the first edition having been replaced. Its nineteen chapters are divided across six parts with slight changes in the headings of the original five parts and the addition of a sixth part entitled 'World Englishes in the Classroom: Rationale and Resources'. *The Other Tongue* was one of the first major works to bring together a cogent and comprehensive presentation of data from world Englishes, the issues and concerns which they raised, and some indications of the directions that they might take. Its two editions remain a 'classic' for reference in the field.

Kachru, Braj B. (1983) *The Indianization of English: The English Language in India.* New Delhi: Oxford University Press. xvi +280 pp.

The eight chapters of this volume are revised versions of papers written between 1960–1981 (p. xi). As the author writes, they 'have a shared theme and focus concerning the twice-born characteristic of English in India' (p. 1). The collection brings explicitly into prominence the very notions of 'the *Indianness* in Indian English (or in a wider context, the *South Asianness* in South Asian English)' and 'the Indianization of the English language in India' (p. 1), of 'Indianisms' and 'the distinction between a *deviation* and a *mistake*' (p. 2). This work may be said to be among the first which brought the ideas of nativization of English and the concept of world Englishes into the awareness of a scholarly community which has by the present day come to accept such notions and technical vocabulary as commonplace.

The Introduction (pp. 1–14) sets out the author's approach and conceptualization of the field of inquiry, as well as presenting an overview of the contents. The chapters are presented in five parts: I. Historical and Sociolinguistic Context; II. The Indianization: Language in Context; III. Lexical Extension; IV. English and New Verbal Strategies; and V. Indian English and Other Non-Native Englishes. Randolph Quirk, then Vice-Chancellor of the University of London, wrote the foreword.

Kachru, Braj B. (1986) *The Alchemy of English: The Spread, Functions and Models of Non-native Englishes.* Oxford: Pergamon. xi + 200 pp.

The ten chapters of this work, which originally appeared as individual papers from 1976 through 1985, are organized into an introduction (pp. 1–15) and four parts: I. Varieties and Functions; II. Models, Norms and Attitudes; III. Impact of Change; and IV. Contact, Creativity and Discourse Strategies. The bibliography (pp. 174–89) serves the whole volume.

As Kachru writes in the preface (p. vii): 'what is vital is the public attitude toward English, the love-hate relationship with the language, and the acceptance of the functional power of English in all parts of the world'. These papers provide a foundation of reading in the issues relating to meta-aspects of world Englishes, including the ground-breaking observations and interpretations that led to the now commonly cited Three Circles Model. See also B. Kachru (1983).

Kachru, Braj B. (2005) *Asian Englishes: Beyond the Canon.* Hong Kong: Hong Kong University Press [South Asian Edition: New Delhi: Oxford University Press].

This book is in the series *Asian Englishes Today,* Hong Kong University Press, Hong Kong. According to the series editor, Kingsley Bolton: 'The scope of this book is innovative and multidisciplinary, and moves from linguistic description to literary explication, from intercultural communication to critical commentary. This work ... will attract a wide international audience among students and scholars of linguistics, cultural studies, literary criticism, and all those interested in the continuing story of English in the Asian context' (p. xiv).

The eleven chapters of the volume are organized into an Introduction, titled 'Anglophone Asia' and six parts. The remaining ten chapters are in Part I: Contexts (pp. 7–95) — Asian Englishes, South Asian schizophrenia, Past imperfect: The Japanese agony; Part II: Convergence (pp. 97–134) — Asia and beyond, The absent voices; Part III: Mantras (pp. 135–62) — Medium and *mantra,* Talking back and writing back; Part IV: Predator (pp. 163–84) — Killer or accessory to murder?; Part V: Pedagogy (pp. 185–202) — Contexts of pedagogy and identity; and Part VI: Afterword (pp. 203–56) — Present tense: Making sense of Anglophone Asia.

In Part I Kachru establishes the broader context of English in Asia, and the subsequent chapters elaborate the issues related to English in South Asia and Japan. Part II is on the Englishization of Asian languages and impact of language contact and convergence on Englishes in Asia. Part III is on literary creativity, and new canons of English literatures. Part IV asks whether English is killer or an accessory to the murder of indigenous languages. Part V is concerned with approaches to teaching and learning of English in Asia; and Part VI deals with a variety of current debates and controversies in the field of English studies in world contexts.

This book contains an extensive bibliography (pp. 265–318). It is indispensable to those interested in the most recent developments in English as an Asian language.

McArthur, Tom (ed.) (1992) *The Oxford Companion to the English Language*. Oxford: Oxford University Press. xix + 1184 pp.

It would not be an overstatement to call this volume a monumental resource for the scholars and students of any sub-field of 'English', whether on the language or literature side. The editor refers in the Preface to his taking on the challenge of producing such a work as an agreement 'to put my head in the lion's mouth'. Lists of the ten associate editors and of the many contributors and consultants are given on pp. xi–xvi.

There is an extensive and helpful statement of 'The Organization of the *Companion*' on pp. xvii–xxiv; it notes, for example, that entries fall into '22 themes or topic areas' (p. xx), including geography, biography, language and media. There is a list of the relatively few generally used abbreviations — twenty-nine, plus two usual meanings for the asterisk (xxv) — and of the phonetic symbols that are employed (pp. xxvi–xxvii). Entries are arranged alphabetically: the first is '**A, a** [Called *ay*, rhyming with *say*]. The 1st letter of the Roman alphabet as used for English ...' (p. 1), and the last is '**ZUMMERZET**. See MUMMERSET, SOMERSET' (p. 1147). In between are entries on just about any thing and person of importance to the language, numbering over 3,500 in all. Location of entries related to what one has just read is facilitated by the 'see also' lists at the ends of entries where they are appropriate and by the thorough Index of Persons (pp. 1151–84). After a good dictionary, *OCEL* is the fundamental acquisition for any English studies reference shelf.

Mufwene, Salikoko S., Rickford, John R., Bailey, Guy and Baugh, John (eds.) (1998) *African-American English: Structure, History and Use*. NY: Routledge. xiv + 314 pp.

After an introduction by editors Mufwene and Rickford (pp. 1–7), this volume is divided into three parts. Part I: Structure contains three chapters, on 'the sentence' (pp. 11–36), 'aspect and predicate phrases' (pp. 37–68), and 'the noun phrase' (pp. 69–81). Part II: History comprises chapters on phonology (pp. 85–109), 'co-existent systems' of general and African-American English (pp. 110–53, by Labov, drawn on for the African-American chapter in the current work), and 'Creole origins' (pp. 154–200). Part III: Use presents four chapters, on lexicon (pp. 203–25), 'ideology and so-called obscenity' (pp. 226–50), 'verbal genres' (pp. 251–81), and 'educational reform' (pp. 282–301).

The editors and contributors are a 'who's who' of scholars in the variety of English which has been referred to by any number of variations of 'African-American English'. Mufwene and Rickford write in their Introduction that:

> Overall, the chapters of this book reflect more or less the state of current scholarship on AAVE. However, they do not simply summarize the state of the art. They also address new questions, explore new approaches, and sometimes apply current analytical frameworks in novel ways. (pp. 5–6)

This volume is a valuable resource for information on AAVE and also for examples of sociolinguistic investigative methodology and interpretation that will remain worthy of study.

Mesthrie, Rajend (ed.) (2001) *Concise Encyclopedia of Sociolinguistics.* Amsterdam: Elsevier Science Ltd. xxvii + 1031 pp.

This work is a one-volume extraction of articles from the ten-volume *Encyclopedia of Language and Linguistics* (1993), edited by Ronald E. Asher (Amsterdam: Elsevier; also Oxford: Pergamon, 1994). It contains more than 280 topical and biographical entries, some of which are new articles commissioned for the volume. There are ten subject sections, within which articles are arranged alphabetically by title. To assist the user in locating information, there are subject and name indexes, as well as an alphabetical list of articles. The contributors are from various countries, and readers can take this as a sign that the articles offer a range of views and interpretations.

One 'howler' is worth noting for readers of the current work. In the biographical article on B. Kachru (pp. 883–4), there is an apparent mis-statement: 'His PhD thesis ... claimed that the goal of linguistic analysis is to relate a text to the context of situation ... and that Indian English should therefore be analyzed in British or American cultural contexts' (p. 883). It hardly needs to be said that this must be a typographical error, in which a negative form of 'should ... be analyzed' was omitted.

This encyclopedia is an invaluable resource for basic information on the whole range of issues, concerns and topics in sociolinguistics generally, which is the natural background to the study of world Englishes.

Schneider, Edgar W. Two volumes in the series *Varieties of English around the World* (General Editor: Edgar W. Schneider). Amsterdam/Philadelphia: John Benjamins:

Englishes around the World 1. General Studies, British Isles, North America: Studies in Honour of Manfred Görlach. (1997) 21 papers, ii + 329 pp.
Englishes around the World 2. Caribbean, Africa, Asia, Australasia: Studies in Honour of Manfred Görlach. (1997) 22 papers, 357 pp.

As the titles of these two volumes indicate, their content covers the geography of the known English-speaking world. Volume 1 includes a paean to Görlach (1997: 1–5) and a bibliography of his publications (pp. 7–13). The introduction by Schneider (pp. 15–8) includes a listing of the contributors and their titles in Volume 2.

Schneider writes in the introduction that the collections are presented 'to honor [*sic*] [Görlach] with a thematically focused collection of ... contributions which should reflect current activities in a scholarly field which he has shaped to a significant extent' (p. 15). Volume 1 addresses 'the world-wide spread and role of the English language in a broader perspective', 'compare[s] structural features on a global scale', and treats the longest-extant varieties of English. Volume 2 addresses the 'varieties which have increasingly come to be called "New Englishes" ' (p. 15).

This series under Schneider's general editorship presents a wide variety of information and perspectives on the field of world Englishes.

Additional resources

Select list of Asian and African literary works

South Asia

Desai, Anita (1978) *Games at Twilight and Other Stories.* London: Penguin Books.
Desai, Anita (2000) *Diamond Dust and Other Stories.* New York: Mariner Books.
Gooneratne, Yasmine (ed.) (1979) *Stories from Sri Lanka.* Hong Kong: Heinemann Asia.
Hashmi, Alamgir (ed.) (1987) *Pakistani Literature: The Contemporary English Writers.* Second edition. Islamabad: Gulmohar.
Narayan, R. K. (1943) *Malgudi Days.* Mysore: Indian Thought Publications [New York: Viking, 1982].
Narayan, R. K. (1985) *Under the Banyan Tree and Other Stories.* London: Heinemann.
Narayan, R. K. (1993) *Salt and Sawdust: Stories and Table Talk.* New Delhi: Penguin Books India.
Paranjape, Makarand (ed.) (1993) *Indian Poetry in English.* Hyderabad: Macmillan India Limited.

East Asia

Lam, Agnes (1997) *Woman to Woman and Other Poems.* Hong Kong: Asia 2000.
Xu, Xi (2002) *Daughters of Hui.* Second edition. Hong Kong: Chameleon Press.
Xu, Xi and Ingham, Mike (eds.) (2003) *City Voices: Hong Kong Writing in English 1945 to the Present.* Hong Kong: Hong Kong University Press.

Southeast Asia

Abad, Gémino Y. (1993) *A Native Clearing: Filipino Poetry and Verse from English since the '50s to the Present, from Edith L. Tiempo to Cirilo F. Bautista*. Quezon City: University of the Philippines Press.

Bonifacio, Amelia Lapena (ed.) (1994) *12 Philippine Women Writers*. Quezon City: University of the Philippines Press.

Cruz, Isagani R. (ed.) (2000) *The Best Philippine Short Stories of the Twentieth Century: An Anthology of Fiction in English*. Manila: Tahanan Books.

Ho, Louise (1994) *Local Habitation*. Hong Kong: Twilight Books Co./ Department of Comparative Literature, The University of Hong Kong.

Lim, Catherine (1980) *Or Else, the Lightning God & Other Stories*. Singapore: Heinemann Educational Books (Asia).

Thumboo, Edwin (1976) *The Second Tongue: An Anthology of Poetry from Malaysia and Singapore*. Singapore: Heinemann, Educational Books (Asia).

Thumboo, Edwin (1985) *The Poetry of Singapore*. Singapore: ASEAN Committee on Culture and Information.

Yeo, Robert (1978) *Singapore Short Stories*. Singapore: Heinemann Educational Books (Asia).

Africa

Achebe, Chinua (1971) *Girls at War and Other Stories*. Garden City, New York: Doubleday.

Malan, Robin (1995) *New Beginnings: Short Stories from Southern Africa*. Cape Town: Oxford University Press.

Mutloatse, Mothobi (ed.) (1981) *Africa South Contemporary Writings*. London: Heinemann Educational.

Mzamane, Mbulelo Vizikhungo (ed.) (1986) *Hungry Flames and Other Black South African Stories*. Harlow: Longman.

Oliphant, Andries Walter (ed.) (1999) *At the Rendezvous of Victory and Other Stories*. Cape Town: Kwela Books.

Some useful websites

1. Dave's ESL Café (http://eslcafe.com/): This TESL site leads to various sites with English lessons, exercises, games, songs, etc.
2. ELT News (http://www.eltnews.com/home.shtml): 'The Web Site for English Teachers in Japan'.
3. *Four Seasons* (http://web.kyoto-inet.or.jp/people/sampachi/fs/): 'The Wonderful World of Japanese Writers of English'; a compilation of writings (stories, essays, poems, travel pieces) by Japanese teachers of English.

4. International Association for World Englishes (IAWE) home page (http://www.iaweworks.org/): International Association for World Englishes, a non-profit organization which meets annually in various locations in Africa, Asia, Europe and the USA, brings together researchers, scholars and teachers of various Englishes.

5. World-English (http://www.world-english.org/listening.htm): 'The one-stop resource for the English language and more'; an audio component presents accents from some varieties of English.

6. *World Englishes* [journal] (http://www.blackwellpublishing.com/journal.asp?ref=0883-2919&site=1): '*World Englishes* is committed to the study of varieties of English in their distinctive cultural, sociolinguistic and educational contexts. It is integrative in its scope and includes theoretical and applied studies on language, literature and English teaching, with emphasis on cross-cultural perspectives and identities.'

References

Abad, Gemino (1997) in *English Is an Asian Language: The Philippine Context.* The Macquarie Library Pty Ltd., p. 17.

Abercrombie, David (1951 [1965]) R. P. and local accent. *The Listener* **46** [Reprinted in *Studies in Phonetics and Linguistics.* Edited by David Abercrombie. London: Oxford University Press, pp. 10–15.]

Achebe, Chinua (1965) English and the African writer. *Transition,* **18**, 27–30.

Achebe, Chinua (1969) *Arrow of God.* Garden City: Doubleday.

Achebe, Chinua (1971) The madman. In *Girls at War and Other Stories.* Garden City: Doubleday.

Achebe, Chinua (1976) *Morning Yet on Creation Day.* Garden City: Anchor Books.

Alatis, James E. and Lowenberg, Peter H. (2001) The three circles of English: An afterword. In *The Three Circles of English.* Edited by Edwin Thumboo. Singapore: UniPress, pp. 425–39.

Albert, Ethel M. (1972) Culture patterning of speech behavior in Burundi. In *Directions in Sociolinguistics: The Ethnography of Communication.* Edited by John J. Gumperz and Del Hymes. New York: Holt, Rinehart and Winston, pp. 72–105.

Algeo, John (2004) Review of *Three Circles of English.* Edited by Edwin Thumboo. *World Englishes* 22(4), 609–11.

Alisjahbana, S. Takdir (1990) The teaching of English in Indonesia. In *Teaching and Learning English Worldwide.* Edited by James Britton, Robert E. Shafer and Ken Watson. Clevedon: Multilingual Matters, pp. 315–27.

Allan, Keith (1980) Nouns and countability. *Language,* **56**(3), 541–67.

Allsopp, Jeannette (2003) *The Multilingual Caribbean Dictionary of Flora, Fauna and Foods in English, French, French Creole, and Spanish.* Kingston: Arawak Press.

Allsopp, Richard and Allsopp, Jeannette (eds.) (1996) *Dictionary of Caribbean English Usage, with a French and Spanish Supplement.* Oxford: Oxford University Press.

Andersen, Roger W. (ed.) (1983) *Pidginization and Creolization as Language Acquisition*. Rowley: Newbury House.

Andreasson, Ann-Marie (1994) Norm as a pedagogical paradigm. *World Englishes*, **13**(3), 395–409.

Asante, Milefi Kete (1987) *The Afrocentric Idea*. Philadelphia: Temple University Press.

Ashcroft, Bill, Griffiths, Gareth and Tiffin, Helen (1989) *The Empire Writes Back: Theory and Practice in Post-Colonial Literature. New Accents*. London: Routledge.

Asmah Haji Omar (1992) *The Linguistic Scenery in Malaysia*. Kuala Lumpur: Ministry of Education Malaysia.

Asmah Haji Omar (2000) From imperialism to Malaysianisation: A discussion of the path taken by English towards becoming a national language. In *English Is an Asian Language: The Malaysian Context*. Edited by Halimah Mohd Said and Keit Sew Ng. Persatuan Bahasa Moden Malaysia and The Macquarie Library Pty Ltd, pp. 12–21.

Austin, John L. (1962) *How to Do Things with Words*. Cambridge: Harvard University Press.

Avis, Walter S. (1967) *A Dictionary of Canadianisms on Historical Principles*. Toronto: Gage.

Azuma, Shoji (1996a) Borrowing and politeness strategy in Japanese. In *Proceedings of the Twenty-Second Annual Meeting of the Berkeley Linguistics Society*. Edited by Jan Johnson, Matthew L. Juge, and Jeri L. Moxley. Berkeley: Berkeley Linguistic Society, pp. 3–12.

Azuma, Shoji (1996b) Free morpheme constraint revisited. *World Englishes*, **15**(3), 361–8.

Baik, Martin Jonghak (1992) Language shift and identity in Korea. *Journal of Asian Pacific Communication*, **3**(1), 15–31.

Baik, Martin Jonghak (1994) *Language, Ideology and Power: English Textbooks of Two Koreas*. Seoul: Thaehaksa.

Baik, Martin Jonghak (2001) Aspects of Englishization in Korean discourse. In *The Three Circles of English*. Edited by Edwin Thumboo. Singapore: UniPress, pp. 181–93.

Baik, Martin Jonghak and Shim, Rosa Jinyoung (1995) Language, culture, and ideology in the English textbooks of two Koreas. In *Language and Culture in Multilingual Societies: Viewpoints and Visions*. Edited by Makhan L. Tickoo Singapore: SEAMEO Regional Language Centre, pp. 122–38.

Bailey, Guy (1993) A perspective on African-American English. In *American Dialect Research*. Edited by D. Preston. Philadelphia: John Benjamins, pp. 287–318.

Bailey, Guy and Thomas, Erik (1998) Some aspects of African-American vernacular English phonology. In *African-American English: Structure, History and Use*. Edited by Salikoko S. Mufwene, John R. Rickford, Guy Bailey and John Baugh. New York: Routledge, pp. 85–109.

Bailey, Richard W. (1991) *Images of English: A Cultural History of the Language*. Ann Arbor: University of Michigan Press.

Bailey, Richard W. (1996) Attitudes toward English: The future of English in South Asia. In *South Asian English: Structure, Use, and Users*. Edited by Robert J. Baumgardner. Urbana: University of Illinois Press, pp. 40–52.

Baker, Wendy and Eggington, William G. (1999) Bilingual creativity, multidimensional analysis, and world Englishes. *World Englishes*, **18**(3), 343–57.

Bamgboṣe, Ayọ (1971) The English language in Nigeria. In *The English Language in West Africa*. Edited by John Spencer. London: Longman, pp. 35–48.

Bamgboṣe, Ayọ (1992 [1982]) Standard Nigerian English: Issues of identification. In *The Other Tongue: English across Cultures*. Edited by Braj B. Kachru. Urbana: University of Illinois Press, pp. 140–61. [1992 edn.]

Bamgboṣe, Ayọ (1998) Torn between the norms: Innovations in world Englishes. *World Englishes*, **17**(1), 1–14.

Bao, Zhiming (2001) Two issues in the study of Singapore English phonology. In *Evolving Identities: The English Language in Singapore and Malaysia*. Edited by Vincent B. Y. Ooi. Singapore: Times Academic Press, pp. 69–78.

Bao, Zhiming and Wee, Lionel (1998) *Until* in Singapore English. *World Englishes*, **17**(1), 31–41.

Barber, Katherine (1999) *The Canadian Oxford Dictionary*. Oxford: Oxford University Press.

Baron, Dennis (2000) Ebonics and the politics of English. *World Englishes*, **19**(1), 5–19.

Basham, Arthur L. (1954) *The Wonder That Was India*. London: Sidgwick and Jackson.

Baskaran, Loga (1994) The Malaysian English Mosaic. *English Today*, **37**(10), 27–32.

Baugh, John (1983) *Black Street Speech: Its History, Structure, and Survival*. Austin: University of Texas Press.

Baumgardner, Robert J. (1987) Using Pakistani newspaper English to teach grammar. *World Englishes*, **6**(3), 241–52.

Baumgardner, Robert J. (1990) The indigenization of English in Pakistan. *English Today* **6**(1), 59–65. [Reprinted in Baumgardner (1993).]

Baumgardner, Robert J. (ed.) (1993) *The English Language in Pakistan*. Karachi: Oxford University Press.

Baumgardner, Robert J. (1996a) Innovation in Pakistani English political lexis. In *South Asian English: Structure, Use, and Users*. Edited by Robert J. Baumgardner. Urbana: University of Illinois Press, pp. 174–88.

Baumgardner, Robert J. (ed.) (1996b) *South Asian English: Structure, Use, and Users*. Urbana: University of Illinois Press.

Bautista, Maria Lourdes S. (1996) Notes on three sub-varieties of the Philippine English. In *Readings in Philippine Sociolinguistics*. Edited by Maria Lourdes S. Bautista. Manila: De La Salle University Press, pp. 93–101.

Bautista, Maria Lourdes S. (1997a) The lexicon of Philippine English. In *English Is an Asian Language: The Philippine Context*. Edited by Maria Lourdes S. Bautista. Sydney: Macquarie Library Pty Ltd., pp. 49–72.

Bautista, Maria Lourdes S. (2000) *Defining Standard Philippine English: Its Status and Grammatical Features*. Manila: De LaSalle University Press.

Bautista, Maria Lourdes S. (2004) Researching English in the Philippines: Bibliographical resources. *World Englishes*, **23** (1), 199–210.

Bautista, Ma. Lourdes S. and Butler, Susan (2000) *Anvil-Macquarie Dictionary of Philippine English for High School*. Pasig City: Anvil Publishing, Inc.

Bautista, Maria Lourdes S. (ed.) (1997b) *English Is an Asian Language: The Philippine Context*. Sydney: Macquarie Library Pty Ltd.

Bautista, Maria Lourdes S. and Bolton, Kingsley (guest eds.) (2004) Special issue on *Philippine English: Tensions and Transitions*. *World Englishes*, **23**(1), 1–5.

Baxter, J. (1980) How should I speak English? American-ly, Japanese-ly or internationally? *The JALT Journal*, **2**, 31–61.

Belazi, Heidi, Rubin, Edward and Toribio, Almedia Jacqueline (1994) Codeswitching and X-bar theory: The functional head constraint. *Linguistic Inquiry*, **24**(2), 221–37.

Bell, Alan and Kuiper, Koenraad (eds.) (1999) *New Zealand English*. Amsterdam: John Benjamins.

Bernardo, Allan B. I. (2004) McKinley's questionable bequest: Over 100 years of English in Philippine education. *World Englishes*, **23**(1), 17–31.

Berns, Margie, et al. (1998) (Re)experiencing hegemony: The linguistic imperialism of Robert Phillipson. *International Journal of Applied Linguistics*, **8**(2), 271–82.

Bhatia, Tej K. (2001) Language mixing in global advertising. In *The Three Circles of English*. Edited by Edwin Thumboo. Singapore: UniPress, pp. 195–215.

Bhatia, Tej K. and Ritchie, William C. (1996) Bilingual language mixing, universal grammar, and second language acquisition. In *Handbook of Second Language Acquisition*. Edited by William C. Ritchie and Tej K. Bhatia. New York: Academic Press, pp. 627–88.

Bhatia, Tej K. and Ritchie, William C. (1989) (guest eds.) Special issue on *Code-mixing: English across Languages*. *World Englishes*, **8**(3), 261–4.

Bhatia, Vijay K. (1993) *Analysing Genre: Language Use in Professional Settings*. London: Longman.

Bhatia, Vijay K. (1996) Nativization of job applications in South Asia. In *South Asian English: Structure, Use, and Users*. Edited by Robert J. Baumgardner. Urbana: University of Illinois Press, pp. 158–73.

Bhatia, Vijay K. (1997) The Power and Politics of Genre. Special Issue on *Genre Analysis and World Englishes*. *World Englishes*, **16**(3), 359–71.

Bhatt, Rakesh M. (1995) On the grammar of code-switching. *World Englishes*, **15**(3), 369–75.

Bhatt, Rakesh M. (guest ed.) (1996) Symposium on *Constraints on Code-mixing*. *World Englishes*, **15**(3), 359–404.

Biber, Douglas (1987) A textual comparison of British and American writing. *American Speech*, **62**, 99–119.

Biber, Douglas (1988) *Variation across Speech and Writing*. Cambridge: Cambridge University Press.

Biber, Douglas, Conrad, Susan and Reppen, Randi (1998) *Corpus Linguistics: Investigating Language Structure and Use. Cambridge Approaches to Linguistics*. Cambridge: Cambridge University Press.

Bickerton, Derek (1983) Comments on Valdman's 'Creolization and second language acquisition'. In *Pidginization and Creolization as Language Acquisition*. Edited by Roger W. Andersen. Rowley: Newbury House, pp. 235–40.

Bloomfield, Leonard (1933) *Language*. New York: Holt, Rinehart and Winston.

Blum-Kulka, Shoshana and Olshtain, Elite (1984) Requests and apologies: A cross-cultural study of speech act realization patterns (CCSARP). *Applied Linguistics*, **5**(3), 196–213.

Blum-Kulka, Shoshana, House, Juliane and Kasper, Gabriele (eds.) (1989) *Cross-cultural Pragmatics: Requests and Apologies*. Norwood: Ablex.

Bokamba, Eyamba G. (1992) The Africanization of English. In *The Other Tongue: English across Cultures*. Edited by Braj B. Kachru. Urbana: University of Illinois Press, pp. 125–47.

Bolton, Kingsley (2000) The sociolinguistics of Hong Kong and the space for Hong Kong English. *World Englishes*, **19**(3), pp. 265–85. [Reprinted in Bolton 2002c, pp. 29–55.]

Bolton, Kingsley (2002a) Chinese Englishes: From Canton jargon to global English. *World Englishes*, **21**(2), 181–99.

Bolton, Kingsley (2002b) Introduction: Hong Kong English: Autonomy and creativity. In *Hong Kong English: Autonomy and Creativity*. Edited by Kingsley Bolton. Hong Kong: Hong Kong University Press, pp. 1–25.

Bolton, Kingsley (2003) *Chinese English: A Sociolinguistic History*. Cambridge: Cambridge University Press.

Bolton, Kingsley (2004) World Englishes. *The Handbook of Applied Linguistics*. Edited by Alan Davies and Catherine Elder. Oxford: Blackwell Publishing, pp. 367–96.

Bolton, Kingsley and Lim, Shirley (2000) Futures for Hong Kong English. In *Special Issue on Hong Kong English: Autonomy and Creativity*. Edited by Kingsley Bolton. *World Englishes*, **19**(3), 429–43.

Bolton, Kingsley and Butler, Susan (2004) Dictionaries and the stratification of vocabulary: Towards a new lexicography for Philippine English. *World Englishes*, **23**(1), 91–112.

Bolton, Kingsley (ed.) (2002c) *Hong Kong English: Autonomy and Creativity.* Hong Kong: Hong Kong University Press.

Booker, M. Keith (1998) *The African Novel in English: An Introduction.* Portsmouth: Heinemann.

Branford, Jean (1978) *A Dictionary of South African English.* Cape Town: Oxford University Press.

Britton, James, Shafer, Robert E. and Watson, Ken (eds.) (1990) *Teaching and Learning English Worldwide.* Clevedon: Multilingual Matters.

Brown, Adam (1986) The pedagogical importance of consonantal features of the English of Malaysia and Singapore. *RELC Journal: A Journal of Language Teaching and Research in Southeast Asia,* **17**(2), 1–25.

Brown, Adam (1992) *Making Sense of Singapore English.* Singapore: Federal Publications.

Brown, Kimberley (1995) World Englishes: To teach? Or not to teach? *World Englishes,* **14**(2), 233–45.

Brown, Penelope and Levinson, Stephen C. (1987) *Politeness: Some Universals in Language Usage.* Cambridge: Cambridge University Press.

Brutt-Griffler, Janina (2002) *World English: A Study of Its Development.* Buffalo: Multilingual Matters.

Butler, Susan (1992) The publishing history of the Macquarie Dictionary: A personal narrative. In *Words in a Cultural Context.* Edited by Anne Pakir. Singapore: UniPress, pp. 7–14.

Butler, Susan (1997) World English in the Asian context: Why a dictionary is important. In *World Englishes 2000.* Edited by Larry E. Smith and Michael L. Forman. Honolulu: University of Hawai'i Press, pp. 90–125.

Calalang, Casiano (1928) Story settings. *The Philippines Herald,* January 29, 3–5.

Canagarajah, A. Suresh (1994) Competing discourses in Sri Lankan English poetry. *World Englishes,* **13**(3), 361–76.

Canagarajah, A. Suresh (1999) *Resisting Linguistic Imperialism in English Teaching.* Oxford: Oxford University Press.

Canagarajah, A. Suresh (2000) Negotiating ideologies through English: Strategies from the periphery. In *Ideologies, Politics and Language Policies: Focus on English.* Edited by Thomas Ricento. Amsterdam: John Benjamins, pp. 121–32.

Candlin, Christopher N., Bhatia, Vijay K. and Jensen, Christian H. (2002) Developing legal materials for English second language learners: Problems and perspectives. *English for Specific Purposes,* **21**(4), 299–320.

Cassidy, Frederic G. and LePage, Robert B. (eds.) (2003) *Dictionary of Jamaican English.* Kingston: UWI Press. [First Published 1967; second edition, 1980, Cambridge: Cambridge University Press.]

Celce-Murcia, Marianne (1991) *Teaching English as a Second or Foreign Language* (Second edition). Boston: Heinle and Heinle.

Cenoz, Jasone and Jessner, Ulrike (eds.) (2000) *English in Europe: The Acquisition of a Third Language*. Clevedon: Multilingual Matters.

Chan, Brian Hok-Shing (2003) *Aspects of the Syntax, the Pragmatics, and the Production of Code-switching: Cantonese and English. Berkeley Insights in Linguistics and Semiotics 51*. New York: Peter Lang.

Chan, Ronald (1991) The Singaporean and Malaysian speech communities. In *Multilingualism in the British Isles (Africa, Middle East and Asia)*. Edited by Sagder Alladina and Viv Edwards. New York: Longmans, pp. 207–20.

Chen, Su-Chiao (1996) Code-switching as verbal strategy among Chinese in a campus setting in Taiwan. *World Englishes*, **15**(3), 267–80.

Cheng, Chin-Chuan (1992) Chinese varieties of English. In *The Other Tongue: English across Cultures*. Edited by Braj B. Kachru. Urbana: University of Illinois Press, pp. 162–77.

Cheshire, Jenny (ed.) (1991) *English Around the World: Sociolinguistic Perspectives*. Cambridge: Cambridge University Press.

Clyne, Michael (1987) Discourse structure and discourse expectations: Implications for Anglo-German academic communication. In *Discourse Across Cultures: Strategies in World Englishes*. Edited by Larry E. Smith. New York: Prentice-Hall, pp. 73–83.

Clyne, Michael (1995) Establishing linguistic markers of racist discourse. In *Language and Peace*. Edited by Christina Schäffner and Anita L. Wenden. Amsterdam: Harwood Academic Publishers, pp. 111–8.

Coates, Jennifer (1983) *The Semantics of Modal Auxiliaries*. London: Croom Helm.

Collins, Peter (1991) The modals of obligation and necessity in Australian English. In *English Corpus Linguistics: Studies in Honor of Jan Svartvik*. Edited by Karin Aijmer and Bengt Altenberg. London: Longman, pp. 145–65.

Collins, Peter and Blair, David (eds.) (1989) *Australian English: The Language of New Society*. St. Lucia and New York: University of Queensland Press. Reprinted in the series on *Varieties of English Around the World*. Vol. 15. Amsterdam: John Benjamins.

Connor, Ulla (1996) *Contrastive Rhetoric: Cross-cultural Aspects of Second Language Writing*. Cambridge: Cambridge University Press.

Cooper, Robert L. (ed.) (1982) *Language Spread. Studies in Diffusion and Language Change*. Bloomington: Indiana University Press.

Courtright, Marguerite S. (2001) Intelligibility and context in reader responses to contact literary text. Unpublished PhD dissertation, University of Illinois, Urbana.

Crewe, William J. (ed.) (1977) *The English Language in Singapore*. Singapore: Eastern University Press.

Crowley, Tony (1989) *Standard English and the Politics of Language*. Urbana: University of Illinois Press.

Cruz, Isagani R. and Bautista, Maria Lourdes S. (compilers) (1995) *A Dictionary of Philippine English*. Metro Manila: Anvil Publishing Inc.

Crystal, David (1985a) How many millions? The statistics of English today. *English Today,* **1**, 7–9.

Crystal, David (1985b) Commentator 2 on Quirk 1985. In *English in the World: Teaching and Learning the Language and Literatures.* Edited by Randolph Quirk and Henry G. Widdowson. Cambridge: Cambridge University Press, pp. 9–10.

Crystal, David (1995) *The Cambridge Encyclopedia of Language.* Cambridge: Cambridge University Press. [First published in 1987.]

Crystal, David (1997) *English as a Global Language.* Cambridge: Cambridge University Press.

Dako, Kari (2002) Code-switching and lexical borrowing: Which is what in Ghanaian English? *English World-Wide,* **20**(2), 48–54.

Dalby, David (1972) The African element in American English. In *Rappin' and Stylin' Out: Communication in Urban Black America.* Edited by Thomas Kochman. Urbana: University of Illinois Press, pp. 170–86.

Daruwalla, Keki N. (1993) The mistress. In *Indian Poetry in English.* Edited by Makarand Paranjape. Hyderabad: Macmillan India Limited, pp. 185–6.

Das, Kamala (1997) An introduction. In *Nine Indian Women Poets: An Anthology.* Edited by Eunice deSouza. Delhi: Oxford University Press, p. 10.

Davidson, Fred (1993) Testing English across Cultures: Summary and comments. *World Englishes,* **12**(1), 113–25.

Davies, Alan (2003) *The Native Speaker: Myth and Reality.* Clevedon: Multilingual Matters.

De Kadt, Elizabeth (1993) Attitudes towards English in South Africa. *World Englishes,* **12**(3), 311–24.

de Klerk, Vivian (ed.) (1996) *Focus on South Africa.* Amsterdam: John Benjamins.

de Souza, Eunice (ed.) (1997) *Nine Indian Women Poets: An Anthology.* Delhi: Oxford University Press.

De La Toree, Visitacion R. (ed.) (1978) *A Survey of Contemporary Philippine Literature in English.* Philippines: National Book Store, Inc.

DeBose, Charles and Faraclas, Nicholas (1993) An Africanist approach to the linguistic study of Black English: Getting to the roots of tense-aspect-modality and copula systems in Afro-American. In *Africanisms in Afro-American Language Varieties.* Edited by Salikoko S. Mufwene. Athens: University of Georgia Press, pp. 364–87.

Desai, Anita (1978) A devoted son. In *Games at Twilight.* London: Penguin Books, pp. 70–81.

Desai, Anita (1992) Interview by Feroza Jussawalla. In *Interviews with Writers of the Post-Colonial World.* Edited by Feroza Jussawalla and Reed W. Dasenbrock. Jackson: University Press of Mississippi.

Desai, Anita (1996) A coat of many colors. In *South Asian English: Structure, Use, and Users.* Edited by Robert J. Baumgardner. Urbana: University of Illinois Press, pp. 221–30.

Devonish, Hubert (1991) Standardization in a Creole continuum situation: The Guyana case. In *English around the World*. Edited by Jenny Cheshire. Cambridge: Cambridge University Press, pp. 585–94.

Dhillon, Pradeep A. (1994) *Multiple Identities: A Phenomenology of Multicultural Communication*. New York: Peter Lang.

Di Sciullo, Anne-Marie, Muysken, Pieter and Singh, Rajendra (1986) Government and code-mixing. *Linguistics*, **22**, 25–67.

Dillard, Joey Lee (1972) *Black English: Its History and Usage in the United States*. New York: Vintage House.

Dissanayake, Wimal (1985) Towards a decolonized English: South Asian creativity in fiction. *World Englishes*, **4**(2), 233–42.

Dissanayake, Wimal (1997) Cultural studies and world Englishes. In *World Englishes 2000*. Edited by Larry E. Smith and Michael L. Forman. Honolulu: University of Hawaii Press, pp. 126–45.

Dixon, Robert M. W., Ward, Malcom, Ramson, William Stanley and Thomas, Mandy (1990) *Australian Aboriginal Words in English: Their Origin and Meaning*. Melbourne: Oxford University Press.

D'souza, Jean (2001) Indian English and Singapore English: Creativity contrasted. In *The Three Circles of English*. Edited by Edwin Thumboo. Singapore: UniPress, pp. 3–17.

Dunn, Ernest F. (1976) Black-Southern white dialect controversy. In *Black English: A Seminar*. Edited by Deborah S. Harrison and Tom Trabasso. Hillsdale: Erlbaum, pp. 105–22.

Dustoor, Phiroze E. (1954) Missing and intrusive articles in Indian English. *Allahabad University Studies*, **31**, 1–70.

Eisikovits, Edina (1981) Inner-Sydney English: An investigation of grammatical variation in adolescent speech. Unpublished PhD dissertation, University of Sydney, Sydney.

Eisikovits, Edina (1989) Girl-talk/boy-talk: Sex differences in adolescent speech. In *Australian English: The Language of New Society*. Edited by Peter Collins and David Blair. St. Lucia: University of Queensland Press, pp. 35–54. [Reprinted in the series on *Varieties of English Around the World*. Vol. 15. Amsterdam: John Benjamins.]

Eliot, T. S. (1943) *Four Quartets*. New York: Harcourt, Brace and Co.

Ewers, Traute (1996) *The Origin of American Black English: Be Forms in HOODOO Texts*. New York: Mouton de Gruyter.

Ferguson, Charles A. (1992 [1982]) Foreword. In *The Other Tongue: English across Cultures*. Edited by Braj B. Kachru. Urbana: University of Illinois Press, pp. vii–xi.

Ferguson, Charles A. (1996a) English in South Asia: Imperialist legacy and regional asset. In *South Asian English: Structure, Use, and Users*. Edited by Robert J. Baumgardner. Urbana: University of Illinois Press, pp. 29–39.

Ferguson, Charles A. (1996b) Sociolinguistic settings of language planning. In *Sociolinguistic Perspectives: Papers on Language in Society 1959–1994. Charles Ferguson.* Edited by Thom Huebner. Oxford: Oxford University Press, pp. 277–94. [First published in 1977 in *Language Planning Processes.* Edited by J. Rubin, B. H. Jernudd, J. Das Gupta, J. A. Fishman, and C. A. Ferguson. The Hague: Mouton, pp. 9–29.]

Ferguson, Charles A. and Dil, Afia (1996) The sociolinguistic variable(s) in Bengali: A sound change in progress? In *Sociolinguistic Perspectives: Papers on Language in Society 1959–1994. Charles Ferguson.* Edited by Thom Huebner. Oxford: Oxford University Press, pp. 181–8. [First published in *Studies in the Linguistic Sciences* **9**(1), 129–37.]

Ferguson, Charles A. and Dil, Anwar S. (1979) Universals of language planning and national development. In *Language in Society: Anthropological Issues.* Edited by William C. McCormack and Stephen A. Wurm. The Hague: Mouton, pp. 693–701.

Ferguson, Charles A. and Heath, Shirley Brice (eds.) (1981) *Language in the USA.* Cambridge: Cambridge University Press.

Fernando, Chitra (1996) The ideational function of English in Sri Lanka. In *South Asian English: Structure, Use, and Users.* Edited by Robert J. Baumgardner. Urbana: University of Illinois Press, pp. 206–17.

Firth, Alan and Wagner, Johannes (1998) SLA property: No trespassing! *Modern Language Journal,* **82**(1), 91–94.

Firth, Alan (ed.) (1995) *The Discourse of Negotiation: Studies of Language in the Workplace.* Oxford: Pergamon.

Flynn, Suzanne (1987) *A Parameter-setting Model of Second Language Acquisition.* Dodrecht: Reidel.

Flynn, Suzanne (1989) The role of head-initial/head-final parameter in the acquisition of English relative clauses by adult Spanish and Japanese learners. In *Linguistic Perspectives on Second Language Acquisition.* Edited by Susan Gass and Jacqueline Schachter. Cambridge: Cambridge University Press, pp. 89–108.

Foucault, Michel (1980) *Power/Knowledge: Selected Interviews and Other Writings 1972–1977.* Edited by Colin Gordon. New York: Pantheon Books.

Foucault, Michel (1981) *The Archaeology of Knowledge.* New York: Pantheon Books.

Francis, W. Nelson (1958) *The Structure of American English.* New York: The Ronald Press Co.

Frederickson, Kirstin M. (1996) Contrasting genre systems: Court documents from the United States and Sweden. *Multilingua,* **15**, 275–304.

Frenck, Susan and Min, Su Jung (2001) Culture, reader and textual intelligibility. In *The Three Circles of English.* Edited by Edwin Thumboo. Singapore: UniPress, pp. 19–34.

Garapati, U. Rao (1991) Subgrouping of the Gondi dialects. In *Studies in Dravidian and General Linguistics: A Festschrift for Bh. Krishnamurti*. Edited by B. Lakshmi Bai and B. Ramakrishna Reddy. Hyderabad: Osmania University Publications in Linguistics, pp. 73–90.

Gardner, Robert C. and Lambert, Wallace E. (1972) *Attitudes and Motivations in Second Language Learning*. Rowley: Newbury House.

Gass, Susan M. (1997) *Input, Interaction, and the Second Language Learner*. Mahwah: Lawrence Erlbaum Associates.

Gaudart, Hyacinth (2000) Malaysia English, can or not? In *English Is an Asian Language: The Malaysian Context*. Edited by Halimah Mohd Said and Keit Sew Ng. Persatuan Bahasa Moden Malaysia and The Macquarie Library Pty Ltd., pp. 47–56.

Gikandi, Simon (1987) *Reading the African Novel*. London: J. Currey.

Gikandi, Simon (ed.) (2003) *Encyclopedia of African Literature*. London: Routledge.

Gill, Saran Kaur (1993) Standards and pedagogical norms for teaching English in Malaysia. *World Englishes*, **12**(2), 223–38.

Goffman, Erving (1967) *Interaction Ritual: Essays in Face-to-Face Behavior*. Chicago: Aldine Publishing Co.

Gonzalez, Andrew (1983) When does error become a feature of Philippine English? In *Varieties of English in Southeast Asia*. Edited by R. B. Noss. Rowley: Newbury House, pp. 150–72.

Gonzalez, Andrew (1997) The history of English in the Philippines. In *English Is an Asian Language: The Philippine Context*. Edited by Maria Lourdes S. Bautista. Sydney, Australia: Macquarie Library Pty Ltd., pp. 25–40.

Goodrich, Peter (1987) *Legal Discourse*. London: Macmillan.

Görlach, Manfred (1991a) Lexicographical problems of new Englishes. In *Englishes. Studies in Varieties of English 1984–1988*. Edited by Manfred Görlach. Amsterdam: John Benjamins, pp. 36–68.

Görlach, Manfred (1991b) *Englishes. Studies in Varieties of English 1984–1988*. Amsterdam: John Benjamins.

Görlach, Manfred (1995) Text types and Indian English. In *More Englishes: New Studies in Varieties of English 1988–1994*. Edited by Manfred Görlach. Amsterdam: John Benjamins, pp. 93–123.

Görlach, Manfred (ed.) (1995b) *More Englishes: New Studies in Varieties of English 1988–1994*. Amsterdam: John Benjamins.

Görlach, Manfred (ed.) (1998) *Even More Englishes*. Amsterdam: John Benjamins.

Görlach, Manfred (ed.) (2002) *Still More Englishes*. Amsterdam: John Benjamins.

Gough, David (1996a) Black English in South Africa. In *Focus on South Africa*. Edited by Vivian de Klerk. Amsterdam: John Benjamins, pp. 53–77.

Gough, David (1996b) English in South Africa. In *A Dictionary of South African English on Historical Principles*. Edited by Penny Silva, Wendy Dore, Dorothea Mantzel, Colin Muller, and Madeleine Wright. Oxford: Oxford University Press, pp. xvii–xix.

Grace, Patricia (1998) *Baby No-Eyes*. Honolulu: University of Hawaii Press.

Graddol, David (1997) *The Future of English?: A Guide to Forecasting the Popularity of English in the 21st Century*. London: British Council.

Green, Georgia M. (1989) *Pragmatics and Natural Language Understanding*. Hillsdale: Lawrence Erlbaum.

Green, Lisa J. (2002) *African American English: A Linguistic Introduction*. Cambridge: Cambridge University Press.

Greenbaum, Sydney (1991) ICE: The international corpus of English. *English Today*, **28**(7.4), 3–7.

Greenbaum, Sidney and Nelson, Gerald (guest eds.) (1996) Special issue on *Studies on International Corpus of English (ICE)*. *World Englishes*, **15**(1), 69–81.

Grice, H. Paul (1975) Logic and conversation. In *Syntax and Semantics 7: Speech Acts*. Edited by Peter Cole and Jerry Morgan. New York: Academic Press, pp. 41–58.

Griffiths, Gareth (1978) *A Double Exile: African and West Indian Writing between Two Cultures*. London: Boyars.

Grosjean, François (1989) Neurolinguists, beware! The bilingual is not two monolinguals in one person. *Brain and Language*, **36**, 3–15.

Grote, David (1992) *British English for American Readers: A Dictionary of the Language, Customs and Places of British Life and Literature*. Westport: Greenwood.

Gumperz, John J. (ed.) (1982a) *Discourse Strategies*. Cambridge: Cambridge University Press.

Gumperz, John J. (ed.) (1982b) *Language and Social Identity*. Cambridge: Cambridge University Press.

Gumperz, John J. and Cook-Gumperz, Jenny (1982) Introduction: Language and communication of social identity. In *Language and Social Identity*. Edited by John J. Gumperz. Cambridge: Cambridge University Press, pp. 1–21.

Gyasi, Ibrahim K. (1991) Aspects of English in Ghana. *English Today*, **26** (7.2), 26–31.

Hall, Edward (1976) *Beyond Culture*. New York: Anchor Press.

Halliday, Michael A. K. (1973) *Explorations in the Function of Language*. London: Edward Arnold.

Halliday, Michael A. K. (1978) *Language as Social Semiotic*. London: Edward Arnold.

Halliday, Michael A. K. and Matthiesson, C. M. I. M. (1999) *Construing Experience Through Meaning: A Language-based Approach to Cognition*. London: Cassell.

Hasan, Ruqaiya (2003) Globalization, literacy and ideology. *World Englishes*, **22**(4), 433–48.

Hashmi, Alamgir (1980) Appendix 1: Pakistan. *Journal of Commonwealth Literature*, **15**(2), 151–6.

Hawkins, R. E. (1984) *Common Indian Words in English*. Delhi: Oxford University Press.

Hayashi, Reiko (1996) *Cognition, Empathy, and Interaction: Floor Management of English and Japanese Conversation*. Norwood: Ablex.

Hayashi, Takuo, and Hayashi, Reiko (1995) A cognitive study of English loanwords in Japanese discourse. *World Englishes*, **14**(1), 55–66.

Hearn, Lafcadio (1925) The dream of a summer day. In *Stories and Sketches by Lafcadio Hearn*. Compiled by R. Tanabe. Tokyo: Hokuseido, pp. 90–110.

Heimann, Betty (1964) *Facets of Indian Thought*. London: George Allen and Unwin.

Hermerén, Lars (1978) *On Modality in English: A Study in the Semantics of Modals*. Lund: Lund University Press.

Higa, Masanori (1973) Sociolinguistic aspects of word borrowing. *Topics in Culture Learning* **1**, 75–85.

Hilgendorf, Suzanne and Martin, Elizabeth (2001) English in advertising: Update for France and Germany. In *The Three Circles of English*. Edited by Edwin Thumboo. Singapore: UniPress, pp. 217–40.

Hinds, John (1987) Reader versus writer responsibility: A new typology. In *Writing Across Languages: Analysis of L2 Text*. Edited by Ulla Connor and Robert Kaplan. Reading: Addison-Wesley, pp. 141–52.

Hinton, Linette N. and Pollock, Karen E. (2000) Regional variations in the phonological characteristics of African American Vernacular English. *World Englishes*, **19**(1), 59–71.

Ho, Chee Lick (1992) Words in a cultural context: Term selection. In *Words in a Cultural Context*. Edited by Anne Pakir. Singapore: UniPress, pp. 202–14.

Ho, Mian-Lian (1993) Variability of *be* realization in the Singaporean English speech continuum. *International Review of Applied Linguistics*, 101–102, 141–65.

Ho, Mian-Lian and Platt, John (1993) *Dynamics of a Contact Continuum: Singapore English*. Oxford: Clarendon Press.

Hoffman, Charlotte (2000) The spread of English and the growth of multilingualism with English in Europe. In *English in Europe: The Acquisition of a Third Language*. Edited by Jasone Cenoz and Ulrike Jessner. Clevedon: Multilingual Matters, pp. 1–21.

Hogan, Patrick Colm (2000) *Colonialism and Cultural Identity: Crises of Tradition in the Anglophone Literatures of India, Africa, and the Caribbean*. Albany: State University of New York Press.

Holm, John and Shilling, Alison W. (1982) *Dictionary of Bahamian English.* Cold Spring: Lexik House.

Horiuchi, Amy (1963) Department store ads and Japanized English. *Studies in Descriptive and Applied Linguistics,* **2**, 49–67.

Horvath, Barbara M. (1985) *Variation in Australian English: The Sociolects of Sydney.* Cambridge: Cambridge University Press.

Huddleston, Rodney (1984) *Introduction to the Grammar of English.* Cambridge: Cambridge University Press.

Hughes, E. ([1967]1977) Epistemological methods in Chinese philosophy. In *The Chinese Mind.* Edited by Charles Moore. Honolulu: The University Press of Hawaii [1977 edn.], pp. 77–103.

Hulme, Keri (1982) E Nga Iwi O Ngai Tahu. In *Into the World of Light.* Edited by Witi Ihimaera and D. S. Long. Auckland: Heinemann, pp. 257–8.

Hulme, Keri (1986) *The Bone People.* New York: Viking Penguin Press.

Hundt, Marianne (1998) *New Zealand English Grammar, Fact or Fiction? A Corpus-Based Study in Morphosyntactic Variation.* In the series *Varieties of English Around the World.* Vol. 23. Philadelphia: John Benjamins.

Hyde, Barbara (2002) Japan's emblematic English. *English Today,* **71** (18.3), 12–16.

Hymes, Dell (1974) *Foundations in Sociolinguistics.* Philadelphia: University of Pennsylvania Press.

Ihimaera, Witi (1974) *Whanau.* Auckland, NZ: Heinemann.

Ihimaera, Witi and Long, D. S. (eds.) (1982) *Into the World of Light.* Auckland, NZ: Heinemann.

Ike, Minoru (1995) A historical review of English in Japan. *World Englishes,* **14**(1), 3–11.

Ilson, Robert (1995) A(n)-dropping. *English Today,* **11**(1), 42–4.

Irele, F. Abiola (2001) *The African Imagination: Literature in Africa & the Black Diaspora.* Oxford: Oxford University Press.

Irele, F. Abiola and Gikandi, Simon (2004) *The Cambridge History of African and Caribbean Literature.* Cambridge: Cambridge University Press.

Iyengar, K. R. S. (1985) *Indian Writing in English.* (Revised and updated edition; first published in 1962). New Delhi: Sterling.

Jenkins, Jennifer (2000) *The Phonology of English as an International Language.* Oxford: Oxford University Press.

Jenkins, Jennifer (2003) *World Englishes: A Resource Book for Students.* London: Routledge.

Jose, F. Sionil (1968) *The God Stealer and Other Stories.* Quezon City: R. P. Garcia Publishing Co.

Jose, F. Sionil (1997) *see under* Standards in Philippine English: The Writers' Forum. In *English Is an Asian Language: The Philippine Context.* Edited by Maria Lourdes S. Bautista. Sydney: Macquarie Library Pty Ltd., pp. 167–9.

Jung, Kyutae (2001) The genre of advertising in Korean: Strategies and 'mixing'. In *The Three Circles of English*. Edited by Edwin Thumboo. Singapore: UniPress, pp. 257–75.

Jung, Kyutae and Min, Su Jung (1999) Some lexico-grammatical features of Korean-English newspapers. *World Englishes*, **18**(1), 23–37.

Kachru, Braj B. (1969) *A Reference Grammar of Kashmiri*. Prepared under a contract with the Institute of International Affairs, Office of Health, Education and Welfare, Washington, DC. Urbana: University of Illinois.

Kachru, Braj B. (1973) Toward a lexicon of Indian English. In *Issues in Linguistics: Papers in Honor of Henry and Renée Kahane*. Edited by Braj B. Kachru, Robert B. Lees, Sol Saporta, Angelina Pietrangeli and Yakov Malkiel. Urbana: University of Illinois Press, pp. 352–76. [A revised version in Kachru, Braj B. (1983) *The Indianization of English: The English Language in India*. Delhi: Oxford University Press, pp. 165–89.]

Kachru, Braj B. (1976) Models of English for the Third World: White man's linguistic burden or language pragmatics? *TESOL Quarterly* **10**(1), 221–39. [Reproduced in *New Varieties of English: Issues and Approaches*. Edited by Jack C. Richards. Singapore: Regional Language Centre, 1979, pp. 1–17; and in *Teaching English Pronunciation: A Book of Readings*. Edited by Adam Brown. London and New York: Routledge, 1992, pp. 31–52.]

Kachru, Braj B. (1979) The Englishization of Hindi: Language rivalry and language change. In *Linguistic Method: Papers in Honor of H. Penzl*. Edited by I. Rouch and G. F. Carr. The Hague: Mouton, pp. 199–211.

Kachru, Braj B. (1980) The new Englishes and old dictionaries: Directions in lexicographical research on non-native varieties of English. In *Theory and Method in Lexicography: Western and Non-Western Perspectives*. Edited by Ladislav Zgusta. South Carolina: Hornbeam Press, pp. 71–101.

Kachru, Braj B. (1982a) Models for non-native Englishes. In *The Other Tongue: English across Cultures*. Edited by Braj B. Kachru. Urbana: University of Illinois Press (1992 edition), pp. 48–74.

Kachru, Braj B. (1983) *The Indianization of English: The English Language in India*. New Delhi: Oxford University Press.

Kachru, Braj B. (1985) Standards, codification and sociolinguistic realism: The English language in the outer circle. In *English in the World: Teaching and Learning the Language and Literatures*. Edited by Randolph Quirk and Henry Widdowson. Cambridge: Cambridge University Press, pp. 11–30.

Kachru, Braj B. (1986a) *The Alchemy of English: The Spread, Functions and Models of Non-native Englishes*. Oxford: Pergamon Press. [South Asian edition, New Delhi: Oxford University Press, 1989; US edition, Urbana: University of Illinois Press, in the series *English in the Global Context*, 1990.]

Kachru, Braj B. (1986b) The bilingual's creativity and contact literatures. In *The Alchemy of English*. Edited by Braj B. Kachru. Oxford: Pergamon Press [reprinted 1990 edition], pp. 159–73.

Kachru, Braj B. (1987) The power and politics of English. *World Englishes*, **5** (2/3), 121–40.

Kachru, Braj B. (1988) The spread of English and sacred linguistic cows. In *Language Spread and Language Policy: Issues, Implication, and Case Studies. GURT 1987*. Edited by Peter H. Lowenberg. Washington, DC: Georgetown University Press, pp. 207–28.

Kachru, Braj B. (1990a) World Englishes and applied linguistics. *World Englishes*, **9**(1), 3–20.

Kachru, Braj B. (1990b) Cultural contact and literary creativity in a multilingual setting. In *Literary Relations East and West*. Edited by J. Toyama and N. Ochner. Honolulu: University of Hawaii Press, pp. 194–203. [Modified version in *Dimensions of Sociolinguistics in South Asia*. Edited by Edward C. Dimock, Braj B. Kachru, and Bh. Krishnamurti. New Delhi: Oxford IBH Publications, pp. 149–59.]

Kachru, Braj B. (1992a) Meaning in deviation: Toward understanding non-native English texts. In *The Other Tongue: English across Cultures*. Edited by Braj B. Kachru. Urbana: University of Illinois Press, pp. 301–26.

Kachru, Braj B. (1992b) Teaching world Englishes. In *The Other Tongue: English across Cultures*. Edited by Braj B. Kachru. Urbana: University of Illinois Press, pp. 355–65.

Kachru, Braj B. (1992c) The second diaspora of English. In *English in its Social Contexts: Essays in Historical Sociolinguistics*. Edited by Tim William Machan and Charles T. Scott. New York: Oxford University Press, pp. 230-52.

Kachru, Braj B. (1993) Ethical issues for applying linguistics: Afterword. Special issue on *Ethical Issues for Applying Linguistics. Issues in Applied Linguistics*, **4**(2), 283–94.

Kachru, Braj B. (1994a) English in South Asia. In *The Cambridge History of the English Language*, Vol. V. Edited by Robert Burchfield. Cambridge: Cambridge University Press, pp. 497–553.

Kachru, Braj B. (1994b) The paradigms of marginality. Annual Plenary in Honor of James E. Alatis, TESOL Convention, 9 March, Baltimore, Maryland, USA.

Kachru, Braj B. (1995a) Transcultural creativity in world Englishes and literary canons. In *Principles and Practice in Applied Linguistics: Studies in Honor of Henry G. Widdowson*. Edited by Guy Cook and Barbara Seidlhofer. Oxford: Oxford University Press, pp. 271–87.

Kachru, Braj B. (1995b) Teaching world Englishes without myths. In *INTELEC '94: International English Language Education Conference, National and International Challenges and Responses*. Edited by Saran K. Gill, I. Abdul Aziz, H. Wong, T. M. M. Tg, Nor Rizan, D. A. H. Bahiyah, A. Hazita, S. Checketts, and S. K. Lee. Bangi: Pusat Bahasa Universiti Kebangsaan Malaysia, pp. 1–19.

Kachru, Braj B. (1996) South Asian English: Toward an identity in diaspora. In *South Asian English: Structure, Use, and Users.* Edited by Robert J. Baumgardner. Urbana, IL: University of Illinois Press, pp. 9–28.

Kachru, Braj B. (1997) World Englishes 2000: Resources for research and teaching. In *World Englishes 2000.* Edited by Larry E. Smith and Michael L. Forman. Honolulu: University of Hawaii Press, pp. 209–51.

Kachru, Braj B. (1999) Asian Englishes: Constructs, contact and convergence. Paper presented at AILA, Tokyo, 2 August.

Kachru, Braj B. (2002) On Nativizing *Mantra*: Identity construction in Anglophone Englishes. In *Anglophone Cultures in Southeast Asia: Appropriations, Continuities, Contexts.* Edited by Rüdiger Ahrens, David Parker, Klaus Stierstorfer and Kwok-kan Tam. Heidelberg: Heidelberg University Press, pp. 55–72.

Kachru, Braj B. (2005a) *Asian Englishes: Beyond the Canon.* Hong Kong: Hong Kong University Press.

Kachru, Braj B. (2005b) English in India: A lexicographical perspective. In *Lexicology 2: An International Handbook on the Nature and Structure of Words and Vocabularies.* Edited by Alan Cruse, Franz Hundsnurscher, Michael Job and Peter Rolf Lutzeier. Berlin: Walter de Guyter, pp. 1274–9.

Kachru, Braj B. and McArthur, Tom (1992) Indian English. In *The Oxford Companion to the English Language.* Edited by Tom McArthur. Oxford: Oxford University Press, pp. 504–8.

Kachru, Braj B. and Nelson, Cecil L. (1996) World Englishes. In *Sociolinguistics and Language Teaching.* Edited by Sandra Lee McKay and Nancy H. Hornberger. Cambridge, UK: Cambridge University Press, pp. 71–102.

Kachru, Braj B. (ed.) (1982b) *The Other Tongue: English across Cultures.* Urbana: University of Illinois Press.

Kachru, Braj B. (ed.) (1992d) *The Other Tongue: English across Cultures.* Second edition. Urbana: University of Illinois Press.

Kachru, Yamuna (1983) Linguistics and written discourse in particular languages: Contrastive studies: English and Hindi. *Annual Review of Applied Linguistics 1982*, **3**, 50–77.

Kachru, Yamuna (1987). Cross-cultural texts, discourse strategies and discourse interpretation. In *Discourse across Cultures: Strategies in World Englishes.* Edited by Larry E. Smith. London: Prentice-Hall, pp. 87–100.

Kachru, Yamuna (1988) Culture and speech acts: Evidence from Indian and Singaporean English. *Studies in the Linguistic Sciences*, **28**, 79–98.

Kachru, Yamuna (1989) Code-mixing, style repertoire and language variation: English in Hindi poetic creativity. *World Englishes*, **8**(3), 311–9.

Kachru, Yamuna (1992) Culture, style and discourse: Expanding noetics of English. In *The Other Tongue: English across Cultures.* Edited by Braj B. Kachru. Urbana, IL: University of Illinois Press, pp. 340–52.

Kachru, Yamuna (1993) Review of L. Selinker (1992). *World Englishes*, **12**(2), 265–73.

Kachru, Yamuna (1994a). Monolingual bias in SLA research. *TESOL Quarterly,* **28**(4), 795–800.

Kachru, Yamuna (1994b). Review of R. Mesthrie (1992). *Language in Society,* **23**(4), 587–91.

Kachru, Yamuna (1995a) Contrastive rhetoric in world Englishes. *English Today,* **11**, 21–31.

Kachru, Yamuna (1995b) Lexical exponents of cultural contact: Speech act verbs in Hindi-English dictionaries. In *Cultures, Ideologies, and the Dictionary: Studies in Honor of Ladislav Zgusta.* Edited by Braj B. Kachru and Henry Kahane. Tübingen: Max Niemeyer Verlag, pp. 261–74.

Kachru, Yamuna (1996) Kachru revisits contrasts. *English Today,* **12**, 41–44.

Kachru, Yamuna (1997a) Cultural meaning and contrastive rhetoric in English Education. *World Englishes,* **16**(3), 337–50.

Kachru, Yamuna (1997b) Culture and argumentative writing in world Englishes. In *World Englishes 2000.* Edited by Larry E. Smith and Michael L. Forman. Honolulu: University of Hawaii Press, pp. 48–67.

Kachru, Yamuna (1998) Culture and speech acts: Evidence from Indian and Singaporean English. *Studies in the Linguistic Sciences,* **28**, 79–98.

Kachru, Yamuna (1999) Culture, context and writing. In *Culture in Second Language Teaching and Learning.* Edited by Eli Hinkel. Cambridge: Cambridge University Press, pp. 75–89.

Kachru, Yamuna (2001a) Discourse competence in world Englishes. In *The Three Circles of English.* Edited by Edwin Thumboo. Singapore: UniPress, pp. 341–55.

Kachru, Yamuna (2001b) World Englishes and rhetoric across cultures. *Asian Englishes: An International Journal of the Sociolinguistics of English in Asia/ Pacific.* Winter, 54–71.

Kachru, Yamuna (2003) Conventions of politeness in plural societies. In *Anglophone Cultures in South-East Asia: Appropriations, Continuities, Contexts.* Edited by Rüdiger Ahrens, David Parker, Klaus Stierstorfer and Kwok-kan Tam. Heidelberg, Germany: Universitätsverlag Winter Heidelberg, pp. 39–53.

Kachru, Yamuna (guest ed.) (1991) Symposium on *Speech Acts in World Englishes. World Englishes,* **10**(3), 295–340.

Kamimura, Takeo (1995) A crosscultural analysis of argumentative strategies in the English essays by American and Japanese students. Paper presented at IAWE, Nagoya, Japan.

Kamimura, Takeo and Oi, Kyoko (1998) Argumentative strategies in American and Japanese English. *World Englishes,* **17**(3), 307–23.

Kamwangamalu, Nkonko (1989) A selected bibliography of studies on code-mixing and code-switching (1970–1988). *World Englishes,* **8**(3), 433–40.

Kamwangamalu, Nkonko (1996) Sociolinguistic aspects of siSwati-English bilingualism. *World Englishes,* **15**(3), 295–305.

Kandiah, Thiru (1996) Syntactic "deletion" in Lankan English: Learning from a new variety of English about. In *South Asian English: Structure, Use, and Users*. Edited by Robert, J. Baumgardner. Urbana: University of Illinois Press, pp. 104–23.

Kaplan, Robert B. (1966) Cultural thought patterns in intercultural education. *Language Learning*, **16**, 1–20.

Kaplan, Robert B. (1972) *The Anatomy of Rhetoric: Prolegomena to a Functional Theory of Rhetoric*. Philadelphia: Center for Curriculum Development.

Kasper, Gabriele and Blum-Kulka, Shoshana (eds.) (1993) *Interlanguage Pragmatics*. New York: Oxford University Press.

Kathpalia, Sujata S. (1997) Cross-cultural variation in professional genres: A comparative study of book blurbs. *World Englishes*, **16**(3), 417–26.

Kay, Gillian (1995) English loanwords in Japanese. *World Englishes*, **14**(1), 67–86.

Kennedy, Graeme D. (1985) Commentator 1 on Quirk (1985). In *English in the World: Teaching and Learning the Language and Literatures*. Edited by Randolph Quirk and Henry G. Widdowson. Cambridge: Cambridge University Press, pp. 7–8.

Kennedy, Graeme D. (1998) *An Introduction to Corpus Linguistics*. London: Longman.

King, Bruce A. (1980). *The New English Literatures: Cultural Nationalism in the Changing World*. New York: St. Martin Press.

Kirk-Greene, Anthony H. M. (1971) The influence of West African languages on English. In *The English Language in West Africa*. Edited by John Spencer. London: Longmans, pp. 123–44.

Kirkpatrick, Andy and Xu, Zhichang (2002) Chinese pragmatic norms and 'China English'. *World Englishes*, **21**(2), 269–79.

Kochman, Thomas (ed.) (1972) *Rappin' and Stylin' Out: Communication in Urban Black America*. Urbana: University of Illinois Press.

Kochman, Thomas (1981) *Black and White Styles in Conflict*. Chicago: University of Illinois Press.

Koyama, Tomoko (1992) *Japan: A Handbook in Intercultural Communication*. Sydney: Macquarie University, National Centre for English Language Teaching and Research.

Krashen, Stephen D. (1981). *Second Language Acquisition and Second Language Learning*. Oxford: Pergamon.

Krashen, Stephen D. (1985). *The Input Hypothesis: Issues and Implications*. London: Longman.

Labov, William (1964) Stages in the acquisition of Standard English. In *Social Dialects and Language Learning*. Edited by Roger Shuy. Champaign: National Council of Teachers of English, pp. 77–103.

Labov, William (1966) *The Social Stratification of English in New York City*. Washington, DC: Center for Applied Linguistics.

Labov, William (1972a) The transformation of experience in narrative syntax. In *Language in the Inner City*. William Labov. Philadelphia: University of Pennsylvania Press, pp. 354–96.

Labov, William (1972b) Objectivity and commitment in linguistic science. *Language in Society*, **11**, 165–201.

Labov, William (1972c) *Language in the Inner City*. Philadelphia: University of Pennsylvania Press.

Labov, William (1972d) *Sociolinguistic Patterns*. Oxford: Blackwell.

Labov, William (1998) Co-existent systems in African-American vernacular English. In *African-American English: Structure, History and Use*. Edited by Salikoko S. Mufwene, John R. Rickford, Guy Bailey and John Baugh. New York: Routledge, pp. 110–53.

Larsen-Freeman, Diane (1976) An explanation for the morpheme acquisition order of second language learners. *Language Learning*, **26**, 125–34.

Lau, Chi-Kuen (1995) Language of the future. *South China Morning Post*, 18 September.

Lawler, John and Dry, Helen Aristar (eds.) (1998) *Using Computers in Linguistics: A Practical Guide*. London: Routledge.

Leech, Geoffrey (1983) *Principles of Pragmatics*. London: Longman.

Leitner, Gerhard and Sieloff, Inke (1998) Aboriginal words and concepts in Australian English. *World Englishes*, **17**(2), 153–69.

Ler, Soon Lay Vivien (2001) The interpretation of the discourse particle *Meh* in Singapore Colloquial English. *Journal of Asian Englishes*, **4**(2), 4–23.

Lewis, Ivor (1991) *Sahibs, Nabobs and Boxwallahs: A Dictionary of the Words of Anglo-India*. Delhi: Oxford University Press.

Li, Dong (1995) English in China. *English Today*, **11**(1), 53–56.

Lim, Shirley Geok-Lin (1994) *Writing South East Asia in English: Against the Grain, Focus on Asian English-Language Literature*. London: Skoob Books Publishing.

Lippi-Green, Rosina (1997) *English with an Accent*. New York: Routledge.

Lisle, Bonnie and Mano, Sandra (1997) Embracing the multicultural rhetoric. In *Writing in Multicultural Settings*. Edited by Carol Severino, Juan C. Guerra, and E. Johnnella. New York: The Modern Language Association of America, pp. 12–26.

Liu, Yameng (1996) Three issues in the argumentative conception of early Chinese discourse. *Philosophy East & West*, **46**(1), 33–58.

Llamzon, Teodoro A. (1969) *Standard Filipino English*. Manila: Ateneo University Press.

Llamzon, Teodoro A. (1997) The phonology of Philippine English. In *English Is an Asian Language: The Philippine Context*. Edited by Maria Lourdes S. Bautista. Sydney, Australia: Macquarie Library Pty Ltd., pp. 41–8.

Longe, V. U. (1999) Student slang from Benin, Nigeria. *English World-Wide*, **20**(2), 237–49.

Low, Ee Ling and Brown, Adam (2003) *An Introduction to Singapore English*. Singapore: McGraw Hill.

Lowenberg, Peter H. (1984) English in the Malay Archipelago: Nativization and its functions in a sociolinguistic area. Unpublished PhD dissertation, University of Illinois at Urbana-Champaign.

Lowenberg, Peter H. (1992) Testing English as a world language: Issues in assessing non-native proficiency. In *The Other Tongue: English across Cultures*. Edited by Braj B. Kachru. Urbana, IL: University of Illinois Press, pp. 108–21. [Originally published in *The Georgetown University Round Table on Languages and Linguistics 1989: Language Teaching, Testing, and Technology*, edited by James E. Alatis. Washington: Georgetown University Press, pp. 216–27.]

Lowenberg, Peter H. (1993) Issues of validity in tests of English as a world language: Whose standards? *World Englishes,* **12**(1), 95–106.

Lowenberg, Peter H. (1995) Language and the institutionalization of ethnic inequality: Malay and English in Malaysia. In *Language and Peace*. Edited by Christina Schäffner and Anita L. Wenden. Amsterdam: Harwood Academic Publishers, pp. 161–72. [Second printing 1999.]

Lukmani, Yasmin (1972) Motivation to learn and language proficiency. *Language Learning,* **22**, 261–73.

Lyons, John (1977) *Semantics* (Volumes 1 and 2). Cambridge: Cambridge University Press.

MacNiece, Louis (1990) *Selected Poems*. Edited and with an introduction by Michael Langley. Winston-Salem, NC: Wake Forest University Press.

Mahootian, Shahrzad and Santorini, Beatrice (1996) Adnominal adjectives, code-switching and lexicalized TAG. In *Proceedings of the Third International Workshop on Tree Adjoining Grammar*. Edited by Anne Abeille, S. Aslanides and Owen Rambow. Paris: Talana, pp. 73–76.

Maltz, Daniel and Borker, Ruth (1982) A cultural approach to male-female miscommunication. In *Handbook of Language and Social Psychology*. Edited by John J. Gumperz. London: John Wiley, pp. 363–80.

Marckwardt, Albert H. (1942) *Introduction to the English Language*. New York: Oxford University Press.

Martin, Isabel Pefianco (2004) Longfellow's legacy: Education and the shaping of Philippine writing. *World Englishes,* **23**(1), 129–39.

Martin, James E. 1992. *Towards a Theory of Text for Contrastive Rhetoric*. New York: Peter Lang.

Matsuura, Kiroko, Chiba, Reiko and Fujieda, Miho (1999) Intelligibility and comprehensibility of American and Irish Englishes in Japan. *World Englishes,* **18**(1), 49–62.

McArthur, Tom (1998) *The English Languages*. Cambridge, UK: Cambridge University Press.

McArthur, Tom (2001) World English and World Englishes: Trends, tensions, varieties, and standards. Review Article. In *Language Teaching: The International Abstracting Journal for Language Teachers, Educators and Researchers.* January, 1–20.

McArthur, Tom (2003) English as an Asian language. *English Today,* **19**(2), 19–22.

McArthur, Tom (ed.) (1992) *The Oxford Companion to the English Language.* Oxford: Oxford University Press.

McInerney, Jay (1985) *Ransom.* New York: Vintage Books.

Melcher, Gunnel and Shaw, Philip (2003) *World Englishes: An Introduction.* The English Language Series. London: Arnold.

Mesthrie, Rajend (1992) *English in Language Shift: The History, Structure and Sociolinguistics of South African Indian English.* Cambridge: Cambridge University Press.

Meshtrie, Rajend (1997) A sociolinguistic study of topicalisation phenomena in South African Black English. In *Englishes around the World 2. Caribbean, Africa, Asia, Australasia: Studies in Honour of Manfred Görlach.* Edited by Edgar W. Schneider. Amsterdam: John Benjamins, pp. 119–40.

Mencken, Henry L. (1936) *The American Language: An Inquiry into the Development of English in the United States.* Fourth edition. New York: Knopf.

Meyerhoff, Miriam (1994) Sounds pretty ethnic, Eh? A pragmatic particle in New Zealand English. *Language in Society,* **23**(3), 367–88.

Milroy, Leslie (1980) *Language and Social Networks.* Oxford: Blackwell.

Miranda, Rocky V. (1978) Caste, religion and dialect differentiation in the Konkani area. *International Journal of Sociology,* **16**, 77–91.

Mishra, Arpita (1982) Discovering connections. In *Language and Social Identity.* Edited by John J. Gumperz. Cambridge: Cambridge University Press, pp. 57–71.

Mitchell, A.G. and Delbridge, A. (1965) *The Speech of Australian Adolescents.* Sydney: Angus and Robertson.

Mitchell, Rosamond and Myles, Florence (1998) *Second Language Learning Theories.* London: Oxford University Press.

Mitchell-Kernan, Claudia (1972) Signifying, loud-talking, and marking. In *Rappin' and Stylin' Out: Communication in Urban Black America.* Edited by Thomas Kochman. Urbana: University of Illinois Press, pp. 315–35.

Modiano, Marko 1996. The Americanization of Euro-English. *World Englishes,* **15**(2), 207–15.

Moody, Andrew (2001) J-pop English: Or, how to write a Japanese pop song. *Gengo Komyunikeeshon Kenkyuu* [*Language Communication Studies*], **1**, 96–107.

Moody, Andrew and Matsumoto, Yuko (2003) Don't touch my moustache: Language blending and code ambiguation by two J-pop artists. *Asian Englishes,* **6**(1), 4–33.

Moore, Charles (1967a) Introduction: The comprehensive Indian mind. In *The Indian Mind: Essentials of Indian Philosophy and Culture*. Edited by Charles Moore. Hawaii: University of Hawaii Press, pp. 1–18.

Moore, Charles (ed.) (1967b) *The Indian Mind: Essentials of Indian Philosophy and Culture*. Hawaii: University of Hawaii Press.

Moore, Charles (ed.) (1967c) *The Japanese Mind*. Honolulu: The University Press of Hawaii [1981 edition].

Morgan, Marcyliena (1998) More than a mood or an attitude: Discourse and verbal genres in African-American culture. In *African-American English: Structure, History and Use*. Edited by Salikoko S. Mufwene, John R. Rickford, Guy Bailey, and John Baugh. New York: Routledge, pp. 251–81.

Mufwene, Salikoko (2001a) What is African American English? In *Sociocultural and Historical Contexts of African American English*. Edited by Sonja L. Lanehart. Philadelphia: John Benjamins, pp. 21–51.

Mufwene, Salikoko (2001b) New Englishes and norm setting: How critical is the native speaker in Linguistics? In *The Three Circles of English*. Edited by Edwin Thumboo. Singapore: UniPress, pp. 133–41.

Mufwene, Salikoko S. and Rickford, John R. (1998) Introduction. In *African-American English: Structure, History and Use*. Edited by Salikoko S. Mufwene, John R. Rickford, Guy Bailey, and John Baugh. New York: Routledge, pp. 1–7.

Mufwene, Salikoko S., Rickford, John R., Bailey, Guy and Baugh, John (eds.) (1998) *African-American English: Structure, History and Use*. New York: Routledge.

Mukherjee, Bharati (1989) *Jasmine: A Novel*. New York: Grove Weidenfeld.

Mukherjee, Meenakshi (1971) *The Twice-born Fiction: Themes and Techniques of the Indian Novel in English*. New Delhi: Sterling Publishers.

Muthiah, S. (1991) *Words in Indian English: A Reader's Guide*. Delhi: Harper Collins.

Muysken, Pieter (1984) The Spanish that Quechua speakers learn: L2 learning as norm-governed behavior. In *Second Language: A Cross-Linguistic Perspective*. Edited by R. Andersen. Rowley: Newbury House, pp. 101–19.

Myers-Scotton, Carol (1996) Afterword. *World Englishes*, **15**(3), 395–404.

Nair-Venugopal, Shanta (2000) English, identity and the Malaysian workplace. *World Englishes*, **19**(2), 205–13.

Narasimhaiah, C. D. (ed.) (1978) *Awakened Conscience: Studies in Commonwealth Literature*. New Delhi: Sterling.

Narayan, R. K. (1990) *The World of Nagaraj*. New York: Viking Press.

Nelson, Cecil L. (1985) My language, your culture: Whose communicative competence? *World Englishes*, **4**(2), 243–50. [Also in Kachru (ed.) (1992).]

Nelson, Gerald (guest ed.) (2004) Special issue on *The International Corpus of English*. *World Englishes*, **23**(2), 225–316.

Nero, Shondel (2001) *Englishes in Contact: Anglophone Caribbean Students in an Urban College.* Cresskill, NJ: Hampton Press.

Newbrook, Mark (ed.) (1999) *English Is an Asian Language: The Thai Context.* Sydney, Australia: The Macquarie Library Pty Ltd.

Ngũgĩ, wa Thiong'o (1981) *Writers in Politics.* London: Heinemann.

Ngũgĩ, wa Thiong'o (1986) *Decolonizing the Mind: The Politics of Language in African Literature.* London: James Currie.

Nihalani, Paroo, Tongue, R. K. and Hosali, Priya (1979) *Indian and British English: A Handbook of Usage and Pronunciation.* New Delhi: Oxford University Press.

Nwankwo, Nkeme (1964) *Danda.* London: Heinemann.

Okabe, Roichi (1987) Ibunka no rhetoric [Rhetorics in different cultures]. In *Ibunka Communication (Intercultural Communication).* Edited by Gyo Furuta. Tokyo: Yuhikaku, pp. 163–83.

Ooi, Vincent B. Y. (ed.) (2001) *Evolving Identities: The English Language in Singapore and Malaysia.* Singapore: Times Academic Press.

Orsman, Harry (1997) *The Dictionary of New Zealand English: A Dictionary of New Zealandisms on Historical Principles.* Auckland: Oxford University Press.

Ọṣundare, Niyi (1995) Caliban's gamble: The stylistic repercussions of writing African literature in English. In *Language in Nigeria: Essays in Honour of Ayọ Bamgboṣe.* Edited by Kọla Owolabi. Ibadan, Nigeria: Group Publishers, pp. 340–63.

Oyelẹyẹ, A. Lekan (1995) Translation and the African writer in English: A sample study of Achebe's *TFA* and *NLAE* [*sic*]. In *Language in Nigeria: Essays in Honour of Ayọ Bamgboṣe.* Edited by Kọla Owolabi, pp. 364–39.

Paikeday, Thomas M. (1985) *The Native Speaker Is Dead!* Toronto: Paikeday Publishing.

Pakir, Anne (1992a) Dictionary entries for discourse particles. In *Words in a Cultural Context.* Proceedings of the Lexicography Workshop, Singapore. Edited by Anne Pakir. Singapore: UniPress, pp. 143–52.

Pakir, Anne (1997) Standards and codification for world Englishes. In *World Englishes 2000.* Edited by L. Smith and M. Forman. Honolulu, HI: University of Hawai'i Press, pp. 169–81.

Pakir, Anne (ed.) (1992b) *Words in a Cultural Context.* Proceedings of the Lexicography Workshop, Singapore: UniPress.

Pandey, Anita (guest ed.) (2000) Symposium on *The Ebonics Debate and African American Language. World Englishes,* **19**(1), 1–106.

Pandharipande, Rajeshwari V. (1983) Linguistics and written discourse in particular languages: Contrastive studies: English and Marathi. *Annual Review of Applied Linguistics* (1982), **3**, 118–36.

Pandharipande, Rajeshwari V. (2001) Constructing Religious Discourse in Diaspora: American Hinduism. *Studies in the Linguistic Sciences,* **31**(1), 231–51.

Parakrama, Arjuna (1995) *De-hegemonizing Language Standards: Learning from (Post)-Colonial Englishes about 'English'.* Basingstoke, UK: Macmillan.

Paranjape, Makarand (ed.) (1993) *Indian Poetry in English.* Hyderabad: Macmillan India Limited.

Pennycook, Alastair (1994) *The Cultural Politics of English as an International Language.* London: Longman.

Pennycook, Alastair (2003) Global Englishes, rip slyme, and performativity. *Journal of Sociolinguistics,* **7**(4), 513–33.

Peña, Phebe S. (1997) Philippine English in the classroom. In *English Is an Asian Language: The Philippine Context.* Edited by Maria Lourdes S. Bautista. Sydney: Macquarie Library Pty Ltd., pp. 87–102.

Phillipson, Robert (1992) *Linguistic Imperialism.* Oxford: Oxford University Press.

Phillipson, Robert (1998) Globalizing English: Are linguistic human rights an alternative to linguistic imperialism? In *Language Rights.* Edited by Phil Benson, Peter Grundy and Tove Skutnabb-Kangas. Special volume. *Language Sciences,* **20**(1), 101–12.

Phillipson, Robert (1999) Linguistic imperialism revisited — or re-invented. A rejoinder to a review essay. *International Journal of Applied Linguistics,* **9**(1), 135–7.

Phillipson, Robert (2003) *English-only Europe? Challenging Language Policy.* London: Routledge.

Phillipson, Robert and Skutnabb-Kangas, Tove (2002) Englishization as one dimension of colonization. In *The English Language and Power.* Edited by Gerardo Mazzaferro. Alessandria: Edizioni dell' Orso, pp. 149–68.

Pinker, Stephen (1994) *The Language Instinct: How the Mind Creates Language.* New York: William Morrow.

Platt, John T. (1987) Communicative functions of particles in Singapore English. In *Language Topics: Essays in Honour of Michael Halliday* Volume I. Edited by Ross Steele and Terry Threadgold. Amsterdam: John Benjamins, pp. 391–401.

Platt, John T. and Ho, Mian Lian (1989) Discourse particles in Singaporean English: Substratum influences and universals. *World Englishes,* **8**(2), 215–21.

Platt, John T. and Weber, Heidi (1980) *English in Singapore and Malaysia.* Kuala Lumpur: Oxford University Press.

Platt, John T., Weber, Heidi and Ho, Mian Lian (1984) *The New Englishes.* London: Routledge and Kegan Paul.

Pongtongchareon, Surai (1999) English in Thailand: Policy and current practice. In *English Is an Asian language: The Thai Context.* Edited by Mark Newbrook. Sydney, Australia: The Macquarie Library Pty Ltd., pp. 59–63.

Pope, Emily (1976) *Questions and Answers in English.* The Hague: Mouton.

Poplack, Shana (1980) 'Sometimes I'll start a sentence in Spanish *y termino en español*: Toward a typology of code-switching. *Linguistics,* **18**(7/8), 581–618.

Poplack, Shana (1982) Bilingualism and the vernacular. In *Issues in International Bilingual Education: The Role of the Vernacular.* Edited by Beverly Hartford, Albert Valdman, and Charles R. Foster. New York: Plenum, pp. 1–23.

Poplack, Shana (ed.) (2000) *The English History of African American English.* New York: Blackwell.

Prasithrathsint, Amara (1999) What is 'good English' for Thais? In *English Is an Asian Language: The Thai Context.* Edited by Mark Newbrook. Sydney, Australia: The Macquarie Library Pty Ltd., pp. 64–70.

Prator, Clifford H. (1968) The British heresy in TESOL. In *Language Problems of Developing Nations.* Edited by Joshua Fishman, Charles Ferguson and Jyotirindra Das Gupta. New York: John Wiley, pp. 459–76.

Preston, Dennis R. (1989) *Sociolinguistics and Second Language Acquisition,* Oxford: Blackwell.

Purves, Alan C. (ed.) (1988) *Writing Across Languages and Cultures: Issues in Contrastive Rhetoric.* Newbury Park: Sage.

Quirk, Randolph (1968) *The Use of English* (second edition). Harlow: Longman [first edition 1962].

Quirk, Randolph (1981) International communication and the concept of nuclear English. In *English for Cross-Cultural Communication.* Edited by Larry E. Smith. New York: Macmillan, pp. 151–65.

Quirk, Randolph (1985) The English language in a global context. In *English in the World: Teaching and Learning the Language and Literatures.* Edited by Randolph Quirk and Henry G. Widdowson. Cambridge: Cambridge University Press, pp. 1–6.

Quirk, Randolph (1988) The question of standards in the international use of English. In *Language Spread and Language Policy: Issues, Implication, and Case Studies. GURT 1987.* Edited by Peter H. Lowenberg. Washington, DC: Georgetown University Press, pp. 229–41.

Quirk, Randolph, Greenbaum, Sidney, Leech, Geoffrey and Svartvik, Jan (1985) *A Comprehensive Grammar of the English Language.* London: Longman.

Quirk, Randolph and Widdowson, Henry G. (eds.) (1985) *English in the World: Teaching and Learning the Language and Literatures.* Cambridge: Cambridge University Press.

Rahman, A. M. M. Hamidur (1996) Acceptability and English curriculum change in Bangladesh. In *South Asian English: Structure, Use, and Users.* Edited by Robert J. Baumgardner. Urbana: University of Illinois Press, pp. 191–205.

Rahman, Tariq (1990) *Pakistani English: The Linguistic Description of a Non-Native Variety of English.* NIPS Monograph Series III. Islamabad: National Institute of Pakistan Studies.

Rahman, Tariq (1991) *A History of Pakistani Literature in English.* Lahore: Vanguard.

Rao, G. Subba (1954) *Indian Words in English: A Study of Indo-British Cultural and Linguistic Relations.* Oxford: Clarendon Press.

Rao, Raja (1938) *Kanthapura.* Reprinted 1963, New York: New Directions; 1974, Madras: Oxford University Press.

Rao, Raja (1978) The caste of English. In *Awakened Conscience: Studies in Commonwealth Literature.* Edited by C. D. Narasimhaiah. New Delhi: Sterling Publishers, pp. 420–2.

Raslan, Karim (2000) Writing fiction. In *English Is an Asian language: The Malaysian Context.* Edited by Halimah Mohd Said and Keit Sew Ng. Persatuan Bahasa Moden Malaysia and The Macquarie Library Pty Ltd., pp. 188–9.

Rastall, Paul (1995) Definite article or no definite article? *English Today,* **42**(2), 37–43.

Reyes, Michiyo Yoneno (2002) Under attack: Mass media technology and indigenous musical practices in the Philippines. In *Global Goes Local: Popular Culture in Asia.* Edited by Timothy J. Craig and Richard King. Vancouver: University of British Columbia Press, pp. 40–57.

Reynolds, Dudley W. (1993) Illocutionary acts across languages: Editorializing in Egyptian English. *World Englishes,* **12**(1), 35–46.

Rickford, John (1973) Carrying the new wave into syntax: The case of Black English *bin.* In *Analyzing Variation in Language.* Edited by Ralph W. Fasold and Roger W. Shuy. Washington, DC: Georgetown University Press, pp. 162–83.

Rickford, John (1998) The creole origin of African American Vernacular English: Evidence from copula absence. In *African-American English: Structure, History and Use.* Edited by Salikoko S. Mufwene, John R. Rickford, Guy Bailey, and John Baugh. New York: Routledge, pp. 154–200.

Ritchie, Donald (ed.) (1997) *Lafcadio Hearn's Japan: An Anthology of His Writings on the Country and Its People.* Tokyo: Tuttle.

Ritchie, William C. and Bhatia, Tej K. (eds.) (1996) *Handbook of Second Language Acquisition.* New York: Academic Press.

Rose, Kenneth R. (1992) Method and scope in cross-cultural speech act research: A contrastive study of requests in Japanese and English. Unpublished PhD dissertation, University of Illinois, Urbana.

Rose, Kenneth R. (1999) Teachers and students learning about requests in Hong Kong. In *Culture in Second Language Teaching and Learning.* Edited by Eli Hinkel. Cambridge Applied Linguistics Series, Cambridge: Cambridge University Press, pp. 167–80.

Roy, Arundhati (1997) *The God of Small Things.* New York: Random House.

Rushdie, Salman (1982) *The Times.* London, October 1982, p. 7.

Sa'adeddin, Mohammed Akram A. M. (1989) Text development and Arabic-English negative interference. *Applied Linguistics,* **10**, 36–51.

Sacks, Harvey, Schegloff, E. and Jefferson, G. (1974) A simplest systematics for the organization of turn-taking for conversation. *Language*, **50**, 696–735.

Sadock, Jerry M. (1974) *Toward a Linguistic Theory of Speech Acts.* New York: Academic Press.

Said, Edward (1993) *Culture and Imperialism.* New York: Alfred Knopf.

Said, Halimah Mohd and Ng, Keit Sew (eds.) (2000) *English Is an Asian Language: The Malaysian Context.* Persatuan Bahasa Moden Malaysia and The Macquarie Library Pty Ltd.

Saro-Wiwa, Ken (1989) *Four Farcical Plays,* London: Saros International Publishers.

Schiffrin, Deborah (1994) *Approaches to Discourse.* Oxford: Blackwell.

Schneider, Edgar W. (ed.) (1996) *Focus on the USA.* Amsterdam: John Benjamins.

Schneider, Edgar W. (ed.) (1997a) *Englishes Around the World 1. General Studies, British Isles, North America: Studies in Honour of Manfred Görlach.* Amsterdam: John Benjamins.

Schneider, Edgar W. (ed.) (1997b) *Englishes Around the World 2. Caribbean, Africa, Asia, Australasia: Studies in Honour of Manfred Görlach.* Amsterdam: John Benjamins.

Schuring, Gerhard K. (1993) Sensusdata oor die tale van Suid-Afrika in 1991. Unpublished working document. HSRC: Pretoria.

Searle, John R. (1969) *Speech Acts: An Essay in the Philosophy of Language.* Cambridge: Cambridge University Press.

Seidlhofer, Barbara (1999) Double standards: Teacher education in the Expanding Circle. *World Englishes*, **18**(2), pp. 233–45.

Seidlhofer, Barbara (2001) Closing a conceptual gap: The case for a description of English as a lingua franca. *International Journal of Applied Linguistics*, **11**(2), 133–58.

Selinker, Larry (1972) Interlanguage. *International Review of Applied Linguistics*, **10**, 209–31.

Selinker, Larry (1992) *Rediscovering Interlanguage.* New York: Longman.

Sey, K. A. (1973) *Ghanaian English: An Exploratory Survey.* London: Macmillan.

Shah, Sayyid Saadat Ali (1978) *Exploring the World of English: A Practical Course in Composition for College Students and Competitive Candidates.* Second edition. Lahore: Ilmi Kitab Khana.

Shapiro, Michael and Schiffman, H. F. (1983) *Language and Society in South Asia.* Dordrecht: Foris.

Shaw, Willard (1981) Asian student attitudes toward English. In *English for Cross-Cultural Communication.* Edited by Larry E. Smith. London: Macmillan, pp. 108–22.

Shim, Rosa (1994) Englishized Korean: Structure, status and attitudes. *World Englishes*, **13**(2), 225–44.

Shim, Rosa (1999) Codified Korean English: Process, characteristics, and consequences. *World Englishes*, **18**(2), 247–58.

Shopen, T. (1978) Research on the variable (ING) in Canberra, Australia. *Talanya*, **5**, 42–52.

Sidhwa, Bapsi (1996) Creative processes in Pakistani creative fiction. In *South Asian English: Structure, Use, and Users*. Edited by Robert J. Baumgardner. Urbana: University of Illinois Press, pp. 232–40.

Siegel, Jeff (1999) Creole and minority dialects in education: An overview. *Journal of Multilingual and Multicultural Development*, **20**(6), 508–31.

Silva, Penny, Dore, Wendy, Mantzel, Dorothea, Muller, Colin and Wright, Madeleine (eds.) (1996) *A Dictionary of South African English on Historical Principles*. Oxford: Oxford University Press.

Silva, Rosangela Souto (1998) Pragmatic competence and transfer abilities: Native and non-native speakers of Portuguese. Urbana-Champaign, IL: Unpublished PhD dissertation, University of Illinois.

Silva, Rosangela Souto (2000) Pragmatics, bilingualism, and the native speaker. *Language and Communication*, **20**, 161–78.

Simo Bobda, Augustin (1994) Lexical innovation in Cameroon English. *World Englishes*, **13**(2), 245–60.

Singh, Khushwant (1959) *I Shall Not Hear the Nightingale*. London: John Calder.

Sinha, Surendra Prasad (1978) *English in India: A Historical Study with Particular Reference to English Education in India*. Patna: Janaki Prakashan.

Skandera, Paul (1999) What do we *really* know about Kenyan English? A pilot study in research methodology. *English World-Wide*, **20**(2), 217–36.

Skutnabb-Kangas, Tove (2000) *Linguistic Genocide in Education or Worldwide Diversity and Human Rights?* Mahwah, New Jersey and London: Lawrence Erlbaum Associates.

Skutnabb-Kangas, Tove (2001) Linguistic human rights in education for language maintenance. In *Language, Knowledge and the Environment: The Interdependence of Cultural and Biological Diversity*. Edited by Luisa Maffi. Washington, DC: The Smithsonian Institute.

Sledd, James H. (1993) Standard English and the study of variation: 'It all be done for a purpose.' In *Language Variation in North American English: Research and Teaching*. Edited by A. Wayne Glowka and Dod M. Lance. New York: The Modern Language Association of America, pp. 275–81.

Smith, Larry E. (1983a) English as an international language: No room for linguistic chauvinism. In *Readings in English as an International Language*. Edited by Larry E. Smith. Oxford: Pergamon, pp. 7–11.

Smith, Larry E. (1992) Spread of English and issues of intelligibility. In *The other Tongue: English across Cultures*. Edited by Braj B. Kachru. Urbana: University of Illinois Press, pp. 75–90.

Smith, Larry E. and Bisazza, John (1982) The comprehensibility of three varieties of English for college students in seven countries. *Language Learning*, **32**, 259–70.

Smith, Larry E. and Nelson, Cecil L. (1985) International intelligibility of English: Directions and resources. *World Englishes*, **4**(3), 333–42.

Smith, Larry E. and Rafiqzad, Khalilulla (1979) English for cross-cultural communication: The question of intelligibility. *TESOL Quarterly*, **13**(3), 371–80.

Smith, Larry E. (ed.) (1981) *English for Cross-Cultural Communication.* London: Macmillan.

Smith, Larry E. (ed.) (1983b) *Readings in English as an International Language.* Oxford: Pergamon.

Smith, Larry E. (ed.) (1987) *Discourse Across Cultures: Strategies in World Englishes.* London: Prentice-Hall.

Smith, Larry E. and Forman, Michael (eds.) (1997) *World Englishes 2000.* Honolulu, HI: University of Hawai'i Press.

Smith, Phillip (1985) *Language, the Sexes and Society.* Oxford: Blackwell.

Smitherman, Geneva (1977) 'It bees dat way sometime': Sound and structure of present-day Black English. In *Talkin and Testifyin*. Geneva Smitherman. Detroit: Wayne State University Press. [Reprinted in *Exploring Language*. Edited by Gary Goshgarian. Second edition, 1980, Boston: Little, Brown, pp. 255–67.]

Smitherman, Geneva (1977) *Talkin and Testifyin: The Language of Black America.* Detroit: Wayne State University Press.

Solomon, Denis (1993) *The Speech of Trinidad: A Reference Grammar.* St. Augustine: University of West Indies, SOCS.

Spolsky, Bernard (1993) Testing across cultures: An historical perspective. *World Englishes*, **12**(1), 87–93.

Sridhar, Kamal K. (1989) *English in Indian Bilingualism.* New Delhi: Manohar.

Sridhar, Kamal K. (1991) Speech acts in an indigenized variety: Sociocultural values and language variation. In *English Around The World: Sociolinguistic Perspectives.* Edited by Jenny Cheshire. Cambridge: Cambridge University Press, pp. 308–18.

Sridhar, Kamal K. and Sridhar, S. N. (1992) Bridging the paradigm gap: Second-language acquisition theory and indigenized varieties of English. In *The Other Tongue: English Across Cultures.* Edited by Braj B. Kachru. Urbana: University of Illinois Press, pp. 91–107.

Sridhar, S. N. (1982) Non-native English literatures: Context and relevance. In *The Other Tongue: English across Cultures.* Edited by Braj B. Kachru. Urbana: University of Illinois Press, pp. 291–306.

Sridhar, S. N. (1992) The ecology of bilingual competence: Language interaction in indigenized varieties of English. *World Englishes*, **11**(2/3), 141–50.

Sridhar, S. N. (1994) A reality check for SLA theories. *TESOL Quarterly*, **28**(4), 800–5.

Sridhar, S. N. (1996) Toward a syntax of South Asian English: Defining the lectal range. In *South Asian English: Structure, Use, and Users*. Edited by Robert J. Baumgardner. Urbana: University of Illinois Press, pp. 55–69.

Sridhar, S. N. and Sridhar, Kamal K. (1980) The syntax and psycholinguistics of bilingual code-mixing. *Canadian Journal of Psychology*, **34**(4), 407–16.

Stanlaw, James (1992) English in Japanese communicative strategies. In *The Other Tongue: English Across Cultures*. Edited by Braj B. Kachru. Urbana: University of Illinois Press, pp. 178–208.

Stanlaw, James (2004) *Japanese English: Language and Culture Contact*. In the series Asian Englishes Today. Hong Kong: Hong Kong University Press.

Stewart, Penny and Fawcett, Richard C. (1994) 'An' to 'A' in American speech: Language change in progress. *English Today*, **10**(1), 18–24.

Strevens, Peter (1980) *Teaching English as an International Language*. Oxford: Pergamon.

Strevens, Peter (1983) What is 'Standard English'? In *Readings in English as an International Language*. Edited by Larry E. Smith. Oxford: Pergamon Press, pp. 87–93.

Strevens, Peter (1985) Standards and the standard language. *English Today*, **1**(2), 5–8.

Strevens, Peter (1992) English as an international language: Directions in the 1990s. In *The Other Tongue: English across Cultures*. Edited by Braj B. Kachru. Urbana: University of Illinois Press, pp. 27–47.

Stubbe, Maria and Holmes, Janet (1999) Talking Maori or Pakeha in English: Signaling identity in discourse. In *New Zealand English*. Edited by Alan Bell and Koenraad Kuiper. Amsterdam: John Benjamins, pp. 249–78.

Swales, John M. (1981) Aspects of article introductions. In *Aston ESP Research Report* No. 1, Language studies Unit, University of Aston in Birmingham, Birmingham, UK.

Swales, John M. (1985) A genre-based approach to language across the curriculum. In *Language Across the Curriculum*. Edited by Makhan L. Tickoo. Singapore: SEAMEO Regional Language Centre, pp. 10–22.

Swales, John M. (1990) *Genre analysis — English in Academic and Research Settings*. Cambridge: Cambridge University Press.

Swales, John M. (1997) English as *Tyrannosaurus rex*. *World Englishes*, **16**(3), 373–82.

Swales, John M. and Feak, C. B. (1994) *Academic Writing for Graduate Students: A Course for Non-native Speakers of English*. Ann Arbor: University of Michigan Press.

Takashi, Kyoko (1990) A sociolinguistic analysis of English borrowings in Japanese advertising texts. *World Englishes*, **9**(3), 327–41.

Talib, Ismail S. (2002) *The Language of Postcolonial Literatures: An Introduction*. London: Routledge.

Tannen, Deborah (1984) *Conversational Style: Analyzing Talk among Friends.* Norwood, NJ: Ablex.

Tannen, Deborah (ed.) (1993) *Gender and Conversational Interaction.* Oxford Studies in Sociolinguistics Series, New York: Oxford University Press.

Tawake, Sandra K. (1990) Culture and identity in literature of the South Pacific. *World Englishes,* **9**(2), 205–13.

Tawake, Sandra (1993) Reading *The Bone People* – cross-culturally. *World Englishes,* **12**(3), 325–33.

Tawake, Sandra K. (1995a) On understanding a text: Reader response and Alan Duff's *Once Were Warriors. World Englishes,* **14**(2), 281–300.

Tawake, Sandra K. (guest ed.) (1995b) Symposium on *World Englishes in the Classroom. World Englishes,* **14**(2), 231–300.

Tay, Mary W. J. (1993a) Code switching and code mixing as a communicative strategy in multilingual discourse. *The English Language in Singapore: Issues and Development.* Edited by Mary W. J. Tay. Singapore: UniPress, pp. 125–44.

Tay, Mary W. J. (ed.) (1993b) *The English Language in Singapore: Issues and Development.* Singapore: UniPress.

Tayao, MA. Lourdes G. (2004) The evolving study of Philippine English phonology. *World Englishes,* **23**(1), 77–90.

Taylor, David S. (1993) A question of concord. *English Today,* **9**(3), 10–17.

Taylor, G. and Chen, T. (1991) Linguistic, cultural, and subcultural issues in contrastive discourse analysis: Anglo-American and Chinese scientific texts. *Applied Linguistics,* **12**(3), 319–36.

Thomas, Jenny (1983) Cross-cultural pragmatic failure. *Applied Linguistics,* **4**(2), 91–112.

Thompson, Eric C. (2002) Rocking East and West: The USA in Malaysian music (an American remix). In *Global Goes Local: Popular Culture in Asia.* Edited by Timothy J. Craig and Richard King. Vancouver: University of British Columbia Press, pp. 58–79.

Thumboo, Edwin (ed.) (1976) *The Second Tongue: An Anthology of Poetry from Malaysia and Singapore.* Singapore: Heinemann Educational Books.

Thumboo, Edwin (1985) Twin perspectives and multi-ecosystems: Tradition for a commonwealth writer. *World Englishes,* **4**(2), 213–21.

Thumboo, Edwin (1992) The literary dimensions of the spread of English. In *The Other Tongue: English across Cultures.* Edited by Braj B. Kachru. Urbana: University of Illinois Press, pp. 255–82.

Thumboo, Edwin (1993) Language as power. *A Third Map: New and Selected Poems.* Singapore: UniPress.

Thumboo, Edwin (2001a) In such beginnings are my ends: Diaspora and literary creativity. In *Diaspora, Identity, and Language Communities.* Edited by Braj B. Kachru and Cecil L. Nelson. Special Issue of *Studies in the Linguistic Sciences,* **31**(1), 19–30.

Thumboo, Edwin (ed.) (2001b) *The Three Circles of English: Language Specialists Talk about the English Language.* Singapore: UniPress.

Tickoo, Asha (2002) On the use of 'then/after that' in the marking of chronological order: Insights from Vietnamese and Chinese learners of ESL. *System,* **30**, 107–24.

Tickoo, Makhan L. (1995a) Authenticity as a cultural concern: A view from the Asian English-language classroom. In *Language and Culture in Multilingual Societies: Viewpoints and Visions.* Edited by Makhan L. Tickoo. Anthology Series 36, Singapore: SEAMEO Regional Language Center, pp. 95–111.

Tickoo, Makhan L. (ed.) (1995b) *Language and Culture in Multilingual Societies: Viewpoints and Visions.* Anthology Series 36, Singapore: SEAMEO Regional Language Center.

Tirkkonen-Condit, S. (1985) *Argumentative Text Structure and Translation.* Jyväskylä, Finland: University of Jyväskylä.

Tongue, Ray (1974) *The English of Singapore and Malaysia.* Singapore: Eastern Universities Press SDN. BHD. [Reprinted 1976, 1979]

Tripathi, P. D. (1990) English in Zambia. *English Today,* **6**(3), 34–38.

Trudgill, Peter (1972) Sex, covert prestige and linguistic change in the urban British English of Norwich. *Language in Society,* **1**, 179–95.

Trudgill, Peter (1990 [1999]) *Dialects of England.* Second edition. Oxford: Blackwell.

Tsang, Wai King and Wong, Matilda (2004) Constructing a shared 'Hong Kong identity' in comic discourse. *Perspectives: Working Papers in English and Communication,* **16**(1), Spring.

Tsuda, Yukio (2002) The hegemony of English: Problems, opposing views and communication rights. In *The English Language and Power.* Edited by Gerardo Mazzaferro. Torino: Edizioni dell'Orso, pp. 19–31.

Turner, George W. (1997) Australian English as a national language. In *Englishes Around the World 2: Studies in Honour of Manfred Görlach: Caribbean, Africa, Asia, Australia.* Edited by Edgar W. Schneider. Amsterdam: John Benjamins, pp. 335–48.

Valentine, Tamara (1988) Developing discourse types in non-native English: Strategies of gender in Hindi and Indian English. *World Englishes,* **7**(2), 143–58.

Valentine, Tamara (1991) Getting the message across: Discourse markers in Indian English. *World Englishes,* **10**(3), 325–34.

Valentine, Tamara (1995) Agreeing and disagreeing in Indian English discourse: Implications for language teaching. In *Language and Culture in Multilingual Societies: Viewpoints and Visions.* Edited by Makhan L. Tickoo. Anthology Series 36, Singapore: SEAMEO Regional Language Centre, pp. 227–50.

Vavrus, Fran (1991) When paradigms clash: The role of institutionalized varieties in language teacher education. *World Englishes*, **10**(2), 181–95.

Verma, Yugeshwar P. (1996) Some features of Nepali newspaper English. In *South Asian English: Structure, Use, and Users*. Edited by Robert J. Baumgardner. Urbana: University of Illinois Press, pp. 82–87.

Vyas, B. S., Tiwari, B. N. and Srivastava, R. N. (1972) *Hindii VyaakaraN aur Racnaa*. (*Hindi Grammar and Composition*). Delhi: National Council of Educational Research and Training.

Wee, Lionel (2003) The birth of a particle: *Know* in Colloquial Singapore English. *World Englishes*, **22**(1), 5–13.

Whatley, Elizabeth (1981) Language among Black Americans. In *Language in the USA*. Edited by Charles A. Ferguson and Shirley Brice Heath. Cambridge: Cambridge University Press, pp. 92–107.

White, Lydia (1989) *Universal Grammar and Second Language Acquisition*. Amsterdam: John Benjamins.

Whitworth, George Clifford (1855) *A Glossary of Indian Terms Used in English, and of Such English or Other Non-Indian Terms as Have Obtained Meanings in India*. London: Kegan Paul Trench.

Widdowson, Henry G. (1979) *Explorations in Applied Linguistics*. Oxford: Oxford University Press.

Widdowson, Henry G. (1997) EIL, ESL, EFL: Global issues and local interests. *World Englishes*, **16**(1), 135–46.

Wilma, Vimala Marie (1987) *A Study of Sentence-Final Particles in Singapore English. Academic Exercise*. Singapore: Department of English Language and Literature, National University of Singapore.

Winford, Donald (1997) On the origins of African American English — a creolist perspective part I: The sociohistorical background. *Diachronica*, **14**, 305–44.

Winford, Donald (1998) On the origins of African American English – a creolist perspective part II: Linguistic features. *Diachronica*, **15**, 99–154.

Wolfram, Walt (1969) *A Sociolinguistic Description of Detroit Negro Speech*. Urban League Series 5, Washington, DC: Center for Applied Linguistics.

Wolfram, Walt (1981) Varieties of American English. In *Language in the USA*. Edited by Charles A. Ferguson and Shirley Brice Heath. Cambridge, UK: Cambridge University Press, pp. 44–68.

Wolfram, Walt (1991) *Dialects and American English*. Englewood Cliffs, NJ: Prentice Hall.

Wolfram, Walt (1993) Ethical considerations in language awareness programs. Special issue on *Ethical Issues for Applying Linguistics. Issues in Applied Linguistics*, **4**(2), 225–55.

Wolfram, Walt (2000) Issues in reconstructing earlier African-American English. *World Englishes*, **29**(1), 39–58.

Wolfram, Walt and Christian, Donna (1976) *Appalachian Speech.* Arlington, VA: Center for Applied Linguistics.

Wolfram, Walt and Schilling-Estes, Natalie (1997) *Hoi Toide on the Outer Banks: The Story of the Ocracoke Brogue.* Chapel Hill: University of North Carolina Press.

Wong, Jock (2004) The Particles of Singapore English: A Semantic and Cultural Interpretation. *Journal of Pragmatics: An Interdisciplinary Journal of Language Studies,* **36**(4), 739–93.

Wyld, Henry C. (1907) *The Growth of English.* London: John Murray.

Yamada, Haru (1992) *American and Japanese Business Discourse: A Comparison of Interactional Styles.* Norwood, NJ: Ablex.

Yule, Henry, and Burnell, A. C. (1886) *Hobson-Jobson: A Glossary of Colloquial Anglo-Indian Words and Phrases and of Kindred Terms, Etymological, Historical, Geographical, and Discursive.* [New edition, 1903, by W. Crooke. London: J. Murray.]

Yunick, Stanley (1997) Genres, register and sociolinguistics. *World Englishes,* **16**(3), 321–36.

Yunick, Stanley (2001) Creativity and ideology in Maori literature in English. In *The Three Circles of English.* Edited by Edwin Thumboo. Singapore: UniPress, pp. 159–77.

Zhang, Hang (2003) Chinese Englishes: History, contexts, and texts. Unpublished PhD dissertation, University of Illinois, Urbana.

Zhao, Yong and Campbell, Keith (1995) English in China. *World Englishes,* **14**(3), 377–90.

Zhu, Hua, Li, W. and Qian, Y. (2000) The sequential organisation of gift offering and acceptance in Chinese. *Journal of Pragmatics,* **32**, 81–103.

Zuraidah Mohd Don (2000) Malay + English → A Malay variety of English vowels and accents. In *English Is an Asian Language: The Malaysian Context.* Edited by Halimah Mohd Said and Keit Sew Ng. Persatuan Bahasa Moden Malaysia and The Macquarie Library Pty Ltd, pp. 35–46.

Index